# Electoral Participation of Muslim Women in India

**Also Available:**

- Globalization and Religion: Interactions and Divergences, editor with Dr. Scaria Pannackal SVD

---

## About the Author

**Dr. (Mrs.) Vasundhara Mohan** acquired her MA degree in History from Manasa Gangotri, Mysore University. After acquiring her PhD for her work on the Muslims of Sri Lanka from the Department of Political Science, Rajasthan University, Jaipur, she joined the Centre of Soviet Studies, Mumbai University in 1984 and retired as Associate Professor in 2006.

From 2007 to 2014 she was associated with the Centre for the Study of Society and Secularism in Mumbai, founded by Late Dr. Asghar Ali Engineer. During this period she developed special in interest in the empowerment of Muslim women and organised a number of workshops for Muslim women in different parts of the country.

She has also written and published a number of books which include Identity crisis of Muslims in post-independent Sri Lanka; Soviet Foreign Policy in South Asia, Soviet Union under Gorbachev, Collapse of Socialism in Russia, Evaluation of Gorbachev Era, Muslim Women and Secular Courts (2010), and Secularism and Pluralistic Democracy in India (2013). She has also published a number of articles on subjects relating to Muslim women. These include Problems of Education and Employment among the Muslim Youth of Sri Lanka (1984), Muslims of Soviet Central Asia (1986), Ethnicity and Power in post-Communist Russia (1993), The Role of Religion and Leadership in Turkmenistan (2003), Sachar Committee Report and Muslims of India (2008), Empowerment of Muslim Women of Karnataka (2008), Muslim Women as Qazis (2015), Educating Muslim Girls (2016), Triple Talaq: The Damocles' Sword (2016) etc.

She has widely travelled in Sri Lanka, USA, UK, Soviet Union/Russia, Thailand etc., for participation and presentation of research papers. Presently, she is working as Programme Director at the Institute of Indian Culture, Mumbai.

# Electoral Participation of Muslim Women in India

## A Comparative Study

Vasundhara Mohan

CONCEPT PUBLISHING COMPANY PVT. LTD.
NEW DELHI-110059

**ISBN-13: 978-93-86682-11-6**

First Published 2018

*Published and Printed by*

Concept Since 1974

**Concept Publishing Company Pvt. Ltd.**
**Regd. Office:**
A/15-16, Commercial Block, Mohan Garden,
New Delhi-110059 (INDIA)
*T* : +91 11 25351460, +91 11 25351794
*E* : publishing@conceptpub.com; *W* : www.conceptpub.com

**Cataloging in Publication Data--Courtesy:** D.K. Agencies (P) Ltd. <docinfo@dkagencies.com>

**Mohan, Vasundhara, 1947- author.**
Electoral participation of Muslim women in India : a comparative study / Vasundhara Mohan.
pages cm
Includes bibliographical references and index.
ISBN 9789386682116

1. Muslim women—Political activity—India—Karnataka. 2. Muslim women—Political activity—India—Uttar Pradesh. 3. Elections—India—Karnataka. 4. Elections—India—Uttar Pradesh. I. Title.

LCC HQ1236.5.I4M64 2017 DDC 305.420954 23

# Preface

Political participation is not restricted to a mere "Right to Vote", but includes noe's political consciousness, political activism and actual participation in decision-making process ether at the local or State-level. Women in India have been participating in elections as voters and were contesting in elections to public office since before independence. Some women have held important positions in political parties and continue to do so even today. Political activism and voting have always been the strongest areas in which women participated in the country's politics. Even at the 2014 Parliamentary elections, women voters constituted over 65 per cent. However, the number of women who were elected as Members of the State Assemblies and the Lok Sabha of the Parliament has always been disproportionate to their numbers in the population. While it is not easy for women in general and Indian women in particular, to participate in elections as contestants, the male dominated political parties have never shown any inclination to bring in more women into the legislatures. Consequently, in terms of representation of women in Parliament, India stands at 20th rank from the bottom. It is true that women have held the posts of President and Prime Minister in India, and there have been women Chief Ministers from time-to-time. Women head three political parties in India. Indian voters have also elected women to various State legislative assemblies and national parliament for many decades. But, the fact remains that women are not getting their due. As of today women comprise just about 11 per cent of the members in the Lock Sabha and 10.6 per cent in the Rajya Sabha. The position in no different in the States.

A Bill introduced in 1996 to provide for 33 per cent reservation for women in the Lok Sabha and State Legislatures is yet to see the light of the day. Male politicians have come-up with one reason or the other and stalled the Bill for over two decades now.

If the above is the situation applicable to women in general, non-Muslim women have been making some headway in politics despite patriarchal attitude. But, it is the Muslim women, who comprise 50 per cent of the Muslim population of India are almost absent in the Parliament and State Assemblies. The few Muslim women that have made it to the Parliament or State Assemblies belong to political families. Yet, Muslim women do not, by and large, form a part of the mainstream women in fighting for a proportional representation. Do not the Muslim women have political ambitions? What prevents them from contesting elections? Why does not the Muslim community send its women to the Parliament and State Assemblies? Does the religion prevent Muslim women's political participation?

This study was undertaken to examine the status of Muslim women's political participation in two States *viz.*, Karnataka and Uttar Pradesh, where Muslims live in different cultural settings.

Mumbai **Vasundhara Mohan**

# Acknowledgments

This study was made possible due to support from the Indian Council of Social Science Research, Government of India, New Delhi. I am grateful to the ICSSR. My thanks are also due to the panel of experts who evaluated my proposal submitted to the ICSSR and made scholastic comments, which I have kept in mind while finalizing this report.

Besides my own efforts, my Research Associate and Field Investigators have made valuable contribution to the project by dint of their hard work in gathering information and data either from the libraries or from the field. I would like to thank Dr. (Ms.) Navashikha Duara, Mumbai; Dr. Arif Mohammad (Varanasi); Mr. Mujahid Deputy and Ms. Afshan Azhar (both of Bangalore) and Mr. Mohamed Mustafa, Research Scholar of Manasa Gangotri, Mysore. My thanks are also due to Mr. Ravi Nair and Ms. Varsha V., who extended support with computer. I am thankful also to the assistance and cooperation extended in my work by the staffers of the Centre for the Study of Society and Secularism, Mumbai; especially Mr. Sharad Bhatt, Gopa Kumar, Kishore Bhagat and Neelam Lotekar.

Among those who offered valuable comments and suggestions, I wish to thank Mr. Syed Tanveer Ahmed, Chief Editor, *Karnataka Muslims* (Bangalore), Quazi Arshed Ali, Bidar, Professor Muzaffar H. Assadi, Department of Political Science, Manasa Gangotri, Mysore, and Professor Abdul Aziz, formerly Head, Department of Economics, Institute for Social and Economic Change, Bangalore.

I would also like to thank my husband for the unstinted cooperation that he extended to me during the course of my work and for offering editorial comments which has helped me in improvising the final report.

Finally, the views expressed in this report are exclusively mine and I take full responsibility. I have discussed my work with experts on Islam regarding the religious aspects and I have taken their views into consideration. I would feel that my efforts are vindicated if the Muslim community rises to the occasion and works with renewed vigour to improve its own socio-economic conditions, instead of depending on the government alone.

I wish the Governments at the Centre and State take further measures in improving the educational infrastructure for, especially, Muslim girls, where such infrastructure does not exist now.

Mumbai **Vasundhara Mohan**

# Contents

*Preface* v
*Acknowledgments* vii
*List of Tables* xi

1. Introduction 1
2. Review of Literature 20
3. Karnataka State 30
4. Uttar Pradesh 90
5. Muslim Women and Women's Reservation Bill 167
6. Muslim women's Political Participation: Religious Aspects 199
7. Responses from the Field 210
8. Conclusion 247

Executive Summary 278

*Bibliography* 283

*Index* 288

# List of Tables


1.1: Election in South Asian Countries 9

3.1: Muslim Population of Karnataka in Different Census Years 32
3.2: Performance of Muslim Women, 1985 General Elections 46
3.3: Karnataka Assembly Constituencies and Muslim Population 47
3.4: Performance of Muslim Women at the 1994 General Elections 48
3.5: Performance of Muslim Women at the 1999 General Elections 49
3.6: Performance of Muslim Women at the 2004 General Elections 50
3.7: Performance of Muslim Women at the 2009 General Elections 51
3.8: Candidates Relation in General Elections 2013 52
3.9: Performance of Muslim Women, 2014 General Elections 54
3.10: Status of Muslims Women Contested from 1952-2013 56
3.11: Muslim women in the Lok Sabha (1st to 15th) 57
3.12: Muslim Women Elected to City Corporations in Karnataka in 2001-02 Elections 62
3.13: Performance of Muslim Women at the Elections to the Urban Local Bodies, 2007 (CC: City Corporation) 63
3.14: Councillor Election Results, Greater Bangalore Municipal Corporation, 2010 70
3.15: Performance of Muslim Woman at the Elections to the City Corporations, 2013 73
3.16: Performance of Muslim Women in the Elections to PRIs, 2013 76

4.1: District-wise Concentration of Muslims in Uttar Pradesh 91
4.2: Literacy Rates of Population: Religion-wise 92
4.3: Women in Uttar Pradesh Legislative Assembly 103
4.4: Performance of Muslim Women at the 1962 Assembly Elections 106
4.5: Performance of Muslim Women at the 1967 Assembly Elections 106

4.6: Performance of Muslim Women at the 1969 Assembly Elections 107
4.7: Performance of Muslim Women at the 1974 Assembly Elections 107
4.8: Performance of Muslim Women at the 1977 Assembly Elections 108
4.9: Performance of Muslim Women at the 1980 Assembly Elections 108
4.10: Performance of Muslim Women at the 1985 Assembly Elections 108
4.11: Performance of Muslim Women at the 1989 Assembly Elections 109
4.12: Performance of Muslim Women at the 1991 Assembly Elections 110
4.13: Performance of Muslim Women at the 1993 Assembly Elections 111
4.14: Performance of Muslim Women at the 1996 Assembly Elections 112
4.15: Performance of Muslim Women at the 2002 Assembly Elections 113
4.16: Performance of Muslim Women at the 2007 Assembly Elections 114
4.17: Performance of Muslim Women, Assembly Elections, 2012 119
4.18: Party-wise Performance of Muslim Women in 2012 Elections 122
4.19: Level Education of Number of Contestants (2012) 122
4.20: Female Candidates in Uttar Pradesh Legislative Assembly 124
4.21: Muslim Women at the 1980 General Elections to 7th Lok Sabha 126
4.22: Muslim Women at the 1984 General Elections to 8th Lok Sabha 127
4.23: Muslim Women at the 1989 General Elections to 9th Lok Sabha 127
4.24: Muslim Women at the 1991 General Elections to 10th Lok Sabha 128
4.25: Muslim Women at the 1996 General Elections to 11th Lok Sabha 129
4.26: Muslim Women at the 1998 General Elections to 12th Lok Sabha 130
4.27: Muslim Women at the 1999 General Elections to 13th Lok Sabha 131
4.28: Muslim Women at the 2004 General Elections to 14th Lok Sabha 132
4.29: Muslim Women among the Elected Presidents of Nagar Palika Parishads, Uttar Pradesh, 2012 (Total Number of Nagar Palika Parishads: 194) 140
4.30: Muslim Women among the Elected Presidents of Nagar Panchayat, Uttar Pradesh, 2012 Total Number of Nagar Panchayats in Uttar Pradesh in 2012: 420 141
4.31: Local Body General Elections, 2012, Uttar Pradesh Details of Contesting candidates for the Post of Chairperson 142
4.32: Age Profile of Successful Muslim Women in the PRI Elections of Uttar Pradesh, 2012 148
4.33: Unanimously Elected Muslim Women 150
4.34: District-wise Participation of Muslim Women 152
4.35: District-wise NP/NPP, Ward, Name of Candidate unopposed 152

5.1: Number of Muslims Elected to tne Lok Sabha (1952-2009) 168
5.2: List of 19 Elected Muslims Women in Lok Sabha (1952-2009) 170
5.3: Muslim Women Candidates to 7th Lok Sabha General Elections 170
5.4: Muslim Women at the Candidates to 8th Lok Sabha General Elections 171

5.5: Muslim Women Candidates to 9th Lok Sabha General Elections 171
5.6: Muslim Women candidates to 10th Lok Sabha General Elections 172
5.7: Muslim Women Candidates to 11th Lok Sabha General Elections 173
5.8: Muslim Women Candidates to 12th Lok Sabha General Elections 174
5.9: Muslim Women at the 1980 General Elections to 13th Lok Sabha 174
5.10: Muslim Women at the 1980 General Elections to 14th Lok Sabha 175
5.11: Muslim Women Candidates to 15th Lok Sabha General Elections 176
5.12: Muslim Women Contestant in Lok Sabha Election 178
5.13: Percentage of Respondents of Muslim in Indian Politics. 191

7.1: Responses about Muslim Women's Participation in Politics 211
7.2: Hardoi, Saharanpur, Sitapur and Rae Bareilly 215
7.3: Literacy Rates of Muslims in 2001 (%) in Bangalore, Karnataka, India 236
7.4: General Opinion on Muslim's Politics Participation in Respondents 242
8.1: Literacy Rate by Religious Communities, Census of India 2011 251

# 1
# Introduction

This study examines the status of electoral participation or political participation of Muslim women in the States of Uttar Pradesh and Karnataka as contestants, seeking representation in the Panchayati Raj Institutions (PRIs) and the respective State Legislatures and Parliament.

At the outset, there is no consensus on the definition of the term 'political representation'—the expression of the urge to be a part of the functioning of the government and have a role in it. In simple terms, political representation is a process by which one is a part of the making of government policy related to the wants, needs and demands of the public. However, "it is a common observation that political representatives tend to be drawn from the elite stratum of society. Even where representatives are chosen through fair and democratic elections, it is often said that legislative assemblies remain "unrepresentative," and, in particular, that they are under-representative of women, ethnic minorities, and the poorer and less educated social classes."[1]

If a parliament should be microcosm of the nation, it should, to some extent at least, mirror the population from which it is drawn and all classes of citizens should have some of their own numbers in the representative body, in order that their feelings and interests may be better understood and attended to. It has become increasingly important that parties and legislatures be (or appear to be) inclusive and demographically representative of the broader society. Of special concern have been two underrepresented groups, women and ethnic minorities.[2] But, although women make up slightly more than 50 per cent of the world's population, they hold only approximately 16 per cent of the world's elected political posts. This is because women are seen as just voters; meant to boost the fortunes of every political party and be happy about it. Political participation includes women's right not only to vote or have their concerns articulated and represented through others, but also to have a wide understanding of and engagement with the political process and their own membership in the legislatures.

A legislature is a key institution which can not only hold tremendous influence over women's lives, but also capable of bringing about changes in women's realities. But, unless specific conditions are met, women find it difficult to participate in the political process, which has so far, by and large, remained a male bastion. The reasons for this are gender-specific. Women are less mobile than men and have domestic responsibilities which limit the time they can devote to such processes. There are also historical prejudices. Even a country like the United States of America has only 16.4 per cent women in the Congress.

Women's entry into public space and the utilization of authority will not only improve their self-esteem, but they can ensure that their rights are upheld or safeguarded by challenging deep-rooted patriarchal practices and feudal mindset that create hurdles in the emancipation of women. US Senator Kirsten Gillibrand said: "We (women) tend to be more results-oriented and less concerned with getting the credit. The female approach is more conciliatory and less combative. We tend to use a more civil tone."[3]

However, bringing women into politics needs consistent efforts over a period of time. Such efforts are afoot in several parts of the World, including India, although they are not always whole-hearted and power-hungry male politicians are always there to scuttle the process. India is a typical example; the Women's Reservation Bill is yet to become a law even though it was initiated in 1996.

Women's political representation in the Lok Sabha has hardly been able to cross the ten per cent mark and the chances are that it may never cross, unless the Reservation Bill is passed. Unless they belong to the elite or privileged class or enter through the caste quotas or at the instance of powerful male politicians, Indian women are unable to stand competition in the political arena. The expectations of the Constituent Assembly that women do not need a separate quota/ reservation and that they would overcome their constraints in a specified period, have proved to be misplaced. It appears that women's political participation is determined by their status and position in the society and the way their roles are viewed.

In fact, in all of South Asia, women's political participation is determined by patriarchal structures and the resultant gender inequality and gender discrimination; a common feature irrespective of the religious affiliation. Gender relations are rooted in the ideology that women are subordinate to men. More often than not, women are consistently denied inheritance rights, freedom of expression and mobility, participation in community activities and a say in personal choices and preferences. They are thus denied a meaningful role in decision-making, and are unable to access even proper education. Their place in the family hierarchy combined with the socially prescribed gendered division of roles determines their levels of exclusion in both the private (household) and public spheres. Since politics is viewed as Public in nature, it is defined in terms of masculinity, as opposed to private space, which is considered feminine and secluded. Consequently, most of the political parties tend to keep women on the periphery, delegating them with tasks like mobilising female voters. If there is no compulsion to do so, political parties will not be inclined to give tickets to women candidates; they have to be part of the political elite to be treated differently. Kinship considerations playing a major role, it is not surprising that most women heads of government and most women in political leadership are from political families.

## Women's Struggle in India

Women's entry into the public and political mainstream began in India with the involvement of some women in the social reform movement at the turn of the 20th century, especially for ending customary practices (*sati,* child marriages, widow remarriage, polygamy etc.) and promoting education. Later, the freedom struggle gave further impetus.

Women's participation in politics in India was initially articulated by educated women like Sarojini Naidu who, in 1918, argued before the Indian National Congress that giving women the right to vote will by no means interfere with the destinies of men and women. Earlier, in 1917, a delegation of Indian women had submitted a demand for franchise to the Secretary of State Edwin Montagu. The ensuing mobilization of women won propertied women the right to vote between 1920 and 1930 though they continued to be denied legislative membership. However, following lobbying by the Women's Indian Association, women were admitted to legislatures in 1930, paving the way for women to be nominated to legislatures; the first woman being Muthu Lakshmi Reddi.

But, for the nationalists the women's question was a non-issue in their political negotiations with the Colonial power. Reservation of seats for women was a contested issue even among women in the sub-continent. During the 1920s, the idea of separate political reservation for women was opposed on the grounds that it deflected from the demand for universal adult franchise and the right to stand for elections on the same terms as men. At the All India Women's Conference in 1930, Sarojini Naidu made it clear that women were not inferior to men that they required any preference in terms of nomination or reservation of seats. On the other hand, at the Round Table Conference in 1930, Begum Jahanara Shah Nawaz and Mrs. Radhabai Subbarayan recommended that five per cent seats be reserved for women. The move was opposed by women's organizations in India who reiterated the demand for universal adult franchise, emphasizing their rejection of "privileges" and "favour" for women.

As the debates continued, greater consensus emerged on universal adult franchise. However, "in the face of opposition from the British, the women's organizations agreed to a compromise which restricted the right to vote for women in the urban areas. The assumption was that the urban women would be in a better position to represent the women of India. But the opposition to reservation remained and merit was to be the only criterion."[4] With respect to communal-based reservations, while Aruna Asaf Ali wanted that the legislature should be filled with those who feel that the country stands above personal or communal considerations, Begum Sakina Mayuzada argued that desiring the good of one's community did not imply harm on others. K.B. Firozuddin felt that the comparative educational backwardness of Muslim women representatives might put them at a disadvantage in joint electorates.[5]

Despite disagreements, women's organizations declared that they were untouched by communalism. Their dissent (over separate or reserved seats based on religion) was ignored even when they came from important figures such as Begum Jahanara Shanawaz. The 1935 Government of India Act provided for the formal induction of women in the political process through a broadened franchise and contesting elections on both reserved and general seats.

Post-independence, women members of the 1949 Constituent Assembly opposed special concessions for women and reservations based on religion. Speaking in the Constituent Assembly on 22 November 1949, Begum Aizaz Rasul (United Provinces) said[6]:

> "... one of the most important and historic features of the Constitution is the abolition of reservation of seats for minorities ... I have consistently supported the thesis for the abolition of these seats... ... which I did ... ... inspired by the conviction that it was absolutely suicidal for a religious minority to keep alive the spirit of separatism by demanding reservation on communal lines. As a matter of fact nothing can protect a minority or group less than a barrier that divides it from the majority. It makes it a permanently isolated group and prevents it from moving closer to the other groups in the country. ... ... I look forward, Sir, to the day when individuals will cease to regard themselves as members of religious minorities. But this, Mr. President, can only be done if and when the majority also cease to be conscious of their majority and members of all communities, big or small, sincerely and simultaneously begin to consider themselves and one another as full and equal citizens of a Secular State."

Years later, in 1975, the Committee on the Status of Women in India rejected the idea of women's reserved seats, although there was a dissenting note from Vina Mazumdar and Lotika Sarkar who saw reservations as a necessary affirmative action for women. However, the Committee did make a strong recommendation for institutionalization of women's participation in local government through special quotas.

Without the benefit of reservations, women's political representation at the legislative level in India has declined from over the years, reflecting the reality that given their disadvantaged position in the society, women are unable to enter or compete in the political arena. Despite their low numbers some women have reached higher positions in the mainstream political parties and in governance. Notwithstanding their standing, such women have failed to push for gender balance in the decision-making bodies within their parties;

the reason being the fact that there are not enough of them in the legislatures to give the necessary push.

While some feel that women do not necessarily want to aim for leadership positions keeping in view their domestic expectations and pressures, the fact remains that they do not get an even-playing field. On the other hand, it is also argued that women need to demand the exercise of more control in areas where they have leverage, and ask for more opportunities for speaking up. Both the arguments are relevant to the Indian context. In spite of the fact that women have often played a subordinate role, changes have been taking place in the role of women in recent times. But, organizations, society and women themselves have not always kept pace with these changes. Civil society, development, and social justice will never find their true meanings without women's presence, role and sharing.

## Muslim Women

In the struggle over women's reservation in independent India, the fact that there are about 60 million Muslim women and they are represented by just three women in the 15th Lok Sabha (2009-2014) raises some questions: are the Muslim women not interested in political participation? Do not they have political ambitions? Does the Muslim society not want to encourage them? Is anybody pleading their case? In this connection, we may quote Jawaharlal Nehru expressing his anguish over the poor representation of women:[7]

> "I am quite sure that our real and basic growth will only come when women have a full chance to play their part in public life. Wherever they have had this chance, they have, as a whole, done well, better if I may say so, than the average man. Our laws are man-made, our society dominated by man, and so most of us naturally take a very lopsided view of the matter. We cannot be objective, because we have grown up in certain grooves of thought and action. But the future of India will probably depend ultimately more upon the women than the men."

As we will see later, some political parties and politicians did try to make out a case for Muslim women when the Women's Reservation Bill was tabled in the Parliament, demanding that unless the Bill makes specific provision of a sub-quota for Other Backward Classes and Muslim women, they will not agree to the passage of the Bill. The fact that they did so for reasons entirely disconnected with promoting OBC and Muslim women's political participation is an open secret. On the other hand, no Muslim leader (male) or Muslim woman of consequence, has forcefully argued the case of Muslim women. Very few, if any, male Muslim leaders have supported Muslim women's representation. Manzoor Alam, General Secretary of the All India Milli Council was one.

*** *** *** ***

When we talk about Muslim women's representation in the Parliament or legislative assemblies in India, it may be relevant to look at the situation in Islamic countries. Speaking at one of the sessions of the Doha Debates in 2005, Dr. Tareq Mohammed Al Suwaidan (a Kuwaiti entrepreneur and leader of Muslim Brotherhood) said[8]:

> "... the situation of woman in the Middle East is miserable, and it is a true situation, it is in politics, in the law, it is in the families. ... ... not only women have problems, but also men have problems, but definitely the situation with woman is much, much worse than the situation with men. But this is not only in the Arab world. It is also in the whole world... ... In studying management we are taught about the glass ceiling where most women have to stop at a certain position. They cannot climb the ladder. Why? Because they are women! ... ... So it is a man's world, and in the Arab world, in the Middle East, it is even worse, much worse than that".

Dr. Suwaidan rejected the argument that Islam is responsible for this situation. He said[9]:

> "Allah Almighty has created us equal. This is stated very clearly by the saying of our Prophet Mohammed (peace be upon him) ... ... Now, what happened is that in the past 400 or 500 years, we have been backward, we have been occupied, and tradition has mastered our society and some people are mixing up between Sharia and Islam and the

> tradition, and thus in the name of Islam, they are putting woman down. ... ... ... we have to admit the problem, it is a traditional problem, and thus it is in politics and economics and because of tradition, it has nothing to do with Islam. Islam is very strong when it comes to the rights of woman. But I would like also to say that a lot of the problem also lies in the hands of woman themselves. They have to pull themselves up, they have to learn, they have to qualify themselves, they have to get skills and stop wasting their time, and again, if they are in the West, they need to break the glass ceiling. They have a double glass ceiling here in this region and they need to work harder to achieve that."

Speaking at the same session of Doha Debates, Sheikh Jihad Brown, an Islamic Scholar, admitted that there is a devaluation of the role of women and questioned[10]:

> "Why is it that a woman, it is automatically assumed that she cannot perform the same task as well as a man, why is that?... If a woman is talented and can play a role in society, can play a role in a certain position, then she should be given the opportunity to take that position alongside other men, and if she performs the same task to the same degree of qualification, she should receive the same pay as men, whether that be in the Middle East or the United States or the West in general".

Compared to the Arab world "South Asia stands out for its dynamic women leaders who reached highest political offices in a region where women as a whole are downtrodden, shackled by illiteracy and customary practices, and denied mobility, inheritance and voice in decision-making" (Table 1.1)[11]. Several initiatives have been taken in South Asia over the years to induct women into the political mainstream, with mixed results.[12]

Though Muslims constitute a sizeable population in India and account for about 13.4 per cent of the population (2001 Census), their representation in the country's Parliament and State legislatures has been disproportionately low, right from the first general elections. Within the Muslim community, the representation of Muslim women in the Parliament and State legislatures is abysmally low.

**Table 1.1:** Election in South Asian Countries

| *Country* | *Month and Year of Elections* | *Lower House* | | | *Upper House* | | |
|---|---|---|---|---|---|---|---|
| | | *Seats* | *Women* | *%* | *Seats* | *Women* | *%* |
| Pakistan | 5/2013 | 323 | 67 | 20.70 | 104 | 17 | 16.30 |
| **India** | **4/2009** | **545** | **60** | **11.00** | **245** | **26** | **10.60*** |
| Bangladesh | 12/2008 | 350 | 69 | 19.70 | – | – | – |
| Sri Lanka | 4/2010 | 225 | 13 | 5.80 | – | – | – |
| Nepal | 4/2008 | 594 | 197 | 33.20 | – | – | – |
| Bhutan | 7/2013 | 47 | 3 | 6.40 | 25 | 2 | 8.00 |
| Maldives | 5/2009 | 77 | 5 | 6.50 | – | – | – |

(*) In 1/2012

*Source:* Inter-Parliamentary Union, *Women in National Parliaments* (data as on 1 September, 2013. Available at http://www.ipu.org/wmn-e/classif.htm)

There are a number of reasons as to why the Muslim community is not represented in the Parliament and State legislatures in proportion to their population. In the absence of a religion-based quota in India, the chances of Muslims getting elected to the legislatures depend upon the mainstream political parties. Among the others, the major reason appears to be the lack of effective Muslim leadership in the country. As a majority of the Indian politicians following partition have been non-Muslim, the country's Parliament and State Legislatures came to be dominated by them. Nepotism and perpetuating the hegemony of a particular family or clan naturally resulted in a higher representation of non-Muslims in the legislatures. Also, many political parties are not optimistic about the electability of Muslims. Talukdar contends: "The non-Muslims electorate, parties think, will not vote for them because of their religious identity."[13] It is also a fact that the Muslims abandon their links with a political party the moment they perceive that it is veering away from its secular character. This is evident from the Muslims shifting their loyalties from the Congress party to other Regional parties and also from one regional party to the other. Their loyalties, thus, become suspect resulting in poor nomination.

Together, the above factors have led to a condition where the Muslim community, the largest minority group in the country, has poor representation in the country's politics. Under the circumstances, the Muslim community has to no time to think about women's participation.

The above situation had prompted this author to examine the political participation of Muslim women in India in 2008.[14] The present study is in continuation of the last one and an attempt is made here to study the political participation of Muslim women in Uttar Pradesh (a North Indian State) and Karnataka (a South Indian State). The reasons for choosing these two states are explained below.

### Muslim Women and Politics

If women, *per se*, have not been able to enter the Parliament and State Legislatures in sufficient numbers even after 70 years of independence, Muslim women are almost absent. Sheema Mohsin, Member of Karnataka Wakf Board observes:[15]

> "On the issue of empowerment of Muslim women, the traditional quarters have always squirmed. There has not been much work in the area. There is an urgent need to empower them on every level through the tool of empowerment like education, creating awareness among them about their rights. What is also important is that they be given representation at the higher decision-making bodies, so that they should raise the problems of Muslim women at that level. This is how they will be able to influence and formulate the policy-making so that the concrete decisions would be made for their welfare and development. It should be kept in mind that if we are working for the development and empowerment of Muslim women it is actually the community itself which is being empowered and developed."

It is an established fact that women in India suffer discrimination; even if it is covert. Muslim women suffer more compared to their Hindu and Christian sisters; most of which are community-specific. They are told that Islam prohibits women from politics and the primary duty of a Muslim woman is to look after her husband and children.[16]

The twentieth century has been witnessing re-awakening among Muslim women in the areas of political thought, literature and knowledge. Muslim women of India have also been fighting for the redressal of their grievances and injustices in matters relating to the domestic sphere. Simultaneously, they have also been attempting to gain representation in the country's Panchayati Raj Institutions, State

Assemblies and the Parliament. If women, as a category by themselves, have unique problems of their own and without their representation such problems may go unnoticed and not considered in a male-dominated parliament, Muslim women have their own religion-specific issues. While Hinduism neither precludes nor encourages its women to take active part in politics, Muslims in almost all Islamic countries have not only never encouraged their women to enter politics, but have, instead, discouraged them from doing so. While Indian Muslim religious leaders frown upon Muslim women contesting elections, they have not at least stopped them from voting unlike in Bangla Desh.[17]

Apart from the religious leaders, even Muslim families do not encourage their women to take-up politics, unless they are "political families."[18] It is for this reason that several Muslim women disappear from the scene after contesting one or two elections. On the other hand, most often the electorate find it difficult to accept a woman to represent them, unless she is already a popular social worker and has proved her mettle and commitment to the societal problems. In all other cases, it appears that the community itself ignores her. The question is why? Does not the community take pride if a woman from the community rises to a politically important position?

The Women's Reservation Bill is based upon the understanding that women's increased political participation does not take place automatically and certain specific measures are necessary for the reinforcement of the level of such participation. In the absence of a guaranteed return system, women, including Muslim women, who tried to enter the parliament or legislatures as independents have had little luck. Yet, Muslim women have realised that while they may stand some chance if the Women's Reservation Bill becomes an Act, demanding a quota for Muslim women within the women's quota, i.e. a quota based on religion, which is not permissible under the Constitution, will only delay the passing of the Bill. As Brinda Karat observed[19]:

> "While there is no Constitutional provision for religion-based reservation, the demand for separate reservation for Muslim women within the Women's Bill is for obvious reasons untenable. That is why many Muslim women have taken a pragmatic stand requesting Muslim MPs in the Parliament

not to stall the Bill as it will give them some hope to contest elections in women reserved seats."

Thus, Muslim women who want the Reservation Bill to be passed in its present form, have termed the demand from the male politicians for a sub-quota for Muslim women is nothing but an attempt to delay and keep the issue alive (of reservation for women) for their own political gains.[20] It is also argued that if the Bill is passed in its present form, it will benefit women belonging to SC/ST categories as well as the minorities and as such there is no need for special quota for Muslim women. They point out that the results of civic polls show that a number of Muslim women have been participating in the elections even when there is no such sub-quota.

By the 1990s, the socio-economic development had helped many women to become educated, financially independent, and reach positions of authority and responsibility. They had begun to reflect Muslim women's aspirations and potential achievements. Muslim women have become increasingly conscious of the gap between their human rights and social needs on the one hand, and their objective conditions, on the other. When they started to make public demands and "women's rights" became a serious issue, challenging the patriarchy. "Even in India many Muslim women began to take an active interest in theological arguments regarding women. They claim the right to interpret laws and religious texts themselves and to learn the skills necessary for such interpretation; they challenge androcentric and misogynist interpretations of texts; and they are determined to find in Islam justifications for demanding individual freedom and women's rights. They have, in other words, joined the political struggle over the right to make their religion work for them".[21]

Thus, there are highly competent Muslim women in different walks of life in India. The presence of such women in the State Legislatures and Parliament will immensely benefit the community; its women and children particularly. But then, it is for the community to allow them to take the plunge. Yusuf Muchhala, legal advisor and member of the AIMPLB observes that in the Muslim society very few women are socially active and felt that "unless Muslim women demand their legitimate rights they will continue to suffer. Women themselves are not demanding their rights and male ego would not allow it to concede their demands. Women have to fight their own battle."[22]

Muslim women-led groups and networks began appearing during the late 1980s and 1990s in urban centres across the country. Their voices were increasingly gaining national attention though their debates related to Muslim women's rights and multiple forms of discrimination on issues like personal law, the orthodox position taken by the All India Muslim Personal Law Board, as well as highlighting wider issues faced by Muslim women that have not been addressed by the *Ulema,* the state, or in any depth by the women's movement. But, political rights were not on the agenda.

## Present Study

Muslim society in India is heterogeneous in nature because of the influence of several factors, including the caste system, which has, it is held, led to *Indianisation* of Islam. There being is no homogeneity among the Muslims of India, it was considered unwieldy to study the political behaviour of Muslim women in the entire country. As such, it was decided to study the subject with reference to two States viz., Uttar Pradesh and Karnataka. Though from the point of view of religion there is no difference between the Muslims of the north and the south, there are differences in more ways than one. Talking about Kerala Muslims, for instance, Yoginder Sikand writes:[23]

- North Indian Muslim culture, as articulated by north Indian Muslim elites, continues to be represented in a feudal mould, reflecting a nostalgic longing for the past, stemming from centuries of the political dominance of Muslim elites, the '*Ashraf*', now long since ended. This feudal culture is reflected in the *huge hiatus* between the Muslim elites and the masses;
- There is a striking difference in the work culture of Muslim institutions in Kerala and in the Urdu-Hindi belt, where many such institutions suffer from a distinct lack of professionalism and from the stern authoritarianism of their managers;
- From the late-nineteenth century onwards, Islamic reformist movements in Kerala continue to be vastly influential. They have played a key role in bridging the sharp dualism between the *Ulema* and the 'modern'-educated class, in promoting 'modern' as well as religious education, including women's education. They have also set up literally thousands of

institutions that cater to the community—not just *madrasahs* and mosques, as in much of north India, but also schools, colleges, hospitals, orphanages, industrial centres, banks, newspapers and so on. In this way, the *Ulema* in Kerala have played a more socially engaged role than their counterparts in the north as far as community work is concerned;

- The middle class among the Muslims in Kerala steadily grew in the post-Partition period, especially due to the Gulf boom from the 1970s onwards. They played a key role in mobilizing the Muslims politically as a strong, effective force. Being taken seriously by various political parties, they were able to get many of the demands of the community met. While in north India Muslim politics have been dominated by symbolic, although not unimportant, issues—Babri Masjid, Urdu, Muslim Personal Law and so on—in Kerala Muslim political discourse has been very different, focusing more on social and economic issues;
- The Partition affected the north Indian Muslims particularly, in contrast to Kerala, which was virtually untouched by its consequences. Few Kerala Muslims migrated to Pakistan. In north India, on the other hand, the bulk of the Muslim middle-class, which could have played a key role in institution building, political mobilisation and promoting modern education, migrated to Pakistan. The majority of the Muslims who remained behind were poor, mainly from the 'lower' castes. Being accused, rightly or wrongly, of being responsible for the Partition, and faced with constant anti-Muslim pogroms, pervasive discrimination and the growing strength of Hindutva chauvinism, the north Indian Muslims were too afraid to mobilize politically as a strong force. … … Hence, lacking a strong independent political identity, the Muslims of north India were politically divided and weakened. The north Indian Muslim political leadership, for whatever it was worth, was divided between different political parties, but even these so-called 'secular' parties used them to gain Muslim votes, but actually did little at all for the Muslim masses. Afraid to alienate their political bosses, these Muslim political elites consistently refrained from addressing the manifold problems of the Muslim masses.

The differences identified by Yoginder Sikand between the North Indian Muslims and those of Kerala are equally, if not wholly, applicable to the Muslims of Karnataka. In the absence of stringency, Karnataka Muslim women are better placed over their counterparts in Uttar Pradesh in terms of educational achievements and work-force participation. For, "education has a positive effect on the decision to participate in the labour market for two reasons; first, education is an investment in human capital and the recipient has to work in order to recover cost of education. Second, education is considered as a consumption activity and the recipient induced to work because of higher earning potential since the opportunity cost of not working is higher. ... ... Data also suggest that the participation of Muslim women (185 for rural and 128 for urban areas) is much less than the overall women's participation in labour force.[24]

If education is an essential determinant of political participation, there should be a larger participation of Muslim women of Karnataka in elections as compared to those of Uttar Pradesh. Is that the case? Studies have shown that "Muslims have lower literacy and educational attainments in the States having higher concentration of their population. Muslim girls in Maharashtra, Karnataka, Andhra Pradesh and Kerala are doing much better than the States like Uttar Pradesh and Bihar.[25] Uttar Pradesh fits this pattern with 18.50 per cent Muslim population, compared to 12 per cent of Karnataka. Secondly, by and large, Muslim women of Karnataka who live in the penumbra region of Darul Uloom are hardly affected by the *fatwas* as are their sisters in Uttar Pradesh. It is not that the Karnataka Muslim women are 'less-Islamic' than those of Uttar Pradesh. But being better educated than the Muslim women of Uttar Pradesh, and living in a different socio-cultural setting, Muslim women of Karnataka have mustered enough courage to question the validity and relevance of the various *fatwas*; especially those that affect that socio-economic well-being.[26] However, there have hardly been any Muslim women in the Karnataka Legislative Assembly ever since the first elections in 1952. On this score, Muslim women of Uttar Pradesh are a shade better, despite the fact that those who got elected have made it have not done so on their own strength, but owing to solid backing of male politicians.

In spite of Muslim women forming a sizable chunk of the country's female population and despite contesting elections since 1952, they are very poorly represented at the federal and State levels. They were almost non-existent on the ballot. Comparatively, non-

Muslim women have been enthusiastic participants in electoral politics, as organisers, voters and contestants. Why do not Muslim women show similar enthusiasm at the Assembly and Parliament elections? Do not they aim for leadership positions? Or are they being discouraged?

## Methodology

This study has been taken up to examine the performance of Muslim women of Karnataka and Uttar Pradesh in the elections to the PRIs as well as State Assemblies and the Parliament. The election statistics of the Election Commission of India and the State Election Commissions form the source of basic data for this study. The views of a cross section of the Muslim community were collected through a questionnaire, personal discussions through the field investigators and personal communication. This author also held discussions with reputed Islamic scholars and senior journalists like Tanweer Ahmed (of Karnataka Muslims, Bangalore) and academicians on political participation of Muslims in India. We agree that compared to the Muslim population of the two States studied, the sample size is too small. But, still we could glean the opinions of the respondents and we are sure that the views expressed will be no different if the sample size had been larger. Even with this constraint, we hope that this study will make the Muslim community sit up and think of improving the community's socio-economic and political status, especially of its women, instead of sticking to the ole ideologies and notions and let itself be bypassed.

## Chapter Scheme

We begin this study with a survey of literature as it relates to the political participation of Muslim women in general and with specific reference to India. The next two chapters are devoted to the examination of the electoral performance of Muslim women in the elections to the PRIs, ULBs, Assembly and the Parliament in Karnataka and Uttar Pradesh. This is followed by a Chapter on Women's Reservation Bill and the position of Muslim women. As the conservatives believe that Islam prohibits women's political participation, the next chapter is devoted to consider this aspect. The responses from the field to our questionnaire are discussed in a separate chapter before concluding.

## NOTES AND REFERENCES

1. Bird, Karen (2003), *The Political Representation of Women and Ethnic Minorities in established Democracies*, Working Paper presented for the Academy of Migration Studies in Denmark (AMID), Aalborg University, 11 November, (Available at http://www.hks.harvard.edu/fs/pnorris/Acrobat/stm103%20articles/Karen%20Bird%20amidpaper.pdf.)
2. *Ibid.*
3. Senator Kirsten Gillibrand quoted by Goudreau, Jenna (2011), A Few Reasons Why Women Should Not Go Into Politics, in *Forbes Woman*, 7 July, (Available at http://www.forbes.com/sites/jennagoudreau/2011/07/07/why-women-shouldnt-go-into-politics-michele-bachmann-sarah-palin/)
4. Raman, Vasanthi (2002). *The Implementation of Quotas for Women: The Indian Experience,* Paper prepared for workshop hosted by International Institute for Democracy and Electoral Assistance (IDEA) on 25 September, 2002 in Jakarta, Indonesia. (Available at http://www.quotaproject.org/cs/cs_india.pdf)
5. Quoted in Mary E. John, (2011), The Politics of Quotas and Women's Reservation Bill in India in Miyoki Tsujimura and Jackie F. Steele (Eds.) *Gender Equality in Asia*, Tohoku University Press, Japan, pp. 169-195. (Available at http://www.cwds.ac.in Politics%20of%20quotas%20and%20WRB-MJ-Ch.8.pdf)
6. Government of India, *Constituent Assembly of India,* Debate on 22 November, 1949, (Available at http://www.indiankanoon.org/doc/1415231). Begum Aizaz Rasul was the only Muslim woman elected to the Constituent Assembly. Born into the princely family of Malerkotla, she was married to Nawab Aizaz Rasul, *a Talukdar* (landowner) of the former Princely State of Oudh.
7. Jawaharlal Nehru, *Letters to the Chief Ministers,* Volume II, pp. 615-16.
8. *The Doha Debates*, June 01, 2005. (Available at http://www.thedohadebates.com/debates/item/?d=25&s=1&mode=transcript)
9. *Ibid.*
10. *Ibid.*
11. *Women's Representation, Effectiveness and Leadership in South Asia*, February 2005, Fifth South Asia Regional Ministerial Conference, Celebrating the Beijing Plus Ten, Islamabad, Pakistan, 3-5th May, 2005, Women's Representation, Effectiveness and Leadership in South Asia, Khawar Mumtaz *(*Available athttp://www.unifem.org.in/PDF/Women_representation.pdf)

12. Currently, reserved seats are provided for women in the legislatures of Pakistan and Nepal (those in Bangladesh having lapsed in 2001), and at the local government level in India, Pakistan, Bangla Desh and Nepal. Sri Lanka has no special provision for women's representation at any level. Notwithstanding the progress made by some individual states in South Asia, the average membership rate of women in parliaments is one of the lowest in the world—lower even than that of East Asia and Sub-Saharan Africa.
13. Talukdar, Shahidur Rashid. *Low Political Representation of Indian Muslims and the Way Out*. (Available at http://www.srtalukdar.com/articles/indian-muslims/low-representaion-of-muslims).
14. Mohan, Vasundhara. *Political Participation of Muslim Women in India.*(Available at http://webspace.webring.com/people/gh/husociology1/1/muslimwomen2008.pdf). A revised version of the paper was presented at the *International Conference of Women and Politics in Asia* at Hildesheim, Germany. (Published as Political participation of Muslim women in India in *Women and Politics in Asia:* LITVerlag *A Springboard for Democracy?* (Eds.) Andrea Fleschenberg and Claudia Derichs, Berlin (2010), LIT-Verlag).
15. In *Two Circles.net*. (Available at http://twocircles.net/2008sep10/sheema_mohsin_first_muslim_woman_karnataka_wakf_board.html)
16. Basheer, K.P.M. Where Muslim League lets Muslim Women down, in *the Hindu* dated 6 October, 2001.
17. Halder, Nomita (2004), "Female Representation in Parliament: A Case Study from Bangladesh" in *New Zealand Journal of Asian Studies,* 6, 1 (June 2004):27-63, (Available at http://www.nzasia.org.nz/downloads/NZJAS-June04/6_1_3.pdf.) Nomita Halder refers to a "recent discovery (which) indicates that millions of Bangladeshi women have never had the experience of voting due to *fatwa* that voting involves women's public interaction. During the last 3-4 years, the government and several NGOs have taken the initiative to teach these women how to vote and for the first time thousands of women cast their votes in the 2001 general election."
18. Dr. Najma Heptulla, former Deputy Speaker of the Rajya Sabha, belongs to the elite class and has a sound educational background, besides being the great grand niece of Maulana Abul Kalam Azad. She enjoyed the support for her work from both her natal and marital family. Margaret Alva, a Christian, former Minister of State and Founder Chair of the National Commission for Women of India, is from a similar background. In both cases the families were involved in the national movement, were influenced by liberal ideology and were highly educated. (Rai, Shirin, "Class, Caste and Gender: Women in Parliament in India" in *International IDEA*, 2002, Women in Parliament, Stockholm. (Available at http://www.idea.int/publications/wip/upload/CS_India.pdf)
19. It is in this connection that the opposition of Muslim women for reservation of quota for them within the 33 per cent demanded for women in general, is

intriguing. Why do they object? Brinda Karat provides an answer Karat, Brinda. *Survival and Emancipation: Notes from Indian Women's Struggles,* Gurgaon, India (2005), Three Essays Collective, p. 142). Similar view was expressed by Rajinder Sachar (Women's Reservation Bill: A Social Necessity, National Obligation. (Available at http://www.pucl.org/Topics/Gender/2003/reservation-bill.htm)

20. Muslim Women question male locus standi in the *Indian Express*, July 16, 1998.
21. Afkhami, Mahnaz and Erika Friedl. (1997), *Muslim Women and the Politics of Participation: Implementing the Beijing Platform*, Syracuse University Press. (Available at http://www.questia.com/PM.qst?a=o&d= 59644978)
22. Lakdawala, M.H., Supreme Court Judgement on Maintenance, in *Milli Gazette,* (Available at http://www.milligazette.com/Archives/01112001/29.htm)
23. Sikand, Yoginder (2007). Muslims in Kerala and Elsewhere: Accounting For the Difference, in *Countercurrents.org*, 30 June. (Available at http://www.countercurrents.org/sikand300607.htm)
24. Masood, Tariq and Md. Izhar Ahmad. (2009), *An Econometric Analysis of Inter-State Variations in Women's Labour Force Participation in India*, 10th October. (Available at http://mpra.ub.uni-muenchen.de/19376/1/MPRA_paper_19376.pdf)
25. Nayar, Usha. (2007), *An Analytical Study of Education of Muslim Women and Girls inIndia,* October 1. (Available at http://www.jeywin.com/wp-content/uploads/2009/12/An-Analytical-Study-of-Education-of-Muslim-Women-and-Girls-in-India.pdf)
26. Ataulla, Nigar, (2010), *FATWA*: An Open Letter to the *Fatwa*-Makers, May 16, In *Indian Muslim Observer.* (Available at http://www.indianmuslimobserver.com/2010/05/issues-open-letter-to-*fatwa*-makers.html. Nigar Ataulla is Executive Editor of the Bangalore-based *Islamic Voice).*

# 2

# Review of Literature

While there are several studies in India and abroad on the socio-economic conditions of the Muslim community on one hand and specifically on Muslim women on the other, there are hardly any studies devoted exclusively to their political participation. The problems faced by Muslim women on issues like marriage, divorce, maintenance, custody of children etc., and the influence of Muslim Personal Law on such issues have been written about at great length. But questions relating to the participation in politics as candidates seeking election to the Parliament and State Assemblies have not attracted much attention. It appears as though it has been taken for granted that Muslim women's political participation is a non-issue and does not merit any extensive and separate discussion, removed from that of women in general. For instance, a report prepared by the National Institute of Advanced Studies (Gender Studies Unit) on "Women and Political Participation in India", which has discussed women's political participation in India has not considered Muslim women as deserving any special mention, in spite of the fact that they form a substantial single group among women.

The few books by well-known authors and reports devoted to Muslim women's political participation are discussed below.

Karin Deutsch Karlekar has paid exclusive attention to Muslim Women in Indian Politics during the period 1947 to 2002. (*In a Minority: Essays on Muslim Women in India,* (Eds.) Zoya Hasan and Ritu Menon, 2005, Oxford University Press, New Delhi). According to Karlekar, "much of the attention has focussed on the educational, legal, and socio-economic disadvantages faced by Muslim women, *with little interest being shown in their involvement in political sphere*"

(p. 222). She has given a historical background to the participation of Indian women in politics, while mentioning that a small number of Muslim women entered public sphere and "they came typically from elite families with a progressive outlook" (p. 222). Such women were already educated, discarded *purdah* and had become involved in social work. "A relatively small number of Muslim women have participated in electoral politics over the past 57 years and an even smaller number have been elected to office." (p. 223) Analysing the data, Karlekar has concluded that Muslim women's electoral prospects have been hampered by their gender and their religious minority status. She provides a portrait of the type of Muslim women who have been involved in politics and the role of political parties in improving women's representation; not Muslim women *per se*. She has identified that female Muslim politicians at both national and provincial-levels have been overwhelmingly associated with the Congress party. (p. 253) The reasons adduced for this phenomenon were that the Congress party was considered as one practicing inclusive politics, protector of minority interests and as one committed to women. However, even Karlekar's study has not touched the constraints being faced by Muslim women from the religious angle. Religious figures have played spoil-sport with the ambitions of Muslim women by issuing *fatwas*. On the other hand, Karlekar states that Muslim women's lower rate of success as compared to Hindu women could be attributed to "discrimination on the part of the political parties or the electorate at large" (p. 248). She has rightly identified the problem, but has not been studied in detail.

*Political Representation of Muslims in India,* 1952-2004 by Iqbal A. Ansari is a marathon effort to analyse the electoral statistics, in his effort to identify the political dynamics that have affected the political participation of Muslims in India. However, not a word is said about Muslim women in the entire analysis. Ansari has observed that "the number of *Muslim candidates* elected will largely depend on the number of candidates nominated by the Party, though their chances of success will be more favourable in constituencies having fair to sizable per centage of Muslim voters." (p. 96) But, this observation does not seem to hold good for Muslim women.

Yet another book [*Unequal Citizens: A Study of Muslim Women in India* (Eds.) Zoya Hasan and Ritu Menon, New Delhi (2004): Oxford University Press] deals with Women's political participation in India, but not specifically with reference to Muslim women. Muslim women are found to be more enthusiastic in queuing up at the election booths than Hindu women (p. 207). The authors find that Muslim women were not interested in contesting elections. In response to their question whether, given an opportunity, they would like to contest elections, an overwhelming majority (78%) of all women responded with a negative reply; with the proportion of Muslims being significantly higher at 81 per cent as against 78 per cent of Hindus" (p. 216). The reasons for the high proportion of Muslim women showing their disinclination to contest elections have not been probed. The authors have also found that "independent candidates fare extremely poorly in elections both at the national and provincial-levels and the support from a political party is absolutely vital to a candidate's success in politics. The party's attitude towards supporting female candidates, in general, plays a major role." (p. 255) This observation is equally applicable to Muslim women. Rather, our study will show that political parties, including Muslim-based ones, have not shown much enthusiasm in supporting Muslim women.

J.K. Chopra [*Women in the Indian Parliament: Critical Study of their Role,* New Delhi (1993): Mittal Publications] writes that "opinion polls suggest that people tend to vote for a party rather than for a particular candidate" (p. 244). This observation especially applies to Muslim women, who invariably lose the election when they contest as independents. On the other hand, we propose to show that even when Muslim women contest under the banner of an established political party, the Muslim electorate have ignored them. Similarly, the success of a Muslim woman candidate is not assured even when she contests from a predominantly Muslim populated area as contended by Karlekar.

Quazi Arshed Ali [*Karnataka Muslims and Electoral Politics*, Bangalore (2012): Bookware] has made a detailed analysis of the political behaviour of Muslims of Karnataka right from the first general elections in 1952 to the elections to the general elections to the Lok Sabha held in 2009. He also has analysed the results of elections to the Karnataka Assembly during the same period and the Legislative Council elections. But, he has just devoted a single paragraph to Muslim women (p. 122), stating that "their share in the political process is negligible."

The Sachar Committee Report (2006) has extensively studied the socio-economic status of Muslims in India. However, the report has not dealt with the issue of political participation of Muslim women.

Pradeep Chibber (*Why some Women are Politically Active: The Household, Public Space, and Political Participation in India*, Department of Political Science, Berkeley: University of California) deals with the general question of women's political participation or the lack of it and the reasons there for. Muslim women are not specifically mentioned.

Nazia Jalali (The Role of Women in Politics *Khilafah* magazine, (August 2003 edition), (http://www.oocities.org/zq83_uk/archives/women_in_polity.htm) looks at women's empowerment and her role in politics from an Islamic perspective. Jalali observes that "despite such changes in recent thinking, the idea of women engaging in politics continues to be a matter that raises much debate in the West and particularly in the Muslim world, which often bears the brunt of criticism in its inequitable regard towards women. She criticises the Western models of democracy, which are imposed on Islamic countries. "If one were to examine every Muslim country today, one would find that *kufr* man-made laws have been implemented, which serve nothing other than to enslave, humiliate and oppress men, women and children".

Azra Khanam and P.K. Mathur have analysed the status of Muslim women on the basis of the Sachar Committee Report. (Status of Muslim Women: An analysis of Sachar Committee Report, in *Islam and Muslim Societies*, Vol. 4, No. 1, 2011, Aligarh: Aligarh Muslim University).(Available on line at http//www. muslimsocieties.org/Vol_4_No_1_Status_of_Muslim_Women_in_ India.html).http://www.muslimsocieties.org/Vol_4_No_1_ Status_of_Muslim_Women_in_India.html. But, as the Sachar Committee has not devoted any attention to the political participation of Muslim women, the analysis deals with only education and work-participation aspects.

Mona Lena Krook's book [*Quotas for Women in Politics, Gender and Candidate Selection Reform Worldwide*, (New York (2009): Oxford University Press] discusses the patterns of political representation and the most common reforms providing for increased representation of women. It also refers to the various methods adopted for improving women's political participation and the role of political elites in their attempt to overcome the quote regime. Muslim women are not specifically discussed.

Satya Pal Ruhela (Ed.) [*Empowerment of the Indian Muslim Women*, New Delhi (1998): MD Publications Pvt. Ltd.] The book contains 40 sociological studies concerning Indian Muslim women, which provide a wide spectrum of socio-cultural, economic and other factors as well as motivations and aspirations of Indian Muslim women in post-Independent India. However, political participation is not discussed.

Shahida Lateef's contribution, Muslim Women in India: A Minority within a Minority [in *Women in Muslim Societies: Diversity Within Unity*, (Eds.) Herbert L. Bodman, Nayereh Esfahlani Tohidi, Boulder, Colorado, USA (1998), Lynne Reinner Publishers Inc., pp. 251-272] deals with the status and role of Muslim women in the context of the political, economic and social survival of the Muslim community in India. The author traces the historical and contemporary changes that have influenced the community action and the status of women. As she rightly points out, in the recent decades, the status of Muslim women has been subject to pressures from the predominantly conservative Muslim leaders in the community. However, the discussion of the effect of the pressures from such conservative forces is limited to Muslim Personal Laws and not to Muslim women's political participation.

In her essay on An Islamic Perspective on Women in the Political System, (Islamic Research Foundation International Inc., Louisville, KY USA) (Available at www.irfi.org/articles/articles_251_300/an_islamic_perspective_on_women.htm) Farhat Naz Rahman states that "the *Qur'an* does not propose or support a singular role or single definition of a set of roles, exclusively, for each gender across every culture. This thus allows individuals the freedom to decide on their functions and roles best suited to their contexts. This must, of course, be done by maintaining fairness and equality through mutual consultation, mercy, consideration and compassion between those affected by the decision. Women can also hold political positions in Islam. No *Qur'anic* verses exist that prevent women from holding positions of leadership.

Other books referred to by this author include:

- Lateef, Shahida. [*Muslim Women in India: Political and Private Realities*, New Jersey (1990): Zed Book].
- Lateef, Shahida. Modernisation in India and the Status of Muslim Women, in *Modernisation and Social Change among Muslims in India*, (Ed.) Imtiaz Ahmad, New Delhi (1983): Manohar (pp. 152-183).
- Vasanthi Raman. Identity Formation, Nationhood and

Women: An Overview of Issues, in *Identity Formation, Nationhood and Women*, (Ed.) Anshu Bharatiya, New Delhi: CWDS, (Available at http://www.academia.edu/1308011/Identity_Formation_Nationhood_and_Women An Overview of Issues).

- Shirin Rai. *Class, Caste and Gender: Women in Parliament in India*, International IDEA, 2002, Women in Parliament, Stockholm (http://www.idea.int) (The case study was originally published in International IDEA's Handbook: *Women in Parliament: Beyond Numbers*, Stockholm, International IDEA, 1998).(Available at http://www.cccindia.co/corecentre/Database/Docs/DocFiles/cs_india.pdf).
- Iqbal A. Ansari. *Political Representation of Muslims in India,* 1952-2004, [New Delhi (2006): Manak Publications Ltd.]. This books deals with the political representation of Muslims in general. Muslim women have not been discussed.
- Bernard Lewis. *The Middle East: A Brief History of the Last 2000 Years*, New York (1997): Simon and Schuster Inc.

Besides the above works, there are a number of studies devoted to Muslim women's political participation in countries like Indonesia, Iran, Pakistan and Bangladesh. The following need mention as they deal with women's political participation, though Muslim women are mentioned in passing.

In her essay on *Obstacles to Women's Political Participation in Indonesia* Kofifah Indar Parawansa (International IDEA, 2002, Women in Parliament, Stockholm)(http://www.idea.int/publications/wip/upload/CS_Indonesia_Parawansa.pdf) observes that "in a country that follows a patriarchal value system, like Indonesia, the chances for women to become politicians are limited because society's perceptions regarding the division of roles between men and women tends to be biased towards thinking that a woman's role should be limited to managing the household". This observation is equally applicable to Indian Muslim society. Parawansa has identified the following as the factors influencing the election of women as legislators in Indonesia:

- The heavily patriarchal Indonesian society perceives that the political arena is for men, and that it is inappropriate for women to become members of parliament;

- Selection of candidates is usually conducted by a small group of officials or party leaders, almost always men. As male leaders of political parties have a disproportionate influence over party politics, women do not receive much support from political parties because of domination of the irstructures by men;
- Media has an important effect in developing public opinion regarding the importance of the representation of women in parliament; and
- Absence of network of organizations, NGOs, and political parties to fight for the representation of women.

The following are the other books/articles consulted during the course of this study. But, once again, they deal mainly with religious and socio-economic of the lives of Muslim women.

- Gail Minault. (1982) *The Khilafat Movement: Religious Symbolism and Political Mobilisation in India,* New York: College University Press.
- Hasina Hashia (ed.), (1998) *Muslim Women in India since Independence: Feminine Perspectives*, New Delhi: Institute of Objective Studies.
- Rozina Vishram. (1992) *Women in India and Pakistan: The Struggle for Independence from British Rule*, Cambridge University Press.
- Maulvi Sir Mohammed Yakub. (1932), *Notes on Women's Franchise* in the Report of the Indian Franchise Committee, Vol. 1. London: HM Stationery Office.
- Qamar Hasan. (1988), *Muslims in India: Attitudes, Adjustments and Reactions,* New Delhi: Classic Bookman Pvt. Ltd.
- Women's political empowerment: The Unrosy picture, in *Karnataka Muslims,* May 15, 2012. (Available at http://karnatakamuslims.com/portal/womens-political-empowerment-the-unrosy-picture/).
- In her thesis on the *Role of Women in Social and Political Development of Pakistan:* 1896 to 1995, Samar Sultana cites poverty, illiteracy, opposition from the spouses and the society and finally the reluctance of the political parties to field women who cannot guarantee a win. All these factors are

also applicable to the Indian scene, as our study will show. Yet, in South Asia, women have fared better in Pakistan's political field due to reservations and have occupied significant positions in the government.

- In her article on "*Muslim Women and their representation in South Asian Politics in Islam and Muslim Societies,*" Vol. 6, No. 2, 2013. (Available at http://www.muslimsocieties.org/Vol_6_No_2_Muslim_Women_and_their_Representation.html), Azra Abidi rightly points out that "the denial of basic education (to Muslim women) means that the majority of women do not realize that they are not receiving their full rights. It is difficult to teach them when they cannot read and difficult for them to stand up for themselves when they cannot write." She also observes that "the reasons and obstacles why only a few Muslim women are in politics even today can be attributed to religious and economic factors, social biases, obstacles, and negative attitudes based on gender roles and stereotypes that continue to persist."
- Ruhaini Dzuhayatin Siti (*Islam, Patriarchy and the State in Indonesia*) refers to the State Guidelines issued in 1989 listing the functions of Indonesian Muslim women, which remain unchanged. These functions do not include her political participation.
- M. Afkhami and E. Friedl (Eds.) (1995), *Faith and Freedom: Women's Human Rights in the Muslim World*, (New York: IB Taurus).
- Ahmed, L. (1992) *Women and Gender in Islam: Historical Roots of Modern Debate*, (New Haven: Yale University Press).
- Dipankar Gupta. (1997), Ethnicity and Politics, in (Ed.) Kaviraj, *Politics in India.*
- M. Hasan. (1997), *Legacy of Divided Nation: India's Muslims since Independence*, New Delhi: Oxford University Press.
- O. Khalidi. (1995), *Indian Muslims since Independence*, New Delhi: Vikas Publishing House Pvt. Ltd.
- Shahida Lateef. (1990), *Muslim Women in India: Political and Private Realities,* 1890*s* to 1980s, Kali for Women.
- A.K. Verma. Muslim Resurgence in Urban Local Bodies of Uttar Pradesh, in *Economic and Political Weekly*, Vol. XLVII No. 40, October 06, 2012. The analysis of Dr. Verma about the resurgence of Muslims in elections to the Urban Local

bodies of Uttar Pradesh in 2012 does not take into account similar resurgence of Muslim women.

A number of articles have appeared in the print media from time to time on Muslim women's political participation and analysing the reasons for their interest in politics and the reaction of the religious leaders and Muslim society at large. Of these the most significant are those by P.M. Basher, Journalist and Zarina Bhatti, Sociologist. Muslim women's rightful place both in society and politics in the general political milieu cannot be separated. But, as Danish Khan, News editor, *Milligazette,* a community paper published from Delhi, says there is a need for change in the outlook and "it should come from within the community." But he has "little hope that it will."

Other articles that we have perused include:

- Alavi, S. "Muslim Women do not need Reservation", in *Times of India*, 15, July, 1988.
- *Baseline Report: Women and Political Participation in India*, National Institute of Advanced Studies, Gender Studies Unit, Prepared by NIAS *et al.*, and Coordinated by IWRAW Asia Pacific: Report of the Core Group.
- Bhatty, Z. Socio-Economic Status of Muslim Women in Z. Siddiqui and A. Zuberi (Eds.) *Muslim Women: Problems and Prospects*, New Delhi: Manohar Publishers, 1985.
- Debroy, Bibek. *Ensuring legal equality for Women*, Punjab, Haryana and Delhi Chamber of Commerce and Industry, Ph.D. Policy Paper, Digitalised 28th October, 2008, University of Michigan.
- Iftekhar, Pumma. *Muslim Women and their Participation in Public Life: A Case Study of UP*, Doctoral Thesis submitted to Jamia Millia Islamia, February 1998.
- Jalal, A., "The convenience of subservience: Women and the State of Pakistan" in Deniz Kandiyoti (Ed.) *Women, Islam and the State*, London (1991): MacMillan.
- Jeffrey, Robin. *Politics, Women and Well-being: How Kerala Became a Model*, Cambridge: Commonwealth Series, MacMillan Press (1992).
- Kazi, Seema. *Muslim Women in India*, Minority Groups International, 1999.

- Mehta, Pratap Bhanu, "The Dilemma of Muslim Politics-1", *The Hindu*, 17th May, 2002.
- Mernissi, Fatima. *Beyond the Veil: Male Female Dynamics in the Muslim World*, Bloomington and Indiana (1987): Indiana University Press.
- Shaheed, F., *et al.*, *Women in Politics: Participation and Representation in Pakistan*, Special Bulletin, Lahore, May 1988.
- WRAG Report on Aspects of Culture and Society: Muslim Women in India, Malappuram, Women's Research Action Group, Mumbai, 1997.
- Zahid, Naghma. *Political Participation of Muslim Women: A Case Study of Delhi*, Ph.D. Thesis (2002) Jamia Millia Islamia, New Delhi.
- Talukdar, Shahidur Rashid. *Low Representation of Muslims in Indian Politics: Causes and Concerns.* (Available at http://www.policymic.com/articles/476/low-representation-of-muslims-in-indian-politics-causes-and-concerns)
- Anne Marie Goetz Women's Education and Political Participation, Background paper prepared for the Education for All Global Monitoring Report 2003/4, *Gender and Education for All: The Leap to Equality,* UNESCO, (New York, 2003).


In view of the above the proposed project intends to seek reasons for Muslim women's failure to make it to the Parliament and state legislatures in the realm of religion and Muslim society. Our study also covers the elections to the Panchayati Raj Institutions in the two States (for certain years only) of Karnataka and Uttar Pradesh to glean the performance of Muslim women. The purpose of this work is to ascertain the factors that still continue to prevent them and show that religion is not the only reason.

# 3

# Karnataka State

The southern State of Karnataka, a successor to the Princely State of Mysore, was formed on 1st November, 1956 following the enactment of the States' Reorganization Act. The earlier name, Mysore State, was later changed to Karnataka in 1973. Mysore State had a distinctive position among all the native states because the rulers were very attentive towards the development of the state and gave priority to education.

With democracies and democratic system of governance taking shape across the world, C.V. Rangacharlu, then Prime Minister of the Mysore State, had formed a Representative Assembly with 144 nominated members in 1881. In 1891 election system was introduced for the Representative Assembly, though on a small scale.

Later, the Mysore Legislative Council was established in 1907 with a view to associating some non-officials with practical experience and knowledge of local conditions and requirements to assist the Government in making Laws and Regulations. The Council was to consist of 10 to 15 members to be nominated by the Government and of this not less than two-fifths were required to be non-officials. *Seats for Muslims, Christians and depressed classes were reserved and the Government nominated them if they were not elected.* The strength of the Council was increased in 1940.

On 24 September, 1947, the Maharaja of Mysore agreed to join the Indian Union. The very next day a responsible government was formed with K.C. Reddy as the Chief Minister. As the State Congress demanded a separate Constitution for Mysore State, the Maharajah issued a Proclamation on 29th October, 1947 setting-up a Constituent Assembly to frame the Constitution of the Mysore State. Elections were held in 1948 for the Mysore Constituent Assembly. But, as by 1948 all the native States had joined the Indian union, the question of separate Constitution for Mysore State was given up and the Mysore Constituent Assembly was converted into an Interim Assembly, which functioned till the general elections held in 1952.

The present geographical structure of Karnataka State has come about in stages. On first October, 1953 seven *talukas* of Bellary district of Madras Province were pulled out and merged with Mysore State. In a second stage of reorganization of the States on linguistic basis, some districts of Andhra, Hyderabad, Bombay and Madras States were clubbed with Mysore State. By 1956 the reorganization of the Mysore State was complete and a United Mysore State was formed on 1st November, 1956 and the small state Coorg was merged with Mysore and given a district status. The districts merged with Mysore State brought with them additional Assembly seats along with the already elected members.

Following the adoption of the Constitution of India and its enforcement across the country, general elections were held all over the country between 1951 and 1952. Elections were held in Mysore also and the first State Assembly came into being on 23 March, 1952.

Of the 99 members of the first Mysore Assembly, there was only one Muslim representative, J.M.M. Imam Saab, who had won from Jagalur constituency in Chitradurga district on Kisan Mazdoor Praja Party ticket. All the nine Muslim contestants were men. As the elections were held in the early years after partition, the time was not yet ripe for Muslim women to venture into politics. In fact, there were no women among the 394 contestants at the 1951 general elections.

Due to reorganization and transfer of assembly segments to Mysore state as aforesaid, the total number of members in the Mysore Assembly rose to 210 on 1st November, 1956 and remained as such on the eve of general elections to the Mysore Assembly in 1957.

## Muslim Population

In 1961, there were only 19 districts in Karnataka. Of these, Bidar district had the highest population of Muslims (18.6%) while Mandya district had the lowest Muslim population at 3.49 per cent. Following the carving out of new districts, Dakshina Kannada (Mangalore) emerged as the district with highest Muslim population of 22.07 per cent, while Mandya maintained its last place.

According to the available official records, Muslim population in Karnataka constituted 8.64 per cent of the population in 1911. The 1931 census records the percentage of Muslims at 9.36 per cent, which went up to 10.05 per cent in 1951, dipping to 9.87 per cent in 1961.[1] The following Table gives the Muslim population of Karnataka at the different Census years.

**Table 3.1:** Muslim Population of Karnataka in Different Census Years

| *Census Year* | *Total population of the State (lakh)* | *Muslim population (in lakh)* | *Percentage of Muslims in the total population (%)* |
|---|---|---|---|
| 1961 | 230 | 23.28 | 9.87 |
| 1971 | 293 | 31.13 | 10.63 |
| 1981 | 371 | 41.63 | 11.21 |
| 1991 | 449 | 52.34 | 11.64 |
| 2001 | 585 | 64.46 | 12.23 |
| 2011 (provisional) | 611 | 77.79 | 12.72 |

*Source:* Quoted from *Muslim Population in Karnataka: An Analysis*-1. Qazi Arshad Ali.

According to the 2001 Census, 17 of the (then) State's 27 districts had more than 10 per cent of Muslim population, with lesser percentage in other 10 districts. In 12 districts of Belgaum and Gulbarga divisions of North Karnataka, the percentage of Muslim population was 14.39, whereas in 15 districts of South Karnataka, the percentage was 10.15. Later, following the carving out of three more districts, the number of districts rose to 30, leading to a readjustment of the population. The percentage of Muslim population in Dakshina Kannada (Bidar, Gulbarga and Dharwad divisions) rose to more than 20 per cent and to more than 15 per cent in Kodagu, Haveri, Bijapur and Raichur districts. Mandya and Chamrajnagar are the two districts where Muslim population is less than 5 per cent, whereas in Mysore, Tumkur, Hassan, Chikmagalur and Bangalore Rural districts it is less than 10 per cent.

At the 2001 Census, the total population of Karnataka was 52.85 million of which 26.90 million (50.89%) were male and 25.95 million (49.11%) were female. The literacy rate among the Muslims of the State was estimated at 67 per cent; with 76 per cent of males and 57 per cent of females being literate. 83.8 per cent of the population were Hindu, 12.23 per cent Muslim, 1.91 per cent Christian, 0.78 per cent Jains, 0.73 per cent Buddhist, with the remainder belonging to other religions.

Kannada is the official language of Karnataka and spoken as a native language by about 64.75 per cent of the people. Other linguistic minorities in the state as of 1991 were Urdu (9.72%), Telugu (8.34%), Marathi (3.95%), Tamil (3.82%), Tulu (3.38%), Hindi (1.87%), Konkani (1.78%), Malayalam (1.69%) and Kodava Takk (0.25%).

## Muslims of Karnataka

The arrival of Muslims in what now constitutes Karnataka had begun soon after the advent of Islam in Arabia. In fact, Arab traders arrived in Karnataka even before the founding of Islam in 7th century AD. Arab traders settled along the coast in Kerala, Karnataka and Tamilnadu.

Tracing the origins of Muslim community in Karnataka, Qazi Arshad Ali (a Member of the Legislative Council of Karnataka State and a senior journalist) writes that after two centuries of establishment of Muslim colonies in South Karnataka and coastal Kerala, Muslims from North India started arriving in north Karnataka and later scattered across the state gradually. Qazi Arshad Ali writes[2]:

> "Muslims' advent to the present Karnataka had begun very soon after the advent of Islam in Arabia. The connection of Muslim Arab businessmen with the coastal region of Kerala and Karnataka is very ancient. They established their colonies in the west coast of India. Ibn-e-Batuta, in his travelogue, written in 1342, has mentioned a Muslim State in Honnavar, and has revealed that even at that time separate institutions were established for girls' education. The generations of Arab Muslims present in the Dakshina Kannada, Udupi and Uttara Kannada districts of south-west coastal Karnataka are Mappila, Byari and Navayathi. These people speak Malayalam, Konkani, Navayathi and Byari languages".

Muslims progressed and strengthened the foundations of Islamic civilization in Karnataka during the rule of Bahamani and Bareed Shahi regimes in Gulbarga and Bidar, and the Adil Shahi and Asaf

Jahi regimes in Hyderabad and Bijapur. Islamic rule in Karnataka contributed immensely to the architecture, painting, music, calligraphy and numismatics, adding several distinct features of its own. Many Hindu shrines took up these features and incorporated them into their own artistic styles. In addition to these processes of assimilation, the Muslim Kings have created some of the most splendid and famous monuments in Karnataka, situated in Bidar, Gulbarga, Bijapur and Srirangapattana.

A majority of the Muslims, who came from North India, speak Urdu language while all the Muslims of Karnataka are conversant with Kannada and other local languages. Owing to different roots in their origin, there is obviously no cultural homogeneity among the Muslims of the State. Muslims of Bidar, Gulbarga, Raichur and Koppal districts, which were earlier a part of Hyderabad State, have a different identity in terms of culture and language compared to the Muslims of other parts of the State. Urbanisation has its own effects. According to one source, in the City of Bangalore, which has 8,89,000 Muslims, "various Muslim communities intermingle with each other and intermarry. Most Muslims speak Urdu as their mother tongue, though not all can read and write Urdu."[3]

Following the migration of Muslims from rural to urban areas, Muslim population of Karnataka is mostly concentrated in urban areas; a phenomenon similar to other parts of the country. According to the 2001 census, of the 6.46 million Muslims (about 12.23%) in the total population of Karnataka, 3.82 million, i.e. 59 per cent lived in Urban areas and 2.65 million, i.e. 41 per cent, in rural areas.

## Educational Status

As we are concerned with the electoral participation of Muslim women in Karnataka, it is relevant to consider the educational status of women, as it is one of the factors (although not the sole determining factor), which determine or affect their socio-economic status and by extrapolation, their electoral participation.

According to a report attributed to noted researcher and demographer Mahendra K. Premi, the literacy rate among Muslim males was high—above 80 per cent—in Kerala, Chhattisgarh, Tamil Nadu, Maharashtra and Gujarat. With regard to Muslim women, a high literacy rate of about 70 per cent was recorded in Kerala, Tamil Nadu, Maharashtra and Chhattisgarh. The percentage of literate

Muslim women was higher than that of the Hindu community in nine States—Andhra Pradesh, Chhattisgarh, Gujarat, Jharkhand, Karnataka, Madhya Pradesh, Maharashtra, Orissa and Tamil Nadu.[4]

It is well established that a majority of Muslim women in India are among the most disadvantaged, least literate, most economically impoverished and politically marginalized sections of the society. According to an ORG-Marg Muslim Women's Survey commissioned by the Nehru Memorial Museum and Library, New Delhi, conducted in 2000-2001 in 40 districts spanning 12 States, the enrolment percentage of Muslim girl children was a mere 40.66 per cent. As a consequence, the proportion of Muslim women in higher education was a mere 3.56 per cent, lower even than that of scheduled castes (4.25%). On all-India basis, 66 per cent Muslim women are stated to be illiterate. However, if illiteracy among Muslim women is most widespread in Haryana, Kerala has least illiteracy among Muslim women, closely followed by Tamil Nadu. Muslim women are found to be more literate than their Hindu counterparts in the states of Madhya Pradesh, Maharashtra, Andhra Pradesh, Karnataka and Tamil Nadu.[5]

The Sachar Committee report records that among the southern States, the literacy rate of Karnataka Muslims (2001 Census) was 70.1 per cent as compared to 89.4 per cent of Kerala, 82.9 per cent of Tamilnadu and 68 per cent of Andhra Pradesh. Muslim Female Literacy rate in Karnataka was 63 per cent compared to 76.9 per cent for Muslim males. Muslim Rural Female Literacy was 52 per cent as against 70.61 per cent in urban areas. However, twelve of the State's districts recorded a literacy rate that was below the State average and 5 districts below the national average. As could be expected, in rural Karnataka, the Muslim female literacy is 52 per cent as against 70.61 per cent in urban areas. Within the state, Muslim Female Literacy ranges from a low of 29.47 per cent in District Gulbarga to 83.9 per cent in District Udupi in rural areas and from 53.76 per cent in District Koppal to 86.69 per cent in District Kodagu.[6]

M.S.A. Siddiqui, Chairman of the National Commission for Minority Educational Institutions had an occasion to observe that the gender-gap in the literacy rates within the Muslim community was the highest among the three largest minority communities viz., Muslims, Christians and Sikhs, and such gap was higher in rural areas. He attributes social taboo attached to education as one of the reasons for the educational backwardness of Muslim girls and states that such taboos feed on existing social reality, severely undermining the public mobility of girls in general.[7]

A few special schemes were floated by the Government of India for education of Muslims, some especially for girls, after 1992. But, studies and field observations show that the implementation of such schemes has been uneven and ineffective. This may be on account of poor dissemination of information about the schemes and even indifference of the States. However, a healthy trend is the growing realization of the necessity to combine religious instructions with secular education. According to available statistics, though at the elementary level the enrolment of Muslim girls appears to be "quite fair", but in comparison to Christians and Sikhs, it comes almost to half.[8]

A number of Sociologists have pointed out that formal education is strongly associated not only with the socio-economic status of a given community, but also with political participation of both men and women. It is held that education is an "especially powerful predictor of political participation." The direct effects of formal education include the acquisition of knowledge and communication skills useful for public debate, and training in political analysis through courses with current events content. Its indirect effects are many and include the benefits of voluntary engagement in school, government, clubs, sports, and school newspapers; these provide young people with an early apprenticeship for politics, where they can exercise leadership, develop civic skills of cooperation and negotiation, and acquire bureaucratic and organizational skills useful for political activity. Education enhances other factors supporting political engagement, such as access to high-income jobs that provide the resources and contacts for political activity, and access to non-political associations such as charitable organizations or religious establishments that can be a recruitment ground for political activity.[9]

It should, however, be acknowledged that educational or economic backwardness is not confined to the Muslim community alone. It cuts across religious, regional and caste boundaries. But, the most common factors for high incidence of non-enrolment, drop outs and low achievement among Muslims girls are stated to be poverty, lack of women teachers, absence of separate schools for girls, observance of *Purdah*, opposition to secular education for girls, early marriages and conservative attitudes.

Abida Samiuddin, a renowned scholar, has observed that the history of Muslim women's education in India is a history of restriction and superstition. Social inequalities have prevented them from fulfilling their needs individually, and playing roles adequately in the family, at work, in the community and in the society in general. The reasons usually attributed to the educational backwardness of Indian Muslims are[10]:

- religious traditionalism and backwardness of those professing Islam;
- partition of India and the psychological crisis of identity it created for Indian Muslims; and
- the alleged deliberate neglect and discrimination against the Muslims by the majority (Hindu) society which professed to be secular, but was, in fact, discriminatory whether in education or employment.

Moreover, the conservative Islamic injunction restricting girls from seeking education in public places or in co-educational institutions—especially higher co-educational institutions—still seem to influence the minds of many Muslim parents. Unlike the Hindu, Christian and Sikh communities which had set up a network of good educational institutions to provide general and professional courses of education, the Muslim community failed to take similar steps soon enough and in large numbers to provide its youth with modern education. Besides, over 70 per cent of the Muslims in India live in rural areas and are marginal and small farmers or self-employed artisans and of the remaining 30 per cent, who are living in towns, roughly 80 to 85 per cent are skilled workers, tailors, retailers and in such other professions which do not require a person to be highly literate.

Higher dropout rate among Muslim students continues to be a cause for concern in Karnataka. In October 2013, the State Mass Education Minister Revu Naik Belamagi is reported to have told the media that "While the national dropout rate for Muslims is 5 per cent, in Karnataka it is 6.2 per cent." The reasons adduced include early childhood education in religious schools (which make it difficult for the children to adjust to mainstream schools) and availability of less number of schools in Muslim localities. But, the silver lining seems to be that Karnataka has a comparatively good gender balance among Muslim students, with an increased number of young women enrolling in high school. The Minister is also reported to have said that there is an educational awakening among Muslims in Karnataka and the rate of enrolment in high schools has increased since 2010 by 15 per cent."

However, educational backwardness of Indian Muslims cannot be attributed to any 'religious fanaticism' or 'minority complex' alone, but to the small size of the middle class whose members can be expected to seek educational opportunities. As stated above, lack of adequate number of schools and infrastructural facilities in the Muslim dominated areas continues to be a major cause of educational backwardness of the community. On the other hand, the reason as to why the literacy rate of Muslims in the southern states is above 70 per cent is because a majority of the Muslims residing in the southern States are engaged in tertiary activities that enhanced the need for acquiring education.[11]

Besides poor education, there are several other reasons that influence women's political participation that are equally applicable to women of all religions. These include time constraints from their domestic and other work commitments, and "gendered perceptions of political and community leadership." The last factor compels women to stay out of politics or develop a notion that women are not cut out for politics, even if they wish to participate.

## Socio-Economic Condition of Muslims of Karnataka

Commenting on the socio-economic status of Muslims in Karnataka, Dr. Abdul Aziz writes:[12]

> "It is a well-known fact that the Muslim population has been a product of conversion of the low caste backward Hindu population from time to time. As a result, the social and living conditions of the majority of Muslims continue to be poor. The condition of the rural-based and urban slum-based Muslims is even worse. Studies carried out by the Karnataka State Minorities Commissions and by some independent scholars hold testimony to this fact. During the pre-Independence period, Muslims had own land resources, controlled business and held government jobs in a large measure. But after independence, with the decline in their influence and the rise of dominant communities into power and influence, Muslims were marginalised particularly in

government and organised industrial and service sectors. The tendency to bask on past glory, ostentatious living, low priority to savings and investment, reluctance to provide modern education to children and a tendency to keep women out of work force are some of the inherent reasons for their social and economic backwardness."

"Recognising these factors, the Union Government and Government of Karnataka formulated programmes for development of weaker sections including Muslims, which range from poverty alleviation to social and political development programmes. Of these, the Swarna Jayanti Swarojgar Yojana and Sampoorna Grameena Rojgar Yojana provide self and wage employment opportunities, programmes of micro-finance, educational loans, housing and sanitation, concessional credit for artisans and agriculturists under priority sector lending, bank finance for industry and trade and so on. There are a large number of programmes, which are specifically meant for Muslim community. The State initiatives seem to be more comprehensive and focussed. They are comprehensive in that they cover all aspects of development of Muslim society, economy, polity and culture. They are focussed in that promoting growth, human resource development, development of women and children, political participation and development, cultural development, social development and developing community assets among Muslims of the Karnataka State".

The following are some of the policies initiated by the Government of Karnataka for economic development of Muslims.

- Starting of Urdu Medium Schools in Muslim dominant areas and providing facilities to learn Kannada language and permitting the minorities to set up schools, colleges and professional educational institutions and teachers' training colleges;
- Providing four per cent reservation of seats in higher education institutions and jobs in the government departments under the OBC (IIB) category;
- The Dalits among Muslims (*Darvesh, Pinjars, Ladafs,*

*Khasai, Fakirs, Phoolmali, Takara*, and *Chapparband)* are entitled to reservation under Category-I of the OBC. Some 33 occupational categories of these social groups are identified as the most backward communities; and
- Providing capital assistance through the Minorities Development Corporation and Commercial Banks to the minority community traders and businessmen.

The Karnataka State Minorities Commission is empowered to review the work done in this regard by the district administration.

## Reservation for Muslims

Muslim community in Karnataka had an edge over those in other States. For, the socio-economic status of the Muslim community was not lost sight of by the Maharaja of Mysore, who considered the Muslim community as a backward class and gave them reservation way back in 1921, following the recommendations of the Justice Miller Committee (1918). This continued till Independence.[13]

In the post-Independence period there were a series of efforts to include Muslims under sections of the backward classes' quota. In 1960, after the re-organisation of State of Mysore as Karnataka, all non-Brahmin Hindu castes and all non-Hindu minority communities like Muslims and Christians were declared as backward classes.

Later, the R. Nagana Gowda Commission (1961) brought Muslims under the backward classes list and identified more than 10 castes within Muslims as most backward. On the recommendations of the Commission, the backward classes were bifurcated into backwards (28%) and more-backwards (22%). Together with the quota for SC/ST, the extent of reservations rose to 68 per cent. However, even when in a land-mark judgement, the Supreme Court placed 50 per cent ceiling on the quantum of reservations, Muslims as a whole continued to be considered as among the backward communities. But, a Government Order issued based on the recommendations of the Nagana Gowda Commission in 1962, was challenged in the court and the issue was kept pending between 1962 and 1973.

In 1972 the Havanur Commission recommended the creation of a distinct category of minority group with reservation not exceeding 6 per cent. The State classified Backward Classes into three categories:

(a) Most backward, (b) More backward, and (c) Backward. All Muslims whose income was less than Rs. 2 lakh per annum were declared backward and placed exclusively in one of the sub-categories of "More Backwards" with four per cent of the seats reserved for them.

In 1977, the Devaraj Urs government passed an order providing reservation to Muslims under Other Backward Classes (OBCs). This was challenged in the High Court, which upheld the order. But it was subsequently questioned in the Supreme Court, which directed (1983) the government to set up another commission to review the backward classes list. Accordingly, the Venkataswamy Commission set up in 1984 suggested continuation of reservation for Muslims. Following protests by Vokkaligas, the Commission's report was not implemented. In 1990, the Chinnappa Reddy Commission again said that Muslims were a backward community. Based on this, the government issued an order in 1994 bringing Muslims under Category II and allocated a 6 per cent quota for Muslims under Category II (B), along with Buddhists and Christians.

However, the same year the Mandal case resulted in fixing a maximum ceiling for all reservations at 50 per cent, which meant capping backward classes reservation at 27 per cent. In the process of trimming down all quotas, the Muslim quota too was fixed at 4 per cent in Category II (B) and a Government Order passed in 1995. The same norm continues to this day.

## Muslims in the Electoral Politics of Karnataka

Before we consider the status of electoral participation of Muslim women in Karnataka, it is relevant to briefly examine the political participation of the community as such. In his detailed analysis of the Muslim community and electoral politics of Karnataka, Quazi Arshad Ali writes: "In the two general elections held in 1952 and 1957 the position of Muslims was weak and a leadership was yet to take shape".[14]

Under such a situation, nobody paid any attention to Muslim women's electoral participation at these two elections. The entry of Muslim women in the electoral politics of Karnataka has a bearing on the fortunes of the community as a whole. Hence, the latter aspect needs a little more attention, keeping in view, at the same time, the fact that the politics of Mysore State, and later of Karnataka, were and continue to be influenced by caste system, like in most other States. If *Vokkaligas* dominated the state politics until 1956, later the *Lingayats* acquired equal dominance. The effect of these changes had an impact on the Muslim community also.

The participation of Muslims as candidates in the elections increased from the third general elections held in 1962, at which, of the total 679 candidates who contested for 208 Assembly seats, 24 were Muslims; all males. Muslims were yet to test the political waters. Hence, most of the candidates flocked to the Congress party, which they considered secular. Seven of the eleven Muslim candidates put up by the Congress were successful. Muslim candidates sponsored by other parties and seven independents lost the election. Quazi Arshad Ali observes[15]:

> "As the democratic experience was gaining ground in the post-Independence era, better sense started prevailing upon Muslims in India. By 1962, the fear and despair psychosis which had engulfed them with the partition of the country (was) extinguished to a larger extent. The political equations were also changing across the country. The Congress sway went away with the death of Pandit Jawaharlal Nehru. The fourth Assembly of Mysore had a different colour now".

At the 1967 Assembly elections held for 216 seats, nine Muslims contested on Congress ticket. But, still no Muslim woman contested the elections. Of the nine male candidates, only four were successful.

After the general elections of 1967, Indira Gandhi emerged as a power to reckon with. In 1969 the old Congress leaders formed a 'Syndicate" and expelled Indira Gandhi from the Congress Party for "fostering a cult of personality." This resulted in a split in the Party. Devaraj Urs, who sided with Indira Gandhi, became the Chief Minister of Karnataka following the 1972 elections. Urs stood for the poor and drown-trodden of the society. He was also instrumental in abolishing the practice of carrying night-soil by Dalits.

The 1972 elections proved to be beneficial both for the backward classes and Muslims. In the elections held for 216 seats, 34 Muslims contested. The 'Indira Congress' gave tickets to 15 Muslims, of whom 12 were successful. Muslim candidates nominated by the main opposition, the Congress (Organisation), were defeated. It was for the first time that there were 12 Muslims in the Assembly. Although

28 non-Muslim women contested the elections, none could win. Muslim women were not yet ready to take the plunge and as such there were no Muslim women contestants at the 1972 elections. The post-partition generation was yet to emerge.

The decade of 1970-1980 witnessed the rise and fall of Indira Gandhi. When elections were held for the Karnataka Assembly in 1978 (post-Emergency), there was no Congress government at the Centre. But in Karnataka the Congress was in power under Devaraj Urs from 1972 to 1978. There was a silent revolution under Devaraj Urs, with the weaker sections getting exposed to a new awakening about their economic and political rights. This had a positive impact on the 1978 election results, which witnessed the emergence of Congress as the single largest party in the State. In the 1978 Assembly polls, the strength of Muslims went up to 16 and 12 of them were from the Congress. For the first time a Muslim woman, Shaukat Qureshi, contested the election from Binnypet Constituency in Bangalore as a Congress candidate. But, she just polled 906 votes (about 1.44% of the total valid votes polled) and lost to an independent non-Muslim candidate.[16]

When the Janata Party had gained popularity across the country in the post-emergency period, Karnataka still voted Congress to power. Later in 1980 the party got full majority in the Parliamentary elections. However, Devaraj Urs had fallen out of favour of Indira Gandhi and quit the Congress party and set up his own party; the *Karnataka Kranti Ranga*. Gundu Rao of the Congress party replaced him as the Chief Minister. Unhappy with his style of governance, Karnataka voters rejected the Congress at the 1983 Assembly elections. By now the Janata Party had become weak, and after the death of Devaraj Urs, his party, the *Karnataka Kranti Ranga*, had almost become defunct.

Following the 1983 elections, a non-Congress government came to power in Karnataka for the first time. This change of political situation had a negative impact on Muslims who continued to depend on the Congress party. Consequently, their representation in the House was reduced to two. At the 1983 elections, 16 Muslims had contested on Congress ticket and only one could win. One Muslim candidate was elected on Janata Party ticket. Others who contested on Republican Party of India and the CPI banner, lost. In so far as Muslim women are concerned, there was a lone woman, Shahajadiamma (Shahajadi Begum), among the 98 Muslim candidates. She contested as an independent from Krishnaraja Constituency, poling just 29 votes

(0.07% of the valid votes polled) and lost her deposit. Neither the performance of Shaukat Qureshi in 1978 nor that of Shahajadiamma later in 1983, offered any encouragement to the Muslim women of Karnataka to enter the electoral arena in large numbers.

The political situation changed following Ramakrishna Hegde's accession as the Janata Party Chief Minister in Karnataka. If Devaraj Urs had taken up issues like Social Justice and Land Reforms, Rama Krishna Hegde was concerned with Value-based Politics.

Following the assassination of Indira Gandhi, the nation went polls in 1984 and in November 1984, Congress party swept the polls on a sympathy wave, capturing 26 out of 28 parliamentary seats in Karnataka. Accepting moral responsibility for the Janata Party's poor performance, Hegde stepped down as Chief Minister. The Assembly was dissolved paving the way for fresh elections. When the Assembly elections were held in 1985, there was a Congress government at the Centre under the leadership of Rajiv Gandhi, but the voters brought back the Janata Party to power in Karnataka for a second time. The dismal performance of Muslim candidates was repeated this time too.

## Muslim Women in Karnataka Elections

Although there was no explicit prohibition against women's participation in elections, Muslim women do not seem to have evinced any interest in participating in the elections nor was there any effort from the community to promote their participation. Thus, in the first general elections held for the Legislative Assembly of Mysore State in 1951, there were no Muslim women contestants. Similarly, as we have seen from the above narration, there were no Muslim women contestants in the elections held to the Mysore/Karnataka Assembly during 1952, 1957, 1962, 1967 and 1972.

Slowly, but surely, Muslim women started evincing interest in political participation and contesting elections. At the 1978 elections, of the total number of 30 women contestants, only 8 were declared elected. As stated above, a lone Muslim woman, Shaukat Qureshi contested the 1998 election from Binnypet Constituency in Bangalore on Congress ticket. She polled 906 votes, i.e., just about 1.44 per cent of the total valid votes polled. She lost the election and forfeited her deposit. Similar was the fate of Shahajadiamma (Shahajadi Begum), who contested as an Independent candidate from Krishnaraja Constituency in Mysore district at the 1983 elections and lost. The fact that Shahajadiamma also lost her deposit goes to show that the Muslim community did not support its own women.

The absence of Muslim women candidates at the general elections to the Assembly during the years 1951 to 1978 is not unique to the Muslim community alone. When more-and-more non-Muslim women started showing interest, most of them were from SC/ST and OBC families. In fact, Quazi Arshad Ali notes that "the number of applications by SC/ST and OBC women seeking ticket from our party (Congress) was twice the number of those for general seats. If there were women from upper caste families, they belonged to political families."[17] The thinking among the traditional 'upper caste' families appeared to be that women should be protected by being kept out of public life and made to stay at home. Corroborating this view, other politicians said that "It is not easy for women from communities such as Brahmin, Lingayat, Maratha and Vaishya to enter politics."[18]

Professor Abdul Aziz of the Institute for Social and Economic Change sees an economic pattern underlying this trend. He wrote: "It is true that 'upper caste' women are less enthusiastic about politics. That is because a smaller proportion of women from upper class and caste backgrounds go out to work, compared to families from the deprived classes. Such behaviour is reflected in politics too."[19]

If the above trend was applicable to non-Muslim families, the chances of Muslim women taking part in elections, at least during the period under consideration, have been bleak. However, those concerned with women's empowerment were optimistic that women leaders will emerge from all sections once an opportunity is created for women to enter public life. Professor Abdul Aziz, who is one of the framers of the Karnataka Panchayat Raj Act, cites an example: "At one time, Muslim women did not go out of their homes. But now, two of my sisters are Panchayat members in Kolar district. Now, they know that there is an advantage to be in politics. It is a continuous process of learning."[20] If women have been subjected to artificial political barriers and long been denied empowerment, the rising intelligentsia were questioning these barriers severely for quite some time pointing out that if "human development is not engendered it is endangered".

Keeping in view the level of their earlier participation, the 1985 general elections to the Assembly witnessed a 'quantum jump' in that there were eight Muslim women contestants (Table 3.2). Only one woman, Mukhtarunnisa of the Congress won from Narasimharaja constituency. While Shaukat Qureshi and Aliya Begum fighting under

Congress ticket lost from Binnypet and Tumkur constituencies, respectively, the remaining five Muslim women who contested as independents lost their deposits, garnering as little as 0.09 per cent to 0.55 per cent of the valid votes polled.

**Table 3.2:** Performance of Muslim Women, 1985 General Elections

| *Constituency* | *Candidate* | *Party* | *Result* |
|---|---|---|---|
| Binnypet | Shaukat Qureshi | INC | Lost |
| Tumkur | Aliya Begum | INC | Lost |
| Jayamahal | Shameem Banu | IND | DF |
| Narasimharaja | Mukhtarunnisa | INC | Won |
| Udupi | Sara S. Amin | IND | DF |
| Bhadrawati | Sabira Begum | IND | DF |
| Hassan | H.M. Yakatunnisa Begum | IND | DF |
| Bijapur | Najma Ajajuddin Bangi | IND | DF |

*Source:* Election Commission of India. DF: Deposit forfeited.

It will be seen that during a period of over three decades, between 1951 and 1985, only eight Muslim women contested Assembly polls and only one—Mukhtarunnisa Begum—won at the 1985 polls. The very fact that eight Muslim women contested the polls at the 1985 elections, of whom five as independents, showed the rising interest, although the Muslim community did not favour them even in constituencies which had sizeable Muslim population (Table 3.3).

The 1989 Assembly elections coincided with Lok Sabha elections. Though Congress was defeated at the Centre, it was brought back to power in Karnataka. Twelve Muslims had gained entry to the Assembly; eleven from Congress (out of 17) and one from the Muslim League. Women fared badly at the election. Only ten women could get elected out of 78. But, the lone Muslim woman (Mastan Bi) who fought the election from Bidar lost her deposit. She secured only 223 votes (0.28% of the valid votes polled).

The demolition of Babri Masjid had not only traumatized the Muslims, but had disturbed all the peace-loving people. In Karnataka, Janata Dal had united and BJP was gaining ground. When Assembly elections were held under such circumstances in 1994, Congress fared badly and Janata Dal regained power. As the Muslim community had hitched itself to the Congress, as and when Congress lost the battle the Muslim representation in Karnataka also came down. Babri Masjid demolition made Muslims suspect the secular credentials of even the

**Table 3.3:** Karnataka Assembly Constituencies and Muslim Population

| *Constituency and Percentage of Muslim voters* | | | | |
|---|---|---|---|---|
| More than 40% | More than 30% | More than 25% | More than 20% | More than 15% |
| Mangalore<br>Pulakeshi nagar<br>Gulbarga<br>Bijapur City<br>Narasimharaja<br>Sarvagna nagar<br>Chamrajpet | Kudachi<br>Belgaum (N)<br>Humnabad<br>Raichur<br>Bidar<br>Shiggaon<br>Kolar<br>Hebbal<br>Shivajinagar<br>Jayanagar<br>Ramanagaram<br>Bidar South | Raibag<br>Chincholi<br>Sirsi<br>Davanagere<br>Shimoga<br>Tumkur City | Gokak<br>Jamkhandi<br>Muddebihal<br>Raichur Rural<br>Hangal<br>Bellary City<br>Bhadrawati<br>Padmanabhanagar<br>Bantwal<br>Chikkodi | Kagwad, Hukkeri;<br>Khanapura; Terdal;<br>Bailahongal; Sundatti;<br>Hunagunda; Jewargi;<br>Chittapur; Manavi;<br>Gulbarga (S); Gadag;<br>Sindanur; Gangawati;<br>Ron; Dharwad;<br>Hubli-Dharwad-E<br>Hubli-Dharwad-C<br>Haveri; Byadagi;<br>Ranibennur;<br>Shikaripura;<br>Chikkamagalur;<br>Chikkanayakana Halli<br>Chikkaballapur;<br>Malur; Shantinagar;<br>Govindarajnagar;<br>Channapatna; Hasan |

*Source:* Syed Tanveer Ahmed, *Karnataka Muslims*, October 28, 2012.

Congress and they were yet to identify an alternative political party, which they could consider secular.

In so far as Muslim women are concerned, there were just four contestants at the 1994 elections (Table 3.4); three contesting as independents and one under *Kannada Chalavali Vatal Paksha* of Vatal Nagaraj. All the four women contestants lost the election, forfeiting their deposits. What is disturbing is the meager number of votes that they polled, in spite of contesting from constituencies like Tumkur, Dharwad, Hukkeri and Bijapur, which had sizeable Muslim population among the voters.

Following the 1994 elections, only six Muslims could enter the Assembly, although there were 145 Muslim contestants, a record in itself, including 97 independents. Of the 15 candidates from Congress, only C.R. Saghir Ahmed could win from Chikkamagalur. The other winners included three of the Janata Dal, one of Bahujan Samaj Party (Zulfikar Hashmi from Bidar) and Qamarul Islam from Gulbarga (Muslim League). None of the 17 candidates fielded by former Chief Minister S. Bangarappa's Karnataka Congress and those fielded by the BJP could win.

**Table 3.4:** Performance of Muslim Women at the 1994 General Elections

| *Constituency* | *Candidate* | *Party* | *Result* |
|---|---|---|---|
| Tumkur | Dilshad Begum | IND | DF |
| Dharwad | Khaderbi G. Bagewadi | IND | DF |
| Hukkeri | Pathan Parveenbi Kasimsaab | KCP | DF |
| Bijapur | Najma Ajajuddin Bangi | IND | DF |

IND: Independent; KCP: *Kannada Chalavali Vatal Paksha*; DF: Deposit forfeited.

*Source:* Statistical Report on General Elections 1994.

It will be seen that Ms. Najma Ajajuddin Bangi had also contested the 1985 elections from the same constituency and lost. Although she was not disheartened with the defeat at the 1985 elections, the electorate did not bother to encourage her; she polled fewer votes during 1994 than what she polled during 1985.

One view is that the Muslim voters of Bijapur rejected Ms. Najma Ajajuddin Bangi. Professor Sandeep Shastri, Political Analyst and Pro-Vice Chancellor of Jain University opined that "the voting pattern of minority communities is determined by a variety of socio-economic factors and political context of specific elections rather than a tendency to vote en-bloc on the basis of religious identity alone". Prof. Shastri pointed out: "as many as 21 of the Assembly constituencies in Karnataka had more than 20 per cent Muslim voters, but few among them have elected a Muslim MLA in the last election. Bijapur city, which has 40 per cent Muslim voters, does not have a Muslim MLA".[21]

In spite of Muslims comprising 13 per cent of the state's 5.27 crore population and were expected to determine the outcome in 38 out of 224 assembly constituencies, the outcome in the elections has repeatedly shown that it did not happen; more so in the case of Muslim women candidates. It is sad that when analysis of Muslim representation in the elections is done, every analyst has taken into account only the male contestants, totally ignoring the prospects of female candidates.

The defeat of Congress in 1996 Parliamentary polls led to a National Front Government at the centre, with Deve Gowda becoming the Prime Minister. In 1996 Parliamentary polls Janata Dal performance in Karnataka was good, but with Deve Gowda's shift from Karnataka caused the down fall of the party. His successor Chief Minister J.H. Patel was frail.

The split in Janata Dal into two factions gave an opportunity to the Congress to regain power at the 1999 Assembly polls. As usual the Muslim strength in the Assembly jumped to double. Of the 93 Muslims who had contested, twelve Muslims entered the Assembly and eleven of them were from Congress and one from Janata Dal. However, the electorate did not favour women. There were only six winners out of a total of 62 women contestants; the latter including 2 Muslim women, who lost.

**Table 3.5**: Performance of Muslim Women at the 1999 General Elections

| *Constituency* | *Candidate* | *Party* | *Result* |
|---|---|---|---|
| Jayanagar | Shahtaj Khanam | JD (S) | DF |
| Indi | Korabu Rajabi Husseinsab | IND | DF |

*Source:* Statistical Report, on General Elections 1999, to the Legislative Assembly of Karnataka, Government of India, Election Commission of India, http://eci.nic.in/eci_main/StatisticalReports/SE_1999/StatisticalReport-KT99.pdf

The contesting Muslim women polled 0.41 per cent and 2.81 per cent of the valid votes, thus losing their deposits. [22]

The fortunes of the Muslims were once again affected when the Congress lost the majority at the 2004 Assembly elections. Muslims' strength in the Assembly was reduced to six. Of the total of 108 Muslims contestants, only four of Congress and two of Janata Dal could get elected. Bahujan Samaj Party, founded by Dalit leader Late Kanshi Ram, basically a north Indian Political Party, now headed by Ms. Mayawati, was new to Karnataka. Muslims contesting under Bahujan Samaj Party, *Kannada Nadu* and BJP lost the elections.

But, the 2004 general elections to the Karnataka Legislative Assembly saw an upsurge in the number of Muslim women contesting the polls in as much as the 108 Muslim contestants included 10 Muslim women (Table 3.6). However, not a single Muslim woman contestant could get elected. The blame could again be pinned on the Muslim community, which refused to see their women as politicians.

As usual, the Muslim women polled 0.27 per cent to 3.2 per cent of the valid votes in their respective constituencies and not a single Muslim woman could get elected even when contesting from Muslim-dominated constituencies. It is interesting to note that on the eve of the next general elections to the Assembly, the fear that the Congress might field a non-minority Congress candidate from the Bidar South made the Muslims demand ticket for a member of their community. A section of the Congress minority leaders pressed for a ticket to minority candidate to cash in on the large chunk of minority votes.

**Table 3.6:** Performance of Muslim Women at the 2004 General Elections

| *Constituency* | *Candidate (Age)(Education)* | *Party* | *Result* |
|---|---|---|---|
| Bidar | Rafat Mateen (41) (PG) | INC | DF |
| Tumkur | Shabeena d/o Abdul Rehman (26) (Graduate) | IND | DF |
| Bagepalli | Rahatunnisa Hafiz (38)(NA) | IND | DF |
| Vittal | Aminabi Sheikh (40)(NA) | MUL | DF |
| Surathkal | Suraiyya d/o Ismail (40) (school education) | IND | DF |
| Dharwad | Hazratbi Anwarsab Mirji (48)(NA) | IND | DF |
| Hubli | Irshad Begum K.M. Adhoni (37) (NA) | IND | DF |
| Mundargi | Bagali Khatunbi Peer Sab (45) (Primary) | JP | DF |
| Athani | Inamdar Khurshidbanu Bashir Ahmed (38) (NA) | SPSP | DF |
| Bharati nagar | Begum A W/O N. Venkatesh (27) (SSLC) | IND | DF |

MUL: Muslim League (Kerala State Committee); JP: Janata Party; SPSP: Sarpanch Samaj Party

*Source:* Election Commission of India, Statistical Report on General Election, 2004 to the Legislative Assembly of Karnataka.

But, why did the community let down Rafat Mateen at the 2004 polls? Because she was a woman?

In the 2008 Assembly elections Congress was defeated and a government of the Bharatiya Janata Party, a Party considered communal and responsible for the demolition of the Babri Masjid, was formed (Table 3.7). Muslim representation was also reduced. Only eight Muslims could get elected. The winners included 7 from the Congress (out of 16) and one from Janata Dal (out of 11). Bahujan Samaj Party, which was yet to take roots in Karnataka, gave tickets to more than 30 Muslims. There was no Muslim woman on the Party's list. It is another matter that none of the Party's candidates could win. Of the total of 128 Muslim contestants, there were only two Muslim women. As no political party supported them, they contested as independents and lost, forfeiting their deposits.

## Muslim Women at the 2013 Assembly Elections

The decline of BJP government's fortunes started with the departure of the Chief Minister, B.S. Yeddyurappa, following allegations of nepotism and other misdeeds, by the Lokayukta.

In selecting candidates for the May 2013 general elections to the Karnataka Assembly, Political Parties did not show any interest in fielding women candidates, both Muslim and non-Muslim, although every party swore by 33 per cent reservation. Out of 2,948 candidates who contested for 224 assembly seats, only 170 were women

**Table 3.7:** Performance of Muslim Women at the 2009 General Elections

| *Constituency* | *Candidate (Age) (education)* | *Party* | *Result* |
|---|---|---|---|
| Hanur | Reshma Banu (49 Yrs.) | IND | DF |
| Bijapur City | Zarina Firoz Shaikh (26 yrs.)(SSLC) | IND | DF |

*Source:* Election Commission of India, Statistical Report on General Elections 2008 to the Legislative Assembly of Karnataka.

contestants i.e., about 5.77 per cent. As usual, the political parties were ready with explanations as to why they could not field more women. Besides the argument about the 'winnability' of a female candidate, which every political party offered as the main reason, there were others. For instance, G. Parameshwara, KPCC President opined that "women contesting against men can prove to be an unequal battle and if it is a battle of the same sexes, it should be OK."[23]

The 2013 elections were not expected to see any increase in the number of women (as also Muslim women) entering the Assembly. For, no political party has been generous in offering tickets to women. While the BJP gave tickets to only 7 women, the Congress nominated 11 women. The third major political party, the JD (S) sponsored 8 women. In fact, the list of candidates submitted by the Congress Party's State Election Committee to the Congress High Command for approval contained the name of only woman (Actress Umashree from Terdal constituency), which upset the Congress President, Mrs. Sonia Gandhi, who returned the list.[24] The revised list submitted for her approval contained eleven women. While they could have included the names of some Muslim women in the revised list, *there was no Muslim woman among them*. Incidentally, Umashree was successful. The NCP, JD (S), KJP, Samajwadi Party and Communist Party (M-L) have sponsored one Muslim woman each.

Thus, at the 2013 elections, there were only 170 women contestants, including 13 Muslim women contestants, out of the total of 2,948 candidates, i.e., a mere 5.76 per cent; a far cry from the 33 per cent that the Women's Reservation Bill sought to introduce. Muslim women constituted 7.65 per cent of the total women contestants. What is disturbing is that the mainstream political parties viz., Nationalist Congress Party, Samajwadi Party, Communist Party (Marxist-Leninist) and Janata Dal (Secular), nominated only 4 of the 13 Muslim women contestants and the other two major parties (Congress and BJP) had none.

In view of the importance of the 2013 general elections to the Assembly, with Congress trying to wrest Karnataka from the BJP and the latter trying to retain Karnataka in the wake of allegations of corruption and parting ways with B.S. Yeddyurappa, neither of the two wanted to take a chance, as the final outcome depended on the 'winnability' of the candidates. Hence, the parties resorted to the time-tested formula of nominating the relatives of established politicians, than betting on a new candidate, especially a Muslim woman candidate. Even the three Muslim candidates sponsored were a son, a son-in-law and a grandson. Why could not they nominate daughters or granddaughter? The following are some examples (Table 3.8).

**Table 3.8:** Candidates Relation in General Elections 2013

| *Congress candidate and constituency* | *Related to* |
|---|---|
| S.S. Mallikarjuna, Davanagere (S) | Son of KPCC Treasurer, S. Shivashankarappa |
| B.K. Shivram, Malleswaram | Brother of B.K. Hariprasad, AICC General Secy., |
| S. Kumar Bangarappa, Sorba | Son of Late S. Bangarappa, former CM |
| Dinesh Gundu Rao, Gandhinagar | Son of former CM, Gundu Rao |
| Kailash V. Patil, Gulbarga (S) | Son of Veerendra Patil, former CM |
| Ajay Dharam Singh, Jewargi | Son of Dharam Singh, former CM |
| Tanveer Sait, Narasimharaja | Son of former Minister Aziz Sait |
| Syed Yasin | Son-in-law of C.K. Jaffar Shariff, former Union Minister |
| Rehman Shariff | Grandson of C.K. Jaffar Shariff, former Minister |

*Source:* ECI, Statistical Reports on General Election 2013.

The above examples are enough to show that for the Congress, and other parties, winning an election is more important than women's empowerment. Instead of giving tickets to the kith and kin of present or erstwhile politicians, women candidates could have been promoted. But, neither the Indian National Congress (which is blamed of minority appeasement) nor the Bharatiya Janata Party, nominated a single Muslim woman. A question may arise as to whether Muslim women would have accepted a nomination from the BJP? They have done so in Karnataka and other States, be it in Assembly elections or in elections to the PRIs. Some were appointed to important positions. The following are some examples:

- Syed Haseena Taj, who polled 11,428 votes from Mangammanapalya ward in Bangalore, is the first Muslim candidate from the Bharatiya Janata Party to win by one of the largest margins in the Bangalore Municipal Corporation elections. Ms. Taj, a homemaker, contested at the insistence of her husband.

- Sheema Mohsin, a journalist and social activist, is the lone female member of the 11-member Karnataka Waqf Board at the instance of Mumtaz Ali Khan, Minority Welfare Minister in the BJP Cabinet of Karnataka. He promised to ensure that Muslim women are appointed to the Minority Development Corporation. He faced objections from the conservative quarters of the community over the appointment of Sheema Mohsin. He told them that he was not doing anything against Islam. "Whatever I am doing is sanctioned by Islam itself because Islam gives equal status to women."

To a question whether the Muslim community has accepted the BJP, Maulana Imtiyaz Hyder, renowned Shia Islamic Scholar and Editor of *Misbah* Magazine who opined that no Party is secular, said in an interview: "Yes. Like they have accepted Congress; there is no much difference between the two parties". Hafiz Syed Shamsul Huda, Social Activist and BSP leader said: "I think no. It is the contestants who are accepting it (the BJP)". However, as Vice President of the BJP's unit at Basavana Bagewadi, Bijapur, Mrs. Fathima Peer Mohammed Girgavi, had a different view. She told us in an interview: "It is wrong to blame BJP. Though people perceive it as communal party, it is concerned towards Muslim community too". However, Ms. Sheema Mohsin, National Convener, Welfare Party of India and Social Activist, opined that the Muslim community has not accepted the BJP.[25]

It is a problem for Muslim women. If the Congress party, perceived to be secular, does not give them tickets (unless one is somebody) and other secular parties have no standing in Karnataka and if they cannot approach BJP for a ticket, how do they expect to enter the portals of *Vidhan Saudha*? Consequently, in their quest for a seat in the Assembly, 6 of the 13 women candidates at the 2013 general elections decided to try their luck as independents. Others have flocked to different parties, who, in their belief, were 'secular'.

Consequently, Ms. Ishrat Jahan, the Chitradurga candidate contested as a candidate of *Rani Chennamma Party* (RCP). The RCP was launched in 2009 from Gadag and on the date of registration, the Party had 2,860 members. Similarly, Chandini *alias* Aslam Pasha, the candidate from Narasimharaja constituency in Mysore district fought the election under the banner of Bharatiya Dr. B.R. Ambedkar Janata Party, a non-starter. They must have known that they would not win even as they signed the papers.

If the idea is to fight under the banner of a secular parity it is interesting to see that the Chamrajpet candidate (Shahtaj Khanam) sought Karnataka Janata Party's (KJP) ticket, switching over from Congress. The KJP was launched by B.S. Yeddyurappa, who had just resigned as BJP's Chief Minister. With his long stint with Rashtriya Swayamsevak Sangh and Bharatiya Janata Party, did he become secular the moment he resigned from the Party?

M. Ghousia Khan a graduate social worker who runs the Raza Justice and Democracy, Mahila and Youth Protection Andolan, fought as an independent only to lose. She had declared that even if she wins the elections, she would serve as an independent leader and would not join or even support any political party.

Party-wise, the following is the list of Muslim women candidates who fought the 2013 general elections to the Karnataka Assembly (Table 3.9). None of the 13 Muslim women could not only get elected, but also lost their deposits.

**Table 3.9**: Performance of Muslim Women, 2014 General Elections

| *Constituency* | *Name of candidate* | *Age (yrs.)* | *Education* | *Party* |
|---|---|---|---|---|
| Chamrajpet | Shahtaj Khanam | 41 | PUC | KJP |
| Sarvagna nagar | Rahath Bee | 45 | SSLC | NCP |
| Belgaum North | Akhila Ayubkhan Pathan | 41 | 10th class | IND |
| Vijayanagar | M. Ghousia Khan | 29 | PUC & DOT | IND |
| Bellary City | Sarmas Bee | 38 | Not stated | IND |
| Chitradurga | Ishrath Jahan | 47 | Not stated | RCP |
| Hiriyur | Rashida Isaq | 45 | B.Com. | IND |
| Dharwad | Azala Farida G. Ronad | 41 | SSLC | IND |
| Jewargi | Akhtar Parveen | 44 | BA | SP |
| Gulbarga North | Syed Razia Begum | 46 | 7th class | IND |
| Narasimharaja | Aslam Pasha (Chandini)* | NK | NK | BAJP |
| Raichur | Noorjahan | 35 | BA | CPI (ML) |
| Baindur | Surayya Banu | 44 | NK | JD (S) |

(NK) Not known as the affidavit does not show the educational qualification of the candidate.

NCP: Nationalist Congress Party; RCP: Rani Chennamma Party; SP: Samajwadi Party; BAJP: Bharatiya Dr. B.R. Ambedkar Janata Party; CPI (M-L): Community Party of India (Marxist-Leninist); JD (S): Janata Dal (Secular) (*) Transgender

*Source:* ECI Reports, Statistical Reports on General Election 2013.

It is seen from the affidavits filed by the contestants that all of them are housewives and 3 out of the 13 are graduates. The remaining 10 have some basic educational qualification. Some of them are engaged in social service and their spouses are engaged in small business activities or agriculturists.

In the Karnataka voters' determination to bring in a stable government, no votes were 'wasted' on Muslim women even in constituencies that had sizeable Muslim voters; in Raichur, for example, Muslims constitute over 40 per cent of the voters. Consequently, not a single Muslim woman listed above, has been successful. Thus, except in the year 1985, when Mukhtarunnisa Begum was elected on a Congress ticket, no Muslim woman has ever been successful and the Muslim community has not shown any interest in sending its women to the Assembly.

Quazi Arshad Ali observes: "It is generally believed that a Muslim candidate wins from Muslim majority area only. But in several cases Muslims have won from areas where their population is thin."[26] This observation is equally true with Muslim women in particular.

Unlike women of non-Muslim communities, Karnataka Muslim women's share in the political process is negligible. As we have seen from the data furnished above, only 41 Muslim women have contested Assembly polls during the entire period from 1952 to 2013 and only one—Mukhtarunnisa Begum—has won in 1985 (Table 3.10).

## Muslim Women in the Legislative Council (Upper House)

The history of Karnataka (earlier Mysore) Legislative Council dates back to 1907, when it was established with a view to associating with the Government a few non-official persons having practical experience and knowledge of local conditions to assist government. As already stated, the Council consisted of 10 to 15 nominated members, in addition to the *ex-officio* members. The minimum and maximum number of nominated members was increased to 15 to 21 respectively by Regulation I of 1914 and the maximum was further increased to 30 by Regulation II of 1919.

In 1923, under the Mysore Legislative Council Regulation, the strength of Legislative Council was fixed at 50. Of the 50 seats, 28 were allotted to the nominated members (official 20 and non-official 8)

**Table 3.10:** Status of Muslims Women Contested from 1952-2013

| *Year* | *Number of Muslim women contested* | *Number of Muslim women elected* |
|---|---|---|
| 1952 | Nil | Nil |
| 1957 | Nil | Nil |
| 1962 | Nil | Nil |
| 1967 | Nil | Nil |
| 1972 | Nil | Nil |
| 1978 | 1 | Nil |
| 1983 | 1 | Nil |
| 1985 | 7 | 1 |
| 1989 | 1 | Nil |
| 1994 | 4 | Nil |
| 1999 | 2 | Nil |
| 2004 | 10 | Nil |
| 2008 | 2 | Nil |
| 2013 | 13 | Nil |

*Source:* ECI Reports

and 22 to elected members. The term of the Council was three years in 1917 and four years in 1940. After the implementation of the States Reorganization Act in 1956, the strength of the Legislative Council was increased to 63 and later to 68. Of the 68 seats, two seats were set apart for women under the 'special interests' category. Four seats were reserved for Muslims. The strength of the Council was increased to 75 with effect from 8 September, 1987.

Muslim women's presence in the Legislative Council is just a shade better. The State Legislative Council has had three members so far. Besides Mukhtarunnisa Begum, two more Muslim ladies (Nafeesa Fazal and Abbasia Begum) have been members of the Legislative Council. The latter two were members of the Council twice. Ms. Fazal was also a Minister of State for five years, becoming the first Muslim woman to be a Minister.[27]

## Karnataka Muslim Women in the Lok Sabha

Keeping in view the fact that Muslim women of Karnataka have done poorly at the State-level, it does not come as a surprise that they were virtually absent in the Lok Sabha. Viewed differently, when the Muslim community of Karnataka was not interested in sending its women to the State Assembly, it is futile to expect it to send them to the Lok Sabha. Consequently, not a single Muslim woman from

Karnataka has ever made it to the Lok Sabha as the following Table 3.11 shows:

**Table 3.11:** Muslim women in the Lok Sabha (1st to 15th)

| *No. of the Lok Sabha* | *Total no. of women* | *No. of Muslim women* | *Name of the Member* | *State and Constituency* | *Party* |
|---|---|---|---|---|---|
| 1 | 23 | Nil | – | – | – |
| 2 | 24 | 2 | Mafida Ahmed | Jorhat (Assam) | INC |
| | | | Maimoona Sultan | Bhopal (MP) | INC |
| 3 | 37 | 2 | Zohraben A. Chavda | Banaskantha (Gujarat) | INC |
| | | | Maimoona Sultan | Bhopal (MP) | INC |
| 4 | 32 | Nil | – | – | – |
| 5 | 26 | Nil | – | – | – |
| 6 | 18 | 3 | Akbar Jahan Begum | Srinagar (J&K) | NC |
| | | | Rashida H. Chowdhury | Silchar (Assam) | INC |
| | | | Mohsina Kidwai | Azamgarh (UP) | INC |
| 7 | 32 | 2 | Begum Abida Ahmed | Bareilly (UP) | INC |
| | | | Mohsina Kidwai | Meerut (UP) | INC |
| 8 | 46 | 3 | Begum Akbar Jahan Abdullah | Anantnag (J&K) | NC |
| | | | Begum Abida Ahmed | Bareilly (UP) | INC |
| | | | Mohsina Kidwai | Meerut (UP) | INC |
| 9 | 28 | Nil | – | – | – |
| 10 | 42 | Nil | – | – | – |
| 11 | 41 | 1 | Begum Noor Bano | Rampur (UP) | INC |
| 12 | 44 | Nil | – | – | – |
| 13 | 52 | 1 | Begum Noor Bano | Rampur (UP) | INC |
| 14 | 45 | 1 | Sayda Rubab | Bahraich (UP) | SP |
| 15 | 39 | 3 | Tabassum Begum | Kairana (UP) | BSP |
| | | | Kaisar Jahan | Sitapur (UP) | BSP |
| | | | Mausam Noor | Malda Uttar (WB) | INC |

*Source:* Compiled from Election Commission reports.

Justice (Retd.) Rajinder Singh Sachar, who headed the committee that surveyed the condition of Muslims in the country, said that he did not favour a sub-quota for Muslim women within the 33 per cent reservation for women in the Lok Sabha and state assemblies. He argued that creation of a sub-quota as demanded by some of the political parties would further weaken the women, as it will split women into Muslim women and others. Justice Sachar observed that women as a block are the most deprived in the country, whether Hindus, Muslims or Christians. In view of the rampant gender injustice in the country, the sole aim should be women's empowerment as a whole.[28]

In an article published in *Indian Muslims* (March 10, 2010), Md. Mudassir Alam, journalist, has asked: "If the government and the opposition were really serious about the rights and upliftment of the women in the country, then why Muslim women were neglected in the Bill?" [29] This author fails to understand as to why the government alone should be blamed for not setting apart a sub-quota for Muslim women. Has there been a demand from the Muslim leaders and the community for such separate quota? The Political parties which tried to scuttle the Women's Reservation Bill by raising the question of separate reservation for Muslim women and others, were doing so not out of any genuine concern for Muslim women, but with a hidden agenda of their own; delay the passing of the Reservation Bill as long as possible. But, has there been any genuine concern from the Muslim community itself?

For, not only certain political parties, but even some influential Islamic scholars and clerics are strongly opposed to the women's reservation bill. Their opposition seems to stem from the fact that such a provision will not only entitle, but also encourage more-and-more Muslim women to take a plunge into politics, where it would not be possible for them to strictly adhere to the tenets of the *Shariat*.

Maulana Saeed-ur Rehman, Principal of the Lucknow-based *Nadwat-ul-Ulema* seminary is reported to have said: "It is un-Islamic for any Muslim woman to contest an election in a secular nation. Muslim women could contest elections in theocratic Islamic states because they would have to necessarily remain in '*purdah*' while there is no such restriction in secular societies."[30]

Although Muslim women of Karnataka have performed poorly at the Assembly and Parliament levels, they seem to be doing better in the elections to the PRIs and Urban Local Bodies.

## Muslim Women in Elections to Panchayati Raj Institutions

Chief Minister Ramakrishna Hegde and his Panchayati Raj Minister Abdul Nazir Saab were instrumental in making Karnataka the first State in the country to implement the Panchayat Raj Act, which mandated 25 per cent reservation for women, in 1987. In the very first elections held after the enactment of the Law, as many as 14,000 women were elected to the PRIs, with women from Dalit and backward communities gaining a large presence. Even as the 73rd and 74th Constitutional Amendments sought provide for 33 per cent reservation for women in Panchayati Raj Institutions, Karnataka had exceeded the 33 per cent mark. In the elections held in 2005, women had won 43.7 per cent of the seats in Gram Panchayats, 41.2 per cent in Taluk Panchayats and 37.1 per cent in Zilla Panchayats.

Subsequently, on May 7, 2012, the Karnataka State Cabinet decided to increase the reservation for women in all Urban Local Bodies (ULB), including the municipal corporations, from the 33 per cent to 50 per cent. Fifty per cent reservation was already made available for women at the Panchayat level. Though it was a welcome move, the ground realities and challenges faced by the women in politics, especially for Muslim women, were plenty. Political parties grumbled: "It is really difficult to identify winnable women candidates in such large numbers, as we will have to first convince their husbands to allow their spouses to contest. The competition is intense as all the three main political parties BJP, Congress and JD (S) are determined to get the best. The caste reservation and other factors further compound the problem."

With the opportunity for political participation available nearer their homes, Muslim women's participation has been better in the elections to the PRIs and Urban Local bodies of the State compared to their participation and performance in the elections to the Assembly or the Parliament. In general, the rise of Indian women in PRIs both as ordinary members and as *Panchayat* leaders is claimed to be a spectacular achievement, at least from the numbers point of view, what with India's poor record of gender discrimination. Malnourished, suppressed, uneducated, violated and discriminated against, Indian women have the odds stacked against them. But, within Indian women, Muslim women have shown that they do not shy away from politics given an opportunity.

Mani Shankar Aiyar, Union Minister for Panchayati Raj revealed at a National Conference on *Two Decades of Panchayati Raj in Karnataka* on April 1, 2007 that besides SC/ST women, Muslim women have also been elected in large numbers. According to a study, "Muslim women of Karnataka have definitely proved that *hijab* does not stand in the way of standing for or winning an election, or running the administration. They have proved that Muslim women are equal to women from all other communities in running Panchayati Raj."[31]

In illustrating the spirit of political participation among the Muslim women of Karnataka, Mani Shankar Aiyar narrated the case of a 23 year old *purdah*-clad Muslim girl, who had been widowed within a few weeks of her election to the Panchayat. He said: "I made the mistake (*gusthakhi)* of asking her what her family thought of her presiding over a conclave in which a large number of men participated. What does it matter what they think, I am the one who got elected, she is reported to have retorted."[32]

Contesting in an election itself is an achievement for Muslim women, subject as they are to the religious and cultural constraints within which they have to operate. There are, however, indications of a change in the social and political conservatism of the husbands and parents, whose cooperation is primarily essential for a Muslim woman to enter politics.

- In 2008, Hasina Bi (BJP) was elected Deputy Mayor of Bellary Municipal Corporation. She was elected unopposed along with G. Shobha as Mayor.
- In 2009, four-time Corporator Sayeeda Begum (Congress) was elected Mayor of Gulbarga Municipal Corporation. She defeated Chandrakala Alandkar of the Bharatiya Janata Party by a margin of 18 votes. She was the first Muslim woman Mayor of the Gulbarga City Corporation.
- In 2010, Syed Sajjad Ali Inamdar, was the Deputy Mayor of Bellary Municipal Corporation, having been elected to the Corporation as an independent. The same ward was earlier represented by his wife, Noorjahan.
- Shahtaj Khanam was a former Deputy Mayor of Bangalore Municipal Corporation. She lost the November 2001 elections to the Corporation when she contested as an independent candidate.

It should, however, not be ignored that for many women, especially Muslim women, the euphoria of winning the elections stops soon and problems start after winning. For, attending a *Panchayat* meeting involves forgoing a day's wage if the woman is a daily wage worker, ensuring that she first fulfils her obligations as a wife and mother and behaving in such a way that they do not cross paths with the conservatives from the point of view of observing the dress code, and in their interaction with outsiders, especially unrelated males. By and large, the women members of Panchayat focus on healthcare, education, and the funds to make these two things happen, although solving health and education is a common concern among all *Panchayat* leaders, whether they are men or women. [33]

As we have seen, while only 41 Muslim women contested the general elections to the Karnataka Assembly from 1952 to 2013, the number of Muslim women who contested elections to the Panchayati Raj Institutions and Urban Local Bodies are many times this number. The reason for this appears to be:

- The place of work of an elected PRI member is much closer to the home and the responsibilities are not so onerous that a woman ignores her household;
- A PRI member will not be spending time away from home unlike a MP or MLA;
- Contesting an election to the PRI is less expensive;
- A PRI representative need not be highly educated and her knowledge of politics need not be too high;
- As a contestant is widely known within the constituency, the chances of getting elected to the PRI are better than when contesting an Assembly or Parliamentary seat;
- Her interaction with unrelated and unknown males is minimal.

In the above background, it would be relevant to examine the extent of participation of Muslim women in PRIs and ULBs in Karnataka.

## Urban Local Body Elections

Ever since reservation was introduced for women in the Panchayati Raj institutions by the Karnataka government, women have been enthusiastically participating in the elections. Muslim women did not lag behind, although they took cautious steps. As stated above, they had better chances at the elections to the ULBs as the voters were limited to smaller localities, the contestants are known to the voters and the issues are more local than they are at the Assembly elections.

Karnataka has nine city corporations, 205 other municipalities: 43 CMCs, 94 TMCs and 68 TPs (Table 3.12). As it is difficult to consider and analyse several elections, we propose to consider the performance of Muslim women at the 2001-02 elections to City

Corporations in Karnataka for the years 2007 and 2010 and local body elections for 2013.

**Table 3.12:** Muslim Women Elected to City Corporations in Karnataka in 2001-02 Elections

| *Name of City Corporation* | *Name of Ward/ Ward Number* | *Name of Muslim woman elected* | *Party* |
|---|---|---|---|
| Mangalore | Katipalla | Rehana Banu | INC |
| | Katipalla | Gulzar Banu | INC |
| | Kunjathabail | Shahnaz | INC |
| | Kudroli | Nafeesa B Aboobakr | IND |
| Dharwad-Hubli | 65 | Fahmida Killedar | JDS |
| | 18 | S. Razia Begum Imam Sab | INC |
| | 20 | G. Muniza Begum Imam sab | INC |
| | 43 | Y. Rabiabi Mohiddin sab | INC |
| | 50 | M. Meharunnisa Allabaksh | INC |
| Belgaum | 9 | Shamshad Allabaksh U | IND |
| | 37 | Wahida Rafiq | IND |
| | 42 | Shahtaj Fujufla | IND |
| Bangalore | Padarayanapura | Zareena begum | JDS |
| | Richmond Town | Jabeen Taj | IND |
| | Shivajinagar | Mumtaz Begum N Mujib | INC |
| Mysore | – | Shamshad Begum | JDS |
| | – | Asia Jan | JDS |
| Gulbarga | 5 | Akila begum Syed bar | INC |
| | 13 | Zahira Ahmed Khan# | INC |
| | 14 | Akhtari Rawoof M | JDU |
| | 15 | Ilyas Khatun | IND |
| | 16 | Shamima KM Nizamuddin | IND |
| | 20 | Noorjahan Begum SS Ali | IND |
| | 25 | Ameena Begum Qureshi | JDS |

#Elected Unanimously.
*Source:* SEC Statistical Report.

In all, 24 Muslim women were elected to the six Municipal Corporations in Karnataka against 405 seats i.e., about 5.92 per cent, which is not bad considering the various hurdles that they have to face in contesting elections.

In the next 6 years, there was a quantum jump in the number of Muslim women entering the electoral battle, as the following data for the 2007 ULB elections Table 3.13 show.

**Table 3.13:** Performance of Muslim Women at the Elections to the Urban Local Bodies, 2007 (CC: City Corporation)

| *Ward No.* | *Name of the Candidate* | *Party* | *Result* |
|---|---|---|---|
| **Mysore CC** | | | |
| 3 | 1. Akhila Begum | IND | Lost |
| 11 | 2. Jabeen Banu | BSP | Lost |
| 37 | 3. Imtiyaz Begum | IND | Lost |
| 40 | 4. Rihana Banu | INC | Won |
| | 5. Jakeer Banu | NCP | Lost |
| | 6. Anees Fatima | JDS | Lost |
| | 7. Jabeen Taj | IND | Lost |
| | 8. Pyari Jan | IND | Lost |
| | 9. Shakira Begum | IND | Lost |
| | 10. Bilalji | BSP | Lost |
| 45 | 11. Nigar Sultana | INC | Won |
| | 12. Nikhat Banu | JDS | Lost |
| | 13. Hajira Khanam | BSP | Lost |
| 46 | 14. Farida Begum | INC | Won |
| | 15. Nasima Khan | JDS | Lost |
| | 16. Syed Razia Sultana | NCP | Lost |
| | 17. Zareen B | IND | Lost |
| | 18. Aisha Sultana | BSP | Lost |
| 47 | 19. Shamshad Begum | INC | Won |
| 48 | 20. Haseena Taj | BSP | Lost |
| 53 | 21. Zubeda Begum | IND | Lost |
| 54 | 22. Neelofar Jabeen Taj | BJP | Lost |
| 59 | 23. Sajeeda Bi | INC | Won |
| | 24. Jahida | BSP | Lost |
| | 25. Ayesha Sk. | IND | Lost |
| | 26. Yasmin Taj | IND | Lost |
| **Mangalore CC** | | | |
| Katipalla-N | 1. Gulzar Banu | INC | Won |
| Bajal | 2. Sumaiya | INC | Lost |
| | 3. Rehana | IND | Lost |
| Bangre | 4. Raziya | INC | Lost |
| -do- | 5. Rubina | IND | Lost |
| **Gulbarga CC** | | | |
| Kapnoor | 1. Maalanbi Kasim Saab | INC | Won |
| | 2. Haseena Begum | JD (S) | Lost |
| Nehru Nagar | 3. Nasreena | INC | Won |
| | 4. Shaheen Sultana | JD (S) | Lost |
| | 5. Akhtar Begum | IND | Lost |
| | 6. Fatima Sadaf | IND | Lost |
| Mominpura | 7. Shahista Naim Serikar | INC | Won |
| | 8. Fatima Shaikh | JD (S) | Lost |
| | 9. Rehana Begum | IND | Lost |

*(Contd.)*

| Ward No. | Name of the Candidate | Party | Result |
|---|---|---|---|
| -do- | 10. Syeda Begum | INC | Won |
| | 11. Tanveer Jamal | JD (S) | Lost |
| | 12. Maimuna Begum | IND | Lost |
| | 13. Anjum Fatima | IND | Lost |
| | 14. Sharifa Bee | IND | Lost |
| 12 | 15. Mirza Gayaz Begum | INC | Won |
| 14 | 16. Fahima Banu | IND | Lost |
| 21 | 17. Jameela Begum | INC | Won |
| | 18. Yasmin Begum Sk. Baba | JD (S) | Lost |
| 24 | 19. Meharunnisa Begum | IND | Won |
| | 20. Sajeeda Begum | JDS | Lost |
| | 21. Shahnawaj Begum Shabdi | IND | Lost |
| 26 | 22. Zahida Khanam | INC | Lost |
| | 23. Ameena Begum | JD (S) | Won |
| | 24. Parveen Sultana | IND | Lost |
| 37 | 25. Shabana Sk. | JD (S) | Won |
| | 26. Munira Sk. Yusuf Ali | INC | Lost |
| 52 | 27. Yasin Begum | INC | Won |
| **Bellary CC** | | | |
| 9 | 1. Rabiya Begum | INC | Lost |
| | 2. Munna Bi | BJP | Won |
| | 3. K. Rahmath Bi | JD (S) | Lost |
| 15 | 4. Haseena Begum | INC | Lost |
| | 5. Zareena Begum | IND | Lost |
| | 6. T. Rahmath | IND | Lost |
| 25 | 7. Sabiya Arshi | INC | Lost |
| | 8. Shamshad Begum | BJP | Won |
| 26 | 9. Sultana Begum | INC | Lost |
| | 10. Hasina Bi | BJP | Won |
| | 11. K. Parvin Banu | JD (S) | Lost |
| | 12. Sahira Bi | IND | Lost |
| 34 | 13. Malan Bi | INC | Lost |
| | 14. Nurjahan | BJP | Won |
| **Davanagere CC** | | | |
| 3 | 1. Abida Bi | INC | Lost |
| | 2. Zubaida Banu | BJP | Lost |
| | 3. Jahida Bi | JD (S) | Won |
| | 4. Asma Parvin | IND | Lost |
| | 5. Shahtaj Bi | IND | Lost |
| 9 | 6. Haji Karimunnisa | IND | Lost |
| 16 | 7. Mumtaz | CPI | Lost |
| 19 | 8. Dilshad Khanam | JD (S) | Lost |
| 35 | 9. Sahera Banu | JDS | Lost |

*(Contd.)*

| Ward No. | Name of the Candidate | Party | Result |
|---|---|---|---|
| **Belgaum CC** | | | |
| 5 | 1. Mulla Kurshida Dadapir | IND | Lost |
| | 2. Sk. Kurshida Begum Abdul Khader | IND | Lost |
| 6 | 3. Zainuddina Imamsaheb D | IND | Lost |
| 33 | 4. Mumtaz Sikandar V | IND | Lost |
| 35 | 5. Ghori Wahida Rafiq | IND | Lost |
| 48 | 6. Baby Ayesha Murad V | IND | Lost |
| 52 | 7. Akila Ayubkhan Pathan | IND | Lost |
| | 8. Imamuddina Nabisab Nawaz | IND | Lost |
| 54 | 9. Pathan NaziyaAfzal khan | IND | Lost |
| | 10. Kamrunnisa B. Ayubkhan | IND | Lost |
| | 12. Mehjabin A.A. Salagar | IND | Lost |
| | 13. Yasmin Rahim Sk. | IND | Lost |
| **Hubli-Dharwad CC** | | | |
| 4 | 1. Rasulbi R Doddamani | INC | Won |
| | 2. Modinbi Reshamwale | IND | Lost |
| 5 | 3. Raziya Begum Kotbagi | JD (S) | Lost |
| | 4. Shamshad Ayyati | IND | Lost |
| 6 | 5. Shahmshad Ayyati | JDS | Lost |
| 10 | 6. Muniza Imamsaheb Guttal | IND | Lost |
| 11 | 7. Farida Begum Shabuddin Sk. | BJP | Lost |
| | 8. Razia Begum I Sangoli | INC | Lost |
| | 9. Khatunbi Tamatgar Md. Jamil | JDS | Won |
| 26 | 10. Nadaf Surayya | IND | Lost |
| 51 | 11. Rashida Begum | NCP | Lost |
| | 12. Hungundi Shama Md. Ashraf | INC | Won |
| | 13. Gulnar Arasikere | JD (S) | Lost |
| 54 | 14. Y. Rabiya Bi Mahaboob Saab | INC | Lost |
| 58 | 15. S. Mumtaz Banu Ghoususab | JDS | Lost |
| 60 | 16. Rabiya Begum Abdul Sattar | INC | Won |
| 64 | 17. J. Rasoobi Hussain Saab | INC | Won |
| | 18. Fahmida Killedar | JD (S) | Lost |
| | 19. Udupi Ashabi Basha Saab | IND | Lost |
| | 20. Noorjahan Bookbinder | IND | Lost |

*Source:* State Election Commission, Karnataka, Results of elections to urban local bodies, 2007. (http://karsec.gov.in/ResultsULB-fs.html)

It will be seen that at the 2007 elections to the Mysore City Corporation, 5 Muslim women were elected as against 2 in 2001. What is heartening is that there were as many as 26 winners in all, drawn from middle-class families.

The fact that a number of Muslim women have lost the elections to the ULBs does not mean that they are inferior to the wining non-

Muslim men/women, if any, but on account of the simple fact that the community considered that they should not have contested in the first place. For instance, Syeda Khushtara Banu, who lost the election to the Hassan Municipal Corporation in 1978 *by a single vote*, said[34]:

> "Many Muslims of the town were very upset about my standing for elections. They felt this was 'un-Islamic', and not something that a Muslim woman, who, in their view, ought to remain house-bound, should do. They went around telling people not to vote for me because I did not veil myself. When I addressed meetings, they would scold me saying that I had come out of my house without *purdah*. Although I narrowly lost that election, I later contested the Hassan municipal elections twice and on both occasions I was elected".

Commenting on the Muslim leadership, she said[35]:

> "At the pan-Indian level, Muslims suffer from a lack of meaningful leadership. The cream of the Muslim intelligentsia and political elite migrated to Pakistan in the wake of the Partition. They thought they could corner all the top posts there, but they were soon disappointed when Pakistan came under Punjabi hegemony and the migrants from India were reduced to virtually second-class status. The Muslims who remained behind in India were largely from the poorer classes. They turned to the conservative Maulvis for leadership, who soon filled the leadership vacuum created as a result of the migration of the Muslim elites to Pakistan".

She further elaborated[36]:

> "In pre-Partition India, Muslims were able to produce several enlightened leaders, some of whom had a traditional *Madrasah* education, but this is not the case today. Maulana Azad, who rose to become India's first Education Minister, was a traditionally-trained Maulavi, but yet he took a leading role in India's freedom struggle, advocated modern education and economic empowerment, and worked for good relations between Muslims and others. Sadly, we do not have Moulavis

of this sort today, who are truly *Ulema* in the actual sense of the term—people with knowledge, not just of the scriptures, but also of the real world in which they live. Today, everywhere *mullahs*, whom I contrast with real *Ulema*, want to monopolise all our community platforms and rule over others. They have little or no knowledge of the real world, of changing social conditions, of the problems and concerns of the marginalized, including Muslim women. Many of them are simply power-hungry power-mongers. Obviously, this is not the sort of leadership we want or need.

"We need leaders who have a good education—both modern as well as Islamic—and who are of a liberal outlook. They should have risen from the grassroots, not handpicked by political parties because of their family connections or because they hold top posts in this or the other *Tanzeem*, *Anjuman* or *Jamaat*. They must have strong, organic relations with the Muslim masses, know their problems and concerns, and represent them accordingly. They must also be strongly committed not just to the welfare of the Muslims alone, but the country as a whole as well; that, however, is something quite missing among those who project themselves as Muslim 'leaders'. Rarely, if ever, do the problems of other marginalized communities, such as Dalits or Adivasis, evoke their concern. That probably has to do with a sort of internal communalism, but also the fact that, generally, Muslims are apprehensive about being too vocal about such issues for fear of being targeted by the police and other arms of the state machinery".

"Besides political leaders, we also need Muslim leaders in various social fields, for which we need a lot more Muslim NGOs than we have at present. I regret to say this, but Muslims have not learnt how to be socially relevant at all, and nor have they understood why they continue to lag behind others. Few Muslim organizations are professionally run, and almost all of them lack far-sightedness. Many of them keep harping on religion, but this is more in the nature of show off-ism. Today, the vast majority of NGOS run by Muslims are madrasas and other such institutions that are concerned mainly or entirely with religious education. We have relatively very few Muslim-run institutions working in diverse fields such as health, modern education, protection of the environment, and so on.

"We need organizations working to promote inter-community harmony as well. Till recently, Muslims generally stayed away from close interaction with secular, non-Muslim social activists and NGOs. But, from the 1990s onwards, with the rise of Hindutva chauvinism, I think they increasingly realized the need to work with secular forces because they now know that they cannot fight anti-Muslim communalism on their own. We need to further strengthen this process. We also need leaders in the intellectual field who can provide Muslims with proper direction and take-up the various economic, social, political and gender-related issues and problems. Unfortunately, in this the Muslim media, which is largely in Urdu, has largely failed. In any case, the number of Muslim readers of Urdu newspapers is rapidly declining as they prefer to read English papers or papers in vernacular languages instead, which do a better job. Urdu papers generally suffer from a lack of professionalism. They give only a very limited coverage of local issues while they constantly highlight issues in far-off Muslim lands such as Palestine and Afghanistan. Naturally, this has little appeal for Muslims who want to know about what is happening in the places where they live".

"The fact remains that no number of fatwas against Muslim women studying, working or participating in politics is going to drive them out from the public sphere, from jobs, from institutions of higher learning, because these women are already there—and in ever increasing numbers. In fact, nowadays, Muslim girls' enrolment in institutions of higher education is higher than that of Muslim boys in large parts of India, because Muslim boys often drop out as soon as they enter their teens and take-up jobs as auto-rickshaw drivers and automobile mechanics in order to supplement their families' incomes. Interestingly, the *burkha* has played a facilitating, rather than restraining, role for some Muslim girls who don it because their parents feel that they are thereby protected and safe thereby and so allow them to attend college. These girls then go on to take-up jobs as teachers or social workers and, besides being more educated than the

> men whom they marry, they might even earn more than their spouses. This is one factor for the increasing rates of divorce today since many men cannot tolerate a wife who is economically independent and who is more educated than them. Nor can educated women put up with the consistent oppression of their husbands".
>
> "The *fatwas* targeting Muslim women's empowerment are not taken seriously by educated, working women. In my view, they reflect a deep-rooted patriarchy that has nothing to do with the spirit of the *Quran*, if it is understood properly. They reflect a mentality, so deeply-ingrained among the conservative *Maulvis*, but which I strongly disagree with; that the more restricted a woman is within the four walls of her home the more pious she is. They also reflect a completely unacceptable assumption that women are the root cause of evil and strife—but this has no sanction at all in the *Quran*".[37]

Yet another Muslim woman, Sajeeda Begum, founder of *Aasra* (Shelter), home for destitute and abandoned Muslim women in Karnataka, deplored: "The patriarchal domination in our society is so much that it is a big task for me to change their mind-set. We are conditioned to believe that the father, husband, brother or son has to be the care-taker of women and that women must always be dependent on men. That is why I think Muslim women need their own economic and educational independence and space."

In spite of the hurdles for their electoral participation, Muslim women continued to contest in the elections to the local bodies in increasing numbers, thanks to the support of their husbands/parents. However, unlike in Uttar Pradesh, Muslim women in Karnataka had no *fatwas* to contend with.

The following Table 3.14 gives the details of Muslim women who contested the elections to the Greater Bangalore Municipal Corporation during 2010.

It will be seen from the presented data that a large number of Muslim women contested the elections to the BBMP. In fact the 72 Muslim women contestants accounted for 53 per cent of the total (134) women contestants. While 48 of the 72 Muslim women contested as independents, except Ms. Farida from Shivaji Nagar ward, all the other independents lost.[38] It is sad that some of them received just less than 10 votes.

**Table 3.14:** Councillor Election Results, Greater Bangalore Municipal Corporation, 2010

| *Ward* | *No. of contestants* | | *Name of the Muslim woman candidate and Party* | *Result* |
|---|---|---|---|---|
| | *Muslim women* | *Others* | | |
| Manorayana Palya (Reserved for women) | 6 | 1 | Fauzia Begum (INC) | Won |
| | | | Asma Tahir (IND) | Lost |
| | | | Aisha Begum (IND) | Lost |
| | | | Khadija Amir Shah (IND) | Lost |
| | | | Zainu Bi (IND) | Lost |
| | | | Qamar Taj (IND) | Lost |
| Dhanisandra (Reserved for women) | 3 | 2 | Fahmudunnisa (INC) | Won |
| | | | Nilofer (IND) | Lost |
| | | | Safina Banu (IND) | Lost |
| Kuvempu Nagar (General) | 3 | 4 | Jabeena (IND) | Lost |
| | | | Naseem Taj (IND) | Lost |
| | | | Fakrunnisa (IND) | Lost |
| Nagavara (Reserved for women) | 3 | 3 | Irshad Begum (INC) | Won |
| | | | Aisha Muhammadi (IND) | Lost |
| | | | Shakeela Begum (IND) | Lost |
| Kadu Gondanahalli (reserved for women) | 8 | 1 | Dilshad Begum (JDS) | Lost |
| | | | Rahath Bi (NCP) | Lost |
| | | | Shahin Taj (INC) | Won |
| | | | Zakir Banu (IND) | Lost |
| | | | Tabassum Fatima (IND) | Lost |
| | | | Naima Akhtar (IND) | Lost |
| | | | Shakeela Begum (IND) | Lost |
| | | | Sumaiya Begum (IND) | Lost |
| Kushal Nagar (Reserved for women) | 8 | 4 | Noorjahan (INC) | Won |
| | | | Gauhar Jahan (JDS) | Lost |
| | | | Sajia Ashraf (IND) | Lost |
| | | | Kausar Mukhtar (IND) | Lost |
| | | | Nasreen Taj (IND) | Lost |
| | | | Reshma Sultan (IND) | Lost |
| | | | Wahidunnisa (IND) | Lost |
| | | | Naim (IND) | Lost |
| Kaval Bari Sandra (Reserved for women) | 1 | 4 | Hajira Samia (JDS) | Lost |
| Vigyana Nagar (Reserved for women) | 1 | 3 | Haseena Begum (IND) | Lost |

(*Contd.*)

| Ward | No. of contestants | | Name of the Muslim woman candidate and Party | Result |
|---|---|---|---|---|
| | Muslim women | Others | | |
| Shivaji Nagar (Reserved for women) | 6 | | Naima Begum (INC) | Lost |
| | | | Nazreen Mujib (JDS) | Lost |
| | | | Noorjahan (IND) | Lost |
| | | | Farida (IND) | Won |
| | | | Farida Begum (IND) | Lost |
| | | | Yasmin Taj (IND) | Lost |
| Shanti Nagar (Reserved for women) | 2 | 8 | Parveen Sultana (IND) | Lost |
| | | | Seema Khanam (IND) | Lost |
| Dharmarayana Devasthana Road (Reserved for BC) | 1 | 12 | Yasmin Taj (IND) | Lost |
| Nayanda Halli (Reserved for women) | 1 | 9 | Mehar Jan (IND) | Lost |
| Padarayanapura (Reserved for women) | 6 | | Zareena Begum (JDS) | Lost |
| | | | Tahira Begum (INC) | Lost |
| | | | Naseem I. Doddamani (CPI-M) | Lost |
| | | | Noorunnisa (BJP) | Lost |
| | | | Nazni Begum (IND) | Lost |
| | | | Noor Alamas Begum (IND) | Lost |
| Jagjivanram Nagar (reserved for women) | 6 | | Navida Banu (BJP) | Lost |
| | | | Bibijan (JDS) | Lost |
| | | | Seema Khanam (INC) | Won |
| | | | Khadija Khanam (IND) | Lost |
| | | | Isha Banu (IND) | Lost |
| | | | Shanawaz (IND) | Lost |
| Mangammana Palya (Reserved for women) | 2 | 4 | Syed Haseena Taj (BJP) | Won |
| | | | Nazmunnisa (IND) | Lost |
| Karisanddra (Reserved for women) | 2 | 2 | Mumtaj (JSD) | Lost |
| | | | Parveen Taj (IND) | Lost |
| Jayanagar (Reserved for women) | 7 | 4 | Shahtaj Khanam (BJP) | Lost |
| | | | Nazrin Idris (IND) | Lost |
| | | | Asma Khalil (IND) | Lost |
| | | | Abida Begum (IND) | Lost |
| | | | Rabiya Basri (IND) | Lost |
| | | | Shakeera Khanam (IND) | Lost |
| | | | Shahida Khalid (IND) | Lost |

http://karsec.gov.in/Urban%20Local%20Bodeis/BBMP/Result%20of%20198%20wards.html)

*Source:* BBMP Elections, 2010. http://karsec.gov.in/Urban%20Local%20Bodeis/BBMP/Form%2025/3.pdf

Among those supported by political parties, 6 Muslim women contesting under the banner of Indian National Congress scored victories. On the other hand, Mrs. Syed Haseena Taj was the first Muslim candidate from the Bharatiya Janata Party to win by one of the largest margins in the BBMP elections from Mangammanapalya ward. Ms. Taj, once a home-maker, contested the elections at the instance of her husband. Speaking on her behalf, her husband Syed Salam, one of the Vice Presidents of the BJP Minority Cell, said [39]:

> "She is very happy. People have supported her wholeheartedly. I was with the JD (S) for 15 years. But we both realised that parties that discriminate on the basis of religion are the JD (S) and the Congress, not the BJP. She would have won even as an independent candidate as people had faith in her reputation as a helpful person".

Similarly, Gulbarga City Corporation had 8 Corporators out of 55 and one of them, Syeda Begum, was the elected the Deputy Mayor. In the Hubli-Dharwad Municipal Corporation, there were two Muslim women out of a total strength of 33 Corporators and 3 out of 35 Corporators of Bijapur Municipal Corporation were Muslim women.

### ULB Elections 2013

Rising to the second level of the PRI system, Muslim women of Karnataka have been participating in large numbers in the elections to the Urban Local Bodies. The following results of the ULB elections held to the 7 City Corporations in 2013 give the picture (Table 3.15).

Overall, out of the 381 seats in the 7 City Corporations, Muslim women could capture 25 seats (6.56%). It will also be seen from the Table that four Muslim women could secure second positions and with a little more voter cooperation and luck, the total number of women in the Corporations would have been around 30 i.e., about 8 per cent (Table 3.16):

- It will be seen from the data that the performance of Muslim women in the ULB elections has not been unsatisfactory. As many as 104 Muslim women were elected to the City Municipal Councils against a total number of 1,393 seats (i.e., about 7.50%), with a good number of them trailing in

**Table 3.15:** Performance of Muslim Woman at the Elections to the City Corporations, 2013

| *Name of the City Corporation* | *Ward No.* | *Name of the winning candidate and Party* | *Name of the first runner-up and Party* |
|---|---|---|---|
| Davanagere | 03 | Dilshad (INC) | Jahida B (BSRC) |
| Mysore | 03 | Sameena Jabeen (BSRC) | NMW |
| | 40 | Tasneem (INC) | Asma Khanam (SDP) |
| | 46 | Haseen Taj (JDS) | NMW |
| | 47 | Shamshad Begum (INC) | NMW |
| | 59 | Reshma Jabeen (SDP) | Sajeeda Bi (INC) |
| | 45 | NMW | Mubin Taj (INC) |
| Mangalore | 60 | NMW | T.K. Naseema (INC) |
| | 35 | K. Zubaida (INC) | NMW |
| | 44 | Rameeja Banu (JDS) | NMW |
| | 53 | Sumaiya (INC) | NMW |
| | 05 | MM | Gulzar Banu (INC) |
| Belgaum | 54 | NMW | Naziya A. Pathan (IND) |
| Hubli-Dharwad | 05 | Bijri Fatima M. Pathan (INC) | NMW |
| | 11 | Khatunbi Tamatgar (JDS) | MM |
| | 51 | Tabassum Md. Ilyas (JDS) | Shamabanu Md. Ashraf (INC) |
| | 60 | Rabiya Begum Amatoor (JDS) | NMW |
| | 64 | Fahmida M. Killedar (JDS) | Jammagi Rasoobi H. (INC) |
| | 67 | NMW | G. Hussain Begum (KJP) |
| Bellary | 25 | Nasreena Begum (INC) | Moti (JDS) |
| | 26 | Rizwana Begum (INC) | Sahera Bi (IND) |
| | 34 | Malan Bi (INC) | NMW |
| | 15 | NMW | Haseena Begum (IND) |
| Gulbarga | 01 | Putali Begum (INC) | NMW |
| | 04 | Nadira Jamal (INC) | Akhtari Begum N. Ahmed (IND) |
| | 09 | Ameena Begum (JDS) | NMW |
| | 11 | Anjum Fatima (JDS) | Saida Begum (INC) |
| | 21 | Yasmin Begum Sk. Baba (INC) | Zameeda Begum (JDS) |
| | 26 | W. Aquila Begum (IND) | Ameena Begum Qureshi (JDS) |
| | 27 | Aisha Firmesh (IND) | Shabana Sk. Hussain (JDS) |
| | 52 | Shabana Begum (IND) | Yasmin Begum (JDS) |

*Source:* Infoelection.com

**Table 3.16:** Performance of Muslim Women in the Elections to PRIs, 2013

| *Name of the District/Taluk Municipal Council/Town Panchayat* | *Ward No.* | *Name of the winning candidate and Party* | *Name of the first runner-up and Party* |
|---|---|---|---|
| (1) | (2) | (3) | (4) |
| **Koppal Dt.** | | | |
| Koppal CMC | 07 | Naseema begum (INC) | Begum Apsarmia (JDS) |
| | 21 | NMW | Rashida Begum (INC) |
| | 30 | NMW | Sabera Begum Hussainpeer-INC |
| Gangawati CMC | 12 | Lubeena Mahboob Ali (JDS) | NMW |
| | 24 | Shakira S. Hussain (JDS) | NMW |
| | 15 | NMW | Raziabegum M. Maniyar (INC) |
| | 21 | NMW | Hasmat Begum Usman Ali (JDS) |
| Kustagi CMC | 02 | Rasoolbi B. Sullad (IND) | NMW |
| | 21 | Fatima Begum NG (INC) | NMW |
| | 22 | Fatima H. Laddi (INC) | Tara Begum KK (JDS) |
| **Raichur Dt.** | | | |
| Raichur CMC | 07 | Seema Sadaf (JDS) | Asmat Begum (INC) |
| | 15 | M.K. Kamlbi Babar (INC) | Sajida Begum Sumeera ( JDS) |
| | 26 | Raziya Begum (INC) | NMW |
| | 29 | Khaja Bee (INC) | NMW |
| | 32 | Wazida Parvin (INC) | Shameena Begum (IIND) |
| Sindanur CMC | 12 | Ayesha Begum (INC) | Badebi (JDS) |
| | 15 | Kausar Begum Alisab (INC) | Begumbi Md. K. Hussain (BSRC) |
| | 17 | Ashabi Abdul Sattar (INC) | NMW |
| | 18 | Mubarak Begum (INC) | Shashabi Abdul Sattar (BSRC) |
| | 20 | Anwar Begum (INC) | NMW |
| | 23 | Rashida Anwar Ali (INC) | NMW |
| Manvi TMC | 07 | Tabassum (IND) | NMW |
| | 15 | Hajira Begum (INC) | Zainab Bi (BSRC) |
| | 17 | Ashabi (INC) | Salima (KJP) |
| | 18 | NMW | Ameena begum (BSRC) |
| | 19 | NMW | Haseena (!NC) |
| Lingasugur TMC | 09 | Annubegum Jalaluddin (INC) | Shamshad Begum (JDS) |
| | 11 | Zareena begum Abdul (JDS) | NMW |
| | 13 | Chotima Hussain Saab (INC) | Roshan Begum (JDS) |
| Devadurga TMC | 07 | Fatima (BJP) | NMW |
| | 10 | Mariyambi (INC) | MM |
| | 16 | Al Haji Tahira Begum (BJP) | Mahaboobi (IND) |
| | 17 | Peeramma Begum (JDS) | NMW |
| | 21 | Tabassum Uddar (JDS) | NMW |
| Mudgal TMC | 03 | Sahira Banu (JDS) | Ameena Begum (INC) |
| | 04 | NMW | Sadika Begum (JDS) |
| | 14 | Rahima begum C (JDS) | Hussein bi A.M (BSRC) |
| **Yadgir Dt.** | | | |
| Yadgir CMC | 09 | Roshan Begum (KJP) | Saijad Begum (INC) |
| | 14 | Tasneema Banu (INC) | NMW |
| Shorapur TMC | 13 | Zaharabi Usmansab (INC) | Shahida Begum MG (IND) |
| | 20 | Zakir Begum Md. Usman (IND) | Khuteja Begum GM (INC) |

*(Contd.)*

| (1) | (2) | (3) | (4) |
|---|---|---|---|
| Shahapur TMC | 14 | Salima Begum (IND) | MM |
| | 15 | Bashira Begum Chand (INC) | NMW |
| Gurumitkal TP | 03 | Nafeesa Khatun (INC) | NMW |
| Shahabad CMC | 15 | Farzana Rasheed (INC) | NMW |
| | 25 | Salima Begum M.A (INC) | Zareena Begum B.(IND) |
| Aland TMC | 10 | Mashak bi Arif Ansari (JDS) | Asifa Md. Ansari (KJP) |
| | 11 | Farzana Begum AA (JDS) | NMW |
| | 18 | Asha Begum Md. A.(JDS) | Anisa Begum Abdul Majid (KJP) |
| | 17 | NMW | Badrunnisa Abdul Latif (KJP) |
| Sedan TMC | 04 | Quirunnisa begum AK-JDS | NMW |
| | 20 | Sajeeda begum R P (INC) | NMW |
| Chittapur TMC | 05 | NMW | Ayesha begum Sirajuddin (KJP) |
| | 13 | Rahmath begum G. Rasool (INC) | NMW |
| Afzalpur TP | 04 | Saipana bi Moulasab (KJP)* | |
| | 08 | Allama Bi MahaboobSaab (KJP) | Raziabi Arif SK (JDS) |
| Chincholi TP | 06 | Farzana Begum S (INC) | NMW |
| | 08 | NMW | Khaja Begum (INC) |
| | 15 | NMW | Arshiya Jabeen (KJP) |
| Jewargi TP | 04 | Fatima begum Abdulgani (INC) | Hajira Begum (IND) |
| | 14 | Md. Hanifa (JDS) | Md. Eijaja (INC) |
| **Bidar Dt** | | | |
| Bidar CMC | 02 | NMW | Rehana Begum (INC) |
| | 10 | Anees Sultana (JDS) | Kausar Begum (INC) |
| | 24 | Fatima Anwar Ali (INC) | Irfan Begum (BSRC) |
| | 25 | Rafat Begum Yusuf (INC) | NMW |
| Basavakalyan CMC | 03 | Jaibunbee (JDS) | NMW |
| | 07 | NMW | Mumtaz Begum (INC) |
| | 25 | Zakiya Begum (BSRC) | Sufiya Bee (JDS) |
| | 31 | Hazeera Bi (IND) | NMW |
| Humnabad TMC | 13 | Yasmin Begum (INC) | NMW |
| | 18 | Roshan Begum (INC) | NMW |
| Chitaguppa TMC | 01 | Reshma (BJP) | Nowsheen (KJP) |
| | 09 | Ghousia Begum ((KJP) | Rehana Bi (JDS) |
| | 11 | Salarbee (JDS) | Halima Bi (INC) |
| | 19 | Jalees begum (JDS) | NMW |
| | 21 | NMW | Yasmin Begum (JDS) |
| Bhalki TMC | 03 | Halima bee (INC) | Baby Fatima Jamaal (BJP) |
| | 19 | Chand Bibi Allauddin (INC) | NMW |
| Aurad TP | 10 | NMW | Yasmin Begum K (BJP) |
| **Bellary Dt.** | | | |
| Hospet CMC | 09 | Noorjahan (INC) | NMW |
| | 16 | Anipa Bi (IND) | Malan bi (IND) |
| | 17 | Ghousia (INC) | Khajabi (IND) |
| | 23 | Noorjahan (INC) | NMW |
| Kampli TMC | 02 | Hussainbee (INC) | NMW |
| Siraguppa TMC | 10 | NMW | S. Sharifa Banu (IND) |
| | 12 | NMW | Banubee (INC) |
| | 14 | Maharaja Begum (INC) | NMW |
| | 17 | NMW | Ruksana (BJP) |
| H. Hadagalli TMC | 07 | Vajrana Bee (IND) | NMW |

(*Contd.*)

| (1) | (2) | (3) | (4) |
|---|---|---|---|
| | 11 | Mardan Bee (JDS) | MM |
| | 20 | NMW | Salma (BJP) |
| | 21 | NMW | Haseena Bi (IND) |
| Sandur TMC | 04 | Noorjahan (INC) | NMW |
| | 16 | Shahajad bi CH (INC) | K. Allabi (IND) |
| | 20 | NMW | Beebi M (IND) |
| Tekkalakote TP | 07 | M.Kadiramma (IND) | S. Shekanbi (BJP) |
| Kamalapur TP | 04 | Khajabi N (INC) | H. Hanifabi (IND) |
| | 10 | NMW | Beebi (IND) |
| Kottur TP | 15 | Ashabegum (INC) | NMW |
| Kudligi TP | 04 | K. Maimoona (IND) | Rahmath (INC) |
| **Uttar Kannada Dt.** | | | |
| Dandeli CMC | 05 | A. Mahmuda Begum MS (INC) | Shabana MH Sanadi (JDS) |
| | 02 | NMW | Pathan Bibi Ayesha (JDS) |
| | 21 | Rahisa MRB (INC) | NMW |
| | 30 | NMW | Dilshad GR (INC) |
| | 31 | NMM | Yasin DY (JDS) |
| Karwar CMC | 10 | Rameeja Banu Sk. (INC) | NMW |
| | 15 | Hafiza Maqbool Sk.(INC) | NMW |
| Sirsi CMC | 17 | Razia Banu AKJ (INC) | S. Shamim Banu (JDS) |
| | 19 | Fatima Musa (BSRC) | Shamshad KA (INC) |
| Bhatkal TMC | 01 | Khudsai Begum MA (IND) | UNANIMOUSLY ELECTED |
| | 02 | Sabina KM Tayyeb (IND) | UNANIMOUSLY ELECTED |
| Honnavar TP | 08 | Jainabi Ismail Saab (INC) | MM |
| | 15 | Sk. Jameelabi AM (INC) | NMW |
| Haliyal TP | 05 | Riyanbi Betageri (INC) | Shamshad Begum SM (JDS) |
| Yellapura TP | 08 | Basheer begum NASK (INC) | Khan Noorjahan (JDS) |
| | 16 | Noorjahan Md. Iqbal Sk. (INC) | Aminabi Ismail Khan (JDS) |
| Mundagod TP | 06 | NMW | Mumtaz begum Nadaf (KJP) |
| | 13 | NMW | Mehar Banu MK (INC) |
| **Haveri Dt.** | | | |
| Rane Bennur CMC | 13 | Fatima SK (IND) | MM |
| | 16 | NMW | Akhtari Begum JM (IND) |
| Haveri CMC | 16 | NMW | Jameela Banu YK (KJP) |
| | 24 | Najibunnisa BN (BJP) | Jatunbi BN (INC) |
| | 28 | NMW | Jairabi IQ (BSRC) |
| Hanagal CMC | 06 | Dilshad Banu S (INC) | Kureshabi Pathan (KJP) |
| | 10 | Haseena begum N (KJP) | Shakeela Banu R (INC) |
| | 23 | NMW | Haseenabi Sk. Sanadi (INC) |
| Savanur TMC | 08 | Navajabi IM (BJP) | Maimunnisa MD (INC) |
| | 09 | D. Sugarabi RK (INC) | NMW |
| | 12 | Seema Md. Rafi QS (INC) | Bibijan BJ (JDS) |
| | 13 | Sufiabi SJ (JDS) | Fatimabi RB (INC) |
| | 16 | NMW | K. Mansurabi AS (INC) |
| Bankapura TMC | 08 | Kutejabi YM (INC) | NMW |
| | 16 | Sabeerabi YM (INC)* | |
| | 23 | Fatimabi KD (INC) | Fatimabi KK (IND) |
| | 01 | NMW | Quairunnisa AM (INC) |
| Shiggaon TMC | 14 | Valeebi MD (INC) | NMW |
| | 18 | S. Rehana Begum AK (INC) | Zaibunnisa MM (JDS) |
| | 04 | NMW | Ruksana JJ (JDS) |
| Herikerur TP | 04 | Sabira bi AMN (INC) | NMW |
| | 10 | Razia Assadi (INC) | NMW |

(*Contd.*)

| (1) | (2) | (3) | (4) |
|---|---|---|---|
| **Gadag Dt.** | | | |
| Gadag Betageri CMC | 18 | Kamar Sultana JN (INC) | NMW |
| Mundargi TMC | 11 | NMW | Mumtaz Begum ME (INC) |
| | 22 | Rehana Begum H Patel (IND) | NMW |
| Rona TMC | 18 | Naziya Begum AY (INC) | NMW |
| | 19 | NMW | Sharifa Bi BK (BJP) |
| Naragunda TMC | 03 | Mumtajbi MS (BSRC) | M. Mahaboobi (BJP) |
| | 14 | NMW | Husna bi AN (INC) |
| Gajendragad TMC | 04 | Matumbi M. Hanagi (INC) | NMW |
| Lakshmeswara TMC | 22 | Banubi HA (INC) | NMW |
| | 05 | Hazratbi PK (BSRC) | Bibijan HK (INC) |
| Mulagunda TMC | 04 | Bibijan MB (INC) | NMW |
| | 09 | NMW | Modina Bi FD (BSRC) |
| **Dharwad Dt.** | | | |
| Annigeri TMC | 02 | Maktumbi M. Thaned (JDS) | Fatima B Thaned (INC) |
| | 09 | NMW | Raziabegum S Tahasildar (BSRC) |
| | 17 | N Kurshida begum K (JDS) | Mahaboobi Chandsab M (INC) |
| | 22 | Haseena Modinsab D (JDS) | NMW |
| Navalgunda TMC | 02 | NMW | Bibijan MG (JDS) |
| | 10 | NMW | Rajnabi Hussain Saab H (JDS) |
| Kundagal TP | 04 | C. Hashimbi Gaffar (INC) | NMW |
| | 13 | Raziabegum DH (JDS) | Bibijan Razak H (INC) |
| Alnavar TP | 05 | NMW | Naseem Banu N. Khatib (INC) |
| **Bangalore Rural** | | | |
| Doddaballapur CMC | 23 | Shamsunnisa (JDS) | NMW |
| Vijapura TMC | 03 | Jabeen Taj (INC) | NMW |
| | 22 | Rizwana Kausar Azaj (INC) | Badrunnisa (JDS) |
| | 23 | Shabeena Hanif (INC) | Roshan (JDS) |
| Hosakote TMC | 17 | Gulab Jan (INC) | Hasma Yasmin (BJP) |
| | 18 | Roshni (BJP) | Haseena (INC) |
| Nelamangala TMC | 03 | Raffia L (INC) | Ayesha Tarannum (JDS) |
| **Bangalore Urban** | | | |
| Anekal TMC | | | |
| **Ramanagaram Dt.** | | | |
| Ramanagaram CMC | 14 | Sameena Taj (INC) | Naveeda Tabassum (JDS) |
| | 19 | Tahseen Taj (INC) | Parvin Taj (JDS) |
| | 23 | Shabana Banu (JDS) | Shahnavaj Khanam (INC) |
| | 24 | Syed Parvin Taj (JDS) | Syed Banu (INC) |
| | 29 | Hasina Banu (JDS) | Zeenatunnisa (INC) |
| Channapatna TMC | 11 | Najmunnisa (INC) | Azra Banu (JDS) |
| | 13 | Khurshidunnisa (INC) | Fatima Tabassum (JDS) |
| | 21 | Syed Kubra Banu (INC) | NMW |
| | 22 | Uzma Ishrat (JDS) | Bibijan (BSRC) |
| | 23 | Kammar Nijami (JDS) | Rizwana Begum (INC) |
| | 24 | Akita Banu (INC) | Asmathunnissa (JDS) |

(*Contd.*)

| (1) | (2) | (3) | (4) |
|---|---|---|---|
| | 28 | Farzana Banu (JDS) | NMW |
| Kanakapura TMC | 01 | Zahida Banu (INC) | Farida Banu (JDS) |
| | 04 | Farhana Begum (INC) | Fatimabi (JDS) |
| | 14 | Gulzar Begum (INC) | Asma (JDS) |
| Magadi TMC | 16 | Fatimunnisa (INC) | Anjumara Aslam (JDS) |
| | 18 | Akila Banu (INC) | Salma (JDS) |
| | 23 | Hajira Banu (JDS) | Rahamatunnisa (INC) |
| **Chitradurga Dt.** | | | |
| Chitradurga CMC | 12 | Shakeela Banu (INC) | Noorjahan Begum (JDS) |
| | 14 | Ramiza Banu (INC) | NMW |
| | 24 | MM | Sakina Banu (JDS) |
| | 10 | NMW | Abida Banu (IND) |
| Challakere TMC | 14 | HF Reshma Banu (JDS) | Noorunnisa (BJP) |
| Hiriyur TMC | 06 | Imran Banu (INC) | Shakeela (IND) |
| | 07 | Syeda Firdaus (IND) | Sameena Banu (JDS) |
| Hosadurga TMC | 05 | NMW | Farzana Begum (INC) |
| | 09 | Shahina Banu (INC) | NMW |
| | 13 | Shahida Begum (KJP) | Tahira Banu (INC) |
| Molakalmuru TP | 13 | Kausar (IND) | NMW |
| | 14 | Ulfatunnisa (JDS) | Bilkis Banu (INC) |
| **Davanagere Dt.** | | | |
| Harihara CMC | 07 | Parveen Banu (INC) | Mehajabin (KJP) |
| | 09 | Gulnaz Begum (JDS) | Shamim Banu (INC) |
| | 17 | Nagina Subhan Saab (JDS) | Rashida Asif Ali Khan (INC) |
| | 19 | Shahajadi Sk.(INC) | NMW |
| | 21 | NMW | Nagina Banu (JDS) |
| Harapana Halli TMC | 10 | Razia BanuKathhib (BSRC) | NMW |
| Honnalli TP | 08 | Gulshira Khanam (BJP) | Shabana Begum (INC) |
| | 11 | Naseema Banu (INC) | Farzana Banu (BJP) |
| Channagiri TP | 03 | Sokarbi (INC) | Asiyabi (JDS) |
| | 08 | Gulzar Banu (INC) | Jamshida Banu (KJP) |
| | 10 | Kamrunnisa (INC) | MM |
| | 13 | Shaheena Banu (INC) | NMW |
| Jagalur TP | 08 | Noorjahan (INC) | Ashrafunnisa (BJP) |
| **Kolar Dt.** | | | |
| Kolar CMC | 22 | Arshiya Sultana (JDS) | Zakiya Sultana (INC) |
| | 31 | Sultana (IND) | Zarina Taj (IND) |
| | 32 | Shabana Azmi (INC) | Noorie (IND) |
| | 33 | Sarala Taj (JDS) | Nashiya Taj (INC) |
| Robertsonpet CMC | 32 | NMW | Tazila Begum (JDS) |
| | 34 | Mahmooda Begum (RPI) | Mahroon Nisha (INC) |
| Bangarpet TMC | 04 | Jabeen Taj (INC) | Naveen Taj (JDS) |
| | 14 | Akila Begum (INC) | NMW |
| Mulbagil TMC | 14 | Hamida Bi (IND) | NMW |
| | 16 | Najima Taj (JDS) | Gulnaz Begum (INC) |
| | 19 | Shaheen Taj (JDS) | Farzana (INC) |
| Malur TMC | 16 | Gulab Jan (BJP) | Zareena Taj (JDS) |
| Srinivasapura TMC | 13 | Jabeen Taj (INC) | Almas Begum (JDS) |

(*Contd.*)

| (1) | (2) | (3) | (4) |
|---|---|---|---|
| | 15 | Sahera Banu (INC) | Kubra (JDS) |
| | 16 | Naveen Taj (INC) | Shaheena (JDS) |
| **Chikkaballapur Dt.** | | | |
| Chikkaballapur CMC | 03 | NMW | Bibijan (IND) |
| | 21 | Jabeen Taj (IND) | NMW |
| Chintamani CMC | 26 | Jabeen Taj (JDS) | Shamim H (IND) |
| | 28 | Rehana (JDS) | Zareena Begum (IND) |
| Gauri*bid*.anur TMC | 16 | Meharunnisa (JDS) | Riyazunnisa (INC) |
| Sidhlaghatta TMC | 12 | Shabana (INC) | Bibijan (JDS) |
| | 14 | Shahida (INC) | N. Jabeena (JDS) |
| | 17 | Mushtari (INC) | Naseem Taj (JDS) |
| | 25 | Nasreen Taj (JDS) | Bibijan (INC) |
| | 26 | Wahida Kausar (INC) | Shaheen Taj (JDS) |
| Bagepalli TMC | 11 | Hussain Bi (JDS) | Shakeela (IND) |
| | 18 | NMW | Shabana Parvin (INC) |
| Gudibande TP | 09 | Jabin Taj (INC) | Nishad Khanam (BSRC) |
| **Shimoga Dt.** | | | |
| Shimoga CMC | 11 | NMW | Tabassum Ara (INC) |
| | 23 | Kurshida Banu (INC) | NMW |
| | 28 | Tarannum Banu (SDP) | NMW |
| | 29 | NMW | Zarina (JDS) |
| | 31 | Shahista Banu (KJP) | NMW |
| Bhadrawati CMC | 30 | NMW | Nasreen Taj (INC) |
| Sagar CMC | 06 | Shahana Banu (INC) | NMW |
| | 22 | Nadira Parvin (INC) | NMW |
| | 25 | Jahida Begum (KJP) | NMW |
| Shikaripura TMC | 08 | Shabana Banu (IND) | NMW |
| | 20 | NMW | Apsara Banu (INC) |
| | 22 | Firoza Banu (KJP) | NMW |
| | 23 | Zarina Rahamtulla (KJP) | NMW |
| Shiralakoppa TP | 05 | Noorjahan (IND) | UNANIMOUSLY ELECTED |
| | 10 | Jameela Khatun (INC) | Shamshad Begum (KJP) |
| | 13 | Rashida Begum (JDS) | NMW |
| Tirthahalli TP | 15 | Shabnam (JDS) | Dilshad (INC) |
| Soraba TP | 03 | Mahaboobi (JDS) | NMW |
| | 09 | BB Zulekha (JDS) | NMW |
| Hosanagara TP | 07 | NMW | Gauhar Jahan (INC) |
| **Mysore Dt.** | | | |
| K.R. Nagar TMC | 19 | Salima Bi (INC) | Tahseen (JDS) |
| | 20 | Farida Khanam (INC) | Rukhsar Banu (SDP) |
| | 21 | Firdaus Khanam (JDS) | Zamina Banu (INC) |
| Hunsur TMC | 19 | Wahida Banu (INC) | Parvin Taj (JDS) |
| | 25 | Gulnaz (INC) | Aajri (JDS) |
| | 26 | Fatimunnisa (INC) | NMW |
| Bannur TMC | 02 | Shahjahan (INC) | Shaheena (JDS) |
| | 13 | Maimunnisa (INC) | Umme Kulsum (JDS) |
| | 15 | Asia Khanam (INC) | Nahida Begum (JDS) |
| **Tumkur Dt.** | | | |
| Tumkur CMC | 12 | Rahamatunnisa (INC) | Sabrina Taj (IND) |

(*Contd.*)

| (1) | (2) | (3) | (4) |
|---|---|---|---|
| | 18 | Muzida Khanam (INC) | NMW |
| | 24 | Farzana Khanam (IND) | Mujibunnisa (INC) |
| Tiptur TMC | 04 | Fauzia Khanam (IND) | NMW |
| | 20 | Khushtarunnisa (KJP) | Shabana (INC) |
| | 23 | Zohra Jabin (INC) | NMW |
| | 22 | NMW | Hoor Banu (INC) |
| | 05 | NMW | Asma Begum (INC) |
| Sira CMC | 11 | Tabassum Banu (JDS) | Imtiaz Banu A Pasha (IND) |
| | 15 | Rehana Banu (IND) | Irshad Begum (INC) |
| | 18 | Akhila Banu (INC) | Maqbool Jan (JDS) |
| | 19 | Razia Khanam (INC) | Salimunnisa (JDS) |
| | 24 | Shahina Banu (INC) | Safia Begum (JDS) |
| C.N. Halli TMC | 06 | NMW | Shahida KS (JDS) |
| Madhugiri TMC | 03 | Rukiyabi (JDS) | NMW |
| | 07 | Zubaida Banu (IND) | NMW |
| | 12 | Salimunnisa AR (JDS) | Sabiha Banu (IND) |
| Pavagada TMC | 08 | NMW | Mallika Bi (INC) |
| | 15 | NMW | Reshma Banu (BSRC) |
| | 22 | NMW | Malin Taj (JDS) |
| Koratagere TP | 03 | Bargees (INC) | NMW |
| | 05 | Noorjan (IND) | Haseena Taj (INC) |
| Gubbi TP | 06 | Ayesha Thasina (INC) | Shakeela Bi (JDS) |
| **Chamrajnagar Dt.** | | | |
| Chamrajnagar CMC | 02 | NMW | Jabeen Taj (INC) |
| | 04 | Wahida Khanam (SDP) | Farida Begum (INC) |
| | 06 | Shabana Begum (INC) | Razia Sultana (SDP) |
| Kollegal CMC | 02 | Asma Parvin (INC) | UNANIMOUSLY ELECTED |
| Gundlupet TMC | 06 | Shafiha (INC) | Barkhatunnisa (KJP) |
| Hannuru TP | 06 | NMW | Mumtaj Banu (KJP) |
| **South Kannada Dt.** | | | |
| Bantwal TMC | 15 | Yasmin (INC) | Jainabi (SDP) |
| | 17 | Mumtaz (SDP) | NMW |
| Ullala TMC | 10 | Zarina Banu (IND) | Jameela Hussain (INC) |
| | 21 | Raziya Ibrahim (INC) | NMW |
| | 11 | NMW | Naseema (SDP) |
| Sulya TP | 17 | NMW | Hajira (BJP) |
| Belthangadi TP | 06 | Mushtari Jan Mahmud (INC) | NMW |
| **Chikkamagalur Dt.** | | | |
| Chikkamagalur CMC | 11 | Asma Khanam (INC) | Bibi Fathima (JDS) |
| | 16 | Zubaida Banu (INC) | NMW |
| | 17 | Ghousia Khanam (JDS) | Khurshidunnisa INC |
| | 30 | NMW | Najima Khanam (INC) |
| | 23 | NMW | Jahira (JDS) |
| Kadur TMC | 02 | NMW | Abida (JDS) |
| | 15 | NMW | Zareena bi (INC) |
| | 16 | NMW | Farida Banu (INC) |
| | 17 | Ruksana Parvin (JDS) | Fathima Nusrat (KJP) |
| | 23 | Hajira Bi (INC) | NMW |

(*Contd.*)

| (1) | (2) | (3) | (4) |
|---|---|---|---|
| Tarikere TMC | 06 | NMW | Shakeela Banu (JDS) |
| | 17 | Parvin Taj (INC) | Najma Dadapeer (KJP) |
| Mudigere TP | 03 | Rameeja Bi (INC) | Naima Parvin (IND) |
| | 09 | NMW | Akhtarunnisa (INC) |
| | 07 | NMW | Fathima (INC) |
| Narasimharajpur TP | 05 | Samira AB (IND) | NMW |
| **Hasan Dt.** | | | |
| Hasan TMC | 26 | NMW | A.P. Naseeba (IND) |
| | 31 | NMW | Shabana (IND) |
| Arasikere TMC | 19 | Reshma Banu (INC) | Hamida Banu (JDS) |
| | 25 | Naseema Banu ASK (JDS) | Gulnaz Begum (INC) |
| Sakleshpura TMC | 01 | NMW | Zareena (INC) |
| | 20 | Tajunnisa (JDS) | NMW |
| Belur TMC | 21 | Shahida Banu (IND) | NMW |
| | 23 | Salma Akhtari (JDS) | Ummiah Banu (KJP) |
| | 12 | NMW | Nahaya Banu (JDS) |
| Alur TP | 06 | Neelofar (IND) | Gulshan Khanam (JDS) |
| **Udupi Dt.** | | | |
| Karakala TMC | 23 | Rahmath (INC) | NMW |
| **Kodagu Dt.** | | | |
| Kushalnagar TP | 05 | Surayya Banu (JDS) | Abida Banu (INC) |
| Virajpet TP | 05 | Tasneem Akhtar (IND) | NMW |
| | 08 | NMW | Haseena Banu (INC) |
| **Mandya Dt.** | | | |
| Mandya CMC | 26 | Shahjahan (INC) | Fathimuthusohara (IND) |
| | 31 | Salma Taj (INC) | Rumana Farhin (JDS) |
| Maddur TMC | 19 | NMW | Kausar Jabeen (INC) |
| Srirangapattana TMC | 18 | Ameena (IUML) | Maqbool Jahan (JDS) |
| K.R. Pete TMC | 04 | Tanzeema Kausar (INC) | Fasiha Banu (JDS) |
| Nagamangala TP | 14 | Parveen Taj (JDS) | Naziya Parveen Taj (INC) |
| **Belgaum Dt.** | | | |
| Gokak CMC | 01 | M Maimunnisa Iqbal (IND) | NMW |
| | 10 | Surayya AMS (IND) | NMW |
| | 20 | Ghousia Bi AR Desai (IND) | Kaliph Shakira Kasim (IND) |
| Nippani CMC | 21 | Najahat Parvin NM (IND) | NMW |
| | 28 | Zayda DB (IND) | NMW |
| | 18 | NMW | Dilshadbi HN (IND) |
| Ramdurga TMC | 04 | B Hajarabi MG (INC) | Ruksana R Mullah (BJP) |
| Sankeshwar TMC | 09 | Katunbi JK (BJP) | NMW |
| Bailahongal TMC | 17 | Bagewadi Rizwana Aiyaz (INC) | NMW |
| | 21 | Mullah Nazrina Banu RA (INC) | Jayarabi IM (BJP) |
| Chikkodi TMC | 01 | Parveen KK (IND) | Atiya Muhammadi N (IND) |
| | 09 | Rashida Hasan K (IND) | Zulekha RM (IND) |
| Mudalagi TMC | 02 | K Jayada Begum M (BJP) | NMW |
| | 15 | Hajma BS (IND) | Shyanabi DG (BJP) |
| | 18 | NMW | Yasmin AT (INC) |

(*Contd.*)

| (1) | (2) | (3) | (4) |
|---|---|---|---|
| Savadatti TMC | 13 | Husenabi DC (KJP) | NMW |
| | 17 | NMW | Ameena M.A. (INC) |
| Hukkeri TMC | 09 | Noorjahan Begum BM (BJP) | Bibi Tabassum RM (INC) |
| | 13 | Naseema J Attar (BJP) | Raju bi Y Mohsin (INC) |
| | 17 | Gulshan Bi MP (BJP) | NMW |
| Khanapura TP | 14 | NMW | Zubaida S Paniwale (IND) |
| | 12 | NMW | Farida Bi MN (IND) |
| Sadalaga TP | 16 | Shahida Rafiq (IND) | NMW |
| Raibag TP | 10 | NMW | Yasmin I Momin (BJP) |
| | 12 | NMW | Momin Fatima Modin (BJP) |
| | 13 | Humasera Mushtak Mullah (BJP) | Jayarabi HK (IND) |
| Kudachi TP | 03 | Afsana AK Rohile (INC) | Sardar Bi IS (IND) |
| | 10 | Khudsiya FP (INC) | NMW |
| | 11 | Ruksana MB (IND) | Shahida GM (INC) |
| | 14 | Shahista AR (INC) | Sadikunnisa MI (IND) |
| | 15 | Mahaboobi MJ (INC) | Amina Amin J (IND) |
| Konnur TP | 16 | NMW | Begum AJ (BJP) |
| **Bijapur Dt.** | | | |
| Bijapur CMC | 19 | Bakshi Anees Fathima SIP (INC) | A Hashim Bi Razak (IND) |
| | 20 | Mahaboobi SD (JDS) | H Khaderbi B (INC) |
| | 25 | Quairunnisa AHS (KJP) | Pathan Sabira Begum MA (INC) |
| | 28 | Inamdar Shahnaz Begum AM (INC) | Pathan Sakina Bi LB (JDS) |
| | 32 | NMW | Shabana Parvez G (JDS) |
| Muddebihal TMC | 18 | Fathima M Dhavalagi (IND) | M Kulsumbi Jalalsa (JDS) |
| | 21 | Fathima L Naikodi (IND) | K Mehroonbi M (JDS) |
| | 22 | H Shahajad Bi A (IND) | I Noorjahan M (IND) |
| Talikote TMC | 06 | M Karim Bi Khalid (INC) | NMW |
| | 18 | NMW | Lalbi MK (IND) |
| | 23 | Hussainbi H. Mullah (IND) | NMW |
| Indi TMC | 09 | Katunbi M Tangewale (INC) | NMW |
| | 15 | H Maktumbi S Basha (INC) | Natikar Zarina H (IND) |
| Sindhgi TMC | 21 | K Rajanbi Saifansab (JDS) | NMW |
| | 22 | M.B. Khajabi Rafiq (JDS) | C Mahaboobi Modinsab (INC) |
| **Bagalkot Dt.** | | | |
| Bagalkot CMC | 24 | Afrin A Kaladagi (INC) | NMW |
| | 25 | NMW | Attar Parvin (INC) |
| | 31 | Tured Mahaboobi (INC) | NMW |
| Jamkhandi CMC | 07 | Ashabi A Sangtras (BSRC) | Sagar Juhurabi Usman9INC) |
| | 09 | Reshma Md. Akbar Kadri (INC) | NMW |
| | 23 | Haseena Illahi A (BSRC) | Naushad Illahi H (INC) |
| | 31 | Noorjanbi H Aparad (BSRC) | NMW |
| Ilakal CMC | 27 | NMW | Sonar Afrina Begum K (INC) |
| Mahalingapura TMC | 22 | NMW | Dilshad Appasab N (JDS) |
| Guledagudda TMC | 15 | Aminabi B Mujahid (INC) | NMW |
| Badami TMC | 13 | B Tahera BanuLalsaab (INC) | U Mumtaz Husseinsab (JDS) |
| | 22 | Shamshad begum AN (JDS) | K Shabana Begum AR (BJP) |
| Hunagunda TP | 16 | NMW | Noorjanbi MB (BJP) |
| Kerur TP | 11 | Peer Khan Bibijan (INC) | NMW |

(*Contd.*)

| (1) | (2) | (3) | (4) |
|---|---|---|---|
| | 01 | NMW | Jayarabi HD (JDS) |
| Bilagi TP | 06 | Mumtaz Begum SG (INC) | NMW |
| | 11 | N. Mustafa Hashimbi (IND) | NMW |
| **Gulbarga Dt.** | | | |
| Shahabad CMC | 15 | Farzana Rasheed (INC) | NMW |
| | 25 | Salima Begum MA (INC) | Zareena Begum B (IND) |
| Aland TMC | 10 | Mashakbee Arif Ansari (JDS) | Asifa Mahmud Ansari (KJP) |
| | 11 | Farzana Begum Arif A (JDS) | NMW |
| | 17 | NMW | Badrunnisa Abdul Latif (KJP) |
| | 18 | Aisha Begum MA (JDS) | Anisa Begum AM (KJP) |
| Sedam TMC | 04 | Quairunnisa Begum AK (JDS) | NMW |
| | 20 | Sajeeda Begum R. Patel (INC) | NMW |
| Chittapur TMC | 13 | Rahmath Begum G R (INC) | NMW |
| | 05 | NMW | Ayesha Begum S (KJP) |
| Afzalpur TP | 04 | Saipanabi Moulasab (KJP) | UNANIMOUSLY ELECTED |
| | 08 | Allamabi Mahaboob Saab (KJP) | Raziabi Arif Sk.(JDS) |
| Chincholi TP | 06 | Farzana begum Saudagar (INC) | NMW |
| | 08 | NMW | Jhaja Begum (INC) |
| | 15 | NMW | Arshiya Jabeen (KJP) |
| Jewargi TP | 04 | Fathima Begum AG (INC) | Hazara begum (IND) |
| | 14 | Md. Hanifa (JDS) | Md. Ejaja (INC) |
| **Yadgir dt.** | | | |
| Yadgir CMC | 09 | Roshan Begum (KJP) | Saijad Begum (INC) |
| | 14 | Tasneema Banu (INC) | NMW |
| Shorapur TMC | 13 | Zaharabi Usmansab (INC) | Shahida Begum MG (IND) |
| | 20 | Zakir begum MU (IND) | Khuteja begum GM Anwar (INC) |
| Shahapur TMC | 14 | Salima Begum (IND) | MM |
| | 15 | Bashira Begum C (INC) | NMW |
| Gurumitkal TP | 03 | Nafeesa Khatun (INC) | NMW |

NMW: Non-Muslim woman; MM: Muslim Male

*Source:* State Election Commission, Karnataka.

the second position. Further, against 2,199 seats in the Town Municipalities, Muslim women could capture 167 seats (11.99%) and in the Town Panchayats, 64 Muslim women were elected against 1,003 seats (6.38%).

- A number of Muslim women have also been elected without contest owing to the goodwill that they had established in the community through their social service; for, none of the Muslim women elected, through contest or unanimously, are related to any senior political leader.
- Surprisingly, a number of Muslim women have contested the elections under the BJP banner and some have even been elected. Some others have contested under the *Karnataka Janata Paksha* (KJP) banner; a party launched by former BJP leader and Chief Minister of Karnataka, B.S. Yeddyurappa, who left BJP for reasons already stated above.
- Muslim women have mainly contested under the banner of either the Congress Party or the Janata Dal (Secular). Some have sought the nomination of the Socialist Democratic Party. Only two Muslim women have contested, one each, under the Republican Party of India and Indian Union Muslim League (Kerala Committee). Both could win.

The results of PRI elections show that for Muslim women of Karnataka *hijab* does not stand in the way of contesting an election, or running administration. They have proved that Muslim women are equal to women from all other communities in running Panchayati Raj.[40]

It has also been observed that Muslim women elected as Members of PRIs are not content to be mere members, attending meetings and marking their attendance. Some of them have been pro-active with regard to civic matters and willing to take-up additional responsibilities.

- Noor Jahan Shariff (Congress) Kushalnagar Councillor and Nazni Begum (Independent) Padarayanapura Councillor (Brihat Bangalore Mahanagar Palike) raised the issue of drinking water problems in their wards.[41]
- Kushal Nagar Corporator Noor Jahan Shariff continued to raise issues like absence of proper drainage system in her ward, on account of which filth overflows onto the road.

She also complained that garbage was not collected properly and whatever is collected is dumped in the ward itself.
- Noor Jahan Sharief was elected unopposed to the Standing Committee for Taxation and Finance.[42]

In fact, Councillors Varalakshmi J. and Noor Jahan, representing Marthahalli and Kushalnagar wards respectively, challenged a notification issued by the Karnataka government on February 8, 2013 changing the reservation of Mayor's post of Bangalore City Corporation to the General category from the General (Woman) category, reflecting their urge to occupy the Mayor's Chair.

Mani Shankar Aiyar, Union Minister for Panchayati Raj had an occasion to observe that in the case of women, "there are still formidable problems to be overcome. Many women are hesitant and tentative in rising to the occasion. Often, the men of the village do not accord them the respect and regard that is their due. Officials take advantage of their inexperience and poor education. Effective devolution is so uneven and inadequate that oftentimes even the most able women are crippled for want of the rightful allocation of functions, finances and functionaries without which effective Panchayati Raj is rendered impossible. Some of these hurdles are gender-specific. Some are generic in nature and related to the larger issue of the empowerment of the Panchayats".[43]

There have been attempts, though not concerted, to create awareness among Muslim women about the importance of their joining mainstream politics and contesting the Lok Sabha and Assembly elections. Sugra Humayun Mirza, the first woman activist in Hyderabad, worked for women's rights, dignity and self-respect. She actively promoted education and established schools for girls way back in 1919. Masuma Begum contested elections from the Hyderabad constituency in 1952 and represented her constituency for 11 years. She was Minister for Social Welfare in 1962. Jamalunissa Baji, who was active in political movements during 1945-47, formed small groups of women to spread awareness about political movements and bring them into the mainstream politics.

It is relevant to refer to a workshop for Muslim women activists on 'Leadership and visibility' organized by *Asmita* Resource Centre for Women in Hyderabad on 17-19 March, 2011. The workshop focused on issues of political visibility of Muslim woman: why is the Muslim woman invisible, not only in the political scenario, but in all other spheres as well? Was it always like this? Despite having dynamic, exemplary Muslim women from the past, there are myriad reasons that are hindering the progress of Muslim women today. The workshop felt that only a collective strength can break the walls of discrimination and marginalization, the patriarchal set up, the stereotypes, the politics of religion and all other encumbering structures. But, the consensus that emerged shows that Muslim women would like to leave politics aside and focus on peace and harmony on one hand and education on the other than on leadership and visibility. The reasoning seemed to be: What good is leadership if there is no *ta'lim* and what good is *ta'lim* if there is no *Aman*?[44]

Unlike some other north Indian states, Karnataka has not witnessed any major communal incident in the last several years. There is, thus, *Aman* in the state. But, what is needed now is *ta'lim* (education), especially secular education, for both Muslim boys and girls. In a charter of demands submitted by the *Karnataka Muslim Muttehada Mahaz* (an umbrella organisation of Muslim bodies in Karnataka) to political parties in April 2013, the Mahaz sought fair representation of the community in the political life and social and economic development of the state, and remedial measures coaching scheme for nearly 50,000 Muslim children dropping out of schools annually.[45] The charter of demands covered a variety of subjects. But, neither the Mahaz included any Muslim women nor the charter of demands sought increasing Muslim women's political representation. It appears as though talking about Muslim women's political representation is anathema. With no backing from the KMMA, Muslim women of Karnataka have to chart their own course.

## NOTES AND REFERENCES

1. Quoted by Qazi Arshad Ali (2010), Muslim Population in Karnataka: An Analysis-1, in *Karnataka Muslims*, September 28, (Available at http://karnatakamuslims.com/portal/muslim-population-in-karnataka-an-analysis-1/)
2. *Ibid.*
3. Muslims of Bangalore: A Major City of India, in 30-*days Prayer Network*, 18 February, 2013. (Available at http://www.30-days.net/muslims/muslims-in/asia-south-central/india/india-bangalore/)
4. Lakhani, Abdul Hafiz (2012), Muslim literacy Lowest: Demographic Report, in *The Milli Gazette*, Published Online: December 28, (Available at http://

www.milligazette.com/news/5359-muslim-literacy-lowest-demographic-report)

5. Jalil, Rakhshanda (2010), Educating Muslim Women in Modern India: Problems and Perspectives, in *Dialogue,* January-March, Volume 11, No. 3. (Available at http://www.asthabharati.org/Dia_Jan10/rakh.htm)
6. Available at http://www.jeywin.com/wp-content/uploads/2009/12/An-Analytical-Study-of-Education-of-Muslim-Women-and-Girls-in-India.pdf)
7. Available at http://www.hindu.com/2011/05/26/stories/2011052660270900.htm
8. Available at http://www.jeywin.com/wp-content/uploads/2009/12/An-Analytical-Study-of-Education-of-Muslim-Women-and-Girls-in-India.pdf
9. Goetz, Anne Marie (2003), Women's Education and Political Participation, Background Paper prepared for the Education for All Global Monitoring Report 2003/4, *Gender and Education for All: The Leap to Equality.* (Available at http://unesdoc.unesco.org/images/0014/001467/146770e.pdf)
10. Kamat, A.R. (1981), Literacy and Education of Muslims: A Note, in *Economic and Political Weekly*, Vol. 6, No. 23, June 6, 1981.
11. Kaur, Gurinder and Divjot Kaur. Literacy of Major Religious Groups in India: A geographical perspective. *Abstracts of Sikh Studies,* October-December 2012/544 NS (Available at http://sikhinstitute.org/oct_2012/5-divjot.pdf)
12. Aziz, Dr. Abdul (2012), Socio-Economic Status of Karnataka Muslims—1, in *Karnataka Muslims*, November 7, Features, (Available at http://karnatakamuslims.com/portal/socio-economic-status-of-karnataka-muslims-1/) *Dr. Abdul Aziz, is a renowned Economist and visiting Professor, Center for the Study of Social Exclusion and Inclusive Policy (CSSEIP), at National Law School of India University, Bangalore).*
13. Bageshree, S. (2012), The Saga of OBC reservation for Muslims in the State, in *The Hindu*, July 23, (Available at http://www.thehindu.com/todays-paper/tp-national/tp-karnataka/article3671742.ece)
14. Ali, Quazi Arshad. (2012), *Karnataka Muslims and Electoral Politics*, Bangalore: Bookware.
15. Ali, Quazi Arshad. Muslims' Participation in Karnataka Legislative Assembly Elections, in *Karnataka Muslims.* (Available at http://karnatakamuslims.com/portal/muslims-participation-in-karnataka-legislative-assembly-elections/.)
16. Mrs. Gnanamba, wife of Vatal Nagaraj, founder of *Kannada Chalavali Vatal Paksha*, a regional party.
17. Qazi Arshad Ali, (2010) Of Class, Gender and Elections, *The Hindu*, December 19.
18. Anil Bhusare, (2010) Maratha leader and former ZP president, quoted in *The Hindu*, December 19.
19. Aziz, Dr. Abdul, *op. cit.*
20. *Ibid.*
21. Professor Shastri at a Seminar on "*Religious Minorities and Politics: The Karnataka Perspective*" organised by the Centre for the Study of Social

Exclusion and Inclusive Policy, National Law School of India, University of Bangalore on 30 September, 2012. Reported in The *Hindu*, 1 October, 2012.

22. Reported in *Bangalore Mirror.com*, 31 March, 2012. (Available at https://vinayak.wordpress.com/category/uncategorized/page/13/) Khanum's case illustrates the uncertainty of political ambitions of a Muslim woman. Shahtaj Khanum was a former Deputy Mayor of Bangalore Municipal Corporation. She lost the November 2001 elections to the corporation when she contested as an independent candidate. Besides losing the election, Khanum suffered at the home front, when her husband gave her the triple *talaq* through a newspaper advertisement. She subsequently joined the Congress party. She said: "I got married to him when I was doing my II PUC. He is a distant relative of my mother. He never stopped me when I joined politics and contested elections to the then BMP from Gurrappana Palya ward in 1995. I became Deputy Mayor and he enjoyed the perks attached to my office. He misused my name and amassed wealth. After I lost in the assembly elections, he must have felt that I am no more useful to him. I have sacrificed a lot for him. I have silently suffered for 10 years."[22]
23. National Parties Ignore Women Candidates, *The Hindu*. (Available at http://www.thehindu.com/todays-paper/tp-national/tp-karnataka/national-parties-ignore-women-candidates/article4645620.ece?)
24. *One India News*, 28 March, 2013. (Available at http://news.oneindia.in/2013/03/28/sonia-gandhi-rejects-karnataka-candidates-list-1181622.html)
25. In interviews with Mujahid Deputy Field Investigator under this Project
26. Ali, Quazi Arshad *op. cit.*, p. 119.
27. A School of Thought, in *the Islamic Voice*, January 2005. (Available at http://www.islamicvoice.com/January2005/Miscellany/). Nafeesa Fazal is a Kutchi Memon and daughter-in-law of Janab Abdul Hameed Fazal Sait, the owner of reputed business house, M. Fazal & Sons and the daughter of Janab Abdul Kareem Sait of Coimbatore. Abbasia Begum Mecci (d.1970) who was a member of the Legislative Council during the 1960s was the wife of Sirajuddin Mecci, an IAS officer and Labour Commissioner. She was a great educationist and founded the New Generation School. She was also the chairperson of the Al-Ameen Educational Society. Her mission to start a school could not be fulfilled due to her untimely death. Her desire was fulfilled by her daughters, by establishing the New Generation Education Society.
28. *DNA*, Kolkata, March 20, 2010.
29. Alam, Md. Mudassir, in *Indian Muslims*, March 10, 2010 (Available at http://indianmuslims.in/women%E2%80%99s-reservation-bill-what-it-means-for-muslim-representation/)
30. India: Muslim Clerics Oppose Women in Parliament, where they could "brush shoulders with men" in *Jihad Watch*. (Available athttp://www.jihadwatch.org/2010/03/india-muslim-clerics-oppose-women-in-parliament-where-they-could-brush-shoulders-with-men.html)

31. Iyar, Mani Shankar (2011) One Step Forward, Two Steps Backward, in *Two Decades of New Panchayati Raj in Karnataka: Issues, Options and Lesson,* Mathew, George (Ed.) Institute of Social Sciences, New Delhi: Concept Publishing Co. (P) Ltd., p. 14.
32. Available at http://infochangeindia.org/governance/analysis/the-challenge-is-to-make-panchayati-raj-institutions-vehicles-for-both-governance-and-delivery.html
33. What Is the Role of Women in Indian Politics? Growing Stronger, in *India Knowledge* @Wharton,...Published: May 21, 2009 (Available at http://knowledge.wharton.upenn.edu/india/article.cfm?articleid=4380)
34. Syeda Khushtara Banu in interview with Yoginder Sikand in *New Age Islam*, 18 August, 2010.
35. *Ibid.*
36. *Ibid.*
37. *Ibid.*
38. A report in *The Hindu* said: "While it is common knowledge that husbands of several women councillors "manage the affairs" of the ward, it was more or less made "official" at a recent *Iftar* party organised by the BJP's Minority Morcha. Ishtiaque Ahmed, husband of Shivajinagar councillor, Farida, was openly referred to as the "area councillor" and was invited to share the *dais* with Chief Minister B.S. Yeddyurappa and other dignitaries. When one of the organisers announced "we invite Shivajinagar councillor to come on the stage", everybody wondered whether Farida would walk up. But they were surprised to see Mr. Ahmed being escorted to the *dais* by his followers. *The Hindu*, September 22, 2010.
39. Available at http://vu-point.blogspot.in/2010/04/muslim-woman-from-bjp-wins-hands-down.html. Out of the 66 Muslim women who contested for a seat in the Bangalore Municipal Corporation, only 8 (12%).
40. *Two decades of New Panchayati Raj in Karnataka: Issues, Options and Lessons*, p. 14, (Ed.) George Mathew, Institute of Social Sciences, (2011) New Delhi: Concept Publishing Company Pvt. Ltd.
41. *The Hindu*, Bangalore, February 1, 2013.
42. *The Hindu,* Bangalore, June 12, 2013.
43. Mani Shankar Aiyar 2008, Minister in Foreword, *Study on EWRs in Panchayatiraj Institutions*, Ministry of Panchayati Raj, Government of India, 24 April.
44. Fatima, Nikhat. 2011, Muslim women activists in Hyderabad discuss history, politics, and society in *The Milli Gazette Online,* Jun 17.
45. *Islamic Voice*, Vols. 26-8, No. 320, August 2013. (Available at http://islamicvoice.com/islamicvoice/karnataka-assembly-elections-muslims-negotiate-charter-of-demands/).

# 4

# Uttar Pradesh

The name North-Western Province was changed to United Provinces of Agra and Oudh in 1902 and to Uttar Pradesh in 1950. Under the provisions of the Government of India Act, 1935, a bicameral legislature came into existence in the United Provinces. The Legislative Assembly was constituted for the first time on 1 April, 1937 with 228 members, with a term of five years. The Legislative Council consisting of not more than 60 members was made a permanent body, with the term of individual members fixed at 9 years and one third of the members retiring every third year.

With the adoption of the Constitution of India on 26 January, 1950, the total membership of the UP Legislative Council was increased to 72. The composition and purpose of the Legislative Council also changed after 1952, when it was reconstituted according to the provisions of the Constitution of India and some kind of functional representation was provided in its composition. With the Constitution (Seventh Amendment) Act, 1956, the strength of the Council was raised to 108. After the reorganisation of Uttar Pradesh in November 2000 and the creation of Uttaranchal, this strength has come down to 100. The Legislative Council Members are elected/nominated for six years and one-third of them retire every second year. After Independence, the Legislative Assembly met for the first time on 3 November, 1947. Under the provisions of the Constitution, the strength of the UP Assembly was fixed at 431 and later revised to 426. Post-Uttaranchal, the strength of the UP Legislative Assembly has become 404 including one nominated member to represent the Anglo-Indian community. The term of the Legislative Assembly is five years, unless dissolved earlier.

## Population

Uttar Pradesh is one of the most populous states in India, with a population of 19,95,81,477 at the 2011 provisional Census. The State has also a high Muslim population, numbering 30,740,158, i.e., about 18.5 per cent of the State's total population. The other religious groups in the State are Christians (0.13%), Sikhs (0.41%), Buddhists (0.18%) and Jains (0.12%).[1]

**Table 4.1**: District-wise Concentration of Muslims in Uttar Pradesh

| *Very High (Above 39.90%)* | *High (30.66-39.90%)* | *Medium (21.42 to 30.66%)* | *Low-level (12.18 to 21.41%)* | *Very Low (Below 12.8%)* |
|---|---|---|---|---|
| Rampur<br>Moradabad<br>Bijnor | Jotiba Phule Nagar<br>Saharanpur<br>Muzaffarnagar<br>Balrampur<br>Bahraich<br>Bareilly<br>Meerut | Siddharth Nagar<br>Shrawasti<br>Baghpat<br>Sant Kabir Nagar<br>Ghaziabad<br>Philibit<br>Barabanki | 27 districts | 18 districts |

*Source:* Election Commission Statistical Report.

The overall distribution pattern of Muslims in Uttar Pradesh shows that they are concentrated in districts located along the northern edge of the state boundary and the southern districts have low concentration of Muslim population (Table 4.1).

## Literacy Rate and Occupational Pattern

A High Powered Panel appointed by Ministry of Home Affairs, Government of India, in the beginning of 1980 (headed by Dr. Gopal Singh) to look into the conditions of the minorities, schedule castes and schedule tribes, had observed that Muslims and neo-Buddhists were educationally most backward at the national level.

The need to take special steps to advance education of Muslims was noted in the National Policy on Education (NPE) 1986 and its programme of Action (revised in 1992) leading to the formulation of the Area Intensive Educational Development as a Central Government Scheme of the Ministry of Human Resource Development. The NPE stated the following with regard to minorities:[2]

> "Some minority groups are educationally backward or deprived. Greater attention will be paid to the education of

these groups in the interest of equality and social justice. This will naturally include the constitutional guarantees given to them to establish and administer their own educational institutions, and protection to their languages and culture. Simultaneously, objectivity will be reflected in the preparation of textbooks and in all school activities and all possible measures will be taken to promote an integration based on appreciation of common national goals and ideas, in conformity with the core curriculum."

But, by and large, the educational status of Muslims has not improved till date despite the Area Intensive and *Madrasah* Modernization programme launched by the Government of India; the reasons adduced being uneven and ineffective implementation. In the absence of concerted efforts, the later Sachar Committee also found that Muslims were still the most educationally backward community of the country. The Committee reported:[3]

> "Muslims are at a double disadvantage with low levels of education combined with low quality education; their deprivation increases manifold as the level of education rises. In some instances, the relative share for Muslims is lower than even the SCs who are victims of a long standing caste system. Such relative deprivation calls for a significant policy shift, in the recognition of the problem and in devising corrective measures, as well as in the allocation of resources."

The following Table 4.2 gives the literacy rates of people belonging to different religions in Uttar Pradesh:

Table 4.2: Literacy Rates of Population: Religion-wise

| *Religion* | *Total* | *Male* | *Female* |
|---|---|---|---|
| UP (2011) | 69.72 | 79.24 | 59.26 |
| Hindu | 57.98 | 71.24 | 43.08 |
| Muslim | 47.79 | 57.29 | 37.38 |
| Christian | 72.85 | 78.14 | 67.36 |
| Sikhs | 71.91 | 72.19 | 52.61 |
| Buddhist | 56.21 | 70.34 | 40.29 |
| Jains | 93.21 | 95.90 | 90.29 |
| Mean | 66.66 | 74.18 | 55.17 |

*Source:* Census of India, 2011. Figures in per cent.

Uttar Pradesh has been educationally backward since the early decades of the 20th century. The 1931 Census points out that "this Province is only 3/5ths as literate as India as a whole and takes a very low position relative to the other provinces." [4] The 1931 census also recorded that "among UP Muslims, there was one literate female for every 6 literate males. In places like the princely state Rampur, there was a virtual ban on women's education."[5] This gives an idea of how Muslim women's education suffered in Uttar Pradesh since decades, for the simple reason that education, beyond the reading of *Quran*, was not considered necessary for girls, and any attempt to transgress the limit was frowned upon.

According to the provisional census figures of 2011, the literacy rate of females belonging to the urban areas of Uttar Pradesh were far behind the national average by 8.24 per cent and in the case of females belonging to rural areas by 3.14 per cent. Within the State, there is disparity in the literacy-levels by religious communities. Only 48 per cent of the State's Muslims are reported literate; the literacy rate ranging from 57 per cent among males to 37 per cent among females. Explaining the educational backwardness of Muslims of the State, the Islamic Society in Mirzapur writes:[6]

> "The state came under many fast developments just after the partition. The major victims of the Zamindari Abolition Act were the Muslim landlords of then the United Province (later named Uttar Pradesh). Benefits of the pre-Partition education and employment were denied to the Muslim youths with de-recognition of Urdu and Persian as the official languages. The state, which was the hinterland of Urdu, grew generations after generation of youths with little knowledge of the language. The aversion of the Muslim rank and file against the British Rule distracted them from learning English for a long time. The creation of Pakistan was also considered to be a conspiracy of the Muslim leadership having deep roots in the Province. Added with a number of other factors, the situation went enormously against the community at least in Uttar Pradesh for some decades. Consequently, the general Muslim masses remained confused, devoid of roots, impoverished and uneducated in the modern sense of the word. This is the reason, why the Muslims who were forward on the front of literacy and general education before Partition

with 42 per cent literacy rate registered just 9 per cent literacy in 1951. The State has yet not come out from the unfortunate situation and the Muslims of the state rank quite low even among the Muslims of various states in term of educational attainments".

"The education of Muslim women is another challenge both for the policy-makers and the Muslim leadership. ... ... Muslim women are lagging behind their counterparts, both the general women and the Muslim men...... According to the census 2001, the literacy rate of the Muslim community in the state is 47.8 per cent and the literacy rate of Muslim women is 37.4 per cent. ... ... Muslims parents generally disregard sending their daughters to coeducational or far-flung schools and colleges. In the process, many talented girls have to drop out at an early stage of their education. The presence of exclusive institutions for girls in a nearby locality most of the time increases Muslim girls' participation beyond primary level to manifold. Hence, it would be an effective strategy to enhance Muslim women's education by establishing more-and-more exclusive and accessible institutions for them. The proverbial statement "Educate a boy educate an individual, educate a girl educate a nation" must be a tested strategy for the overall educational progress of the community. A noteworthy challenge in this regard has been the parents' apathy towards the education of the girl child, which could be done away with by systematically launching of awareness campaigns in the community".

While the Muslims in general and Muslim women in particular, are the most illiterate religious community in the State of Uttar Pradesh, the literacy-levels differ from one district to the other.

- Female literates by district varies between 26.05 per cent in Shrawasti to 70.54 per cent in Mau;
- Muslims literacy rates in 12 districts are 'very high' (above 61.64%) in Mau, Ghazipur, Azamgarh, Jhansi, Ballia, Lalitpur, Chitrakoot, Kanpur Nagar, Ambedkar Nagar, Allahabad, Mahoba and Hamirpur;
- In 21 districts, Muslim literacy rate was found to range from 52.75 per cent to 61.64 per cent;

- There are 23 districts in the medium level category of Muslim literacy;
- A low level (34.94% to 43.84%) literacy rate is observed in the districts of Jotiba Phule Nagar, Kheri, Barabanki, Etah, Shahjahanpur, Philibit, Mathura, Gonda, Bareilly, Moradabad and Budaun; and
- There are only four districts with a very low level of Muslim literacy rate viz., Balrampur, Rampur, Bahraich and Shrawasti.

A closer look between Muslim population and Muslim literacy rate shows that the lesser the percentage of Muslims in a district, the higher is their literacy-level, whereas, the districts in which the Muslims have more than 20 per cent population their literacy-level is less than that of Hindus.[7]

A number of factors are responsible for Muslim women's low literacy rate in the State. While it is not entirely incorrect to say that religious conservatism is one of the major factors for Muslim girls not accessing education, the main reason for educational backwardness of Muslim girls is the abject poverty of the parents, due to which the girls drop out after the first few classes. Girls are expected to look after their younger siblings while their parents go to work. Childlabour is also reported to be high among Muslims as compared to other communities. As only a few good-quality Government schools are available in Muslim areas and the pupil-teacher ratio is high in such schools, Muslim parents are forced to send their children to private schools, if they can afford. Children, especially girls, whose parents cannot afford private schools, simply drop out of the government schools.

Thus, financial constraints, illiteracy of poor parents, lack of neighbourhood schools, faulty curriculum, and paucity of trained teachers, traditional teaching approach, low retention and enrolment, population growth are cited as the major causes that hinder education of the Muslim children. Socio-economic factors contribute significantly to disparities in literacy and educational attainment among women in rural and urban areas. Perceptions of public security—partly associated with increasing incidents of communal violence—prevent parents from sending daughters to schools located at a distance where they would have to use public transport. This is particularly the case when the girls reach upper-primary and middle-school levels, leading to high dropout rates.[8]

In a study covering Moradabad and Barabanki districts, most of the male and female teachers expressed that the two main factors that retarded education of Muslim girls were poverty and acute religious fanaticism. *Purdah* discouraged parents from sending girls, especially older girls, to schools other than *Madrasahs*. Those Muslim girls who received some education through *madrasahs* did so mainly in Arabic language. Conservative Muslim parents wanted that formal and regular education should be provided only in *Madrasahs* and only by those teachers who can instruct the students in Urdu language. Muslim parents have also been demanding separate schools for girls. An additional factor affecting girls' education is that a large number of Muslim girls belonging to low-income group families are engaged in low-paid economic activities like *beedi* rolling, spinning and weaving etc. As the income from these small-scale domestic-based activities being remunerative for the families concerned, parents discourage girls from going to school.

Yet another study of Attitudes of Teachers and Parents of Azamgarh District towards Muslim Girls' Education by Hafiz Mahboob-based on a sample of 70 Muslim teachers in government and government-aided schools and *madrasahs*, brings out the following points:[9]

- While male literacy was fairly high among the Muslims of Azamgarh, the female literacy rates were very low;
- Almost all the *madrasah* teachers believed in the importance of girls' education, but stressed that the ideal education which Muslim girls should receive should be religious in nature, although a modicum of general subjects that enable girls to become good housewives and mothers would be ideal;
- Eighty per cent of the parents believed that as far as religious education is concerned, there should be no distinction between boys and girls. Some parents stressed that girls must study in all-girl schools and under female teachers, and ultimately, they must discontinue their studies after the attainment of puberty; and
- It was deemed imperative that these schools be located within the locality where the girls live.

In the final analysis, the reasons for the educational backwardness of the Muslim community in Utter Pradesh are manifold. While poorly educated parents may not realise the value of education, poor parents also cannot afford to provide the necessary support system at home. Yet another factor is also that Muslim artisans and those engaged in petty businesses do not see the necessity of formal education for their children or do not consider education as necessarily translating into formal employment. The low representation of Muslims in public or private sector employment and the perception of discrimination in securing salaried jobs make them attach lesser importance to formal 'secular' education in comparison to other communities.

The role of religion in the educational backwardness of the Muslim community, especially Muslim girls, cannot be totally ignored. For instance, in December 2007, the National Council for Minority Educational Institutions opined that co-education could hamper education of Muslim girls as it would 'distract' the students. Justice M. S. A. Siddiqui, Chairman of the Council declared that "there should be no co-education till the class XII", as, in his opinion, the young students would take time to understand the concept of co-education before they grow up to a particular age. In his view, girls developed the required mental maturity only after Class XII to deal with the concept of co-education at college level. He felt that the restriction will not only benefit girls, but also the boys in that avoiding co-education will help them to be away from distractions. The Chairman felt that the distractions will hamper the efforts to make a maximum number of Muslim children, particularly girls, literate.[10] Even Darul Uloom, Deoband had also opined that co-education should be banned in schools, colleges, universities and even religious schools because it created the potential for many evils.

The Uttar Pradesh *Madrasah* Board went one step further and banned, in February 2009, co-education in the *madrasahs* across the State. Haji Rizwan Haq, Chairman of the Board justified the ban saying that co-education is against the "spirit of Islam". He emphasised: "In Islam, *purdah* is very important. By allowing co-education we promote *'be-pardgi'* (women without veil), which is against *Shariat*".[11] Out of the more than 16,000 *madrasahs* in the state, 1,900 were affiliated to the Board and of these, about 170 *madrasahs* were meant exclusively for girls and the rest followed co-education. The Chairman threatened to take action against *madrasahs* admitting girls in those meant for boys. The Board's order was expected to interrupt the education of over 25,000 girl students in the state, who were to be given their school-leaving certificates and asked to sit at home.

In a November 2009 resolution on girls' education, the *Jamiat ul-Ulema-e Hind* said:

> "Their education must be fully in accordance with the limits set by the *Shariah* and the rules of *purdah*. Co-education must be fully avoided, or else it is feared that more harm than good would result."

Jamaat-e-Islami Hind chief Moulana Jalaluddin Umri said: "The problem starts with co-education. We are saying educate the girls as much as you want, but give the education separately." When there is paucity of schools, colleges and institutions offering professional courses, how far these orders and resolutions can be adhered to is any body's guess.

Economic reasons on one hand and religious rulings on the other have hampered the educational status of Muslim girls in Uttar Pradesh. The Muslim community should make up its mind if it has to come out of the sorry state of affairs in which it finds itself in.

## Economic Activity

As a group, the role of Muslims in the economic activity in the State is marginal, with most of them engaged in informal skills and trades with poor productivity, primarily because of low levels of education. NSS data shows that urban centres have only 3 per cent Muslim graduates compared to 15 per cent Hindu graduates and over 20 per cent Sikh and Christian graduates. Rural Uttar Pradesh does not have enough graduates to draw any meaningful comparison across religions. It can be safely assumed that most graduates would move to urban centres seeking opportunities and employment. In urban centres nearly 1/3rd Muslims are recorded as having completed primary education, 10 per cent has completed middle and another 11 per cent having completed secondary education. However low these figures may be, they do challenge the conventional bias that suggests reluctance within the community towards pursuit of education.[12]

In the prime age group of 16-25 years, there is a country-wide declining trend in the labour force participation rate (LFPR) amongst Muslims, from 78 per cent to 67 per cent in males and 17 per cent to 12 per cent in females, over the last 10 years, suggesting that more persons are moving away seeking active employment in this age-group, implying a growing trend in the numbers pursuing higher studies or seeking professional education. Among the Muslims of Uttar Pradesh belonging to the same age-group, the LFPR decline has been greater than the national averages, indicating a stronger trend and perhaps a greater willingness amongst young boys and girls to pursue higher studies. In Western UP, which is 35 per cent urban with 32 per cent Muslims population, an examination of the reasons for migration of Muslims to urban centres has revealed that nearly 49 per cent of them have done so for pursuing education and 22 per cent for employment. Clearly, education and better employment are becoming a family priority.[13]

Though the unemployment rates are fairly low across communities, with some variations between the rural and urban sector, the UP Muslims are engaged mostly in traditional skill-based industries. Even with a high LFPR and low unemployment rate, the economic condition of Muslims in Uttar Pradesh is one of the worst in the country viewed from the monthly per capita expenditure (MPCE) angle and comparing it with states like Kerala, J&K and West Bengal.[14] Within the State, the situation of Muslims in Eastern UP is far behind other areas. Overall, the MPCE indicates that although employed, due to low productivity, the earning levels remain in the lower percentile.

The numbers themselves thus demonstrate a narrative, both bleak and full of optimism at the same instance. While it primarily remains a discourse of economic disenfranchisement over time, notwithstanding frequent political promises and political posturing, on the positive side the new narration indicates an increasing effort within the community in seeking education and skills in order to integrate with the mainstream.[15]

The key indicators of social and demographic development in relation to the Muslim minority concentration districts show that the population growth is high and family size is large. Barring Meerut, Saharanpur and Ghaziabad (due to their proximity to Delhi), the use of family planning methods is very poor and in Basti and Bijnor, more than three-fourths of the girls are married before the age of eighteen, and proportion of women receiving skilled attention during pregnancy is reported to be woefully poor.

Irrespective of the issue of electoral participation, it is necessary to create a strong awareness about girls' education in the predominantly Muslim areas and the parents motivated, besides convincing Muslim religious heads. Teachers also feel that in order to promote girls education, separate schools for girls should be set up at the middle level and at least one woman teacher appointed in all primary schools. The teachers also support the demand of Muslim parents for the setting up of vocational-*cum*-school education for girls.[16]

## Muslim Women of Uttar Pradesh in Freedom Movement

A number of Muslim women, from what now constitutes Uttar Pradesh, have made supreme sacrifices right from the first war of independence in 1857. "The participation of Muslim women in freedom movement began from the first war of independence, 1857. This was the time when our society was still dominated by conservative traditions and social customs and denied women their rightful place in it. Nevertheless, leaving the hearths and homes they came forward and fought against foreign domination. They also made supreme sacrifices without asking for a weaker sex treatment from a cruel world around."[17]

Such patriotic Muslim women include Azizan Begum (b.1832) daughter of Husain Khan and Hamida Begum of Lucknow. She raised a Women's Brigade, training the members in arms and horse-riding. She is said to have enjoyed the confidence of Tantiya Tope, Nana Saheb, Azimulla Khan and other leaders. Begum Hazrat Mahal, wife of Wazid Ali Shah, is a house-hold name. Abadi Begum (known popularly as Bi Amman), mother of Ali Brothers (Mohammad Ali and Shaukat Ali) was recognised as a National Leader in the' twenties. She joined the Home Rule League started by Tilak along with her daughter-in-law and other adult members of the family. She was the first woman to address a male audience while wearing the veil. Bi Amman presided over the All India Ladies Conference in Ahmedabad on 30 December, 1921. She advocated Hindu-Muslim unity and the establishment of Panchayats.

Other Muslim women of repute in the national context include Akbari Begum (mother of Barrister Asif Ali, freedom fighter), Nishatunnisa Begum, wife of Sayyid Fazl ul Hasan Rizvi)[18]. The latter was a confirmed nationalist of revolutionary leanings and an ardent supporter of *Swadeshi*. "Pandit Brij Narain Chakbast called her a 'Devi' and advised the younger generation to sit under her feet and learn lessons of devotion to motherland, sincerity of purpose and sacrifice".[19] Mention should also be made of Begum Mohammed Ali (wife of Maulana Md. Ali Johar) and Begum Khursheed Khwaja (wife of well-known nationalist Khwaja Abdul Majeed). The latter discarded *purdah* after marriage and accompanied her husband.

Begum Hajira was in the Congress during 1936-1940 and along with her husband implemented Party's programmes. She later joined the Communist Party. Women from the families of Khwaja Ghulam-us-Saqlain and Soofi Iqbal also took active part in the National Movement. Apart from these few names, "there were hundreds of those unknown women who readily parted with their precious jewellery and suffered economic hardship because of the political involvement of their husbands and silently went through the agony of separation during their husbands' or sons' frequent imprisonment during the freedom struggle."[20]

## Women in Uttar Pradesh Electoral Politics

Thus, although the Muslim women of Uttar Pradesh played significant role in the anti-colonial struggle during the early 1900s and although Uttar Pradesh is a home-state for many Indian national leaders "in terms of the women's movement, it is dismissed as an area of little consequence. While Bengal and Maharashtra are clearly the leaders, the UP lagged behind the burden of *purdah*, child marriage and general sense of social conservatism.[21] "Muslim Women in Uttar Pradesh" a researcher has observed, "became special victims of the partition because of the fact that this state was felt responsible for the creation of the new Islamic State of Pakistan. Moreover, when the *Zamindari* and feudal system ended, the Muslim community was converted into a poor lot. They suffered economically, socially, educationally and politically.[22] Some of the other reasons as to why the Muslim community in Uttar Pradesh remained removed from the mainstream have already been narrated above. If the lives became unsettled after partition, poverty, neglect of secular education right from the colonial days, absence of political leaders and the rise of influence of the Clergy—all added up to Muslim women getting confined to the four walls of their homes. There was no question of their venturing into politics.

However, before independence, Safia Abdul Wajjid was elected to the UP assembly in 1946 and in fact she was the only Muslim woman to be on Congress ticket in pre-independent India. Earlier, Begum Majida Bano contested the 1937 elections from Lucknow on Congress ticket, a most prestigious seat reserved for a Muslim lady. Her rival was Begum Habibullah, contesting on Muslim League ticket. The election "had historical importance as the issue at stake was whether the Muslim League or the Congress represented a majority of the Muslim community.[23] In spite of strong support, Majida Bano lost by a narrow margin."

From the point of view of electoral participation of Muslim women, Uttar Pradesh has fared poorly since the first elections after independence. As we have stated earlier, what defines women's political participation, Hindu and Muslim alike, is the endemic nature of patriarchal structures and the resultant gender inequality and gender discrimination. Gender relations are rooted in the ideology that women are subordinate to men. Women are consistently denied inheritance rights, adequate nutrition, freedom of expression and mobility, participation in community activities and a say in personal choices and preferences. They are thus denied a meaningful role in decision-making, and are not in a position to access educational facilities, or political and financial institutions. Women's place in the family hierarchy and relationships within the home combine with the socially prescribed gendered division of roles to determine their levels of exclusion in both the private (household) and public spheres. Class, caste, religion, ethnicity and location are additional factors that mediate gendered social relations. Sheeba Aslam Fehmi said in an interview:[24]

> "Patriarchal readings of religion and patriarchal prescriptions of personal law are not the only problems of Muslim women. There are other problems, such as poverty and illiteracy, which they share with most Muslim men. But it is also the case that culturally-influenced misreading of Islam as well as unjust legal prescriptions, enforced by the state under pressure from Muslim patriarchs, are a central factor for the continued 'backwardness' of Indian Muslim women. I do not ignore the economic factors for such 'backwardness', and I would insist that besides championing gender-just understandings of Islam and reforming Muslim Personal Law, we need to work to ensure Muslim women's economic security and independence. But, at the same time, I do not

think that mere economic empowerment of Muslim women would suffice, because as the case of women in rich Gulf states, for instance, shows, even if women are financially secure they will still be treated as second-class citizens and subordinated to men if patriarchal readings of Islam and laws flowing out from such readings are not effectively challenged. The cultural and religious realm does have autonomy of its own, distinct from the economic, and we cannot turn a blind eye to it".

Women, in general, are a neglected section in the matter of their representation in the Uttar Pradesh Assembly. In the 15 general elections to the UP Assembly since (Table 4.3) 1952, the average representation of women in the Assembly has been a mere 4.4 per cent. Despite social restrictions, women have tried to get their share of political participation and a substantial number of women have tried their luck contesting as independent candidates, for want of nomination by mainstream political parties.

**Table 4.3:** Women in Uttar Pradesh Legislative Assembly

| *Year* | *No. of women candidates* | *No. of women elected* | *Year* | *No. of women candidates* | *No. of women elected* |
|---|---|---|---|---|---|
| 1952 | 25 | 11 | 1957 | 39 | 18 |
| 1962 | 61 | 20 | 1967 | 39 | 06 |
| 1969 | 55 | 18 | 1974 | 92 | 21 |
| 1977 | 63 | 11 | 1980 | 85 | 23 |
| 1985 | 168 | 31 | 1989 | 201 | 18 |
| 1991 | 226 | 10 | 1993 | 253 | 14 |
| 1996 | 190 | 20 | 2002 | 344 | 26 |
| 2007 | 370 | 23 | 2012 | 583 | 35 |

*Source:* Election Commission, Government of India. Data excludes any Bye Elections.

According to Election Commission data, Kudasiya Begum was the first woman to win as an independent candidate from Sandila seat in 1977. After her, only two women, contesting as independent candidates, could win in 1989 and 1996.[25]

Besides the Congress Party, others like the Socialist Party, Kisan Mazdoor Praja Party, Praja Socialist Party, Janata Dal, Bharatiya Kranti Dal, and Jana Sangh, have all fielded women candidates before the new regional parties came up. But, their number has always been small; neither commensurate with the female population of the State nor with the now proposed 33 per cent reservation.

One of the reasons for the poor performance of women is that not many were nominated by the mainstream political parties. While almost all political parties do a lot of talk about promoting the participation of women in politics, their intentions are not reflected at the time of giving tickets. This has been the case with Uttar Pradesh also. Even at the general elections to the UP Assembly held in 2012, in spite of the three main parties being headed by women they were not enthusiastic about giving tickets to women candidates.[26] In the final list of 1,548 candidates for 403 assembly seats, there were only 146 women candidates sponsored by the main political parties. Apart from keeping the winnability of the female candidates in view, the first priority seemed to be giving most of the tickets to the close relatives of influential political leaders. Thus, at the 2012 elections, all the parties fell far short of reaching the 33 per cent goal. With such attitude, it is no wonder that there have always been very few women in the Legislative Assembly of the State.

In so far as Muslim women are concerned, a study by Shaista Parveen on the political and social status of Muslim women in western Uttar Pradesh has found that they are much behind in political leadership, but are becoming conscious of the value of their votes. Even if they have not understood the present political system, they have started to realize the importance of parties and organizations. Similarly, though very few Muslim women are in active politics, the scenario is changing silently. It was found that their independent political outlook is getting shape and making them prepared for clear-cut political roles in future political activities. Even in the matter of casting votes, though, at present 75 per cent women have been voting according to the wishes of their families, 25 per cent women voted independently.[27]

The study has also brought out the fact that the Muslim women seem to have realised their capacity to play more dynamic roles in their social and political lives. The concept of women's employment is getting clear to them and they seem to be eager to achieve it. An important finding of the study is that religion is no bar to the women's understanding of politics and political system, their views of the modern society, their perspective of family and community life and their attitude towards development. Consequently, the new generation of Muslim women in the two districts (Saharanpur and Muzaffarnagar) studied was found to be gearing up for new social and political roles, with a commitment towards improving their own educational and social upliftment. Their understanding of new dynamism of political parties was found to be very positive, constructive and encouraging. Their enthusiasm to perform better in private as well as public life and their ambition to improve their economic ambition and be independent, was also noted.[28]

Although the number of Muslim women contesting elections has been on the increase, their lack of an in-depth knowledge about the political structures and legal system has been a stumbling block for their political advancement. With a view to politically empowering Muslim women, the Union government introduced a scheme through the Women and Child Development Ministry, to train Muslim women in electoral participation. The intention was that lessons in leadership and a better political representation would help the minority community to fight for better participation in elections and the training would enable them to avail the benefits of the welfare programmes and fight for their rights. In the pilot stage the scheme was to be initiated in some of the Muslim-dominated districts of Uttar Pradesh, Bihar and West Bengal and later cover all 88 Muslim-dominated districts in India.[29]

In the above background, we may look at the participation of Muslim women in the elections to the Uttar Pradesh Assembly.

## Muslim Women in UP Assembly Elections

Uttar Pradesh holds a record of sorts. The State gave India its first woman Prime Minister, first woman Chief Minister, first woman Governor and first woman Dalit Chief Minister. UP also holds the credit of sending maximum number of women to the first Lok Sabha in 1951. Of the 24 women who reached Parliament then, six were from UP, including Vijay Lakshmi Pandit, Rajmata Kamlendumati, Uma Nehru, Shrivarajvati Nehru, Ganga Devi and Shakuntala Nayyar. If the Women's reservation Bill becomes an Act, Uttar Pradesh would be sending the maximum number of women to Parliament. With 33 per cent reservation for women in legislative bodies in place, the number of Lok Sabha seats reserved for women in UP will be 27 out of 80. However, the Bill is yet to become an Act.

Muslim women, however, made a delayed entry into the electoral politics of Uttar Pradesh. Besides the trauma of Partition, Muslim women of Uttar Pradesh were living in a different socio-cultural setting, compared to, for example, Karnataka. At the 1951 general elections to the UP assembly, Begum Safia Abdul Wajjid was the lone Muslim woman to win, contesting on a Congress ticket from Bareilly East constituency.[30]

At the 1957 general elections to the UP assembly, there were 39 women among the 1,759 contestants for 341 seats. Only 18 women were elected. Habib Bano was the lone Muslim woman from Lucknow City Central constituency to contest as an independent candidate. She lost the election, having secured only 19.42 per cent of the valid votes polled.

At the 1962 elections, the number of Muslim women contestants rose to three out of a total of 61 women contestants (Table 4.4). But, only one Muslim woman could win. Habib Bano was once again unsuccessful.

**Table 4.4:** Performance of Muslim women at the 1962 Assembly Elections

| *Constituency* | *Name of candidate* | *Party* | *Result and percentage of votes polled* |
|---|---|---|---|
| Rampur City | Kishwar Ara Begum | INC | Won |
| Lucknow City Central | Habib Bano | SOC | DF (3.20%) |
| Salempur-South (Deoria) | Noorjahan | SOC | DF (4.76%) |

INC: Indian National Congress; SOC: Socialist Party. DF: Deposit Forfeited.
*Source:* State Election Commission Statistical Report.

At the 1967 elections, there were 3 Muslim women among the 39 contestants. While only 6 women were elected, Kishwar Ara Begum and two more Muslim women were defeated, even though all three women contested under the Congress banner (Table 4.5):

**Table 4.5:** Performance of Muslim Women at the 1967 Assembly Elections

| *Constituency* | *Name of candidate* | *Party* | *Result and percentage of votes polled* |
|---|---|---|---|
| Rampur City | Kishwar Ara Begum | INC | DF (8.31%) |
| Haidergarh (Faizabad) | Hamida Habibullah | INC | Lost (26.76%) |
| Nanpara (Barabanki) | H.A. Begum | INC | Lost (28.30%) |

*Source:* State Election Commission Statistical Report.

At the 1969 elections, there were 4 Muslim women among the total 55 women candidates and two Muslim women out of the 18 winners (Table 4.6):

**Table 4.6**: Performance of Muslim Women at the 1969 Assembly Elections

| *Constituency* | *Name of candidate* | *Party* | *Result and percentage of votes polled* |
|---|---|---|---|
| Rampur | Rafat Zamani Begum | IND | Lost (42.31%) |
| Haidergarh (Faizabad) | Hamida Habibullah | INC | Won |
| Sandila (Hardoi) | Kudsia Begum | INC | Won |
| Salempur (Deoria) | Noorjahan | SOC | DF (1.95%) |

IND: Independent.
*Source:* State Election Commission Statistical Report.

Of the four Muslim women, Rafat Zamani Begum belonged to the Royal family of Rampur and Hamida Habibullah was the wife of Major General E. Habibullah, who was responsible for setting-up the National Defence Academy, at Khadakvasla near Poona.

The number of Muslim women contesting polls had gone up to 8 at the 1974 elections. Though there were 92 women contestants in all, only 21 were elected, including one Muslim woman; Mohsina Kidwai of the Congress Party (Table 4.7):

**Table 4.7**: Performance of Muslim Women at the 1974 Assembly Elections

| *Constituency* | *Name of candidate* | *Party* | *Result and percentage of votes polled* |
|---|---|---|---|
| Sahaswan (Budaun) | Sakina Begum | IND | DF (1.29%) |
| | Farouqui | IND | DF (1.05%) |
| Haidergarh (Deoria) | Hamida Habibullah | INC | Lost (23.35%) |
| Masauli (Barabanki) | Mohsina Kidwai | INC | Won |
| Sadulla Nagar (Balrampur) | Qaniz Fatima | IND | DF (1.90%) |
| Farukkabad | Wahida Begum | IND | DF (0.68%) |
| Aligarh | Sahar Bano | RPK | DF (1.42%) |
| Meerut | Husna Begum | INC | Lost (28.52%) |

RPK: Republican Party of India-Khobragade.
*Source:* State Election Commission Statistical Report.

The 1977 elections saw a decrease in the number of Muslim women contesting the elections. There were only two Muslim women out of the total 63 women contestants. Of the 11 winners, only one Muslim woman, Kudsia Begum could win. Mohsina Kidwai, a Congress stalwart lost the election (Table 4.8):

**Table 4.8**: Performance of Muslim Women at the 1977 Assembly Elections

| *Constituency* | *Name of candidate* | *Party* | *Result and percentage of votes polled* |
|---|---|---|---|
| Sandila (Hardoi) | Kudsia Begum | IND | Won |
| Masauli (Barabanki) | Mohsina Kidwai | INC | Lost (38.02%) |

*Source:* State Election Commission Statistical Report.

At the 1980 elections, there was a slight increase in the number of Muslim women contestants over the previous elections. Of the total of 85 women candidates, there were 4 Muslim women. Of the 23 winners, there was a lone Muslim women; Kudsiya Begum won from Sandila, this time as a Congress nominee (Table 4.9):

**Table 4.9**: Performance of Muslim Women at the 1980 Assembly Elections

| *Constituency* | *Name of candidate* | *Party* | *Result and percentage of votes polled* |
|---|---|---|---|
| Sandila (Hardoi) | Kudsia Begum | INC (I) | Won |
| Lucknow Central | Akhtar Jahan | IND | DF (0.43%) |
| Pharenda (Gorakhpur) | D.I. Khan | IND | DF (0.60%) |
| Garhmukteshwar (Ghaziabad) | Aquila Begum | IND | DF (0.26%) |

*Source:* State Election Commission Statistical Report.

However, the 1985 elections witnessed a cognizable jump in the number of Muslim women contestants. There were 11 Muslim women among the 168 women contestants. Only 31 women were elected at the elections and they included two Muslim women (Table 4.10):

**Table 4.10**: Performance of Muslim Women at the 1985 Assembly Elections

| *Constituency* | *Name of candidate* | *Party* | *Result and percentage of votes polled* |
|---|---|---|---|
| Seohara (Bijnor) | Gulshan | IND | DF (1.01%) |
| Bijnor | Zameela | IND | DF (1.29%) |
| Kanth (Moradabad) | Akhtari | IND | DF (0.31%) |
| Amroha (JP Nagar) | Nasim Begum | INC | Lost (20.30%) |
| Kawar (Bareilly) | Qamar Begum | IND | DF (1.33%) |
| Biswan (Sitapur) | Salma | IND | DF (0.82%) |
| Laharpur (Sitapur) | Salma | IND | DF (0.81%) |
| Sandila (Hardoi) | Kudsia Begum | INC | Won |
| Rudauli (Faizabad) | Qamarun Nisha | IND | DF (1.49%) |
| Mirzapur | Ashrafiman | INC | Won |
| Aryanagar (Kanpur) | A. Hussain | IND | DF (0.08%) |
| Garoutha (Jhansi) | Saliman | ICJ | DF (0.29%) |

ICJ: Indian Congress (J)

*Source:* State Election Commission Statistical Report.

Those who contested as independents polled from 0.08% to 1.49%, confirming the fact that the backing and support of a strong political party is essential and independents have no chance of winning, especially when the voters do not consider it worth their while to vote for independent female candidates.

Even at the 1989 elections, the number of Muslim women contestants was quite high, compared to the previous elections. There were 14 Muslim women in the fray among the 201 women contestants. The only Muslim woman elected was Mrs. Reshma Arif, wife of former Union Minister, Arif Mohammad Khan, who had quit Congress over his support to Supreme Court's decision in the Shah Bano case (Table 4.11):

**Table 4.11**: Performance of Muslim Women at the 1989 Assembly Elections

| *Constituency/District* | *Name of candidate* | *Party* | *Result and percentage of votes polled* |
|---|---|---|---|
| Amroha (JP Nagar) | Shamim Bano | IND | DF (0.09%0 |
| Usehat (Budaun) | Parveen Azad | INC | Lost |
| Bareilly City | Meraj Hasan | BSP | DF (0.44%) |
| Dhaurehara (Kheri) | Kanis Fatima | BSP | DF (1.37%) |
| Sandila (Hardoi) | Kudsia Begum | INC | Lost |
| Lucknow Central | Shahnaz | IND | DF (0.29%) |
| Pipraich (Gonda) | Ashrafi | IND | DF (0.15%) |
| Ghazipur | Syeda Faiz | IND | DF (1.44%) |
| Mirzapur | Ashrafi Imam | INC | Lost |
| Aryanagar (Kanpur) | Reshma Arif | JD | Won |
| Garautha (Jhansi) | Saliman | IND | DF (0.09%) |
| Firozabad | Khushnaseeb | IND | DF (0.09%) |
| Agra Cantt | Noor Bano Maisi | IND | DF (0.17%) |
| Muzaffarabad | Shagufta Khan | IND | DF (0.13%) |

BSP: Bahujan Samaj Party
*Source:* State Election Commission Statistical Report.

It will also be seen from the results of the election that Congress party was no longer a guarantor of a win and all the four Muslim women who contested on Congress tickets lost. It may be relevant to quote the following at this juncture[31]:

> "During the first five decades of independence, the vast majority of Muslims saw in the Congress their natural protector, for its commitment to secularism. Attracted to party by its ideology as much as by the promises of assembly seats

> or ministerial portfolios, Muslim politicians joined congress en masse. But these Congress Muslims often proved to be men of straw, whose political longevity was conditional to their docility. Moreover, the protection contract between Muslims and the Congress started showing its limits from the late 1960s onwards, with the escalation of anti-Muslim violence and the economic marginalisation of the community, sometimes at the hands of the Congress-State itself, such as during the Emergency".

In view of the above, Muslims' confidence in Congress having been eroded, it is no wonder that Muslim women keen on a political career were, obviously, advised by their families to fight elections either as independents or under the banner of other parties, which they considered secular.

At the 1991 general elections, there were 17 Muslim women in a total of 226 women contestants. While only 10 women could win, no Muslim woman was successful, including those nominated by the Congress (Table 4.12):

**Table 4.12:** Performance of Muslim Women at the 1991 Assembly Elections

| *Constituency/District* | *Name of candidate* | *Party* | *Result and percentage of votes polled* |
|---|---|---|---|
| Badri Kedar (Chamoli) | Shabnam Rizvi | IND | DF (0.33%) |
| Usehat (Budaun) | Parveen Azad | INC | Lost |
| Philibit | Zahida Begum | IND | DF (0.27%) |
| Sandila (Hardoi) | Kudsiya Begum | INC | Lost |
| Lucknow West | Sajda Parveen | IND | DF (0.06%) |
| -do- | Roshan | IND | DF (0.02%) |
| Ghazipur | Zaibunnisa | IND | DF (0.17%) |
| Varanasi Cantt | Athat Jamal Lari | JD | Lost |
| Mirzapur | Begum Ashram Imam | INC | DF (6.01%) |
| Allahabad South | Kaneez Bano | IND | DF (0.07%) |
| Aryanagar (Kanpur) | Ayesha Begum | ABMDL | DF (0.06%) |
| Garoutha (Jhansi) | Saleeman | IND | DF (0.87%) |
| Bhongaon (Jaunpur) | Faridan | IND | DF (0.14%) |
| Agra Cantt | Noor Bano Maisi | IND | DF (0.07%) |
| Khatauli (Kanpur Nagar) | Shama Zedi | IND | DF (0.08%) |
| Nakur (Saharanpur) | Shagufta Khan | INC | Lost |
| Muzaffarnagar | Shama Zaidi | IND | DF (0.18%) |

ABMDL: Akhila Bharatiya Mahila Dal
*Source:* State Election Commission Statistical Report.

At the 1993 general elections, there were 13 Muslim women among the 253 women contestants. While only 14 women were elected, Muslim women drew blank (Table 4.13):

**Table 4.13:** Performance of Muslim Women at the 1993 Assembly Elections

| *Constituency/District* | *Name of candidate* | *Party* | *Result and percentage of votes polled* |
|---|---|---|---|
| Bijnor | Meena Khan | IND | DF (0.04%) |
| Lucknow-West | Fakrunnisa | IND | DF (0.05%) |
| Bahraich | Rajiya Abbasi | IND | DF (0.07%) |
| Itawah | Farhat Nasim | JP | DF (0.12%) |
| Zamania (Maharajganj) | Shoukat Siddiqui | IND | DF (0.30%) |
| Varanasi-South | Nargis Begum | IND | DF (0.09%) |
| Varanasi-North | Asghari Begum | IND | DF (0.02%) |
| Fatehpur | Noorjahan | IND | DF (0.05%) |
| Kalyanpur (Ballia) | Shahjahan Begum Khan | IND | DF (0.10%) |
| Lalitpur | Rabiya | IND | DF (0.17%) |
| Firozabad | Kudsiya Sherwani | IND | DF (0.03%) |
| -do- | Shabana Anjum | IND | DF (0.05%) |
| Deoband (Saharanpur Dehat) | Shakura | JP | DF (0.17%) |

SP: Samajwadi Party; JP: Janata Party.
*Source:* State Election Commission Statistical Report.

None of the 12 Muslim women contested under the Congress banner. Once again, Muslim women fighting the elections as independents did not have any chance. They polled between 0.02 and 0.17 per cent of the valid votes. It is distressing to note that even when they contested from Muslim-dominated constituencies (e.g., Bijnor, Bahraich), they could not retain their deposits.

At the 1996 general elections, there were only 10 Muslim women among the 190 women contestants. While 20 women were elected, Muslim women drew blank this time also. Incidentally, Zeenat Naaz, who contested as an independent candidate, is the lady who dared the *Darul Uloom fatwa* and took off her veil and addressed public meetings during her campaign. It is beside the point that she lost the contest (Table 4.14) :

At the 1996 elections, Muslim women had options other than Congress viz., the Samajwadi Party and some new parties. But, once again Muslim women fared very poor, although some of them were repeatedly trying their luck. All the 9 candidates who lost their deposits, as usual, polled between 0.14 and 0.29 per cent of the valid votes. It appeared as though the Muslim electorate did not want to elect Muslim women.

**Table 4.14**: Performance of Muslim Women at the 1996 Assembly Elections

| *Constituency/District* | *Name of candidate* | *Party* | *Result and percentage of votes polled* |
|---|---|---|---|
| Bijnor | Meena Khan | IND | DF (0.50%) |
| Naugarh (Basti) | Khalida | IND | DF (0.35%) |
| Paniara (Gorakhpur) | Talat Aziz | SP | DF (10.58%) |
| Barsathi (Jaunpur) | Kamrun | IND | DF (0.23%) |
| Jaunpur | Hameeda Bano | IND | DF (0.14%) |
| Pratappur (Azamgarh) | Aneesa Bano | IND | DF (0.60%) |
| Sardhana (Meerut) | Mehjabi | BHJS | DF (0.29%) |
| Nakur (Saharanpur) | Shagufta Khan | INC | Lost |
| -do- | Kishwar Amir | NLP | DF (0.38%) |
| Deoband (Saharanpur) | Zeenat Naaz | IND | DF (0.59%) |

SP: Samajwadi Party; BHJS: Bahujan Samaj Party—Raj Bahadur; NLP: National Loktantrik Party.

*Source:* State Election Commission Statistical Report.

Uttar Pradesh was bifurcated and Uttaranchal was formed on the 9th November, 2000, carved out of northern Uttar Pradesh and included Garhwal and Kumaon divisions. The poor performance of Muslim women was repeated during the 2002 elections to the UP Assembly, though there was a surge in the number of Muslim women contestants. There were 25 Muslim women among the 344 women contestants. Only 26 women could win, including two Muslim women (Table 4.15).

Twenty five Muslim women at the 2002 elections is the highest number since 1951. It is also for the first time that the Nationalist Congress Party (Sharad Pawar) made its presence in Uttar Pradesh and issued tickets to 3 Muslim women. Similarly, the Muslim League (Kerala State Committee) nominated one Muslim woman. Several other smaller parties also entered the picture at the 2002 elections, which were considered an alternative to the traditional parties. However, only two of the 25 Muslim women could win; one from Salempur on BSP ticket and the other from Kaimganj on Congress ticket. Of the two, Louise Khurshid (Kaimganj) was the wife of Salman Khurshid, a Minister in the Congress government at the Centre and the then Minister for External Affairs.

Muslim women's urge to seek an elected office kept increasing with each election. This is evident from the 2007 elections to the UP assembly, at which as many as 38 Muslim women contested. Out of the total of 370 women contestants, only 23 could win, including two Muslim women who fought on SP ticket (Table 4.16).

**Table 4.15**: Performance of Muslim Women at the 2002 Assembly Elections

| *Constituency/District* | *Name of candidate* | *Party* | *Result and votes polled (%)* |
|---|---|---|---|
| Bijnor | Tasleem | SP | Lost |
| -do- | Meena Khan | IND | DF (0.28%) |
| Moradabad | Asma Aslam | NCP | DF (1.12%) |
| -do- | Israt Mukhtar Ansari | IND | DF (0.31%) |
| Suar Tanda (Rampur) | Sageera Begum | IND | DF (0.34%) |
| Shahabad (Rampur) | Guddi Begum | RTLP | DF (10.61%) |
| Gunnaur (Budaun) | Shahjahan | RTKP | DF (0.82%) |
| Sahaswan (Budaun) | Shama Ali | JD (U) | Lost |
| -do- | Tasleem Jahan | INC | DF (1.35%) |
| Usehat (Budaun) | Parveen Azad | RPD | DF (8.71%) |
| Nanpara (Barabanki) | Kamrunnisa | MUL | DF (0.27%) |
| Domariaganj (Siddharth Nagar) | Parveen Begum | NCP | DF (1.23%) |
| Salempur (Deoria) | Fasiha Murad *alias* Gajala | BSP | Won |
| Mughalsarai (Varanasi) | Shakeela | AD | DF (2.63%) |
| Kalyanpur (Ballia) | Haji Salem Urf Kinner Ramkali | IND | DF (0.96%) |
| Kamal Ganj (Ghazipur) | Munni Begum | AD | DF (0.78%) |
| Kaimganj (Ghazipur) | Louise Khursheed | INC | Won |
| -do- | Sajida Begum | IND | DF (0.54%) |
| Aliganj (Etah) | Chanda Begum | INC | DF (0.93%) |
| Aligarh | Razia Khan | SP | DF (6.25%) |
| -do- | Naureen Khan | INLD | DF (0.11%) |
| Modinagar (Baghpat) | Bismillah | INLD | DF (0.57%) |
| Meerut | Nazma | IND | DF (0.10%) |
| Thana Bhawan (Kanpur Dehat) | Vakila | IND | DF (0.40%) |
| Muzaffarabad (Etawah) | Shaheen Khan | NLP | DF (0.25%) |

RTKP: Rashtriya Kranti Party; RPD: Rashtriya Parivartan Dal; MUL: Muslim League (Kerala Committee); NCP: Nationalist Congress Party; AD: Apna Dal; INLD: Indian National Lok Dal.
*Source:* State Election Commission Statistical Report.

## 2012 Elections

In the seven-phase elections for 403 assembly seats in Uttar Pradesh held in February-March 2012, there has been a near 50 per cent rise of women voters, signaling, as Dipankar Gupta writes, a "gentle, but

**Table 4.16**: Performance of Muslim Women at the 2007 Assembly Elections

| *Constituency/District* | *Name of candidate* | *Party* | *Result and percentage of votes polled* |
|---|---|---|---|
| Amroha (JP Nagar) | Umme Ammara | NBNP | DF (0.32%) |
| | Mehphuja | IND | DF (0.27%) |
| Sambhal (Moradabad) | Tarannum Aqueel | BSP | Lost |
| Moradabad West | Rehana Saifi | RSBP | DF (0.49%) |
| Moradabad | Rahisan | RSBP | DF (0.12%) |
| Moradabad Rural | Hajra Begum | INC | DF (9.68%) |
| Rampur | Atiya Musharrat | IND | DF (0.30%) |
| Shahabad (Hardoi) | Guddi Begum | INC | DF (11.35%) |
| Nawabganj (Faizabad) | Kaisar Jahan | INC | DF (7.41%) |
| Paila (Kheri) | Meera Bano | JM | DF (2.70%) |
| Behta (Hardoi) | Taevun Nisha | IND | DF (0.47%) |
| Laharpur (Sitapur) | Reshma Khan | RLD | DF (0.42%) |
| Sandila (Hardoi) | Ishrat Rasool | SP | Lost |
| Lucknow Cantt | Salma | JM | DF (0.13%) |
| -do- | Shaif Ali Chaudhari | LKPT | DF (0.09%) |
| Tanda (Faizabad) | Azra Sultana | INC | DF (2.95%) |
| -do- | Ashrafa | SBSP | DF (2.26%) |
| Bhinga (Bahraich) | Aneesa Bano | IND | DF (0.65%) |
| Bahraich (Bahraich) | Reshma Arif | IJP | DF (10.51%) |
| Gainsari (Barabanki) | Shahin | IND | DF (0.52%) |
| Utraula (Barabanki) | Akbari | IND | DF (0.21%) |
| Gorakhpur (Gorakhpur) | Sayyad Safia Tabassum | MMUP | DF (0.26%) |
| Seorahi (Basti) | Shahanaj Bano | LJP | DF (0.61%) |
| Salempur (Deoria) | Chaudhari Fasiha Vaseer | SP | Won |
| Azamgarh (Azamgarh) | Atiya Noor Azmi | IND | DF (0.25%) |
| Mohammadabad (Maharajganj) | Sayyada Shadab Fatima | SP | Won |
| -do- | Razia Sultana | IPH | DF (0.55%) |
| Chandauli (Varanasi) | Mirza | RSMD | DF (0.41%) |
| Mughal Sarai (Varanasi) | Roshan Ara | NLP | DF (0.33%) |
| Varanasi-South (Varanasi) | Rabiya Kalam | IND | Lost |
| Machchlishahar (Jaunpur) | Shakeela Khatun | RSBP | DF (0.56%) |
| Fatehpur (Fatehpur) | Fahmeeda Begum | NCP | DF (0.66%) |
| Rajpur (Ballia) | Shabana Begum | IND | DF (1.38%) |
| Kaimganj (Ghazipur) | Louise Khursheed | INC | Lost |
| Patiali (Kanshiramnagar) | Nadira Sultana | INC | Lost |
| Sardhana (Meerut) | Tabassum Begum | RLD | Lost |
| Nakur (Saharanpur) | Saphura Begum | NBNP | DF (0.20%) |
| Muzaffarabad (Etawah) | Khurshida | NLHP | DF (0.31%) |

NBNP: Nav Bharat Nirman Party; RSBP: Rashtriya Swabhiman Party; IJP: Indian Justice Party; LJP: Lok Janashakti Party; IPH: Islam Party (Hind); RSMD: Rashtriya Samata Dal; NLHP: National Lokhind Party.

*Source:* State Election Commission Statistical Report.

determinate shift in the character of Indian politics". Unlike in the previous elections, the voter turnout was the highest ever at 60 per cent; 14 percentage points higher than in the previous assembly election. The turnout of women was higher than that of men and went up by 18 percentage points compared to 2007. The high turnout of women voters is attributed by Dipankar Gupta to years of democratic practice that has encouraged women to break free on Election Day. Panchayati Raj and gender sensitive programmes have given women a better understanding of their rights.[32] According to Gupta, "women are not voting for their self-interest, but are voting for society. Women are more inclined than men to think beyond themselves; with families on their mind, they are given to thinking of the future, of the long term. Unlike men, who would generally want a factory to be set up in the region, which would provide job opportunities, rural woman want a school, a hospital, even a college, so that their children could prosper in the future.[33]

Unlike the past elections at which "short-term caste, community and religious calculations were dominant", the 2012 elections showcased "felt aspirations" rather than "felt needs". "Felt aspirations" can only be addressed over the long term, unlike the "felt needs" which send people scrambling for advantage. "It is a sign of changing times that those who lost in 2012 were the one who played with the same old themes. On the other hand, those who won, thought long term, or, at least, gave that impression. All of this could happen only if people saw themselves principally as voters and not as members of this or that community".[34]

And the women voters were in the thick of it all; all the 60.29 per cent of them. This number was much higher than that of the men, which stood at 58.8 per cent. Gupta cautions that "as women tend to vote against short term tactical considerations, the victors will have to fall in step with them and think strategically too. This is how they can do justice to the women voters and keep them firmly on their side".[35]

The increase in the women voter percentage was also due to the fact that in UP there were as many as 15 million women who were freshly enrolled in the 2012 voters' list. Gupta cautions[36]:

> "Those who have won in the 2012 elections should not take their victory to be an outcome of caste calculations or class positioning or, indeed, of family charisma either. For the first time there was a clear distinction between those who stuck to

> previous tactics of caste and religion and those who talked of general development without community overtones. Politics in India is looking better for it is getting feminised, but not feminist. Women have put "aspirations" on the front page for they are thinking of the future and the long term, as they are wont to. This might pressure the political class to think development and not just growth. If that happens, India will invest in infrastructure and human capital and not just in machines. Villages will have schools and hospitals and not just sweat shops. Men have needs that can easily be met; but because women have aspirations there is hope in this world".

In keeping with the new found enthusiasm among women in general, Muslim women did not lag behind. Large numbers of Muslim women in veils came out of their homes in various districts to join the democratic process by making aware their counterparts in the community about the importance of voting. A report from Akbarpur block, for example, says that "women groups have taken the job in a very impressive manner. They have enthusiastically joined the election campaign while urging the voters, particularly women and young Muslim girls, to go and cast vote for a better change." One of the reasons for the significant change in the outlook of women, who were earlier confined to their homes, is said to be the awareness campaigns launched by the district authorities.[37]

Those who were leading the awareness-creation campaign persuaded the male members of Muslim families not to prevent or discourage the women from going to the polling booths. The campaign, whose aim was to help the women in the region understand the structure, procedure and responsibilities of elections, seems to have yielded results. It was reported that the voters in the villages widely supported the cause with several Muslim women joining the group. Marking a significant change in the Indian women participation in the democratic process, the veiled women were confident of making women aware about elections.

The 2012 general elections to the UP Assembly also witnessed a sea change in the outlook and thinking of Muslim women. Ignoring the sops held out by the political parties, (including the minority quota offered by Salman Khursheed) Muslim women declared that they would judiciously exercise their vote. Most of these women seemed to understand the political pulse and declare that their vote would not be influenced by any religious or family decree, or the assurances made by the parties. Instead, issues like women's education, upliftment and security weighed heavily on their minds. Better Education Through Innovation (BETI), an organisation headed by Sehba Hussain, demanded right to survival, development, protection and growing participation of Muslim women in various spheres.[38]

Sehba Hussain said that she was disillusioned not only with quota-based politics, but also *fatwas*, adding that politicians should adopt a holistic approach rather than a communal one. As regards *fatwas*, Sehba Hussain said: "It is difficult to understand the new found system of *fatwas* which is nothing, but a mere misinterpretation of the holy *Quran*." She wanted Muslim women to strive for a qualitative life instead of the quantitative.

Even young Muslim girls seemed to have understood the politics that the politicians play, as evidenced by the statement of a class 12 student of La Martiniere Girls College and a first-time voter, who was also against quota-based politics. "Quota only helps the white-collar and elite Muslims, where does a commoner go?" She understood empowerment to mean removal of fundamentalism and ending male domination in the Muslim society followed by education. She emphasised that educated Muslim women should not care about the *fatwas*, adding: "I expect the elected candidate not to have a communal approach because when I vote as a citizen of India, I want the candidate to work like the citizen of India and be secular.[39] The young woman's views reflects a departure from the practice where 88 per cent first-time voters used to consult their family members to decide on the party they would vote for, irrespective of whether they were educated or semi-literate.

Sabra Habib, Emeritus Professor of Russian in Lucknow University, referred to the sugar-coated words that flow before the elections, and added that "the pre-and post-picture of election should never be different, which, I am sad to admit, happens all the time." She however felt that it is not the Muslims alone that are suffering. The issue is about all those who are below the poverty line. With regard to Congress' announcement of the 4.5 per cent sub-quota for minorities, Ruqsana, Principal, Karamat Girls College, Lucknow, said that if they really want to give a quota for Muslim women, it should be more, keeping in view the findings of the Sachar Committee report with regard to the representation of Muslims in Services. Parveen Talha, ex-member of Union Public Service Commission, also condemned the quota-based politics, adding that Muslims have not realised that they are used as a vote bank. "Instead of pleasing a community, the political parties should fulfill the commitments they have made earlier. "Why are the Muslim women targeted as weak and not the educated ones? As far as empowerment is concerned, what about educating the male members who are the so-called decision makers and the more responsible ones," she asked.

According to yet another report, "in spite of the *fatwas* and frowning clergy, Muslim women of Uttar Pradesh have realised that they have to take a pro-active stand and make Muslim women and girls know about the importance of their vote and educating the community about the importance of participation in the democratic process and urging them to vote in the elections.[40] Table 4.17 gives the performance of 52 Muslim women who contested the 2012 general elections to the Uttar Pradesh Assembly.

Table 4.18 is an abstract of Party-wise performance of Muslim women at the 2012 elections.

The above data reveals that 94.33 per cent of the Muslim women, who contested under the banner of various parties, including national-level parties, and as independents, either lost the election or forfeited their deposits. Some of the parties had no locus standi in Uttar Pradesh and some could not have been expected to make any dent. By fighting elections under the banner of such parties, the women were only wasting their money, time, and energy. It is also observed that Muslim women had no guarantee of success even while contesting from districts which had substantial Muslim population. Obviously, Muslim women had no guidance or were left to fend for themselves; no heart bled if one lost.

In so far as the contestants are concerned, most of the Muslim women were housewives and more than 50 per cent of them were educated (undergraduates, graduates and post-graduates). In spite of the fact that there were 28educated women among the 52 contestants at the 2012 elections (including one candidate with *Adeeb-e-Kamil* degree from Jamia, Aligarh, which is equivalent to BA degree) the electorate refused to send them to the Assembly (Table 4.19).

Why did the community (assuming that at least Muslim voters cast their vote for Muslim candidates, an assumption that is not always correct) reject them? Unfortunately, all those who lost, have polled very few votes; not exceeding even 1 per cent of the valid votes polled. This situation confirms the fact that one should be a winnable candidate and have a good backing even to get a ticket. For instance, four women from Uttar Pradesh who entered the 15th Lok Sabha for the first time were well-connected.[41] Analysing the background of women Members

**Table 4.17**: Performance of Muslim Women, Assembly Elections, 2012

| *Constituency/District* | *Name of candidate (Age in years)* | *Party* | *Result and votes polled (%)* | *Education* |
|---|---|---|---|---|
| Aliganj (Etah) | Meharunnisa (NK) | MD | DF (0.67%) | Graduate |
| Aligarh (Aligarh) | Sayra Mujammal Khan (38) | RLM | DF (0.09%) | Graduate |
| Amroha (JP Nagar) | Umme Ammara (52) | RPD/IND | DF (0.40%) | Law |
| Ayodhya (Faizabad) | Gulshan *alias* Bindoo (42)(O) | IND | DF | Literate |
| Baheri (Bareilly) | Kaisar Jahan (47) | IEMC | DF (4.93%) | Some school |
| Chamraua (Rampur) | Reshma Ilyas (35) | IND | DF (0.53%) | Illiterate |
| Chandausi (Moradabad) | Sarvesh Urf Shabnam (35) | PECP | DF (2.15%) | Literate |
| Chandpur (Bijnor) | Shabana Parveen (33) | IND | DF (0.26%) | Graduate |
| Chhaprauli (Baghpat) | Nasreen Khan (34) | AITC | DF (0.60%) | Undergrad. |
| Dhampur (Bijnor) | Kahkashan Parveen (40) | AITC | DF (0.21%) | Post-grad. |
| Nagina | Chhoti Amir Ali | MKUP | DF (0.21%) | Illiterate |
| Dhampur | Jahan Ara (27) | SSD | DF (0.09%) | -do- |
| -do- | Zareena Begum ([illegible]8) | RLM | DF (0.15%) | Undergrad. |
| Rampur | Nisha Jaffar Ali (26) | IND | DF (0.68%) | Undergrad. |
| -do- | Safia Wasim (25) | IEMC | DF (0.28%) | Graduate |
| Kidwai Nagar | Shabana Parveen (32) | RVLP | DF (0.09%) | -do- |
| Fatehpur | Fahmida Begum (59) | RsAD | DF (0.15%) | Other |
| Domariaganj (Siddharth Nagar) | Sayyada Khatun (NK) | BSP | Lost | Graduate |
| Farukkabad (F'bad) | Louise Khursheed | INC | DF (13.16%) | Graduate |
| Fatehpur (Fatehpur) | Sahar Naqvi (26) | AITC | DF (0.38%) | Illiterate |
| Gangoh (Saharanpur) | Shagufta Khan (52) | BSP | Lost | Law |
| Ghosi (Mau) | Rana Khatun Fasihuddin (56) | INC | DF (1.68%) | Graduate |
| Gola Gokarnnath (Kheri) | Simmi Bano (37) | BSP | Lost | Literate |
| Handia (Allahabad) | Jaheeda Khatun (38) | LD | DF (0.32%) | Undergrad. |
| Isauli (Sultanpur) | Nargis Nayab (35) | BSP | DF (14.17%) | Post-grad. |

(*Contd.*)

| Constituency/District | Name of candidate (Age in years) | Party | Result and votes polled (%) | Education |
|---|---|---|---|---|
| Jangipur (Ghazipur) | Suraiyya Mazhar (27) | PECP | DF (0.28%) | Post-grad. |
| Karachhana (Allahabad) | Shakila Bano (46) | RJPK | DF (0.78%) | Literate |
| Katra (Shahjahanpur) | Zeenat Khan (36) | IND | DF (1.37%) | Illiterate |
| Khadda (Kushinagar) | Haseena Sujahat Ali (28) | IND | DF (0.73%) | Undergrad. |
| Kidwai Nagar (Kanpur Nagar) | Zakeema Begum (30) | RUC | DF (0.13%) | Some school |
| Kundarki (Moradabad) | Rahil Parveen (42) | AITC | DF (0.37%) | Post-Grad. |
| Lucknow Cantt | Suraiyya Siddiqui (34) | AITC | DF (0.21%) | Others |
| Mariyahu (Jaunpur) | Parveen Akhtar (40) | AITC | DF (0.43%) | Graduate |
| Modi Nagar (Baghpat) | Rahisa Begum (46) | BMKCP | DF (0.15%) | NK |
| Moradabad Nagar (Moradabad) | Yasmeen Haneef (28) | RLM | DF (0.16%) | Some school |
| Muzaffar Nagar (Muzaffarnagar) | Sitara Begum Ansari (46) | NNP | DF (0.19%) | 5th Standard |
| Nagina (Bijnor) | Babli Urf Gulshan Jahan (32) | AITC | DF (0.42%) | Illiterate |
| Nugawan Sadat (JP Nagar) | Fehmeeda Begum (54) | PECP | DF (0.89%) | 12th standard |
| Paniyara (Maharajganj) | Talat Aziz (67) | INC | Lost | Medicine |
| Patiyali (Kanshiram Nagar) | Najeeva Khan Zeenat (50) | SP | Won | Adeeb-e-kamil, Jamia Aligarh |
| Rampur Karkhana (Deoria) | Fasiha Bashir *alias* Gajala Lari (41) | SP | Won | Some school |
| Rampur (Rampur) | Reshma Bi (49) | RLM | DF (2.55%) | Undergrad. |
| Raniganj (Pratapgarh) | Noorjahan Ali Raza (57) | VIP | DF (0.32%) | NK |
| Saiyadraja (Chandauli) | Hamidun Ajeem (58) | JMM | DF (0.14%) | -do- |
| Sandila (Hardoi) | Ishrat Rasool (53) | INC | DF (3.57%) | Graduate |
| Sardhana (Meerut) | Shahin Parvez (51) | RUC | DF (0.13%) | Law |
| Sikandrabad (Bulandshahar) | Farzana Ahsaan (40) | LD | DF (0.20%) | Illiterate |
| Siwalkhas (Baghpat) | Nusrat Bano (44) | PECP | DF (1.18%) | Literate |
| Suar (Rampur) | Mushayyada Mahmood (53) | IND | DF (0.67%) | Undergrad. |

(*Contd.*)

| Constituency/District | Name of candidate (Age in years) | Party | Result and votes polled (%) | Education |
|---|---|---|---|---|
| Tilhar (Shahjahanpur) | Shahanaj Begum (56) | IND | DF (0.31%) | -do- |
| Varanasi North | Rabiya Kalam (44) | INC | Lost | -do- |
| Zahoorabad (Ballia) | Syeda Shadab Fatima (48) | SP | Won | Some school |

(RJP: Rashtriya Janwadi Party (Krantikari); JMM: Jharkhand Mukti Morcha; TMC: All India Trinamool Congress; RAD: Rashtriya Apna Dal; VSIP: Vanchit Samaj Insaf Party; MD: Mahan Dal; RVP: Rashtriya Vikalang Party; RLM: Rashtriya Lok Manch; NNP: Navbharat Nirman Party; NLP: National Loktantrik Party; IMC: Ittehad-e-Millat Council; RPD: Rashtriya Parivartan Dal; (O) Other gender.

*Source:* ceouttarpradesh.nic.in/GE2012/contestants and http://www. empoweringindia.org

**Table 4.18:** Party-wise Performance of Muslim Women in 2012 Elections.

| Party | Number of Muslim women | | | |
|---|---|---|---|---|
| | Contested | Won | Lost | Deposit forfeited |
| Bahujan Samaj Party (BSP) | 4 | – | 2 | 2 |
| Navbharat Nirman Party (NNP) | 1 | – | – | 1 |
| All India Trinamool Congress (AITC) | 7 | – | – | 7 |
| Mazdoor Kisan Union Party (MKUP) | 1 | – | – | 1 |
| Soshit Samaj Dal (SSD) | 1 | – | – | 1 |
| Rashtriya Lok Manch (RLM) | 4 | – | – | 4 |
| Peace Party (PECP) | 4 | – | – | 4 |
| Ittehad-E-Millat Council (IEMC) | 2 | – | – | 2 |
| Rashtriya Ulama Council (RUC) | 2 | – | – | 2 |
| Bharatiya Mazdoor Kisan Congress Party (BMKCP) | 1 | – | – | 1 |
| Lok Dal (LD) | 2 | – | – | 2 |
| Samajwadi Party (SP) | 3 | 3 | – | – |
| Mahan Dal (MD) | 1 | – | – | 1 |
| Indian National Congress (INC) | 5 | – | 2 | 3 |
| Rashtriya Vikalang Party (RVLP) | 1 | – | – | 1 |
| Rashtriya Apna Dal (RsAD) | 1 | – | – | 1 |
| Vanchit Samaj Insaf Party (VIP) | 1 | – | – | 1 |
| Rashtriya Janwadi Party (Krantikari) | 1 | – | – | 1 |
| Jharkhand Mukti Morcha (JMM) | 1 | – | – | 1 |
| Independents | 9 | – | – | 9 |
| **Total** | **52** | **3** | **4** | **45** |

*Source:* State Election Commission Report.

**Table 4.19:** Level Education of Number of Contestants (2012)

| Level of Education | Number of Contestants |
|---|---|
| Legal professionals | 03 |
| Medical professionals | 01 |
| Post-graduates | 04 |
| Graduates | 10 |
| Undergraduates | 09 |
| Some-level of schooling/ home-based education | 07 |
| Urdu /other education | 03 |
| Literate (no formal schooling) | 05 |
| Illiterate | 07 |
| Not known | 03 |
| **Total** | **52** |

*Source:* State Election Commission Report.

of Parliament in the 15th Lok Sabha, Anjali Puri wrote:[42]

> "At least 36 of them (out of 58)—that's close to a depressing two-thirds—are close relatives of male politicians ranging from national leaders and chief ministers to lower-level politicos like MLAs and RSS *pracharaks*; and of personages described colourfully as "cooperative *mafia* leader" and "mining baron's political aide". This is a Lok Sabha with many new female faces and younger ones, too, but a dismaying 17 of the 29 "fresh faces" are in the hallowed-by-proxy, *biwi-beti-bahu-behen* category. But even these figures do not tell the whole tale—a few other women MPs have more convoluted family connections, like Helen Davidson from Tamil Nadu who is related to the DMK clan through Azhagiri's daughter; or they come with backing from influential male patrons not related to them".
>
> "Some cynical old habits die hard when it comes to sending women to Parliament—and parties headed by women are clearly no exception. Even within a broader culture of 'dynastic politics', ... ... political scientists reckon that women MPs are more likely to be from political families than their male counterparts, and clearly, more than one dynamic is at work here. ... ... For a political player, it means consolidating power in safer ways than most—who, for instance, would you trust more than your wife? "It is about keeping the circle of power limited and controllable, and this happens much more in the case of women," says Prof. Niraja Gopal Jayal of the Centre for Law and Governance at Delhi's JNU. Another important criterion, Jayal points out, is 'winnability'—women from political families or elite backgrounds are considered more 'winnable' than the rest. "... ...
>
> "UP is a good case study. It may want to pat itself on the back for having got the largest number of women into the House—12—but who are they—three political widows, two *bahus*, three wives, one daughter. Of the remaining three, one is a film star (Jaya Prada) with the rock-solid support of the redoubtable Amar Singh, the other Annu Tandon, a high-profile wife of a top Reliance executive ... ... the Samajwadi Party's Sushila Saroj ... ... is the wife of an ex-IPS officer close to Mulayam Singh Yadav."

In summing up, the following Table 4.20 gives the representation of Muslim women in the UP Assembly in the various elections:

**Table 4.20**: Female Candidates in Uttar Pradesh Legislative Assembly

| Year | Women Contestants | | | Women Elected | | |
|---|---|---|---|---|---|---|
| | Non-Muslim | Muslim | Total | Non-Muslim | Muslim | Total |
| 1951 | NA | nil | | 11 | nil | 11 |
| 1957 | 38 | 1 | 39 | 18 | nil | 18 |
| 1962 | 58 | 3 | 61 | 19 | 1 | 20 |
| 1967 | 36 | 3 | 39 | 6 | nil | 06 |
| 1969 | 51 | 4 | 55 | 16 | 2 | 18 |
| 1974 | 83 | 8 | 91 | 20 | 1 | 21 |
| 1977 | 61 | 2 | 63 | 10 | 1 | 11 |
| 1980 | 81 | 4 | 85 | 22 | 1 | 23 |
| 1985 | 157 | 11 | 168 | 29 | 2 | 31 |
| 1989 | 187 | 14 | 201 | 17 | 1 | 18 |
| 1991 | 109 | 17 | 226 | 10 | nil | 10 |
| 1993 | 234 | 19 | 253 | 14 | nil | 14 |
| 1996 | 180 | 10 | 190 | 20 | nil | 20 |
| 2002 | 319 | 25 | 344 | 24 | 2 | 26 |
| 2007 | 332 | 38 | 370 | 21 | 2 | 23 |
| 2012 | 530 | 53 | 583 | 32 | 3 | 35 |

*Source:* State Election Commission Statistical Report.

True that following the 2012 general elections, Muslim representation in Uttar Pradesh Assembly has risen to an all-time high of 68 MLAs; very close to being proportional to the Muslim population in the State, i.e., 18 per cent. Credit for the SP's resounding success at the 2012 polls goes, at least in part, to the support for the party by Muslim voters of Uttar Pradesh and not to persona like the Shahi Imam of Jama Masjid, Delhi. The Imam had initially asked UP Muslims to vote for Samajwadi Party, but within one year after the elections, he severed ties with Samajwadi Party and said that Mulayam Singh had cheated the Muslims.[43]

Muslim women of Uttar Pradesh (or any other State for that matter) need someone like the Grand Mufti of Kashmir, Maulana Bashir-Ud-Din, who has welcomed the passage of the Women's Reservation Bill in the Rajya Sabha, describing it as "a great step towards women's empowerment".

The Maulana urged Muslim women to enter politics and get elected to Parliament and State Assemblies so as to empower themselves. He also urged political parties to give tickets to women from minorities so that all the apprehensions about the Bill that it is not aimed to help the minorities are cleared.[44]

But, the fact that a Muslim population of about 31 million is unable to elect even ten women to represent its 15 million women is a sad commentary on the UP Muslim community.

## UP Muslim Women in the Lok Sabha

If the number of Muslim women entering the UP Legislative Assembly is small, their presence in the Lok Sabha is meager still. Election Commission's statistics reveal that there have never been more than three elected Muslim women in the Lok Sabha. It would be relevant to consider Muslim women entering Lok Sabha from various States to get a broader picture.

- In the elections to the first Lok Sabha (1952-1957) there were no Muslim women contestants. There were none in the Rajya Sabha too.
- In the 2nd Lok Sabha (1957-1962) there were two Muslim women viz., Ahmed Mofida (Jorhat, INC) and Maimoona Sultan (Bhopal, INC). The lone Muslim woman contestant from Uttar Pradesh (Sybil Khan, Nainital, PSP) lost.
- Maimoona Sultan (Bhopal, INC) was the only Muslim woman to be elected to the 3rd Lok Sabha (1962-1967). Later she was nominated to the Rajya Sabha from April 1974 to April 1980 and from June 1980 to June 1986. Sybil Khan (Nainital, PSP) was the lone Muslim woman among the 14 women contestants from Uttar Pradesh. She lost.
- No Muslim women were elected to the 4th, 5th and 10th Lok Sabha.
- At the elections to the 6th Lok Sabha, two Muslim women were elected (Rashida Haque Choudhary (Silchar, INC) and Akbar Jahan Begum (JKN, J&K). A third Muslim woman, Mohsina Kidwai was elected in a bye-election held in 1978 and a fourth was added with the election of Begum Abida Ahmed in a bye election held in 1981.[45]
- Mohsina Kidwai was the only one Muslim woman elected at the 1980 elections held for the 7th Lok Sabha from Meerut.
- But, Muslim Women started contesting in a big way from this point. While there were no independent candidates until now, the 1980 elections witnessed a sudden spurt of

enthusiasm among Muslim women to contest elections, as evidenced by a number of Muslim women contesting as independents (Table 4.21):

**Table 4.21:** Muslim Women at the 1980 General Elections to 7th Lok Sabha

| *States* | *Name of Candidates* | *Party Affiliation* | *Result of Election* |
|---|---|---|---|
| Assam (Silchar) | Rashida Haque Chaudhari | INC | Lost |
| Bihar (Hazaribagh) | Azima Hussain | IND | Lost |
| Gujarat (Bharuch) | Hasmat Begum Rehman | INC-U | DF |
| Maharashtra (Chandrapur) | Pratima Nuruddin | JNP-S | -do- |
| U.P (Shahabad) | Meharunnisa | IND | -do- |
| -do-(Hamirpur) | Tahira Khan | -do- | -do- |
| -do-(Aligarh) | Ruhi Zuberi | -do- | -do- |
| -do-(Meerut) | Mohsina Kidwai | INC (I) | Won |
| W.B., (Barasat) | Noorjahan Begum | IND | DF |
| -do-(Diamond Harbour) | Jamila Khatun | -do- | DF |

*Source*: Election Commission's Statistical Report. [JNP (S): Janata Party-Secular] [INC-U: Indian National Congress-United; INC (I): Indian National Congress-Indira].

- Only three Muslim women were elected at the 1984 elections to the 8th Lok Sabha; two from Uttar Pradesh and one from Jammu & Kashmir. There were 44 women contestants from Uttar Pradesh (including 6 Muslim women) of whom only 9 were successful. Of these, only 2 were Muslim women viz., Begum Abida Ahmed (Bareilly, INC) and Mohsina Kidwai (Meerut, INC). The remaining who fought as independents or as nominees of regional parties lost or forfeited their deposits (Table 4.22).
  At the 1989 elections to the 9th Lok Sabha, only one Muslim woman (Subhashini Ali) was elected. Nine Muslim women who contested as independents and three on Congress ticket, lost (Table 4.23).
- As the 9th Lok Sabha could not run its full term, mid-term elections were held for the Tenth Lok Sabha in 1991 and for Punjab State in 1992. In terms of performance in general, of the total of 330 women that contested (both in 1991 and 1992), only 38 were elected and 250 women candidates lost their security deposits. Yet, Muslim women did not lose their interest. As many as 15 Muslim women contested the

**Table 4.22:** Muslim Women at the 1984 General Elections to the 8th Lok Sabha

| *States* | *Name of the Candidate* | *Party Affiliation* | *Result of Election* |
|---|---|---|---|
| Bihar (Siwan) | Bibi Khursheed Jahan | LKD | DF |
| J&K (Anant Nag) | Akbar Jahan Begum | JKN | Won |
| Kerala (Manjeri) | K. Nafeesa Kutty | IND | DF |
| Madhya Pradesh (Bhopal) | Zohra Jamal | IND | DF |
| Uttar Pradesh: | | | |
| Rampur | Aftab Jamani Begum | IND | Lost |
| Bareilly | Abida Ahmad | INC | Won |
| Sitapur | Salma | IND | DF |
| Banda | Shahida Hanif | IND | DF |
| Meerut | Mohsina Kidwai | INC | Won |
| Meerut | Nahid Malik | IND | DF |

*Source:* Election Commission's Statistical Report; LKD: Lok Dal.

**Table 4.23:** Muslim Women at the 1989 General Elections to 9th Lok Sabha

| *States* | *Name of Candidates* | *Party Affiliation* | *Result of Election* |
|---|---|---|---|
| Kerala (Kasargod) | Ayesha Mallath | IND | Deposit forfeited |
| M.P. (Indore) | Mumtaz B. Patel | -do- | -do- |
| Bombay (South) | Sayeeda Bano | -do- | -do- |
| Rajasthan (Udaipur) | Malika Khan | -do- | -do- |
| UP (Bareilly) | Begum Abida Ahmed | INC | Lost |
| UP (Kheri) | Jane Jahan | IND | DF |
| UP (Maharajganj) | Ansari | -do- | -do- |
| UP (Ghazipur) | Sayeeda | -do- | -do- |
| UP (Meerut) | Mohsina Kidwai | INC | Lost |
| -do- | Nahid Malik | IND | DF |
| -d0-(Bahraich) | A.R. Kidwai | INC | Lost |
| -do-(Kanpur) | Subhashini Ali | CPM | Won |
| Andaman & Nicobar | Zubaida Cheku | IND | DF |

*Source:* Election Commission's Statistical Report.

elections in 1991. There were no Muslim women candidates in 1992. Not a single Muslim woman was elected. Table 4.24 gives the results.

- It is apparent from the above list that the established National parties did not entertain Muslim women. This left the Muslim women to try their luck to fight the elections under the banner of some existing party; even if it is obscure and has no history of electoral success. The 10th Lok Sabha did not have a single Muslim woman.

**Table 4.24:** Muslim Women at the 1991 General Elections to 10th Lok Sabha

| States | Name of Candidates | Party Affiliation | Result of Election |
|---|---|---|---|
| Assam (Barapeta) | Halida Khatoon | Janata Party | DF |
| Bihar (Hazaribagh) | Azeema Hussain | -do- | -do- |
| Gujarat (Rajkot) | Farida Kasham Juneja | IND | -do- |
| Gujarat (Ahmedabad | Sk. Ayesha Mohammadali | Jana Dal | -do- |
| M.P. (Mandsaur) | Bano Bi | IND | -do- |
| -do- | Pyari Bai Gurjar | -do- | -do- |
| Bombay (N-W) | Anees Syed | Janata Dal | -do- |
| Rajasthan (Udaipur) | Latifan Chakkiwale | DDP | -do- |
| Rajasthan (Jodhpur) | Mahmooda Begum | IND | -do- |
| -do- | Azeena Khan | -do- | -do- |
| U.P. (Domraiganj) | Mohsina Kidwai | INC | Lost |
| -do- | Seema Mustafa | ICS (CS) | DF |
| U.P. (Kanpur) | Subhashini Ali | CPI (M) | Lost |
| -do- | Tasneem Ali | Janata Party | DF |
| W.B. (Jadhavpur) | Lailunnisa | IND | -do- |

DDP: Doordarshi Party, (ICS-CS) Indian Congress-Socialist, Saratchandra Sinha faction.
*Source:* Election Commission's Statistical Report.

- In the 1996 elections for the eleventh Lok Sabha, a record number of 37 Muslim women tried their luck. It will be seen from the results furnished in Table 4.25 that the Congress Party gave tickets only to two Muslim women. The only winner was Noor Bano Begum of the Rampur Royal family.
- The poor performance of Muslim women continued at the general elections held in 1998 for the 12th Lok Sabha. Table 4.26 gives the results of Muslim women who contested the 1998 elections.
- Elections to the 13th Lok Sabha were held in 1999 due to the collapse of the National Democratic Alliance (NDA) Government (Table 4.27). Only one Muslim woman (Begum Noor Bano) was elected and all others who continued to try to enter the Parliament either as independents and under the banner of established national and/or regional parties could not make it; either they lost, but retained their deposits or lost so miserably as to forfeit their deposits.

**Table 4.25**: Muslim Women at the 1996 General Elections to 11th Lok Sabha

| *States* | *Name of Candidates* | *Party Affiliation* | *Result of Election* |
|---|---|---|---|
| A.P. (Kurnool) | Masoom Bi | IND | DF |
| -do-(Hyderabad) | Amtul Rasheed | -do- | -do- |
| -do-(Secunderabad) | Shahajadi Begum | -do- | -do- |
| Assam (Guwahati) | Nawazis Ara Begum | SP | -do- |
| -do-(Tezpur) | Syeda Husna Begum | IND | -do- |
| -do-(Nowgong) | Nazneen Faruque | INC | Lost |
| Gujarat (Ahmedabad) | Farida Banu J. Khan | IND | DF |
| -do-(Bhavnagar) | Farida Banu J. Pathan | -do- | -do- |
| Jammu & Kashmir | Mehbooba | -do- | -do- |
| Karnataka (Bijapur) | Nazma Ajijuddin Bangi | -do- | -do- |
| Kerala (Ponnani) | A.K. Kuttyassan | -do- | -do- |
| M.P. (Jangir) | Tahira Khan | -do- | -do- |
| -do-(Mandsaur) | Raisa Bano | -do- | -do- |
| -do-(Mandsaur) | Bano Bee | -do- | -do- |
| Mumbai (N-E) | Ashraf Begum Bahadur Khan | -do- | -do- |
| Mumbai (N-E) | Sheikh Akhtar Jamal | -do- | -do- |
| Maharashtra (Latur) | Sk. Mumtaz Noor Mohammad | -do- | -do- |
| Rajasthan (Churu) | Anwar Bano | -do- | -do- |
| -do- | Bismillah | -do- | -do- |
| -do-(Sikar) | Zakiya | -do- | -do- |
| -do-(Udaipur) | Latifan | -do- | -do- |
| -do-(Jodhpur) | Mahmooda Begum | -do- | -do- |
| Tamilnadu (Ramnad) | Abila Begum | -do- | -do- |
| U.P. (Rampur) | Nur Bano Begum | INC | Won |
| -do-(Rae Bareilly) | Mumtaz Sultan | IND | DF |
| -do-(Domraiganj) | Mohsina Kidwai | INC | -do- |
| -do-(Domraiganj) | Seema Mustafa | IND | -do- |
| -do-(Domraiganj) | Rafique Khatun | -do- | -do- |
| -do-(Varanasi) | Madina Begum | -do- | -do- |
| -do-(Allahabad) | Mumtaz Hussain | -do- | -do- |
| -do-(Kanpur) | Subhashini Ali | CPI (M) | Lost |
| -do-(Agra) | Asifa Begum | BKD | DF |
| -do-(Meerut) | Taslim Rizvi | IND | -do- |
| -do-(Meerut) | Pakeeza Begum | -do- | -do- |
| W.B. (Jangipur) | Jahera Begum | -do- | -do- |
| New Delhi | Saira | RAM | DF |
| East Delhi | Shahnaz | IND | DF |

DF: Deposit Forfeited.
*Source*: Election Commission's Statistical Reports.

- In the elections to the 14th Lok Sabha held in 2004, out of the total 355 contestants, 239 women lost the elections losing their deposits. Only 45 women could win the battle of the

**Table 4.26**: Muslim Women at the 1998 General Elections to 12th Lok Sabha

| *States* | *Name of Candidates* | *Party Affiliation* | *Result of Election* |
|---|---|---|---|
| Andhra Pradesh (Nalgonda) | Sakeena Alladdin | IND | DF |
| J & K (Srinagar) | Hafiza Begum | -do- | -do- |
| M.P. (Khajuraho) | Begum Noorjahan | -do- | -do- |
| -do-(Mandsaur) | Bano Bee | -do- | -do- |
| Orissa (Berhampur) | Aliya Begum | RJD | -do- |
| Punjab (Ferozepur) | Amro Bibi | IND | -do- |
| Rajasthan (Jodhpur) | Mahmooda Begum | SAP | -do- |
| Tamilnadu (Madras Central) | Sava Mustafa | IND | -do- |
| -do-(Ramanathapuram) | Nazeera Parvin | PT | -do- |
| Uttar Pradesh (Rampur) | Begum Noor Bano | INC | Lost |
| -do-(Kanpur) | Tarana Sarfuddin | IND | DF |
| -do-(Agra) | Shammi | -do- | -do- |
| -do-(Bulandshahar) | Anisa | -do- | -do- |
| -do-(Meerut) | Mohsina Kidwai | INC | -do- |
| -do-(Meerut) | Shaheen Parvez | JD | -do- |

*Source:* Election Commission's Statistical Report.

ballot. In the bye elections held later, five more women won seats in the Lok Sabha, taking the total to 50. From the point of view of Muslim women's political participation, the Table 4.28 gives the results.

Muslim women continued to seek sponsors among the national and regional parties, resulting in some of them fighting the elections under the banner of different parties. It was also for the first time that a recognised Muslim Party, the Hyderabad-based All India Majlis-e-Ittehadul Muslimeen supported a woman at the elections from Secunderabad in Andhra Pradesh. She lost her deposit.

- In the 15th Lok Sabha, which came into being following the 2009 elections, there were three Muslim women among the 58 women members. The Muslim women members in the Lok Sabha were Tabassum Begum (Kairana, Uttar Pradesh, Bahujan Samaj Party), Kaisar Jahan (Sitapur, Uttar Pradesh, Bahujan Samaj Party) and Mausam Noor (Malda North, West Bengal, Congress).

In the final tally, of the 549 women elected to the Lok Sabha at the various elections since independence, only 19 have been Muslim women. It appears from the above analysis that the established national

**Table 4.27:** Muslim Women at the 1999 General Elections to 13th Lok Sabha

| *States* | *Name of Candidates* | *Party Affiliation* | *Result of Election* |
|---|---|---|---|
| Assam (Guwahati) | Nawazis Ara Begum | SP | DF |
| Bihar (Lohardaga) | Sofia Kachhap | BSP | -do- |
| Gujarat (Gandhinagar) | Mahmooda Riaz Munshi | Ind. | -do- |
| -do-(Bharuch) | Roshanben Shabbirbhai | -do- | -do- |
| J & K (Srinagar) | Mehbooba Mufti | -do- | Lost |
| -do-(Srinagar) | Hafiza Begum | -do- | DF |
| -do-(Srinagar) | Waheeda Shah | -do- | -do- |
| -do-(Srinagar) | Hafiza Begum | -do- | -do- |
| -do-(Srinagar) | Aisha | RJD | -do- |
| M.P. (Khajuraho) | Anisa | JD (S) | -do- |
| -do-(Mandsaur) | Bano Bee | BMSM | -do- |
| Maharashtra (Parbhani) | Noorjahan Rehman Khan | Ind. | -do- |
| -do-(Parbhani) | Mumtaz Md. Yahya Khan | -do- | -do- |
| Rajasthan (Jhalawar) | Razia Bano | RJVP | -do- |
| -do-(Jodhpur) | Mahmooda Abbasi | Ind. | -do- |
| Tamilnadu (Ramnad) | Nazeera Parvin Dr. | PT | -do- |
| -do-(Ramnad) | Ayeravalli alias Ameenal | Ind. | -do- |
| U.P. (Nainital) | Naina Ahmed | BSP | -do- |
| -do-(Rampur) | Noor Bano Begum | INC | Won |
| -do-(Lucknow) | Afaque Parvin | AIMF | DF |
| -do-(Bahraich) | Ruvab Sayeeda | SP | -do- |
| -do-(Maharajganj) | Talat Aziz | BSP | Lost |
| -do-(Farukkabad) | Louise Salman Khursheed | INC | Lost |
| W.B. (Mushirabad) | Khadija Banu | Ind. | DF |
| -do-(Calcutta N-W) | Masarrat Begum | JD (S) | -do- |
| -do-(Bolpur) | Nazma | JP | -do- |

PT: *Puthiya Tamilagam*; RJVP: Rajasthan Vikas Party; BMSM: Bharatiya Minorities Suraksha Mahasangh; AIMF: All India Minorities Front; JD (S): Janata Dal (Secular); JP: Janata Party.
*Source:* Election Commission's Statistical Reports.

parties did not entertain Muslim women unless they already had a track record (e.g., Mohsina Kidwai) or belonged to a dynasty with influence at the grass-roots level and the means to fight the election. The other national parties, including the Left, hardly showed any concern for Muslim women. In comparison, though, the BSP and the Congress have given some space to Muslim women.

## Women's Representation in PRIs in UP

The failure of Muslim women to get elected to the Assembly in

**Table 4.28:** Muslim Women at the 2004 General Elections to 14th Lok Sabha

| *States* | *Name of Candidates* | *Party Affiliation* | *Result of Election* |
|---|---|---|---|
| A.P. (Secunderabad) | Humera Aziz | AIMIM | DF |
| Assam (Dhubri) | Jabeen Borbhuyan | BJP | -do- |
| -do-(Mangaldoi) | Shaheda Begum | SAP | -do- |
| J & K (Srinagar) | Mehbooba | IND | -do- |
| -do-(Anantnag) | Mehbooba Mufti | JKPDP | Won |
| Karnataka (Bellary) | Gousia Begum | IND | DF |
| Madhya Pradesh (Betul) | Shameem Modi | SWJP | -do- |
| Mumbai (N-W) | Saira Bano Md. Patel | IND | -do- |
| Maharashtra (Nanded) | Sk. Waheeda Mehbooba Pasha | BSP | -do- |
| Rajasthan (Jodhpur) | Mahmooda Begum | IND | -do- |
| Tamilnadu (Madras) | Bader Sayeed | ADMK | Lost |
| -do-(Chengalpattu) | Shaheen Banu | IND | DF |
| U.P. (Moradabad) | Faeem Akhtar | -do- | -do- |
| -do-(Rampur) | Noor Bano Begum | INC | Lost |
| -do-(Sambhal) | Tarannum Aqeel | BSP | Lost |
| -do-(Bahraich) | Rubab Sayeeda | SP | Won |
| -do-(Maharajganj) | Talat Aziz | BSP | Lost |
| -do-(Kanpur) | Subhashini Ali | CPM | DF |
| -do-(Farukkabad) | Louise Salman Khurshid | INC | Lost |
| West Bengal (Calcutta-S) | Nafisa Ali Sodhi | INC | DF |
| Outer Delhi | Kaisar | NBNP | -do- |

AIMIM: All India Majlis-e-Ittehadul Muslimeen; SAP: Samata Party; JKPDP: Jammu & Kashmir People's Democratic Party; SWJP: Samajwadi Jana Parishad; ADMK: Anna Dravida Munnetra Kazhagam; SP: Samata Party; NBNP: Nav Bharat Nirman Party.

*Source:* Election Commission's Statistical Reports.

sufficient numbers during the last 6 decades raises the question whether they have missed a step? Should they have first made their mark at lower levels? As Dr. Pritam Singh opines, "as the demand for bringing more women into the political processes and decision-making bodies increases, their involvement at the grassroots levels acquires special significance, not merely in terms of political training, but also to ensure that those at the helm of affairs are the true representatives of people's interest."[46] This means that they should rise from Gram Panchayat level.

In the year 2000, Uttar Pradesh had the largest number of women in the PRIs in the country; 1,20,591 in Gram Panchayats, 13,865 in

Panchayat Samitis and 634 in Zilla Parishads making a total of 1,35,090. Following the 73rd Constitutional Amendment, elections for all three levels of Panchayats were held in 1995 and within the stipulated time of 5 years again in 2000. The reservations under the 73rd and 74th Constitutional Amendments, and overwhelming response from women (and their male relatives) resulted in women capturing more than 33 per cent of the seats reserved for them; Chairpersons, Zilla Panchayat (53.62%); Member, Zilla Panchayat (37.06%); Chairperson, Kshetra Panchayat (36.71%); Member, Kshetra Panchayat (35.82%); Gram Pradhan (35.32%); and Member, Gram Panchayat (37.95%).

It may be true that quite a few women members in the PRIs are yet to come into their own as far as exercising their expected roles in development is concerned. The strings of power continue to be with their spouses or other male members of their families. But, they still have achieved. There is an element of training of women of the PRIs under the Panchayati Raj Department. The impact of this training is yet to be analysed from point of view of its effect in making the women competent in discharging their duties. It goes without saying that educated women appear to handle their political leadership roles relatively much better and it is the lower crust of the PRIs where female literacy and educational levels are extremely low, makes them vulnerable. The situation may soon change.

## Muslim Women in Panchayati Raj Institutions

For the poorly educated or even illiterate rural women, including Muslim women, the 33 per cent reservation of seats for women in the Panchayati Raj Institutions following the 73rd and 74th Amendments to the Constitution has come as an opportunity they never expected. Muslim women, who had entertained ambitions of elected office, but could not take part in elections to the Assembly and Parliament for various reasons, have taken advantage of the opportunity; even if at a slower pace. Mumtaz Mazumdar observes:[47]

> "It can be estimated from our immediate social environments that the Muslim women, except in Kerala, are much slower in performing at par with the majority community. Hesitation due to lack of education, unawareness, apathetic attitude towards politics, shy nature, dominance and interference of

> male members of the family, lack of self-confidence, and lack of political experience are some of the reasons that have kept the pace of the Muslim women at the snail's movement".

In the face of several odds, it was not easy for Muslim women to contest even in the elections to the PRIs. They had to first secure the consent of their spouses if married, or their parents, by convincing them that they would not be ignoring their domestic responsibilities. Secondly, they were to gauge the reaction of the society in which they lived. Besides the expenses involved in contesting elections, they were also to keep in mind the religious leaders. In so far as the last element is concerned, Muslim women in the southern states were not too much worried about *fatwas* from Darul Uloom, unlike Muslim women of Uttar Pradesh.

Thus, in contesting for membership in PRIs, Muslim women had to muster a lot of courage and win the support of their families and society and get over the presumption that Muslim women are incompetent. Consequently, unlike non-Muslim women, Muslim women's entry into PRI was slow in the beginning. But, in spite of the odds, "the representation of Muslim women in the Panchayati Raj is not very large, but the ones who have taken over the reins of the administration are definitely making their mark, in spite of their having less grounding in politics than their male counterparts".[48]

As we have seen from the Karnataka chapter, Muslim women have shown a high level of enthusiasm in contesting elections to the PRIs and ULBs. Assessing the performance of Muslim women in the PRIs, a joint statement issued by 15 Muslim women's organizations in 2010 stated:[49]

> "Mandatory reservations for women in Panchayats and Local Bodies have facilitated the entry of lakhs of women in villages, small towns and cities, into the political arena. As a result, a large number of Muslim women also had the opportunity for the first time to enter the public sphere from which they had been absent. Today, Muslim women are actively carrying out their responsibilities as Sarpanchs, Panchayat members, BDC members, ZP Chairpersons and members, Town Area Chairpersons, Mayors and Councillors in the States of India. They have faced tremendous odds to enter the electoral fray and many of them are role models for

> their community and for all women. This has brought many important women's issues on the agenda of Panchayats and local bodies. This positive experience needs to be strengthened and extended further."

Across the country today, there is a marked presence of women, including Muslim women, in the Panchayati Raj Institutions; an estimated 10 million women in all three tiers of Panchayat Raj Institutions. The entry of women into PRI in such large numbers has shattered the myth that women are not interested in Politics and have neither the time nor the competence to discharge their duties as Members or Presidents of the PRIs.

Even when they secure the permission of the family, the main problem for the Muslim women is to muster the support and acceptance of the Muslim voters. For, it has been observed that even in Muslim-dominated constituencies, Muslim women have fared very poorly, often securing very few votes. Alka Madhok cites the example of a Gram Panchayat election in Rajasthan, at which one of the contestants, a Muslim woman, was supported by "lower castes and not Muslims". Madhok presumes that "there was reciprocal relationship" in this event as her election as President of the Panchayat has benefitted the lower castes.[50] As the Muslim woman in question is described as "young, straight forward and simple" and was elected from a general category seat, it is more of a case of non-Muslim voters supporting her in large numbers as compared to Muslim voters.

Country-wide, a substantial number of women members, particularly at Gram Panchayat level, are illiterate or partially illiterate. This is the case even with Muslim women contesting Assembly elections in Uttar Pradesh, although there are quite a few well-educated women among the aspirants. Further, a substantial number of women representatives are from middle to lower-middle class families; either housewives or engaged in unskilled/semi-skilled activities. Reservation of seats has given these women an opportunity to demonstrate their deep political consciousness and interest in accessing power. For them, politics and elections are instruments of social change.

The reason as to why Muslim men do not encourage women from venturing into politics is explained by Nazreena Bhura.[51]

> "There is still fear in the Muslim community that if a woman

is empowered, she will in some way threaten the family structure and traditions. That she will want to go her own way, become too independent. But I would like to say that while there will be such misuse of empowerment by women who do not understand that independence and decision-making go hand in hand with responsibility, there will be a lot of other who do understand this... It is not selfish to want education and financial empowerment, it is your right. If you are happy with yourself, you will make others happy, including your husband and children. Being educated and financially empowered does not mean that you will turn away from family traditions and practices, that your belief in *Allah* and his *Rahmath* becomes any less. One does not preclude the other. Islam has had highly empowered women."

## Darul-Uloom and UP Muslim Women

Muslim women of Uttar Pradesh, at least those living in the shadow of Darul-Uloom, Deoband, have also to contend with *fatwas* coming out of Darul-Uloom, Deoband. *Fatwas* may not be legally binding and are only in the nature of opinions, but not all the members of the Muslim community, given the nature of the society in Uttar Pradesh, can ignore the *fatwas*. Indian Muslim women, particularly in rural areas, are pushed to the wall; victims of, first, the incorrect interpretation of Islamic laws and, second, low literacy-level.

In a *fatwa* issued on August 16, 2005, the Islamic Seminary ruled that Muslim women should not contest elections and if they have to, they must do it under veil. The *fatwa* said: "Muslim women are not allowed to appear before men without a veil and under the Islamic law. *Pardanashin* women are only allowed to contest elections." This *fatwa* was condemned by all political parties and women's groups.

In November 1995, when 45 Muslim women filed their nomination to participate in the civic bodies' election from the area in the vicinity of Darul-Uloom, Deoband, the *Ulema* became alarmed. They issued a *fatwa* barring Muslim women from participating in elections as it will bring them into contact with men".[52]

Raising objections to Muslim women aspiring for leadership is not confined to India alone. Such phenomenon cuts across countries in South and South-East Asia. Commenting on the situation in Sri Lanka, Ferial Ashraf said: "Muslim society in Sri Lanka is to a large extent a conservative one, with a certain segment still frowning upon female leadership. I think they are more concerned about women in leadership positions maintaining their identity as Muslims. I think the issue should be not what you do, but how you do it. If you maintain your identity as a Muslim and do what you are called upon to do, I do not think there should be any problems".[53]

That the Muslim community of, at least, Deoband area, was wary of the Darul Uloom is evidenced by the fact that there were no Muslim women candidates from Deoband constituency in the Assembly Elections during the years 1951, 1957, 1962, 1967, 1969, 1974, 1977, 1980, 1985, 1989 and 1991. In 1993, there was only one Muslim woman (*Shakura*) out of 24 candidates, who contested on Janata Party ticket. She just polled 237 votes. At the 1996 elections, once again, there was only one Muslim woman, (Zeenat Naaz, Independent, votes polled 915). There were no Muslim women candidates at the 2002, 2007 and 2012 elections.

Indian Muslim women, all over the length and breadth of the country, have always been sincere followers of Islam and in fact, are becoming more conscious of their religion without any compulsion. This is evident from the voluntary donning of the veil, or at least the head scarf, by increasing number of Muslim women. But, they too have to draw a line somewhere. They cannot distance themselves from the country's democratic values and the benefits flowing therefrom. Muslim women seem to have realised that they cannot remain unconcerned in a changing world any longer and continue to be mere voters. The November 1995 *fatwa* did not have any great impact on Muslim women and conscious Muslim voters.

There were courageous Muslim women like Zeenat Naaz, a middle-class housewife, who declared that in a democracy, politics cannot be practised behind the *hijab*, flung off her *burkha* and appeared bare-faced before a crowd at a public meeting symbolising her entry into the male dominion of politics. Though she was ostracised, dedicated social service won her acceptance and admiration. She was the most promising candidate for the chairmanship of the Nagar Palika of Deoband, a seat reserved for women. Although her popularity alarmed the clerics of Deoband, she contested and won. The Clerics' stand on Muslim women joining politics became a subject for debate, but given the international standing of Deoband's Dar-ul-Uloom Islamic University, few were willing to openly contradict its stand.[54]

What, perhaps, caused the rebellion was that in the *fatwa* issued against Muslim women participating in elections, Deoband said that it was *preferable to let a Hindu win*, rather than permit a Muslim woman to shed her veil and enter the political arena. Describing the *purdah* as the symbol of purity in Muslim women, Deoband said that if "women become *Pradhans*", segregation between men and women would end, to the detriment of society. The *fatwa* denounced reservation of seats for women as a ploy to bring *be-purdah* women out of their homes and into the male bastions and suggested that it was best not to vote for such ambitious women.[55]

In a clarification issued later, Darul Uloom declared that the *Shariat* did not *debar* women from serving society as elected representatives, provided they adhered to the code of conduct laid down by Islamic law and observed certain 'restrictions'. Voting for women candidates was thus held to be permissible. Maulana Hajib-ur-Rehman, signatory to the second *fatwa*, opined: "If more-and-more women come out *be-purdah* from their homes, as is happening today, society will suffer. It is best that women stay at home. The external sphere is for men, the internal for women."

But, their clarification did not cut ice with the community. Ironically, the *fatwas* worked to Zeenat's advantage. The town's 65 per cent Muslim population did not like giving away the seat to a Hindu candidate. At the same time, the town's elite felt it was far better to vote for Zeenat, who was already *be-purdah*, than to liberate more women from the veil.[56] The argument against participation of Muslim women in politics centres on the *hijab*, which symbolises segregation of the sexes and their exclusion from public life. Maulana Hajib-ur-Rehman strongly denied that either of the fiats was politically inspired: "We do not issue *fatwas* (on our own). Someone asks us a question on a point of Islamic law and we reply. No particular personality was involved. It was a general direction to the community."

On the issue of Muslim women in politics, the Imam of Delhi's Fathepuri Masjid also insisted that it is better for women to stay away. "In the interests of a clean society, the *Shariat* prescribes that women observe *purdah* and stay at home. But Islam is not as rigid as it is made out to be. I agree that if women want to serve society, they can come forward, but they must stick to the rules. Women can and do work in *burkha*, but too much freedom is bad."

While a Muslim woman Member of the Parliament known for her progressive views criticised the Deoband *fatwas* and pointed out that the best way to fight the orthodoxy is to ignore them and work quietly towards acquiring political clout, the moderates feel that it is high time Muslims took a more practical view of the *Shariat*. Rigid rules are all very well in an Islamic state, but if Muslims living in India try and bring everything into an Islamic framework, they will lose out.

In spite of the odds, a number of Muslim women were successful at the elections to the PRIs. There are 12 Municipal Corporations, 194 Nagar Palika Parishads and 421 Nagar Panchayats in Uttar Pradesh besides hundreds of Gram Panchayats. In view of the voluminous data involved, it is difficult to analyse each election. We propose, therefore, to give only a few examples. In the elections held in 2000:

- In Khurja Municipal Board (Bulandshahar district) Razia Saleem Khan was elected to the Chairman's post. She was the first Muslim to be elected to the post. Muslims constituting only 30 per cent of the city's population and with another formidable Muslim candidate in the fray, Razia Khan attracted a large number of non-Muslim votes.
- Reshma Afroz, Chairman of Rampur Municipal Board, won the seat a second time again trouncing her opponent by a heavy margin.
- Naseebunnisa (Nanpara Nagar Palika Parishad), Tahira Begum (Chairperson of Nagina Nagar Palika Parishad), Shakeela Begum (Muhammadi Nagar Palika Parishad), Atiya Bano (chairperson, Faridpur Nagar Palika Parishad) are some examples of Muslim women being accepted by the society.

A number of other Muslim women candidates have won from several other Municipal Boards. Their representation has also increased in corporations and municipal boards.[57]

The performance of Muslim woman to the various PRIs at the elections held in 2012 is proposed to be examined below Tables 4.29, 4.30, 4.31.

An analysis of the data of the 2012 elections to the PRIs in Uttar Pradesh shows that over 7,000 Muslim women contested the elections seeking to become members of the various Nagar Panchayats, Nagar Palika Parishads and Nagar Nigams of the State and over 1,300 of them were successful. What is surprising is the courage shown by

**Table 4.29:** Muslim Women among the Elected Presidents of Nagar Palika Parishads, Uttar Pradesh, 2012 (Total Number of Nagar Palika Parishads: 194)

| Name of the District | Name of Nagar Palika Parishad | Name of the President Elect (age within parenthesis) |
|---|---|---|
| 1. Saharanpur | Sarsawah | 1. Nafeesa Vazir Ahmed (38) |
| 2. Mirzapur | Chunar | 2. Hasina Begum (48) |
| 3. Sant Ravidas Nagar | Badohi | 3. Mahalka Begum (44) |
| 4. Mau | Mau | 4. Shahina Amjad Khan (43) |
| 5. Siddharth Nagar | Bansi | 5. Chaman Ara (38) |
| 6. Mahoba | Charkhari | 6. Ruksana (49) |
| 7. Kasganj | Ganj Dundwara | 7. Najma Begum (36) |
| 8. Bulandshahar | Gulvati | 8. Nusrat Jahan (41) |
| 9. Bijnor | Syohara | 9. Tarannum Malik (36) |
| | Chandpur | 10. Zeenat Parvin (33) |
| | Kiratpur | 11. Rubina Manan (31) |
| 10. Bareilly | Nawabganj | 12. Shahala Tahir (45) |
| 11. Aligarh | Atrauli | 13. Sazda Begum (40) |
| 12. Mahamaya Nagar | Sikandara Rao | 14. Fanus Begum (41) |

*Source:* http://sec.up.nic.in

such large number of Muslim women offering themselves as candidates at the PRI elections, ignoring the *fatwas* against women's electoral participation and other odds (Table 4.32).

While the socio-economic profile of this huge number of elected women is difficult to come by, it can be assumed that most of them are housewives, and belong to lower-middle or middle class families, with their husbands/parents engaged in farming or petty businesses. Although the actual educational status of the women that have contested in the elections is not known, it may be safely assumed that, except in a very few case, most of the contestants have some basic educational qualifications. The age profiling of all the elected Muslim women has been carried out and given in the Table below (except in the case of 5 women whose age has not been shown in the State Election Commission data). The age profile of the emerging pattern of Muslim women leadership in Panchayats shows that the elected women Sarpanches were around 50 years of age or even less. In fact, most of them were in the age group of 30 to 40 years and married. In a few cases, Muslim women elected as Pradhans are in the 60+ age group. The younger generation, in the age group of 21 to 30 years, opting for political participation denotes a sign of change.

The age profile shows that about 61 per cent of the Muslim women

**Table 4.30**: Muslim Women among the Elected Presidents of Nagar Panchayat, Uttar Pradesh, 2012 (Total Number of Nagar Panchayats in Uttar Pradesh in 2012: 420)

| *Name of the Districts* | *Name of Nagar Panchayat* | *Name of the President Elect. (age in parenthesis)* |
|---|---|---|
| 1. Saharanpur | Sultanpur Chilkhana | 1. Suraiyya Jamal (35) |
| 2. Mirzapur | Kachchwa | 2. Sabeela Begum (51) |
| 3. Sant Ravidas Nagar | Mohammadabad Gohna | 3. Zarina Khatun (48) |
| –do- | Bikapur | 4. Zulekha Khatun (50) |
| –do- | Ashrafpur Kichchaucha | 5. Shabana Khatun (40) |
| 4. Sultanpur | Koireepur | 6. Rubina Bano (31) |
| 5. Barabanki | Satrikh | 7. Mumtaj Begum (42) |
| –do- | Siddaur | 8. Kamrunnisa (45) |
| –do- | Fatehpur | 9. Reshma Mashqur (36) |
| 6. Lakhimpur-Kheri | Singhahi Bedowra | 10. Afroz Jahan (33) |
| 7. Lucknow | Nagram | 11. Zeenat Imran (41) |
| –do- | Malihabad NP | 12. Asmat Ara Khan (56) |
| 8. Unnao | Kursat | 13. Najima Subrati (46) |
| 9. Allahabad | Lal Gopal Ganj | 14. Zulekha (40) |
| -do- | Handia | 15. Kulsum (46) |
| –do- | Bharatganj | 16. Yasmin (45) |
| –do- | Phulpur | 17. Sarbat Jahan (50) |
| 10. Kaushambi | Manjhanpur | 18. Hashmi Begum (55) |
| 11. Mainpuri | Bhogaon | 19. Naseem Bano (36) |
| 12. Mahamaya Nagar | Shadabad | 20. Rihana (45) |
| 13. Aligarh | Charra | 21. Rahiso Jawani (65) |
| –do- | Pilkhana | 22. Habib Jahan (66) |
| 14. Budaun | Sakhanu | 23. Mubina Khatun (48) |
| 15. Bareilly | Fatehganj East | 24. Kishwari Begum (55) |
| 16. Moradabad | Umri Kalan | 25. Farha Khatun (33) |
| –do- | Kanth | 26. Nasreen Bano (30) |
| 17. Amroha | Uzhari | 27. Mahjabeen Nafis (70) |
| 18. Bijnor | Badhapur | 28. Khadija Mohammad (60) |
| 19. Ghaziabad | Faridnagar | 29. Nazma Nasir (45) |
| 20. Meerut | Falwada | 30. Ayisha Khatun (50) |
| 21. Muzaffar Nagar | Purkhaji | 32. Shahida Nasim (57) |
| 22. Shamli | Jalalabad | 32. Rana Ashraf (35) |

*Source:* http://sec.up.nic.in

elected were in the age group of 30-50 years; 26 per cent in the 21-30 age group and 13 per cent in the above 50 years age group. One contestant, who won the election, was 80 years old, although there were quite few women aged between 65 and 70 years.

A study of women's participation in Gram Panchayat election in Odisha has observed: "aged women have some sort of apathy towards politics, whereas young and middle aged women are more interested in politics."[58] Although the study does not specifically comment on

**Table 4.31:** Local Body General Elections, 2012, Uttar Pradesh Details of Contesting candidates for the Post of Chairperson (NPP: Nagar Palika Parishad; NP: Nagar Panchayat; NN: Nagar Nigam)

| Distt. | NPP/NP/NN | Total no. of contestants | | | Elected |
|---|---|---|---|---|---|
| | | NM M&NMW | MW | MM | |
| 1. Saharanpur | Deoband NPP | 3 | 2 | 7 | MM |
| | Gangoh NPP | 2 | 1 | 3 | MM |
| | Sarsawah NPP | 5 | 3 | – | Nafisa W Ahmed (38) |
| | Sultanpur Chilkhana NP | 1 | 2 | – | Surayya J Hussain (55) |
| | Teetaro NP | 6 | 1 | – | NMW |
| | Rampur Maniharan NP | 10 | 9 | – | NMW |
| 2. Muzaffarnagar | Muzaffarnagar NPP | 10 | 1 | 5 | NMM |
| | Khatauli NPP | 9 | 2 | 14 | NMM |
| | Shahpur NP | 10 | 1 | 4 | MM |
| | Purkhaji NP | 5 | 4 | – | Shahida Naseem (57) |
| | Jansath NP | 11 | 2 | 8 | NMM |
| | Charthawal NP | 7 | 5 | – | NMW |
| | Budhana NP | 7 | 1 | 5 | NMM |
| 3. Shamli | Kandhla NPP | 5 | 1 | 6 | MM |
| | Kairana NPP | 2 | 5 | 22 | MM |
| | Jalalabad NP | 1 | 2 | 5 | Rama Ashraf (35) |
| | Banat NP | 9 | 5 | – | NMW |
| 4. Meerut | Sarghana NPP | 6 | 2 | 10 | MM |
| | Mawana NPP | 5 | 5 | – | NMW |
| | Parikshitgarh NP | 9 | 2 | – | NMW |
| | Lawad NP | 4 | 1 | 9 | MM |
| | Hastinapur NP | 10 | 1 | – | NMW |
| | Kharkauda NP | 5 | 1 | 1 | NMW |
| | Falwada NP | – | 5 | – | Ayesha Khatun (50) |
| | Kithaur NP | – | 1 | 5 | MM |
| 5. Baghpat | Badhauth NPP | 17 | 1 | 5 | NMM |
| | Teekri NP | 19 | 2 | – | NMW |
| 6. Ghaziabad | Murad Nagar NPP | 3 | 6 | – | NMW |
| | Loni NPP | 12 | 1 | 13 | NMM |
| | Faridnagar NP | 4 | 7 | – | Nazma Nasir (45) |
| | Dasna NP | 1 | 1 | 14 | MM |
| 7. G.B. Nagar | Dadri NPP | 3 | 5 | – | NMW |
| | Rabupura NP | 5 | 2 | – | NMW |
| | Bilaspur NP | 3 | 3 | – | NMW |
| 8. Bulandshahar | Bulandshahar NPP | 10 | 4 | – | NMW |
| | Jahangirabad NPP | 10 | 5 | – | NMW |
| | Syana NPP | 6 | 7 | – | NMW |
| | Gulawathi NPP | 11 | 7 | – | Nusrat Jahan (41) |
| | Anupshahr NPP | 12 | 2 | – | NMW |
| | Dibai NPP | 11 | 3 | – | NMW |

*(Contd.)*

| Distt. | NPP/NP/NN | Total no. of contestants | | | Elected |
|---|---|---|---|---|---|
| | | NM M&NMW | MW | MM | |
| | Sikandrabad NPP | 7 | 7 | – | NMW |
| | Pahasu NP | 4 | 3 | – | Zayda I– Qureshi (31) |
| 9. Hapur | Hapur NPP | 13 | 1 | – | NMW |
| 10. Bijnor | Syohara NPP | 2 | 8 | – | Tarannum Malik (36) |
| | Chandpur NPP | 4 | 3 | 15 | Zeenat Parvin (33) |
| | Nurpur NPP | 4 | 1 | 7 | MM |
| | Haldaur NPP | 3 | 3 | – | NMW |
| | Kiratpur NPP | 2 | 17 | – | Rubina Md– Manan (31) |
| | Nazibabad NPP | 4 | 2 | 9 | MM |
| | Nahtaur NPP | 4 | 3 | 16 | MM |
| | Sherkot NPP | 4 | 1 | 9 | MM |
| | Nagina NPP | 4 | 1 | 10 | MM |
| | Jhalu NP | 7 | 2 | – | Kishwar Jahan (36) |
| | Mandawar NP | 1 | 1 | 2 | MM |
| | Jalalabad NP | – | 1 | 7 | MM |
| | Badhapur NP | 6 | 1 | 15 | Khatija M– Rani (60) |
| | Saharpur NP | – | 1 | 10 | MM |
| 11. Amroha | Amroha NPP | 3 | 1 | 17 | MM |
| | Hasanpur NPP | 4 | 2 | 10 | NMM |
| | Dhanowra NPP | 8 | 1 | 7 | NMM |
| | Bachrayu NPP | 3 | 1 | 10 | MM |
| | Joya NP | – | 1 | 6 | MM |
| | Uzhari NP | – | 2 | 1 | Mahjabeen Nafis (70) |
| | Naugawan Sadat NP | – | 2 | 11 | MM |
| 12. Moradabad | Bilari NPP | 6 | 2 | 9 | NMM |
| | Thakurdwar NPP | 7 | 2 | 10 | MM |
| | Umari Kala NP | – | 7 | 14 | Farha Khatun (33) |
| | Kundarki NP | 6 | 7 | 15 | MM |
| | Kanth NP | 8 | 8 | – | Nasreen Bano (30) |
| 13. Rampur | Tanda NPP | – | 1 | 8 | MM |
| | Suar NPP | 1 | 3 | 12 | MM |
| | Milk NPP | 10 | 1 | 5 | NMW |
| | Bilaspur NPP | 7 | 1 | 8 | NMM |
| | Shahabad NP | 2 | 4 | 7 | MM |
| | Maswasi NP | 7 | 8 | – | NMW |
| | Kaimari NP | 1 | 2 | 6 | MM |
| 14. Sambhal | Bahjoee NPP | 13 | 4 | – | NMW |
| | Sambhal NPP | 2 | 2 | 13 | MM |
| | Chandausi NPP | 4 | 3 | – | NMW |
| | Narauli NPP | 7 | 9 | – | NMW |
| | Gunaur NP | 4 | 1 | 9 | MM |
| 15. Bareilly | Faridpur NPP | 8 | 1 | 9 | NMM |
| | Nawabganj NPP | 9 | 2 | 9 | Shahala Tahir (45) |
| | Awala NPP | 16 | 2 | 10 | MM |
| | Baheri NPP | 1 | 3 | 11 | MM |
| | Faridpur NP | 3 | 1 | 6 | MM |

(*Contd.*)

| Distt. | NPP/NP/NN | Total no. of contestants | | | Elected |
|---|---|---|---|---|---|
| | | NM M&NMW | MW | MM | |
| | Shishgarh NP | – | 1 | 6 | MM |
| | Sirauli NP | 2 | 6 | 7 | NMW |
| | Shahi NP | 1 | 1 | 7 | MM |
| | Fatehganj West | 10 | 2 | 10 | MM |
| | Mirganj NP | 9 | 1 | 8 | NMM |
| | Sonthal NP | – | 1 | 14 | MM |
| | Dhaura Tanda NP | 1 | 3 | 5 | MM |
| | Rithaura NP | 11 | 7 | – | NMW |
| | Tiria Nijavat Khan NP | – | 1 | 12 | MM |
| | Fatehganj East NP | 5 | 5 | – | Kishwari Begum (55) |
| | Shergarh NP | 5 | 4 | 10 | NMM |
| | Richa NP | – | 1 | 3 | MM |
| 16. Philibit | Bisalpur NPP | 8 | 3 | 4 | NMM |
| | Puranpur NPP | 5 | 1 | 4 | NMM |
| | Barkheda NP | 7 | 1 | 2 | MM |
| 17. Shahjahanpur | Tilhar NPP | 5 | 1 | 8 | MM |
| | Jalalabad NPP | 14 | 2 | 3 | NMM |
| | Allahganj NP | 11 | 1 | 2 | NMW |
| | Khudaganj NP | 8 | 1 | – | NMW |
| | Katra NP | 8 | 1 | 7 | NMM |
| | Khutar NP | 14 | 2 | – | NMW |
| 18. Budaun | Kakrala NPP | 1 | 3 | 4 | MM |
| | Bisauli NPP | 8 | 1 | 2 | MM |
| | Uzhani NPP | 5 | 4 | – | NMW |
| | Sahaswan NPP | 2 | 3 | 9 | MM |
| | Budaun NPP | 10 | 1 | 1 | NMM |
| | Kachchla NP | 4 | 1 | – | NMW |
| | Sakhanu NP | – | 4 | – | Muvina Khatun (48) |
| | Islam Nagar NP | 3 | 1 | 4 | NMM |
| | Bazirganj NP | 5 | 1 | 2 | MM |
| | Faujganj NP | 5 | 4 | – | NMW |
| 19. Aligarh | Aligarh Nagar Nigam | 3 | 6 | – | NMW |
| | Atrauli NPP | 8 | 2 | – | Sajda Begum (40) |
| | Charra NP | 5 | 1 | 1 | Rahiso Jawani Khan (65) |
| | Kauriaganj NP | 5 | 1 | 2 | MM |
| | Pilkhana NP | 9 | 1 | – | Habib Jahan (66) |
| 20. Hathras | Sikandara Rao NPP | 4 | 8 | – | Fanus Begum (42) |
| | Shadabad NP | 13 | 4 | – | Rihana Fajuddin (45) |
| | Mursan NP | 11 | 1 | 2 | NMM |
| | Hasayan NP | 7 | 1 | 1 | NMM |
| 21. Mathura | Mathura NPP | 6 | 1 | – | NMW |
| | Farah NP | 3 | 1 | 2 | NMM |
| 22. Agra | Fatehpur Sikri NPP | 4 | 2 | 4 | MM |
| | Shamshabad NPP | 3 | 1 | 1 | NMW |

(*Contd.*)

| | Distt. | NPP/NP/NN | Total no. of contestants | | | Elected |
|---|---|---|---|---|---|---|
| | | | NM M&NMW | MW | MM | |
| 23. | Firozabad | Shikohabad NPP | 14 | 1 | 4 | NMM |
| 24. | Mainpuri | Kurawali NP | 10 | 1 | 5 | NMM |
| | | Karhal NP | 12 | 1 | 6 | NMM |
| | | Bhogaon NP | 11 | 5 | – | Nasreen Bano (36) |
| 25. | Etah | Nil | – | – | – | – |
| 26. | Kasganj | Ganj Dundwara NPP | 4 | 3 | – | Najma Begum (54) |
| | | Bhargain NP | – | 2 | 10 | MM |
| | | Sidpura NP | 9 | 1 | 3 | NMW |
| | | Sahawar NP | 2 | 2 | 5 | MM |
| | | Bilram NP | 6 | 6 | – | NMW |
| 27. | Farukkabad | Kayamganj NPP | 7 | 1 | – | NMW |
| | | Farukkabad NPP | 12 | 5 | – | NMW |
| 28. | Kannauj | Kannauj NPP | 5 | 5 | – | NMW |
| | | Chhibarmau NPP | 5 | 5 | – | NMW |
| | | Gurusahay Ganj NPP | 10 | 5 | – | NMW |
| | | Talgram NP | 7 | 1 | 3 | NMM |
| | | Saurikh NP | 8 | 2 | 5 | NMW |
| | | Tirwaganj NP | 10 | 1 | 2 | NMW |
| | | Samghan NP | – | 4 | 14 | MM |
| 29. | Etawah | Etawah NPP | 7 | 1 | 3 | NMM |
| | | Jaswant Nagar NPP | 7 | 4 | – | NMW |
| | | Bakedar NP | 9 | 3 | – | NMW |
| | | Lakhna NP | 10 | 1 | 1 | NMM |
| 30. | Aurraiya | Dibiyapur NP | 13 | 1 | – | NMW |
| | | Fafud NP | 9 | 4 | – | Hashmi Begum (38) |
| | | Aatsu NP | 11 | 1 | – | NMW |
| | | Bidhuna NP | 15 | 3 | – | NMW |
| 31. | Kanpur ® | Pukhraya NPP | 9 | 2 | – | NMW |
| | | Amraundha NP | 4 | 2 | 8 | MM |
| | | Sikandara NP | 13 | 2 | 2 | MM |
| | | Akbarpur NP | 14 | 5 | , | NMW |
| | | Rasoolabad NP | 4 | 2 | – | NMW |
| | | Derapur NP | 6 | 5 | – | NMW |
| 32. | Jalaun | Konch NPP | 10 | 5 | – | NMW |
| 33. | Lalitpur | – | – | – | – | – |
| 34. | Jhansi | Chirgaon NPP | 9 | 1 | – | NMW |
| 35. | Mahoba | Charkhari NPP | 13 | 3 | – | Ruksana Moinuddin (49) |
| | | Kabarai NP | 11 | 3 | – | NMW |
| 36. | Hamirpur | Hamirpur NPP | 17 | 2 | – | NMW |
| | | Maudaha NPP | 12 | 11 | – | NMW |
| 37. | Banda | Banda NPP | 19 | 3 | – | NMW |
| | | Naraini NP | 13 | 2 | – | NMW |
| | | Disanda NP | 20 | 4 | – | NMW |

*(Contd.)*

| | Distt. | NPP/NP/NN | Total no. of contestants | | | Elected |
|---|---|---|---|---|---|---|
| | | | NM M&NMW | MW | MM | |
| 38. | Chitrakoot | Chitrakoot Karvi NPP | 12 | 2 | – | NMW |
| 39. | Fatehpur | Fatehpur | 8 | 2 | 4 | NMM |
| | | Bindki NPP | 6 | 2 | – | NMW |
| | | Khaga NP | 14 | 3 | – | NMW |
| | | Bahua NP | 7 | 5 | – | NMW |
| | | Koda Jehanabad NP | 3 | 1 | – | Shahin Hasan (58) |
| | | Hathgam NP | 8 | 1 | 3 | NMM |
| 40. | Kaushambi | Sarai Aakil NP | 5 | 4 | – | NMW |
| | | Manjhanpur NP | 5 | 7 | – | Hashmi Begum (55) |
| | | Ajuba NP | 8 | 2 | – | NMW |
| 41. | Allahabad | Allahabad Nagar Nigam | 24 | 5 | – | NMW |
| | | Lal Gopal Ganj NP | 8 | 11 | – | Zulekha Ahmed (40) |
| | | Phulpur NP | 2 | 2 | 2 | Sarbath Jahan (50) |
| | | Shankargarh NP | 19 | 4 | – | NMW |
| | | Korav NP | 9 | 1 | – | NMW |
| | | Handia NP | 4 | 3 | – | Kulsum Ahmed (46) |
| | | Bharatganj NP | 3 | 4 | – | Yasmin Sirajuddin (45) |
| 42. | Pratapgarh | Pratapgarh City NP | 7 | 6 | – | NMW |
| | | Antu NP | 7 | 1 | – | NMW |
| 43. | Unnao | Kursat NP | – | 1 | 2 | Najima Subrati (46) |
| | | Ganj Muradabad NP | 1 | 1 | 2 | MM |
| | | Shafipur NP | 3 | 3 | – | NMW |
| | | Purva NP | 12 | 6 | – | NMW |
| 44. | Hardoi | Bilgram NPP | 7 | 4 | – | NMW |
| | | Mallaba NPP | 12 | 3 | – | NMW |
| | | Sandi NPP | 6 | 3 | – | NMW |
| | | Shahabad NPP | 6 | 1 | 4 | MM |
| | | Pali NP | 3 | 1 | 2 | MM |
| | | Kachouna Pathseni NP | 9 | 2 | – | NMW |
| 45. | Lucknow | Malihabad NP | 2 | 1 | 2 | Asmat Ara Khan (56) |
| | | Nagram NP | 3 | 2 | – | Zeenat Imran (41) |
| 46. | Sitapur | Khairabad NPP | 2 | 1 | 13 | MM |
| | | Sitapur NPP | 11 | 5 | – | NMW |
| | | Hargaon NP | 4 | 4 | 1 | NMW |
| | | Tambour Ahmedabad NP | 37 | 4 | 20 | MM |
| 47. | Lakhimpur Kheri | Muhammadi NPP | 10 | 10 | – | NMW |
| | | Lakhimpur NPP | 16 | 2 | 3 | NMW |
| | | Kheri NP | 3 | 1 | 18 | MM |
| | | Singahi NP | 10 | 2 | – | Afroz Jahan Md– Yusuf (33) |
| | | Mailani NP | 8 | 2 | – | NMW |

(*Contd.*)

| Distt. | NPP/NP/NN | Total no. of contestants | | | Elected |
|---|---|---|---|---|---|
| | | NM M&NMW | MW | MM | |
| | Barbar NP | 9 | 1 | 3 | NMM |
| 48. Bahraich | Nanpara NPP | 5 | 1 | 7 | MM |
| | Jarawal NP | 3 | 1 | 9 | MM |
| 49. Shrawasti | Ikowna NP | 8 | 1 | 3 | NMM |
| 50. Balrampur | Tulsipur NP | 9 | 2 | 4 | MM |
| 51. Gonda | Nawabganj NPP | 5 | 2 | 2 | NMW |
| 52. Barabanki | Nawabganj NPP | 7 | 1 | 4 | NMM |
| | Banki NP | 5 | 5 | – | NMW |
| | Satrikh NP | 4 | 4 | – | Mumtaz Begum (42) |
| | Dariabad NP | 3 | 2 | 7 | MM |
| | Siddaur NP | 3 | 6 | – | Kamrun Nisha (45) |
| | Fatehpur NP | 4 | 1 | 4 | Reshma Mashkur (36) |
| 53. Sultanpur | Sultanpur NPP | 14 | 1 | 5 | NMM |
| | Kadipur NP | 14 | 2 | – | NMW |
| | Dostpur NP | 10 | 8 | – | NMW |
| | Koiripur NP | 5 | 3 | – | Rubina Bano (31) |
| 54. Ambedkar-nagar | Akbarpur NPP | 16 | 1 | 4 | NMM |
| | Ashrafpur KichchouchaNP | 8 | 4 | – | Shabana Khatun (40) |
| 55. Faizabad | Rudauli NPP | – | 1 | 5 | MM |
| | Gosai Ganj NP | 7 | 1 | 3 | NMM |
| | Bikapur NP | 14 | 3 | – | Zulekha Khatun (50) |
| 56. Amethi | Salon NP | 9 | 1 | 8 | MM |
| | Musafirkhana NP | 5 | 1 | – | NMM |
| | Amethi NP | 3 | 3 | 3 | NMW |
| 57. Basti | – | – | – | – | – |
| 58. Siddharthnagar | Siddharthnagar NPP | 16 | 1 | 1 | MM |
| | Bansi NPP | 6 | 2 | – | Chaman Ara Idris (38) |
| | Badhni Bazaar NP | 9 | 2 | – | NMW |
| | Domariyaganj NP | 10 | 5 | – | NMW |
| | Uska Bazaar NP | 17 | 1 | 2 | NMM |
| 59. Sant Kabir Nagar | Maghar NP | 8 | 2 | 5 | NMM |
| | Mehdawal NP | 11 | 1 | 2 | NMM |
| 60. Gorakhpur | Gorakhpur NN Pipraich NP | 7 | 1 | – | NMW |

(MM: Muslim Male; NMW: Non-Muslim Woman; NMM: Non-Muslim Male; MW: Muslim woman)

*Source:* (http://sec.up.nic.in) No Muslim woman was elected/contested for Kanpur Nagar Nigam.

**Table 4.32:** Age Profile of Successful Muslim Women in the PRI Elections of Uttar Pradesh, 2012

| *Sl. No.* | *District* | *Total number of winners* | *Age profile (in Years)* | | |
|---|---|---|---|---|---|
| | | | *Up to 30* | *Above 30 and up to 50* | *Above 50* |
| 1. | Agra | 11 | 6 | 3 | 2 |
| 2. | Aligarh | 28 | 2 | 23 | 3 |
| 3. | Allahabad | 28 | 9 | 18 | 1 |
| 4. | Ambedkar Nagar | 20 | 3 | 17 | — |
| 5. | Amethi | 15 | 3 | 10 | 2 |
| 6. | Amroha | 30 | 4 | 22 | 4 |
| 7. | Aurraiya | 6 | 3 | 3 | — |
| 8. | Azamgarh | 27 | 5 | 18 | 4 |
| 9. | Badaun | 47 | 15 | 27 | 5 |
| 10. | Baghpat | 7 | 2 | 5 | — |
| 11. | Bahraich | 20 | 11 | 6 | 3 |
| 12. | Ballia | 7 | 1 | 5 | 1 |
| 13. | Balrampur | 16 | 5 | 9 | 2 |
| 14. | Banda | 5 | 1 | 3 | 1 |
| 15. | Barabanki | 27 | 7 | 14 | 6 |
| 16. | Bareilly | 70 | 20 | 43 | 7 |
| 17. | Basti | 3 | — | 2 | 1 |
| 18. | Bijnor | 93 | 28 | 55 | 10 |
| 19. | Bulandshahar | 38 | 7 | 27 | 4 |
| 20. | Chandauli | 4 | 1 | 3 | — |
| 21. | Chitrakoot | 1 | — | 1 | — |
| 22. | Deoria | 9 | 3 | 6 | — |
| 23. | Etah | 14 | 1 | 10 | 3 |
| 24. | Faizabad | 10 | 2 | 7 | 1 |
| 25. | Farukkabad | 10 | 2 | 7 | 1 |
| 26. | Fatehpur | 14 | 9 | 2 | 3 |
| 27. | Firozabad | 5 | 1 | 2 | 2 |
| 28. | Gautam Budh Nagar | 11 | 4 | 7 | — |
| 29. | Ghaziabad | 12 | 6 | 6 | — |
| 30. | Ghazipur | 15 | 3 | 11 | 1 |
| 31. | Gonda | 19 | 1 | 12 | 6 |
| 32. | Gorakhpur | 8 | 1 | 6 | 1 |
| 33. | Hamirpur | 8 | 3 | 3 | 2 |
| 34. | Hapur | 10 | 2 | 8 | — |
| 35. | Hardoi | 40 | 10 | 23 | 7 |
| 36. | Hathras | 11 | 1 | 8 | 2 |
| 37. | Itawah | 2 | — | 2 | — |
| 38. | Jalaun | 15 | 3 | 11 | 1 |
| 39. | Jaunpur | 13 | 4 | 7 | 2 |
| 40. | Jhansi | 2 | 2 | — | — |
| 41. | Kannoj | 19 | 5 | 12 | 2 |
| 42. | Kanpur City | 13 | 3 | 8 | 2 |
| 43. | Kanpur Rural | 10 | 4 | 4 | 2 |
| 44. | Kasganj | 29 | 7 | 14 | 8 |

(*Contd.*)

| Sl. No. | District | Total number of winners | Age profile (in Years) | | |
|---|---|---|---|---|---|
| | | | Up to 30 | Above 30 and up to 50 | Above 50 |
| 45. | Kaushambi | 5 | 1 | 3 | 1 |
| 46. | Kushinagar | 9 | 1 | 6 | 2 |
| 47. | Lakhimpur Keri | 20 | 5 | 14 | 1 |
| 48. | Lalitpur | 4 | — | 4 | — |
| 49. | Lucknow | 19 | 3 | 13 | 3 |
| 50. | Maharajganj | 6 | 2 | 3 | 1 |
| 51. | Mahoba | 3 | — | 3 | — |
| 52. | Mainpuri | 9 | 1 | 7 | 1 |
| 53. | Mathura | 10 | 1 | 8 | 1 |
| 54. | Mau | 24 | 8 | 13 | 3 |
| 55. | Meerut | 32 | 10 | 21 | 1 |
| 56. | Mirzapur | 3 | — | 1 | 2 |
| 57. | Moradabad | 39 | 7 | 24 | 8 |
| 58. | Muzaffarnagar | 32 | 10 | 20 | 2 |
| 59. | Philibit | 19 | 6 | 12 | 1 |
| 60. | Pratapgarh | 12 | 1 | 10 | 1 |
| 61. | Rae Bareilly | 7 | — | 6 | 1 |
| 62. | Rampur | 42 | 11 | 19 | 7* |
| 63. | Saharanpur | 35 | 12 | 20 | 3 |
| 64. | Sambhal | 22 | 6 | 14 | 2 |
| 65. | Sant Kabir Nagar | 5 | 4 | 1 | — |
| 66. | Sant Ravidas Nagar | 11 | 3 | 4 | 4 |
| 67. | Shahjahanpur | 17 | 5 | 10 | 2 |
| 68. | Shamli | 27 | 3 | 20 | 4 |
| 69. | Shrawasti | 5 | 1 | 4 | — |
| 70. | Siddharth Nagar | 13 | 2 | 7 | 4 |
| 71. | Sitapur | 34 | 7 | 22 | 5 |
| 72. | Sonbhadra | 2 | — | — | 2 |
| 73. | Sultanpur | 8 | 1 | 5 | 2 |
| 74. | Unnao | 25 | 7 | 12 | 6 |
| 75. | Varanasi | 10 | 4 | 4 | 2 |
| | **Total** | **1,311** | **332** | **800** | **174*** |

(*) In Rampur district, the ages of 5 Muslim women candidates who won the Elections to the Kaimiri Nagar Panchayat are not known as the State Election Commission's data does not provide this information.

*Source:* State Election Commission, Uttar Pradesh.

the behaviour of Muslim women, our analysis of the age profile of the winning Muslim candidates in the 2012 elections to the PRIs and ULB in Uttar Pradesh throws up the same pattern.

It will be seen from the above data that while the women contestants above the age of 50 years constitute only 13.76 per cent of the total contestants, those in the middle-age group (above 30 and up to 50 years of age) constitute 61.04 per cent of all the contestants. The younger women (up to 30 years of age) make the remaining (25.20%). Thus, while the older women are not very keen to offer themselves as candidates and the younger Muslim women seem to be considered too young to seek an elected office, it is the middle-age group women who have shown the courage to enter the poll-fray.

It is also interesting to see that a number of Muslim women have been unanimously elected, reflecting the popularity that they command in the constituency on account of their social service in the community. The following Table 4.33 are examples of some such women:

**Table 4.33:** Unanimously Elected Muslim Women

| *Name (age)* | *Ward* | *NP/NPP//NN* | *District* |
|---|---|---|---|
| Rabiya Khatun (41) | Ashraf Tola | Sandila NPP | Hardoi |
| Meena Ilyas (53) | Jawahar nagar | Elan NP | Shamli |
| Sabiha Anjum (35) | Sayeed | Kakrala NPP | Badaun |
| Mir Jahan (52) | Ganj Shahida-S | Agnani NPP | Badaun |
| Afroz Jahan (27) | Bank Road | Mudiya NP | Badaun |
| Mala Ishtiaque Ahmed (38) | Pure Achaee | Phulpur NP | Allahabad |
| Shakeela Parvin (51) | West Thok | Dundwara NPP | Kasganj |
| Nazmi Begum (41) | Afzal Thok | Mohanpur NP | Kasganj |
| Aasia Begum (39) | Irda Thok | Mohanpur NP | Kasganj |
| Chhoti Umar (53) | Toli | Dhaura Tanda | Bareilly |

*Source:* State Election Commission Statistical Report, Uttar Pradesh.

Though the number of Muslim women contesting and winning the elections in the below 30 years age group is less compared to the 30-50 years group, a majority of them have just gained their eligibility to vote and contest elections; some of them as young as 21 years of age. If their number is not more, it is perhaps due to families discouraging them over their lack of worldly experience. On the other hand, most women above 50 years of age would have lost their interest in politics and the few that have contested successfully owe it to their popularity in the community, comprising both Hindu and Muslim voters. A majority of the women elected fall in the middle age category i.e., above 30 years and up to 50 years of age. These women have the necessary worldly knowledge, experience and courage to ignore comments that discourage them from contesting.

Analysing the age profile of female Congresswomen in the United States, Kate Dittmar writes:[59]

> "Children and families are not the sole source of delay for women. Women's motivations for office are more likely to emerge from issue involvement over time rather than long-term desire to hold office, which is more common among men. Moreover, women continue to need greater encouragement to run for office, and often feel the need to gather greater experience and/or training than their male peers. Regardless of the causes for delay, women's later entry into office at both the State legislature and congressional levels can have real implications for women's institutional power, political advancement and ambition and/or ability to seek higher office."

While the apprehensions of the young Muslim women in entering politics could be understood, with age and maturity, Muslim women have understood that if they do not take the initiative, they would remain uncared for. We have already cited the reasons adduced by Professor Abdul Aziz, formerly Head of the Department of Economics at the Institute of Social and Economic Change, Bangalore, who is one of the framers of the Karnataka Panchayati Raj Act, in the Karnataka chapter.

Most of the winning women have contested as independents, i.e. without the support or backing of any political party. While the regional parties like the Bahujan Samaj Party and the Samajwadi Party were nowhere in the picture, some of the Muslim women have contested under the banner of the Nationalist Congress Party of Sharad Pawar. A few women have chosen to contest under the banner of Bharatiya Janata Party also.

A list showing the district-wise participation of Muslim women in the elections from each of the 75 districts is annexed. However, Table 4.34 gives an idea of the enthusiastic participation of Muslim women from some of the districts.

It will be seen that the average success rate is about 26 per cent, which is not bad compared to the success rate in the Assembly elections. What is surprising is that in a community in which patriarchy and conservatism rules, Muslim women have dared to contest against all-male opponents in several constituencies and won. There are also instances where Muslim women have been elected unopposed. A few examples (Table 4.35).

**Table 4.34:** District-wise Participation of Muslim Women

| District | Muslim women | | Percentage of success |
|---|---|---|---|
| | Total number of contestants | Number of women elected | |
| Aligarh | 140 | 28 | 20.00 |
| Allahabad | 162 | 28 | 17.28 |
| Ambedkar Nagar | 64 | 20 | 31.25 |
| Amroha | 133 | 30 | 22.56 |
| Azamgarh | 87 | 27 | 31.03 |
| Badaun | 154 | 47 | 30.52 |
| Bahraich | 73 | 20 | 27.40 |
| Bareilly | 339 | 70 | 20.65 |
| Bijnor | 341 | 93 | 27.27 |
| Bulandshahar | 124 | 38 | 30.65 |
| Kasganj | 48 | 29 | 60.42 |
| Lucknow | 122 | 19 | 15.57 |
| Mau | 91 | 24 | 26.37 |
| Meerut | 197 | 32 | 16.24 |
| Moradabad | 167 | 39 | 29.35 |
| Muzaffarnagar | 169 | 32 | 18.93 |
| Rampur | 243 | 42 | 17.28 |
| Saharanpur | 147 | 35 | 23.81 |
| Sitapur | 135 | 34 | 25.18 |

*Source:* State Election Commission Statistical Report.

**Table 4.35:** District-wise NP/NPP, Ward, Name of Candidate unopposed

| District | Nagar Panchayat (NP)/Nagar Palika Parishad (NPP) | Ward | Name of candidate elected unopposed and age |
|---|---|---|---|
| Fatehpur | Kishunpur NP | West Katikhana | Shabana Begum (31) |
| Shamli | Elan NP | Jawahar Nagar | Meena Ilyas (53) |
| Allahabad | Nagar Nigam | Phulpur | Mala Ishtiaque Ahmed (38) |
| Bijnor | Chandpur NPP | Shah Chandan-N | Farzana (39) |
| Badaun | Agnani NPP | Ganj Shahida-S | Mir Jahan (52) |
| Kasganj | Sandila NPP | Ashraf Tola | Rabiya Khatun (41) |
| Kasganj | Dundwara NPP | West Thok | Shakeela Parvin (51) |
| Kasganj | Bhargain NP | Afzal Thok | Nazimi Begum (41) |
| Kasganj | Bhargain NP | Irda Thok | Asia Begum (39) |

*Source:* State Election Commission Statistical Report.

Entering the Gram Panchayat as a Member is a stepping stone to one's political life. As a member of the Village Panchayat or Nagar Palika Parishad or Nagar Nigam, the women will get to know and acquire knowledge of the rules and regulations, fundamentals of planning, administration and execution of schemes for the benefit of the society. Not content with membership of the PRI, Muslim women have also contested for the post of Mayor and Presidents of the institutions. Though no Muslim woman was elected Mayor of any of the 12 Corporations during 2012 elections, 14 Muslim women were elected as Presidents of Nagar Palika Parishads and 32 Muslim women were elected Presidents of Nagar Panchayats.

The above achievement may not be much. But, if it is remembered that Muslim women have to operate within a number of constraints, theirs is no mean achievement. Madhu Kishwar writes:[60]

> "A key component of politics is the art of building alliances. In a culture where even formal interaction with men unconnected to one's own family is frowned upon, women are severely handicapped in politics because they cannot cultivate close association with men without jeopardising their position in the family. A woman operating on her own strength in a party filled with corrupt politicians who think nothing of slandering their own women colleagues would find the going very tough, even if she can somehow mobilise other compensatory resources by her own special efforts. The fact that politics is dominated by the most unsavoury kind of men makes most women themselves reluctant to break taboos regarding free intermixing with men. A woman risks her reputation by even being seen with many of them, whereas a man does not have to prove his credentials by such fierce avoidance".

With the male politicians, including Muslim politicians, oblivious to the problems of the Muslim women, the presence of Muslim women in the Assembly in adequate numbers will have a salutary effect on the community. For, as we have already pointed out, a woman's outlook towards the societal needs differs from a man. Unlike in the first few elections, more-and-more Muslim women have started exercising their franchise, thereby participating in the political process; their right as citizens. But, it is still difficult for a woman, more so for a Muslim woman, to enter politics under the existing circumstances. We may quote Baijayant (Jay) Panda, Member of Parliament (Kendrapada, Orissa), who told a young woman who sought his advice as to how she could join a political party and make a career in politics: "Really, I do not know what to advise you. The time is yet not come. We need lot of level playing field; we need reforms in politics, to enable large number of women like you to join political parties as career politicians like any other profession."[61] Panda's advice sums up the situation.

## NOTES & REFERENCES


1. *Government of Uttar Pradesh*, Statistical Department, Lucknow, Provisional Data, 2011. (Available at http://upgov.nic.in/upstateglance.aspx)
2. *Government of India*, Ministry of Human Resource Development, National Policy on Education, 1986, Programme of Action, 1992, New Delhi, Section: 3.1.4, p. 9.
3. *Government of India*, Sachar Committee, 2006, pp. 50-51.
4. Quoted by Visalakshi Menon, (2003) in *Indian Women and Nationalism: The UP Story*, New Delhi: Har-Anand Publications Pvt., Ltd., p. 29.
5. *Ibid.*
6. *Islamic Society*, Aharaura, District Mirzapur, Uttar Pradesh. (Available at http://www.islamicsociety.org.in/focus.htm)
7. Siddiqui, Farasat Ali, Nazmul Hussain and Akram Hannan, (2011), Literacy and work participation among Muslims in Uttar Pradesh, *Journal of Geography and Regional Planning,* Vol. 4(6), pp. 305-325, June 2011 (Available online at http://www.academicjournals.org/JGRP).
8. Sheikh, Mehraj Ud Din and Qamar Jahan. (2013), Literacy Rate of Muslim Women in Uttar Pradesh (India), in *Educationia Confab*, Vol. 2, No. 4, April 2013 (Available at http://www.confabjournals.com/confabjournals/images/652013817437.pdf).
9. Khan, Azim A. (2011), Socio-economic Status of Muslims in Western UP in *The India Economy Review*, 30 May. (Available at http://www.theindiaeconomyreview.org/Article.aspx?aid=102&mid=5)
10. Co-education will distract Muslim girls: Panel. Reported in Rediff.com, December 9, 2007. (Available at http://www.rediff.com/news/report/coed/20071209.htm)
11. UP Madrasah Board bans co-ed. in its institutions, in *IBNLive.com. (*Available at http://ibnlive.in.com/news/up-madrasa-board-bans-coed-in-its-institutes/84221-3.html).
12. Siddiqui, Farasat Ali, *op. cit.*
13. *Ibid.*
14. *Situation of Muslim Women and Girls.* (Available at http://ncw.nic.in/pdfReports/Gender%20Profile-Uttar%20Pradesh.pdf)
15. Siddhiqui, Farasat Ali, *op. cit.*
16. *Ibid.*
17. Samiuddin, Abida and Rashida Khanam. (Eds.) (2002), *Muslim Feminism and Feminist Movement: India,* New Delhi: Global Vision Publishing House, pp. 47-73.

18. *Ibid.*
19. *Ibid.*
20. *Ibid.*
21. Visalakshi Menon, *op. cit.*
22. Iftekhar, Pumma (1998), *Muslim Women and their Participation in Public Life: A Case Study of UP*, Doctoral Thesis submitted to Jamia Millia Islamia. February.
23. Samiuddin, Abide and Rashid Khanam, *op. cit.*
24. Fehmi, Sheeba Aslam, 2011 in an interview with Yoginder Sikand, in *Countercurrents.org* 11 April, (Available at http://indiaminorities.wordpress.com/tag/women/) Sheeba Aslam Fehmi is one of Islamic feminist writer and Journalist in India and one of the few Indian Muslim women scholars who writes on Islam.
25. Poor representation of women in UP assembly, in *Outlookindia.com*, January 11, 2012. Laljhadi won as an independent candidate from Gauri Bazar in 1989 and Manju, won from Ballia seat in 1996.
26. Mayawati (BSP), Uma Bharati (BJP), and Rita Bahuguna Joshi, Congress.
27. Parveen, Shaista. *Political and Social Status of Muslim Women in Western Uttar Pradesh: A Case Study of Saharanpur and Muzaffarnagar Districts,* Aligarh Muslim University. (Available at http://jmi.ac.in/upload/Research/ab2012_polsc_shaista.pdf)
28. *Ibid.*
29. Chauhan, Chetan. Indian Muslim women to be politically empowered, September 29, 2008.(Available at http://southasia.oneworld.net/news/indian-muslim-women-to-be-politically-empowered#.UckwZevrbZ4). On the recommendations of the Sachar Committee, a scheme for empowerment of women was conceived on January 27, 2010 by the Ministry of Women and Child Development. Later the scheme was transferred to the Ministry of Minority Affairs. For 2 years nothing was done under the scheme. The Minority Welfare Ministry revived project to train at least 40,000 women from the minority communities to develop leadership qualities in them. Uttar Pradesh's 20-odd districts having considerable Muslim population were to be the beneficiaries. A sum of Rs. 8 crore was released in 2009-10 and another Rs. 15 crore in 2010-11. The money, however, had not been put to use. The government now proposes to utilize the amount and implement the scheme in Badaun, Bahraich, Balrampur, Barabanki, Bareilly, Bijnor, Bulandshahar, Ghaziabad, JP Nagar, Lucknow, Meerut, Moradabad, Muzaffarnagar, Philibit, Rampur, Saharanpur, Sant Kabir Nagar, Shrawasti, Siddharthnagar and Baghpat districts of Uttar Pradesh.
    Neha Shukla, *Times News Network*, January 6, 2013. (Available at http://articles.timesofindia.indiatimes.com/2013-01-06/lucknow/36173792_1_minority-women-muslim-women-sachar-committee)
30. Born on September 5, 1905 in an educated and a comparatively liberal Muslim family in Etah, Begum Safia Abdul Wajjid had graduated from Isabella Thowborne College and post-graduated from Allahabad University.

She joined the Indian National Congress, which provided her the opportunity of voicing her opinions at a political level. In 1942, Begum Safia had taken active part in the Quit India Movement because of which she had to lose a lucrative and prestigious job of a lecturer in a government college. After independence, she continued to work for the emancipation of the masses. She was elected to the Uttar Pradesh assembly twice—in 1952 (Bareilly East). Thereafter, she took-up social work, but refrained from taking part in active politics.

31. *Muslims in Indian Cities: Trajectories of Marginalisation* (Eds.) Laurent Gayer and Christophe Jaffrelot, C. Hurst & Co. (Publishers) Limited (2012) London, p. 5).
32. Gupta, Dipankar (2012). Uttar Pradesh polls: Men smart, but women smarter, in *Mail Today*, March 16, (Available at http://indiatoday.intoday.in/story/uttar-pradesh-polls-men-smart-but-women-smarter/1/177991.html).
33. *Ibid.*
34. *Ibid.*
35. *Ibid.*
36. *Ibid.*
37. On line. (Available athttp://articles.timesofindia.indiatimes.com/2012-02-04/lucknow/31024198_1_muslim-women-cast-vote-women-members)
38. Kazmi, Insia (2012), UP polls: Muslim women 'cast' their mark, in *Times of India*, 7 February (Available at http://articles.timesofindia.indiatimes.com/2012-02-07/india/31033731_1_muslim-women-muslim-votes-first-time-voter)
39. *Ibid.*
40. *Muslim Women Campaign for India Elections*, 4 February, 2012. (Available at http://www.onislam.net/english/news/asia-pacific/455659-muslim-women-campaign-for-india-elections.html)
41. Raj Kumari Chauhan was the wife of State Minister Jaiveer Singh; Seema Upadhyay (Fatehpur Sikri), the spouse of Ramveer Upadhyay a Minister in Mayawati government, Tabassum Begum, the widow of a powerful Muslim BSP MP and Kaiser Jahan (Sitapur) is the wife of Sitapur's Former BSP MLA.
42. Puri, Anjali. Your MP... Mrs. MLA, in *Outlook*, June 8, 2009. (Available at http://www.outlookindia.com/article.aspx?240649)
43. Shahi Imam of Jama Masjid severs relations with SP for cheating Muslims. In *DNA*, Lucknow, 16 March, 2013.
44. Indo Asian News Service (Available at http://newshopper.sulekha.com/grand-mufti-urges-muslim-women-to-enter-politics_news_1155510.htm)
45. Mohsina Kidwai was later elected to the Seventh and Eighth Lok Sabha. She held different portfolios in the Ministries of Labour and Rehabilitation, Health and Family Welfare, Rural Development, Transport, Urban Development, and Tourism. She was later elected to Rajya Sabha in July 2004.

46. Singh, Pritam (2003), *Women Legislators in Indian Politics*, New Delhi: Concept Publishing Co.
47. Mazumdar, Mumtaz (2011), *Muslim Women Amidst Decentralization and Rural Development* in India, eEssay, Assam University. (Available athttp://www.grin.com/en/e-book/176808/muslim-women-admist-decentralisation-and-rural-development-in-india)
48. Madhok, Alka, (2002), Panchayati Raj: Participation of Muslim Women, in (Ed.) Hajira Kumar, *Status of Muslim women in India* (Ed.) Sarojini Naidu Centre for women's studies, Jamia Millia Islamia, Delhi: Aakar Books, p. 78.
49. Muslim Women Demand 33 per cent Women's Reservation, 16 April, 2010, in *Pragati*, (Available at http://www.pragoti.in/node/3889)
50. Madhok, Alka, *op. cit.*, p. 78.
51. Bhura, Nazreena, Editor, *Deccan Chronicle (*Chennai edition), Paper presented at the Educational Conference of the Ambur Muslim Education Society's Centenary Celebrations, Ambur, Tamilnadu on September 6, 2006. Reported in *MilliGazette* Online, 24 September, 2006. (Available at http://www.irfi.org/articles/article_651_700/empowerment_of_the_indian_muslim.htm)
52. Ahamed, Ishtiaque. Plight of Muslim women, in *Hindustan Times*. (Available at http://www.sundaytimes.lk/980322/plus8.html)
53. Ferial Ashraf, widow of Mohammad Ashraf, leader of Sri Lanka Muslim Congress, in an interview. She is the first Muslim woman to become a cabinet minister in Sri Lanka and holds the Department of Reconstruction of East and Rural Development. (Available at http://www.milligazette.com/Archives/01032001/inter.htm)
54. Liberated From The Veil, in *Outlook India*, December 20, 1995. (Available at http://www.outlookindia.com/article.aspx?200445)
55. *Ibid.*
56. Zeenat Naaz owed her success to her husband, Mohammad Ershad. A small businessman, he nursed hopes of entering public life, but abdicated his ambitions in favour of his wife saying that "she is more capable than I am." For months she resisted his plea that she abandons her burkha, which he saw as an impediment to a political career. "I obeyed him, but you can imagine my embarrassment as I stood on the dais, face uncovered, before thousands of people. I had been veiled since puberty," said Zeenat. In spite of her emancipation from the *hijab* she remained deeply religious. She rationalises her defiance of the *fatwa* by saying that it was politically inspired. People appreciated Zeenat Naaz saying that, after all, she dropped her veil in a good cause."
57. Rahman, Ubaidur Syed. UP municipal elections and Muslims in *Milli Gazette*. (Available at http://www.milligazette.com/Archives/15-12-2000/Art1.htm)
58. Gochhayat, Artatrana, (2013), Political Participation of women in Gram Panchayat elections in Odisha: A case study of Hindol block in Dhenkanal

district, *Journal of Humanities and Social Science Invention*, Vol. 2, Issue 2, February, pp. 38-46.

59. Dittmar, Kelly (2013), *What is the Hold up? Women's delayed entry into political office,* Centre for American Women and Politics, Rutgers, January 8, (Available at http://cawp.rutgers.edu/foornotes/whats-the-hold-up-womens-delayed-entry-into-political-office
60. Kishwar, Madhu. Women's marginal role in politics, in *Manushi*. (Available at http://www.manushi-india.org/pdfs_issues/PDF%20files%2097/women's_marginal_role_in_politics.pdf)
61. New Age Women seek larger space in politics, in *Uday India* Weekly (Delhi) September 2012. (Available at http://www.udayindia.in/english/content_8septmbert2012/special-report.html)

## Annexure

### *Details of Candidates Contesting for Membership in the Local Body Elections, 2012, Uttar Pradesh*

(MM: Muslim Male; MW: Muslim Woman; NMM: Non-Muslim Male; NMW: Non-Muslim Woman)

| *Distt.* | *NPP/NP/Nagar Nigam* | *Total no. of contestants* | | | *Elected* |
|---|---|---|---|---|---|
| | | *NM M NMW* | *MW* | *MM* | |
| Saharanpur | Deoband NPP | 3 | 2 | 7 | MM |
| | Gangoh NPP | 2 | 1 | 3 | MM |
| | Sarsawah NPP | 5 | 3 | – | Nafisa W Ahmed (38) |
| | Sultanpur Chilkhana NP | 1 | 2 | – | Surayya J Hussain (55) |
| | Teetaro NP | 6 | 1 | – | NMW |
| | Rampur Maniharan NP | 10 | 9 | – | NMW |
| Muzaffarnagar | Muzaffarnagar NPP | 10 | 1 | 5 | NMM |
| | Khatauli NPP | 9 | 2 | 14 | NMM |
| | Shahpur NP | 10 | 1 | 4 | MM |
| | Purkhaji NP | 5 | 4 | – | Shahida Naseem (57) |
| | Jansath NP | 11 | 2 | 8 | NMM |
| | Charthawal NP | 7 | 5 | – | NMW |
| | Budhana NP | 7 | 1 | 5 | NMM |
| Shamli | Kandhla NPP | 5 | 1 | 6 | MM |
| | Kairana NPP | 2 | 5 | 22 | MM |
| | Jalalabad NP | 1 | 2 | 5 | Rama Ashraf (35) |
| | Banat NP | 9 | 5 | – | NMW |
| Meerut | Sarghana NPP | 6 | 2 | 10 | MM |
| | Mawana NPP | 5 | 5 | –, | NMW |
| | Parikshitgarh NP | 9 | 2 | – | NMW |
| | Lawad NP | 4 | 1 | 9 | MM |
| | Hastinapur NP | 10 | 1 | – | NMW |
| | Kharkauda NP | 5 | 1 | 1 | NMW |
| | Falwada NP | – | 5 | – | Ayesha Khatun (50) |
| | Kithaur NP | – | 1 | 5 | MM |
| Baghpat | Badhauth NPP | 17 | 1 | 5 | NMM |
| | Teekri NP | 19 | 2 | – | NMW |
| Ghaziabad | Murad Nagar NPP | 3 | 6 | – | NMW |
| | Loni NPP | 12 | 1 | 13 | NMM |
| | Faridnagar NP | 4 | 7 | – | Nazma Nasir (45) |
| | Dasna NP | 1 | 1 | 14 | MM |
| G–B– Nagar | Dadri NPP | 3 | 5 | – | NMW |

(*Contd.*)

| *Distt.* | *NPP/NP/Nagar Nigam* | *Total no. of contestants* | | | *Elected* |
|---|---|---|---|---|---|
| | | *NM M NMW* | *MW* | *MM* | |
| | Rabupura NP | 5 | 2 | – | NMW |
| | Bilaspur NP | 3 | 3 | – | NMW |
| Bulandshahar | Bulandshahar NPP | 10 | 4 | – | NMW |
| | Jahangirabad NPP | 10 | 5 | – | NMW |
| | Syana NPP | 6 | 7 | – | NMW |
| | Gulawathi NPP | 11 | 7 | – | Nusrat Jahan (41) |
| | Anupshahr NPP | 12 | 2 | – | NMW |
| | Dibai NPP | 11 | 3 | – | NMW |
| | Sikandrabad NPP | 7 | 7 | – | NMW |
| | Pahasu NP | 4 | 3 | – | Zayda I– Qureshi (31) |
| Hapur | Hapur NPP | 13 | 1 | – | NMW |
| Bijnor | Syohara NPP | 2 | 8 | – | Tarannum Malik (36) |
| | Chandpur NPP | 4 | 3 | 15 | Zeenat Parvin (33) |
| | Nurpur NPP | 4 | 1 | 7 | MM |
| | Haldaur NPP | 3 | 3 | – | NMW |
| | Kiratpur NPP | 2 | 17 | – | Rubina Md– Manan 31 |
| | Nazibabad NPP | 4 | 2 | 9 | MM |
| | Nahtaur NPP | 4 | 3 | 16 | MM |
| | Sherkot NPP | 4 | 1 | 9 | MM |
| | Nagina NPP | 4 | 1 | 10 | MM |
| | Jhalu NP | 7 | 2 | – | Kishwar Jahan (36) |
| | Mandawar NP | 1 | 1 | 2 | MM |
| | Jalalabad NP | – | 1 | 7 | MM |
| | Badhapur NP | 6 | 1 | 15 | Khatija M– Rani (60) |
| | Saharpur NP | – | 1 | 10 | MM |
| Amroha | Amroha NPP | 3 | 1 | 17 | MM |
| | Hasanpur NPP | 4 | 2 | 10 | NMM |
| | Dhanowra NPP | 8 | 1 | 7 | NMM |
| | Bachrayu NPP | 3 | 1 | 10 | MM |
| | Joya NP | – | 1 | 6 | MM |
| | Uzhari NP | – | 2 | 1 | Mahjabeen Nafis (70) |
| | Naugawan Sadat NP | – | 2 | 11 | MM |
| Moradabad | Bilari NPP | 6 | 2 | 9 | NMM |
| | Thakurdwar NPP | 7 | 2 | 10 | MM |
| | Umari Kala NP | – | 7 | 14 | Farha Khatun (33) |
| | Kundarki NP | 6 | 7 | 15 | MM |
| | Kanth NP | 8 | 8 | – | Nasreen Bano (30) |
| Rampur | Tanda NPP | – | 1 | 8 | MM |
| | Suar NPP | 1 | 3 | 12 | MM |
| | Milk NPP | 10 | 1 | 5 | NMW |
| | Bilaspur NPP | 7 | 1 | 8 | NMM |
| | Shahabad NP | 2 | 4 | 7 | MM |

*(Contd.)*

| Distt. | NPP/NP/Nagar Nigam | Total no. of contestants | | | Elected |
|---|---|---|---|---|---|
| | | NM M NMW | MW | MM | |
| | Maswasi NP | 7 | 8 | – | NMW |
| | Kaimari NP | 1 | 2 | 6 | MM |
| Sambhal | Bahjoee NPP | 13 | 4 | – | NMW |
| | Sambhal NPP | 2 | 2 | 13 | MM |
| | Chandausi NPP | 4 | 3 | – | NMW |
| | Narauli NPP | 7 | 9 | – | NMW |
| | Gunaur NP | 4 | 1 | 9 | MM |
| Bareilly | Faridpur NPP | 8 | 1 | 9 | NMM |
| | Nawabganj NPP | 9 | 2 | 9 | Shahala Tahir (45) |
| | Awala NPP | 16 | 2 | 10 | MM |
| | Baheri NPP | 1 | 3 | 11 | MM |
| | Faridpur NP | 3 | 1 | 6 | MM |
| | Shishgarh NP | – | 1 | 6 | MM |
| | Sirauli NP | 2 | 6 | 7 | NMW |
| | Shahi NP | 1 | 1 | 7 | MM |
| | Fatehganj West | 10 | 2 | 10 | MM |
| | Mirganj NP | 9 | 1 | 8 | NMM |
| | Sonthal NP | – | 1 | 14 | MM |
| | Dhaura Tanda NP | 1 | 3 | 5 | MM |
| | Rithaura NP | 11 | 7 | – | NMW |
| | Tiria Nijavat Khan NP | – | 1 | 12 | MM |
| | Fatehganj East NP | 5 | 5 | – | Kishwari Begum (55) |
| | Shergarh NP | 5 | 4 | 10 | NMM |
| | Richa NP | – | 1 | 3 | MM |
| Philibit | Bisalpur NPP | 8 | 3 | 4 | NMM |
| | Puranpur NPP | 5 | 1 | 4 | NMM |
| | Barkheda NP | 7 | 1 | 2 | MM |
| Shahjahanpur | Tilhar NPP | 5 | 1 | 8 | MM |
| | Jalalabad NPP | 14 | 2 | 3 | NMM |
| | Allahganj NP | 11 | 1 | 2 | NMW |
| | Khudaganj NP | 8 | 1 | – | NMW |
| | Katra NP | 8 | 1 | 7 | NMM |
| | Khutar NP | 14 | 2 | – | NMW |
| Badaun | Kukrala NPP | 1 | 3 | 4 | MM |
| | Bisauli NPP | 8 | 1 | 2 | MM |
| | Uzhani NPP | 5 | 4 | – | NMW |
| | Sahaswan NPP | 2 | 3 | 9 | MM |
| | Badaun NPP | 10 | 1 | 1 | NMM |
| | Kachchla NP | 4 | 1 | – | NMW |
| | Sakhanu NP | – | 4 | – | Muvina Khatun (48) |
| | Islam Nagar NP | 3 | 1 | 4 | NMM |
| | Bazirganj NP | 5 | 1 | 2 | MM |

(*Contd.*)

| Distt. | NPP/NP/Nagar Nigam | Total no. of contestants | | | Elected |
|---|---|---|---|---|---|
| | | NM M NMW | MW | MM | |
| | Faujganj NP | 5 | 4 | – | NMW |
| Aligarh | Aligarh Nagar Nigam | 3 | 6 | – | NMW |
| | Atrauli NPP | 8 | 2 | – | Sajda Begum (40) |
| | Charra NP | 5 | 1 | 1 | Rahiso J– Khan (65) |
| | Kauriaganj NP | 5 | 1 | 2 | MM |
| | Pilkhana NP | 9 | 1 | – | Habib Jahan (66) |
| Hathras | Sikandara Rao NPP | 4 | 8 | – | Fanus Begum (42) |
| | Shadabad NP | 13 | 4 | – | Rihana Fajuddin (45) |
| | Mursan NP | 11 | 1 | 2 | NMM |
| | Hasayan NP | 7 | 1 | 1 | NMM |
| Mathura | Mathura NPP | 6 | 1 | – | NMW |
| | Farah NP | 3 | 1 | 2 | NMM |
| Agra | Fatehpur Sikri NPP | 4 | 2 | 4 | MM |
| | Shamshabad NPP | 3 | 1 | 1 | NMW |
| Firozabad | Shikohabad NPP | 14 | 1 | 4 | NMM |
| Mainpuri | Kurawali NP | 10 | 1 | 5 | NMM |
| | Karhal NP | 12 | 1 | 6 | NMM |
| | Bhogaon NP | 11 | 5 | – | Nasreen Bano (36) |
| Etah | Nil | – | – | – | – |
| Kasganj | Ganj Dundwara NPP | 4 | 3 | – | Najma Begum (54) |
| | Bhargain NP | – | 2 | 10 | MM |
| | Sidpura NP | 9 | 1 | 3 | NMW |
| | Sahawar NP | 2 | 2 | 5 | MM |
| | Bilram NP | 6 | 6 | – | NMW |
| Farukkabad | Kayamganj NPP | 7 | 1 | – | NMW |
| | Farukkabad NPP | 12 | 5 | – | NMW |
| Kannauj | Kannauj NPP | 5 | 5 | – | NMW |
| | Chhibarmau NPP | 5 | 5 | – | NMW |
| | Gurusahay Ganj NPP | 10 | 5 | – | NMW |
| | Talgram NP | 7 | 1 | 3 | NMM |
| | Saurikh NP | 8 | 2 | 5 | NMW |
| | Tirwaganj NP | 10 | 1 | 2 | NMW |
| | Samghan NP | – | 4 | 14 | MM |
| Etawah | Etawah NPP | 7 | 1 | 3 | NMM |
| | Jaswant Nagar NPP | 7 | 4 | – | NMW |
| | Bakedar NP | 9 | 3 | – | NMW |
| | Lakhna NP | 10 | 1 | 1 | NMM |

(*Contd.*)

| *Distt.* | *NPP/NP/Nagar Nigam* | *Total no. of contestants* | | | *Elected* |
|---|---|---|---|---|---|
| | | *NM M NMW* | *MW* | *MM* | |
| Aurraiya | Dibiyapur NP | 13 | 1 | – | NMW |
| | Fafud NP | 9 | 4 | – | Hashmi Begum (38) |
| | Aatsu NP | 11 | 1 | – | NMW |
| | Bidhuna NP | 15 | 3 | – | NMW |
| Kanpur NN | – | – | – | – | – |
| Kanpur Dehat | Pukhraya NPP | 9 | 2 | – | NMW |
| | Amraundha NP | 4 | 2 | 8 | MM |
| | Sikandara NP | 13 | 2 | 2 | MM |
| | Akbarpur NP | 14 | 5 | , | NMW |
| | Rasoolabad NP | 4 | 2 | – | NMW |
| | Derapur NP | 6 | 5 | – | NMW |
| Jalaun | Konch NPP | 10 | 5 | – | NMW |
| Lalitpur | – | – | – | – | – |
| Jhansi | Chirgaon NPP | 9 | 1 | – | NMW |
| Mahoba | Charkhari NPP | 13 | 3 | – | Ruksana– M (49) |
| | Kabarai NP | 11 | 3 | – | NMW |
| Hamirpur | Hamirpur NPP | 17 | 2 | – | NMW |
| | Maudaha NPP | 12 | 11 | – | NMW |
| Banda | Banda NPP | 19 | 3 | – | NMW |
| | Naraini NP | 13 | 2 | – | NMW |
| | Disanda NP | 20 | 4 | – | NMW |
| Chitrakoot | Chitrakoot Karvi NPP | 12 | 2 | – | NMW |
| Fatehpur | Fatehpur | 8 | 2 | 4 | NMM |
| | Bindki NPP | 6 | 2 | – | NMW |
| | Khaga NP | 14 | 3 | – | NMW |
| | Bahua NP | 7 | 5 | – | NMW |
| | Koda Jehanabad NP | 3 | 1 | – | Shahin Hasan (58) |
| | Hathgam NP | 8 | 1 | 3 | NMM |
| Kaushambi | Sarai Aakil NP | 5 | 4 | – | NMW |
| | Manjhanpur NP | 5 | 7 | – | Hashmi Begum (55) |
| | Ajuba NP | 8 | 2 | – | NMW |
| Allahabad | Allahabad Nagar Nigam | 24 | 5 | – | NMW |
| | Lal Gopal Ganj NP | 8 | 11 | – | Zulekha Ahmed (40) |
| | Phulpur NP | 2 | 2 | 2 | Sarbath Jahan (50) |
| | Shankargarh NP | 19 | 4 | – | NMW |
| | Korav NP | 9 | 1 | – | NMW |

(*Contd.*)

| Distt. | NPP/NP/Nagar Nigam | Total no. of contestants | | | Elected |
|---|---|---|---|---|---|
| | | NM M NMW | MW | MM | |
| | Handia NP | 4 | 3 | – | Kulsum Ahmed (46) |
| | Bharatganj NP | 3 | 4 | – | Yasmin Sirajuddin (45) |
| Pratapgarh | Pratapgarh City NP | 7 | 6 | – | NMW |
| | Antu NP | 7 | 1 | – | NMW |
| Rae Bareilly | Unchahar NP | 4 | 1 | 6 | NMM |
| | Maharajganj NP | 4 | 2 | – | NMW |
| | Dalmau NP | 10 | 1 | – | NMW |
| | Lalganj NP | 18 | 2 | – | NMW |
| Unnao | Kursat NP | – | 1 | 2 | Najima Subrati (46) |
| | Ganj Muradabad NP | 1 | 1 | 2 | MM |
| | Shafipur NP | 3 | 3 | – | NMW |
| | Purva NP | 12 | 6 | – | NMW |
| Hardoi | Bilgram NPP | 7 | 4 | – | NMW |
| | Mallaba NPP | 12 | 3 | – | NMW |
| | Sandi NPP | 6 | 3 | – | NMW |
| | Shahabad NPP | 6 | 1 | 4 | MM |
| | Pali NP | 3 | 1 | 2 | MM |
| | Kachouna Pathseni NP | 9 | 2 | – | NMW |
| Lucknow | Malihabad NP | 2 | 1 | 2 | Asmat Ara Khan (56) |
| | Nagram NP | 3 | 2 | – | Zeenat Imran (41) |
| Sitapur | Khairabad NPP | 2 | 1 | 13 | MM |
| | Sitapur NPP | 11 | 5 | – | NMW |
| | Hargaon NP | 4 | 4 | 1 | NMW |
| | T– Ahmedabad NP | 37 | 4 | 20 | MM |
| Lakhimpur Kheri | Mohammadi NPP | 10 | 10 | – | NMW |
| | Lakhimpur NPP | 16 | 2 | 3 | NMW |
| | Kheri NP | 3 | 1 | 18 | MM |
| | Singahi NP | 10 | 2 | – | Afroz Jahan Md– Y 33 |
| | Mailani NP | 8 | 2 | – | NMW |
| | Barbar NP | 9 | 1 | 3 | NMM |
| Bahraich | Nanpara NPP | 5 | 1 | 7 | MM |
| | Jarawal NP | 3 | 1 | 9 | MM |
| Shrawasti | Ikowna NP | 8 | 1 | 3 | NMM |
| Balrampur | Tulsipur NP | 9 | 2 | 4 | MM |
| Gonda | Nawabganj NPP | 5 | 2 | 2 | NMW |
| Barabanki | Nawabganj NPP | 7 | 1 | 4 | NMM |
| | Banki NP | 5 | 5 | – | NMW |
| | Satrikh NP | 4 | 4 | – | Mumtaz Begum (42) |

(*Contd.*)

| *Distt.* | *NPP/NP/Nagar Nigam* | *Total no. of contestants* | | | *Elected* |
|---|---|---|---|---|---|
| | | *NM M NMW* | *MW* | *MM* | |
| | Dariabad NP | 3 | 2 | 7 | MM |
| | Siddaur NP | 3 | 6 | – | Kamrun Nisha (45) |
| | Fatehpur NP | 4 | 1 | 4 | Reshma Mashkur (36) |
| Sultanpur | Sultanpur NPP | 14 | 1 | 5 | NMM |
| | Kadipur NP | 14 | 2 | – | NMW |
| | Dostpur NP | 10 | 8 | – | NMW |
| | Koireepur NP | 5 | 3 | – | Rubina Bano (31) |
| Ambedkarnagar | Akbarpur NPP | 16 | 1 | 4 | NMM |
| | Ashrafpur Kichchoucha NP | 8 | 4 | – | Shabana Khatun (40) |
| Faizabad | Rudauli NPP | – | 1 | 5 | MM |
| | Gosai Ganj NP | 7 | 1 | 3 | NMM |
| | Bikapur NP | 14 | 3 | – | Zulekha Khatun (50) |
| Amethi | Salon NP | 9 | 1 | 8 | MM |
| | Musafirkhana NP | 5 | 1 | – | NMM |
| | Amethi NP | 3 | 3 | 3 | NMW |
| Basti | – | – | – | – | – |
| Siddharthnagar | Siddharthnagar NPP | 16 | 1 | 1 | MM |
| | Bansi NPP | 6 | 2 | – | Chaman Ara Idris (38) |
| | Badhni Bazaar NP | 9 | 2 | – | NMW |
| | Domariyaganj NP | 10 | 5 | – | NMW |
| | Uska Bazaar NP | 17 | 1 | 2 | NMM |
| Sant Kabirnagar | Maghar NP | 8 | 2 | 5 | NMM |
| | Mehdawal NP | 11 | 1 | 2 | NMM |
| Gorakhpur | Gorakhpur Nagar Nigam | 7 | 1 | – | NMW |
| | Pipraich NP | 13 | 2 | – | NMW |
| Maharajganj | Nautanva NPP | 6 | 3 | – | NMW |
| | Anand nagar NP | 6 | 1 | 2 | NMM |
| | Nachnol NP | 10 | 1 | – | NMW |
| Kushinagar | – | – | – | – | – |
| Deoria | Gaura Barhaj NPP | 8 | 1 | 2 | NMM |
| | Rampur Karkhana NP | 7 | 1 | 3 | NMW |
| | Majhouliraj NP | 18 | 7 | – | NMW |
| | Lar NP | 13 | 6 | – | NMW |
| Azamgarh | Mubarakpur NPP | 1 | 1 | 9 | MM |
| | Azamgarh NPP | 5 | 3 | – | NMW |
| | Azmatgarh NP | 4 | 1 | – | NMW |

(*Contd.*)

| Distt. | NPP/NP/Nagar Nigam | Total no. of contestants | | | Elected |
|---|---|---|---|---|---|
| | | NM M NMW | MW | MM | |
| | Katgarh Lalganj NP | 6 | 1 | – | NMW |
| Mau | Mau NPP | 8 | 8 | – | Shahina A– Jamal (43) |
| | Adari NP | 7 | 1 | 2 | NMM |
| | Kopganj NP | 4 | 1 | 5 | NMM |
| | Muhammadabad Gohna NP | 8 | 3 | – | Zarina Khatun (48) |
| | Ghosi NP | 9 | 1 | 7 | MM |
| | Dohri Ghat NP | 8 | 1 | – | NMW |
| Ballia | Bilthra Road NP | 16 | 1 | – | NMM |
| | Sikandarpur NP | 4 | 1 | – | NMW |
| Ghazipur | Zamania NPP | 8 | 1 | – | NMW |
| | Sadat | 8 | 2 | – | NMW |
| | Bahadurganj NP | 1 | 1 | 3 | MM |
| Chandauli | Mughalsarai NPP | 13 | 2 | – | NMW |
| | Saiyadraja NP | 7 | 1 | 3 | MM |
| | Chandauli NP | 7 | 1 | – | NMW |
| Varanasi | Ramnagar NPP | 10 | 1 | – | NMW |
| Jaunpur | Jaunpur NPP | 15 | 2 | 3 | NMM |
| | Mariyahu NP | 11 | 5 | – | NMW |
| | Machchlishahar NP | 4 | 1 | 3 | NMM |
| | Kerakat NP | 6 | 2 | – | NMW |
| | Khetasarai NP | 7 | 5 | – | NMW |
| | Jaffrabad NP | 6 | 2 | – | NMW |
| Sant Ravidasnagar | Badohi NPP | 4 | 8 | – | Mahalka Begum (44) |
| | Khamariya NP | 5 | 3 | – | NMW |
| | Nai Bazaar Badohi NP | 8 | 1 | – | NMW |
| Mirzapur | Chunar NPP | 4 | 3 | – | Hasina Begum (48) |
| | Mirzapur NPP | 15 | 1 | – | NMW |
| | Kachchwa NP | 10 | 2 | – | Sabila Begum (51) |
| Sonbhadra | Dudhi NP | 8 | 1 | – | NMW |

*Source:* http://sec.up.nic.in

# 5

# Muslim Women and Women's Reservation Bill

In this study we are mainly concerned with the poor performance of Muslim women in the elections to the Lok Sabha and State Assemblies. The electoral participation of Muslim women in Karnataka and Uttar Pradesh discussed in the preceding chapters has shown that while only a single Muslim woman had been elected to the Karnataka Assembly between 1952 and 2012, Uttar Pradesh has fared a shade better, sending 10 Muslim women during the same period; actually six, if we exclude those who were re-elected. There is no single reason for this state of affairs. It is alleged that Muslims, as a group or category, have not received their due, on account of the neglect of the mainstream political parties in nominating Muslims. At the same time, Muslims have also not been sticking to any single political party; their affiliation shifting from one election to the other, depending upon how they perceive the secular character of a given party. Such shifting alliances make them, in the eyes of the political parties, a non-dependable constituency.

In so far as Muslim women are concerned, it is not that the Muslim women are not interested, but statistics show that the mainstream political parties have not been entertaining Muslim women in adequate numbers, leaving them no alternative than fighting elections as independents or seeking nomination from smaller parties. It is suggested in some quarters that the Muslim community should form its own political parties instead of depending on the mainstream political parties. But, will such Muslim political parties promote or encourage Muslim women? Will the Women's Reservation Bill (when enacted) help Muslim women? Even if there is a separate quota for Muslim women, will it benefit Muslim women who are not connected with political families? To get a larger picture, we may, in the first instance, look at the representation of the Muslim community itself in the Lok Sabha. The following Table 5.1 gives the numbers:

**Table 5.1**: Number of Muslims Elected to the Lok Sabha (1952-2009)

| *Year* | *No. of Muslims in the Lok Sabha* | *Year* | *No. of Muslims in the Lok Sabha* |
|---|---|---|---|
| 1952 | 21 | 1957 | 24 |
| 1962 | 23 | 1967 | 29 |
| 1971 | 30 | 1977 | 34 |
| 1980 | 49 | 1984 | 46 |
| 1989 | 33 | 1991 | 28 |
| 1996 | 28 | 1999 | 33 |
| 2004 | 36 | 2009 | 28 |

*Source:* Election Commission, Government of India.

Of the 543 members in the 15th Lok Sabha, only 28 were Muslims; a mere 5.16 per cent of the total elected members. Despite changing political situations, favourable circumstances, emergence of new political groups, and alignment and re-alignment of pro-Muslim entities, Muslims could never win even 50 Lok Sabha seats at any time. Election data also reveals that Muslim representation has been confined to only a few states. Of the 35 States and Union Territories, Muslims could get elected only from 5 States *in all the general elections* held since 1957. While Muslims could get elected from 18 States, including two Union Territories, no Muslim could get elected from the remaining 17 States. No Muslim was ever elected to the Lok Sabha from Gujarat since 1984; much before the rise of Hindutva.

Looked at from a different angle, of the 7,900 odd Lok Sabha constituencies that went to polls since 1957, Muslims were able to win only 449 seats and of these they were able to retain just 26 seats for more than five times and 53 seats had a Muslim MP only once.

Election Commissioner's data also shows that except the Congress, no other political party has given a fair representation to the Muslim community on its list of candidates, leading to the community's complaint that no political party is fair to Muslims and none has allowed a Muslim to grow as a leader at the national level. It is also alleged that denial of tickets to the sitting MPs or abrupt changes in the constituencies was the common strategy adopted by almost all the parties to crush the rise of Muslim leadership.

## Muslim Women in the Parliament

If the number of Muslim men in the Lok Sabha is considered low, the number of Muslim women is still lower; to the extent of being almost non-existent. Election Commission's statistical reports show that there have never been more than three elected Muslim women representatives in the Lok Sabha at any time. Thus:

- There were no Muslim women in the first, fourth, fifth, ninth, tenth and twelfth Lok Sabhas;
- There were only two to three Muslim women in the second, third, sixth, seventh, eighth and fourteenth Lok Sabhas and only one in the eleventh and thirteenth Lok Sabha;
- In the 15th Lok Sabhathere were only three Muslim women among the 58 women members; and
- Over all, of the 549 women elected to the Lok Sabha at the various elections since independence, only 19 were Muslim women.

Table 5.2 is the list of the 19 Muslim women elected to the Lok Sabha in Independent India.

In spite of entertaining aspirations for an elected office or the ambition to enter the legislature, for want of nomination and support from the national parties or strong regional parties, a majority of the Muslim women have contested the Lok Sabha elections as independent candidates, particularly from the Seventh Lok Sabha elections onwards, only to lose. Out of the ten Muslim women contestants for the 7th Lok Sabha, all except Mohsina Kidwai of the INC (I) lost. Later, in a bye election held in 1981, Begum Abida Ahmed (INC) was elected from Bareilly (UP) (Table 5.3).

Eighth Lok Sabha: Out of the nine Muslim women candidates, five were independents; two belonged to the Congress, and one each to the Lok Dal and J&K Conference. Only three were elected (Table 5.4).

Nineth Lok Sabha (1989): Out of the 12 Muslim women candidates, seven contested as independents; three as Congress candidates, and one each from CPM and Janata Party. None was elected (Table 5.5).

**Table 5.2**: List of 19 Elected Muslims Women in Lok Sabha (1952-2009)

| *Year* | *Elected Muslim women members* | *Party and constituency* |
|---|---|---|
| 1952 | Nil | – |
| 1957 | Mafida Ahmad | Congress, Jorhat (Assam) |
| | Maimoona Sultan | Congress, Bhopal (MP) |
| 1962 | Maimoona Sultan | Congress, Bhopal (MP) |
| | Zohraben Akbarbhai Chavda | Congress, Banaskantha (Gujarat) |
| 1967 | Nil | – |
| 1971 | Nil | – |
| 1977 | Rasheeda Haque Chaudhary | Congress (U), Silchar (Assam) |
| | Akbar Jahan Begum | NC, Srinagar (JK) |
| | Mohsina Kidwai (1978 Bye election) | Congress, Azamgarh (UP) |
| 1980 | Mohsina Kidwai | Congress, Meerut (UP) |
| | Begum Abida Ahmed (1981 bye election) | Congress, Bareilly (UP) |
| 1984 | Akbar Jahan Begum | JKN, Srinagar (JK) |
| | Mohsina Kidwai | Congress, Meerut (UP) |
| | Begum Abida Ahmed | Congress, Bareilly (UP) |
| 1989 | Nil | – |
| 1991 | Nil | – |
| 1996 | Begum Noor Bano | Congress, Rampur (UP) |
| 1998 | Nil | – |
| 1999 | Begum Noor Bano | Congress, Rampur (UP) |
| 2004 | Mehbooba Mufti | JKPD, Anantnag (JK) |
| | Rubab Syeda | Samajwadi Party, Bahraich (UP) |
| 2009 | Tabassum Begum | BSP, Kairana (UP) |
| | Qaiser Jahan | BSP, Sitapur (UP) |
| | Mausam Benazir Noor | Congress, Malda-N (WB) |

NC: National Conference; JKPD: Jammu & Kashmir People's Democratic Party.
*Source:* Election Commission, Government of India.

**Table 5.3**: Muslim Women Candidates to 7th Lok Sabha General Elections

| *Candidate* | *Constituency* | *Party* | *Result* |
|---|---|---|---|
| Rashida Haque Chaudhari | Silchar (Assam) | INC (U) | DF |
| Hasmat Begum Rehman | Bharuch (Gujarat) | INC (U) | -do- |
| Pratima Nuruddin | Chandrapur (Maharashtra) | JNP (S) | -do- |
| Meharunnisa | Shahabad (Uttar Pradesh) | IND | -do- |
| Tahira Khan | Hamirpur (Uttar Pradesh) | -do- | -do- |
| Ruhi Zuberi | Aligarh (Uttar Pradesh) | -do- | -do- |
| Mohsina Kidwai | Meerut | INC (I) | Won |
| Noorjahan Begum | Barasat ( West Bengal) | IND | DF |
| Jamila Khatun | Diamond Harbour (West Bengal) | MUL | DF |
| Azima Hussain | Hazaribagh ( Bihar) | INC (I) | DF |

INC-U: Indian National Congress-United, JNP-S: Janata Party-Secular. DF: Deposit Forfeited.
*Source:* Election Commission's Statistical Report.

**Table 5.4:** Muslim Women at the Candidates to 8th Lok Sabha General Elections

| *Candidate* | *Constituency* | *Party* | *Result* |
|---|---|---|---|
| Bibi Khurshid Jahan | Siwan (Bihar) | LKD | DF |
| Akbar Jahan Begum | Anantnag (J&K) | JKNC | Elected |
| Zohra Jamal | Bhopal (MP) | IND | DF |
| Aftab Zamani Begum | Rampur (UP) | IND | Lost |
| Begum Abida Ahmed | Bareilly (UP) | INC | Elected |
| Salma | Sitapur (UP) | IND | DF |
| Shaheda Hanif | Banda (UP) | IND | DF |
| Mohsina Kidwai | Meerut (UP) | INC | Elected |
| Nahid Malik | Meerut (UP) | IND | DF |

*Source:* Election Commission, Government of India. DF: Deposit Forfeited.

**Table 5.5:** Muslim Women Candidates to 9th Lok Sabha General Elections

| *Candidate* | *Constituency* | *Party* | *Result* |
|---|---|---|---|
| Ayesha Mallath | Kasargod (Kerala) | IND | DF |
| Mumtaz Patel | Indore (MP) | IND | DF |
| Sayeeda Bano | Bombay (S) | IND | DF |
| Malika Khan | Udaipur (Raj) | JNP | DF |
| Begum Abida Ahmed | Bareilly (UP) | INC | Lost |
| A.R. Kidwai | Bahraich (UP) | INC | Lost |
| Ansari | Maharajganj (UP) | IND | DF |
| Sayeeda | Ghazipur (UP) | IND | DF |
| Subhashini Ali | Kanpur (UP) | CPM | Elected |
| Mohsina Kidwai | Meerut | INC | Lost |
| Nahida Malik | Meerut (UP) | IND | DF |
| Zubaida Cheku | Andaman Nicobar | IND | DF |

*Source:* Election Commission, Government of India.

Tenth Lok Sabha: As the 9th Lok Sabha could not run its full term, mid-term elections were held for the Tenth Lok Sabha in 1991 and for Punjab State in 1992. Of the 15 Muslim women contestants for the tenth Lok Sabha, seven were independent candidates; three were fielded by the Janata Party and one each by the Janata Dal, Communist Party of India (Marxist), *Door Darshi* Party (DDP), the Indian Congress-Socialist (ICS), and the Congress. All of them lost (Table 5.6).

In the elections to the 11th Lok Sabha, out of the 44 Muslim women, the Congress had fielded three, while the Samajwadi Party, the Bahujan Kranti Dal (BKD), CPM, Indian People's Democratic Party and the *Rashtriya Aikata Manch* nominated one each. Thirty five Muslim

**Table 5.6:** Muslim Women candidates to 10th Lok Sabha General Elections

| Candidate | Constituency | Party | Result |
|---|---|---|---|
| Halida Khatun | Barapeta (Assam) | JP | DF |
| Azeema Hussain | Hazaribagh | JP | DF |
| Farida ben K. Juneja | Rajkot (Gujarat) | IND | DF |
| Sk. Ayesha begum Md. Ali | Ahmedabad | JD | DF |
| B. Mahaboob Bi | Bangalore (N) | IND | DF |
| Bano Bi | Mandsaur (MP) | IND | DF |
| Anees Syed | Bombay (N-W) | IND | DF |
| Latifan Chakkiwale | Udaipur (Raj) | DDP | DF |
| Mahmuda Begum | Jodhpur (Raj) | IND | DF |
| Azeena Khan | Jodhpur (Raj) | IND | DF |
| Mohsina Kidwai | Domariaganj (UP) | INC | Lost |
| Seema Mustafa | Domariaganj (UP) | ICS (SCS) | DF |
| Subhashini Ali | Kanpur | CPM | Lost |
| Tasneem Ashraf | Kanpur | JP | DF |
| Lailunnisa | Diamond Harbor (WB) | IND | DF |

[DDP: Door Darshi Party: The political base of *Doordarshi* party formed in 1980 by Guru Jai Guru Dev was social reform and spiritual upliftment. The party could not make any headway in politics and was wound up; ICS (SC): Nothing much is known about the ICS (SC) party, except that it was a breakaway faction of the Indian Congress (Socialist) and led by former Assam Chief Minister Sarat Chandra Sinha. The party survived during the period from 1984 to 1999 and was later merged with Nationalist Congress Party in 1999].

*Source:* Election Commission, Government of India.

women (about 80% of the contestants) were independents. Mohsina Kidwai, who contested as All India Indira Congress (Tiwari) candidate, lost. Begum Noor Bano (Congress) was the lone winner (Table 5.7).

Of the 15 Muslim women contestants at the elections to the 12th Lok Sabha, nine were independents, two contested on Congress ticket and one each on Janata Dal, the Rashtriya Janata Dal, the *Puthiya Tamizhagam* and the Samata Party tickets. None of them was elected (Table 5.8).

Among the 27 Muslim women contestants to the 13th Lok Sabha, (1999) the BSP fielded three; the Samajwadi Party, the Janata Dal (Secular) and the Congress two each; and one each by the Janata Party, the *Puthiya Tamizhagam*, the Rashtriya Janata Dal, the Rajasthan Vikas Party, the Bharatiya Minorities Suraksha Mahasangh and the All India Minorities Front. The rest contested as independents. Only one woman was elected (Table 5.9).

**Table 5.7:** Muslim Women Candidates to 11th Lok Sabha General Elections

| *Candidate* | *Constituency* | *Party* | *Result* |
|---|---|---|---|
| P. Masoom Bi | Kurnool (AP) | IND | DF |
| Amtul Rasheed | Hyderabad (AP) | IND | DF |
| Shazadi Begum | Secunderabad (AP) | IND | DF |
| Nawazis Ara Begum | Guwahati (Assam) | SP | DF |
| Nazneen Faruque | Nowgong (Assam) | INC | Lost |
| Syeda Husna Begum | Tezpur (Assam) | IND | DF |
| Faridaben J. Khan | Ahmedabad | IND | DF |
| Faridaben J. Pathan | Gandhinagar | IND | DF |
| Mehbooba | J&K | IND | DF |
| Najma Ajijuddin Bhangi | Bijapur (Karnataka) | IND | DF |
| A. Kadeesumma Kuttyassan | Ponnani (Kerala) | IND | DF |
| Mehzabin | Khajuraho (MP) | IND | DF |
| Rabbi khan | Satna (MP) | IND | DF |
| Tahira Khan | Jhanjgir (MP) | IND | DF |
| Raisa Bano | Mandsaur (MP) | IND | DF |
| Bano Bee | Mandsaur (MP) | IND | DF |
| Ashraf Begum B Khan | Mumbai (N-E) | IND | DF |
| Sk. Akhtar Jahan | Mumbai (N-E) | IND | DF |
| Tadvi Joharabi Hamid | Jalgaon (Maha) | IND | DF |
| Sk. Mumtaz Noor Md. | Latur | IND | DF |
| Bismillah | Churu (Raj) | IND | DF |
| Anwar Bano | Churu (Raj) | IND | DF |
| Zakiya | Sikar (Raj) | IND | DF |
| Lateefan | Udaipur (RJ) | IND | DF |
| Mahmuda Begum | Jodhpur (Raj) | IND | DF |
| Abila Begum MNS | Ramanathapuram (TN) | IND | DF |
| Begum Nur Bano | Rampur (UP) | INC | Elected |
| Parveen Azad | Budaun (UP) | INC | DF |
| Mumtaz Sultan | Rae Bareilly (UP) | IND | DF |
| Mohsina Kidwai | Domariaganj (UP) | AIIC (T) | DF |
| Seema Mustafa | Domariaganj (UP) | IND | DF |
| Rafia Khatun | Domariaganj (UP) | IND | DF |
| Mushtari | Varanasi (UP) | IND | DF |
| Madina Begum | Varanasi (UP) | IND | DF |
| Anwar Begum | Phulpur (UP) | IND | DF |
| Mumtaz Hussain | Allahabad (UP) | IND | DF |
| Subhashini Ali | Kanpur (UP) | CPM | Lost |
| Asifa Begum | Agra (UP) | BKD (J) | DF |
| Taslim Rizwi | Meerut (UP) | IND | DF |
| Pakeeza Begum | Meerut (UP) | IND | DF |
| Jahera Begum | Jangipur (WB) | IND | DF |
| Molla Rokiya Begum | Uluberia (WB) | IDPP | DF |
| Saira | New Delhi | RAM | DF |
| Shahnaz | East Delhi | IND | DF |

*Source:* Election Commission, Government of India.

**Table 5.8**: Muslim Women Candidates to 12th Lok Sabha General Elections

| *Candidates* | *Constituency* | *Party* | *Result* |
|---|---|---|---|
| Sakeena Allauddin | Nalgonda (AP) | IND | DF |
| Hafiza Begum | Srinagar (J&K) | -do- | -do- |
| Begum Noorjahan | Khajuraho (MP) | -do- | -do- |
| Bano Bee | Mandsaur (MP) | -do- | -do- |
| Aliya Begum | Berhampur (Orissa) | RJD | -do- |
| Amro Bibi | Ferozepur (Punjab) | IND | -do- |
| Mahmooda Begum | Jodhpur (Raj) | SAP | -do- |
| Sava Mustafa | Madras Central (TN) | IND | -do- |
| Nazeera Parvin | Ramanathapuram (TN) | PT | -do- |
| Begum Noor Bano | Rampur (UP) | INC | Lost |
| Tarana Sarfuddin | Kanpur (UP) | IND | DF |
| Shammi | Agra (UP) | -do- | -do- |
| Anisa | Bulandshahar (UP) | -do- | -do- |
| Mohsina Kidwai | Meerut (UP) | INC | -do- |
| Shaheen Parvez | Meerut (UP) | JD | -do- |

*Source:* Election Commission, Government of India.

**Table 5.9**: Muslim Women Candidates to 13th Lok Sabha General Elections

| *Candidates* | *State* | *Party* | *Result* |
|---|---|---|---|
| Nawazis Ara Begum | Guwahati (Assam) | SP | DF |
| Sofia Kachhap | Lohardaga (Bihar) | BSP | -do- |
| Mahmooda Riaz Munshi | Gandhinagar (Gujarat) | Ind. | -do- |
| Roshanben Shabbirbhai | Bharuch (Gujarat) | -do- | -do- |
| Mehbooba Mufti | Srinagar (J&K) | -do- | Lost |
| Hafiza Begum | -do- | -do- | DF |
| Waheeda Shah | -do-(Srinagar) | -do- | -do- |
| Hafiza Begum | Anantnag (J&K) | -do- | -do- |
| Aisha | -do- | RLD | -do- |
| Anisa | Khajuraho (MP) | JD (S) | -do- |
| Bano Bee | Mandsaur (MP) | BMSM | -do- |
| Noorjahan Rehman Khan | Parbhani (Maha) | IND | -do- |
| Mumtaz Md. Yahya Khan | -do- | -do- | -do- |
| Amro Bibi | Ferozepur (Punjab) | IND | -do- |
| Razia Bano | Jhalawar (Raj) | RJVP | -do- |
| Mahmooda Abbasi | Jodhpur (Raj) | IND | -do- |
| Nazeera Parvin K. (Dr.) | Ramanathapuram (TN) | PT | -do- |
| Ayeravalli alias Ameenal | -do- | IND | -do- |
| Naina Ahmed | Nainital (UP) | BSP | -do- |
| Noor Bano Begum | Rampur (UP) | INC | Elected |
| Afaque Parvin | -do-(Lucknow) | AIMF | DF |
| Ruvab Sayeeda | Bahraich (UP) | SP | -do- |
| Talat Aziz | Maharajganj (UP) | BSP | Lost |
| Louise Salman Khursheed | Farukkabad (UP) | INC | Lost |
| Khadija Banu | Mushirabad (WB) | IND | DF |
| Masarrat Begum | Calcutta N-W | JD (S) | -do- |
| Nazma | Bolpur (WB) | JP | -do- |

*Source:* Election Commission, Government of India.

At the elections for the 14th Lok Sabha, there were 24 Muslim women contestants; eight independents, three each from the BSP and the Congress, and one each from the S.P., the Bharatiya Janata Party (BJP), the CPI (M), the All India Anna Dravida Munnetra Kazhagam, the Samata Party, the Jammu & Kashmir People's Democratic Party, the Samajwadi Jana Parishad, the All India Majlis-e-Ittehadul Muslimeen, the Socialist Democratic Party and the Nav Bharat Nirman Party. Two women could get elected. (Table 5.10):

**Table 5.10:** Muslim Women Candidates to 14th Lok Sabha General Elections

| *Candidates* | *State* | *Party* | *Result* |
|---|---|---|---|
| Humera Aziz | Secunderabad (AP) | AIMIM | DF |
| Jabeen Borbhuyan | Dhubri (Assam) | BJP | -do- |
| Shaheda Begum | Mangaldoi (Assam) | SAP | -do- |
| Mehbooba | Srinagar (J&K) | IND | -do- |
| Darakshana Andrabi | Srinagar (J&K) | SDP | -do- |
| Mehbooba Mufti | Anantnag (J&K) | JKPDP | Elected |
| Gousia Begum | Bellary (Karnataka) | IND | DF |
| Shameem Modi | Betul (MP) | SWJP | -do- |
| Saira Bano Md. Patel | Mumbai (N-W) | IND | -do- |
| Sk. Waheeda M. Pasha | Nanded (Maha) | BSP | -do- |
| Mahmuda Begum A. | Jodhpur (Raj) | IND | -do- |
| Bader Sayeed | Madras-S (TN) | AIADMK | Lost |
| Shayeen Banu | Chengalpattu (TN) | IND | DF |
| Faeem Akhtar | Moradabad (UP) | -do- | -do- |
| Noor Bano Begum | Rampur (UP) | INC | Lost |
| Tarannum Aqeel | Sambhal (UP) | BSP | Lost |
| Rubab Sayeeda | Bahraich (UP) | SP | Elected |
| Talat Aziz | Maharajganj (UP) | BSP | Lost |
| Subhashini Ali | Kanpur (UP) | CPM | DF |
| Louise S. Khurshid | Farukkabad (UP) | INC | Lost |
| Khadija Banu | Murshidabad (WB) | IND | DF |
| Nafisa Ali Sodhi | Calcutta-S (WB) | INC | DF |
| Kaisar | Outer Delhi | NBNP | -do- |

*Source:* Election Commission, Government of India.

At the general elections to the 15th Lok Sabha (2009), there were 48 Muslim women contestants; the largest number ever. But, only three could get elected and all the three were well-connected to the present or past politicians (Table 5.11).

Tabassum Begum Hasan (MP, 15th Lok Sabha from Kairana, Uttar Pradesh, BSP) appears to have entered politics for the first time in 2009 as a Member of the Lok Sabha on a BSP ticket. She is only a

**Table 5.11**: Muslim Women Candidates to 15th Lok Sabha General Elections

| *Candidates* | *State* | *Party* | *Result* |
|---|---|---|---|
| Shiraz Khan | Secunderabad (AP) | UWF | DF |
| Fatima A. | Hyderabad (AP) | PRAP | DF |
| Parveen Sultana | Mangaldoi (Assam) | AIMF | DF |
| Hena Shahab | Siwan (Bihar) | RJD | Lost |
| Ayesha Khatun | Jehanabad (Bihar) | LTSD | DF |
| Memon Fatimaben F. | Gandhinagar (Gujarat) | IJP | DF |
| Patel Meharunnisa VA | Bharuch (Gujarat) | LKJP | DF |
| Ghousia Basheer | Baramulla (J&K) | IND | DF |
| Khalida Begum | Srinagar (J&K) | JKANC | DF |
| Shakila Bano | Jammu (J&K) | IND | DF |
| Ghousia Begum | Koppal (Karnataka) | IND | DF |
| Naheeda Salma S. | Bangalore-S (Karnataka) | BSP | DF |
| CA Haseena | Chalakudy (Kerala) | IND | DF |
| Yasmin Khan | Gwalior (MP) | IND | DF |
| Shabnam | Khajuraho (MP) | IND | DF |
| Bano Bee | Mandsaur (MP) | BMSM | DF |
| Sujata Ibrahim Tadvi | Raver (Maharashtra) | AUDF | DF |
| Sayyad Hasina Md. Naseem | Kalyan (Maharashtra) | NBNP | DF |
| Naushad Ansar Sk. | Ahmednagar (Maharashtra) | IND | DF |
| Mahmuda Begum Abbasi | Jodhpur (Raj) | IND | DF |
| Farheen Khan | Kota (Raj) | SP | DF |
| Zeenatunnisa Begum MB | Chennai-N (TN) | IND | DF |
| Afroz Husna KS | Tiruvannamalai (TN) | LKJP | DF |
| Rameeja Begum ST | Pollachi (TN) | SAP | DF |
| Zafrunnisa A | Trichy (TN) | IND | DF |
| Baby Kamitha Banu | Trichy (TN) | IND | DF |
| Tabassum Begum | Kairana (UP) | BSP | Elected |
| Babli *alias* Gulshan Jahan | Nagina (UP) | NELU | DF |
| Begum Nur Bano | Rampur (UP) | INC | Lost |
| Sameena Bi | Rampur (UP) | RSBP | DF |
| Firdaus Rana | Baghpat (UP) | MKUP | DF |
| Lubna Asif | GB Nagar (UP) | AiMF | DF |
| Kaisar Jahan | Sitapur (UP) | BSP | Elected |
| Nafisa Ali Sodhi | Lucknow (UP) | SP | DF |
| Shahnaz Sidart | Lucknow (UP) | IND | DF |
| Nasreen Bano | Faizabad (UP) | IND | DF |
| Rubab Saida | Shrawasti (UP) | SP | Lost |
| Usmana Faruque | Azamgarh (UP) | IND | DF |
| Mausam Noor | Malda-N (WB) | INC | Elected |
| Monowara Begum | -do- | RDMP | DF |
| Amina Khatun | -do- | IND | DF |

*(Contd.)*

| Candidates | State | Party | Result |
|---|---|---|---|
| Khadija Bano | Murshidabad (WB) | IND | DF |
| Nargis Begum | Burdwan-Durgapur (WB) | INC | Lost |
| Mira Salam | Kanker (MP) | BSP | DF |
| Shahida Begum | Hardwar (Uttaranchal) | IND | DF |
| Shahida Parvin | NCT Delhi | UWF | DF |
| Nasim Begum | -do- | IND | DF |
| Nisha Bano | New Delhi | ANC | DF |

[UWF: United Women's Front; PRAP: Praja Rajyam Party; AIMF: All India Minorities Front; RJD: Rashtriya Janata Dal; LTSD: Lok Tantrik Samata Dal; IJP: Indian Justice Party; LKJP: Lok Tantrik Janata Party; SAP: Samata Party; JKANC: Jammu & Kashmir Awami National Conference; BSP: Bahujan Samaj Party; BMSM: Bharatiya Minorities Suraksha Sangh; AUDF: Assam United Democratic Front; NBNP: Nav Bharat Nirman Party; SAP: Samata Party; RSBP: Rashtriya Swabhiman Party; MKUP: Mazdoor Kisan Union Party; RDMP: Rashtriya Dehat Morcha Party; SP: Samajwadi Party; NELU: Nelopa (United) (earlier known as Rashtriya Parivartan Morcha); ANC: Ambedkar National Congress].

*Source:* Election Commission, Government of India.

Matriculate. But she was made a Member of Committee on Health and Family Welfare, Standing Committee on Ministry of Social Empowerment and Justice etc. She is also a Member of Central Sunni Wakf Board. Kaisar Jahan (MP, Sitapur, BSP, 15th Lok Sabha) was the Chairperson of Nagar Palika Parishad, Laharpur in 2006. As a Lok Sabha member, she was Member of the Committee on Science and Technology, Environment and Forests, although she was not even a matriculate and was 'privately educated'. (Members' Bio profile, 15th Lok Sabha (Table 5.11).

It will be seen from the above data that:

- Out of the total number of 203 Muslim women who contested the elections to the Lok Sabha (excluding bye-elections, if any), 104 fought the election as independent candidates i.e., 51.23 per cent.
- 45 Muslim women (22.17%) contested under the banner of small parties, forfeiting their deposits.
- Muslim (or Muslim-based) political parties like the Muslim League and the Assam United Democratic Front and others, sponsored a negligible number of Muslim women.

**Table 5.12:** Muslim Women Contestants in Lok Sabha Election

| *Party* | *Number of Muslim Women Contestants at the General Elections for the Lok Sabha* | | | | | | | | |
|---|---|---|---|---|---|---|---|---|---|
| **No. of LS→** | **7** | **8** | **9** | **10** | **11** | **12** | **13** | **14** | **15** |
| Congress | 2 | 2 | 3 | 1 | 3 | 2 | 2 | 3 | 3 |
| BSP | – | – | – | – | – | – | 3 | 3 | 5 |
| BJP | – | – | – | – | – | – | – | 1 | – |
| SP | – | – | – | – | 1 | – | 2 | 1 | 3 |
| CPM | – | – | 1 | – | 1 | 1 | – | 1 | – |
| RJD | – | – | – | 1 | – | 1 | 1 | – | 1 |
| MUL | 1 | – | – | – | – | – | – | – | – |
| JP | 1 | – | 1 | 3 | – | – | – | – | – |
| Independents | 4 | 4 | 7 | 7 | 35 | 9 | 12 | 8 | 18 |
| Others | 2 | 2 | – | 3 | 4 | 2 | 7 | 7 | 18 |
| **Total** | **10** | **8** | **12** | **15** | **44** | **15** | **27** | **24** | **48** |

*Source*: Adapted from Election Commission, Government of India.

- Parties like the United Women's Front, the All India Minorities Front and the *Bharatiya Minorities Suraksha Sangh* which were intended to promote women could not find favour with the voters.

It also appears that the mainstream national parties did not nominate adequate number of Muslim women and when they did, the tickets were given to women who already had a track record (e.g., Mohsina Kidwai) or those belonging to the elite class (e.g., the Royal family of Rampur) or those who wielded support at the grass-roots level through their male relatives, who were already politicians of influence and had the means to fight the election. This is clear from the backgrounds of the above 18 winners:

- Begum Mafida Ahmed : Member of Congress Party since 1943
- Mohsina Kidwai : Politician of long standing, both at State and Centre
- Maimoona Sultan : Royal family of Bhopal
- Begum Abida Ahmed : Wife of Faknruddin Ali Ahmed, former President
- Begum Noor Bano : Royal family of Rampur
- Mehbooba Mufti : Daughter of Late Mufti Md. Sayeed former CM of J&K

- Begum Akbar Jahan : Wife Late Shaikh Abdulla, former Chief Minister, J&K
- Tabassum Begum : Wife of Munawwar Hasan, former MLA and MP (RS)
- Qaiser Jahan : Wife J. Ansari, BSP MLA
- Mausam Benazir Noor : Niece of Late ABA Ghani Khan Chaudhari, Congress
- Rubab Syeda : Wife of Dr. Waqar Ahmad Shah, five-times MLA, from Bahraich and Labour Minister in the Akilesh Yadav government. His son Yasar Shah is also a MLA from Matera constituency.

It is unfortunate that the Muslim women of Karnataka did not have a Godfather. Among the national parties, the Congress and the BSP have given some space to Muslim women, although the antecedents of the women that they have sponsored are in keeping with the above observation. Others, including the Left, were hardly liberal in nominating Muslim women.[1]

It is obvious that unless one is well-connected as aforesaid, the chances of Muslim women from non-political and non-affluent families getting even nominated, leave alone getting elected, are far remote; more so when they fight as independents. The fact that Muslim women could not succeed even while contesting from Muslim-dominated constituencies speaks volumes of the community's attitude towards Muslim women seeking election.[2]

## Women's Reservation Bill and Muslim Women

As the chances of Muslim women getting elected when contesting as independents are absolutely zero, and the mainstream political parties have not been generous in sponsoring them, will Muslim women's chances improve if the Women's Reservation Bill becomes an Act? Does the Women's Reservation Bill benefit Muslim women? There are conflicting views within the Muslim community on this issue. Our inquiries show that the community and even the male-dominated Muslim political partiers pay lip service to Muslim women's electoral participation.

Right from the day the Bill was introduced in the parliament, there was opposition to the concept of reservation for women. The opposition has centred on the demand for setting apart sub-quotas for women of the OBC and Muslim community. Although the Bill was passed by the Rajya Sabha, it still has to go through the Lok Sabha.

## Religion-Based Impediments

If the political parties which opposed the Women's Reservation Bill without separate reservations for OBCs and Muslim women had their own agenda, some influential Islamic scholars and Clerics are strongly opposed to the Women's Reservation Bill. Their opposition seems to stem from the fact that a reservation for women will not only entitle, but also encourage more-and-more Muslim women to take a plunge into politics, where it would not be possible for them to strictly adhere to the tenets of the *Shariat*. Maulana Saeed-Ur Rehman, Principal of the Lucknow-based Nadwat-ul-Ulema seminary, said: "It is un-Islamic for any Muslim woman to contest an election in a secular nation. Muslim women could contest elections in theocratic Islamic states because they would have to necessarily remain in *purdah* while there is no such restriction in secular societies."[3] He contended that Islam did not permit participation of women in people's parliament because it would mean close interaction with men. "They could, however, join the proceedings of a parliament where there is ample provision for *purdah* and proper segregation of women." Asked whether contesting elections would not act as a catalyst for Muslim women getting educated, he retorted: "Islam is not against education of women, but the idea is to let them acquire education, but remain within the confines of their homes, as Islam clearly prescribes *purdah* for them and holds that they must look after their homes."[4]

Leading Shia Cleric and scholar Maulana Kalbe Jawwad agreed with the line adopted by the Nadwa principal. When his attention was drawn to Iran, an Islamic State, which allowed women to participate in various political activities, he replied: "Iran does have women members of Parliament, who go through the process of elections, but they strictly follow the *purdah* system. Even when they sit in their Parliament, they observe complete seclusion, which is not possible in Indian parliament". He also added: "Any woman entering the electoral fray would have to go into lanes and by-lanes, stand on dais and brush shoulders with men. How can Islam permit all that?"[5]

Naib Imam Maulana Khalid Rasheed, head of the Lucknow's oldest Islamic Seminary Firangi Mahal, differed from the Maulana. He said: "There is nothing wrong about a Muslim woman participating in active politics and contesting elections. After all, so many Muslim women have done well in politics. However, I am opposed to the Women's Reservation Bill as it is contradictory to the fundamental provisions of any democratic society. In fact, reservation within reservation is against the spirit of the Constitution of India."[6]

A cross-section of Muslim women feel that trivial issues such as dress code or earning to make a living are non-issues that have little or no impact on contemporary and educated women, who believe that there is nothing wrong in contributing to the family's income or in participating in elections. Muslim women feel that since Islam does not discriminate between men and women, there is nothing wrong in a woman contributing to the household's income along with her husband or in contesting elections. For, hundreds of women of the community have now become partners in the development process. The Deoband-based Islamic Seminary Darul-Uloom in Saharanpur district of Uttar Pradesh, which had issued a *fatwa* against Muslim women's employment, later backtracked on the controversial *fatwa* which prohibited Muslim women from mingling with men in workplaces. The seminary also denied that it had asked Muslim women to wear *purdah* in workplaces, adding that it had only expressed an opinion on the dress code and denied having said that it was illegal for a family to depend on the earnings of a woman.

Shahnaz Sidrat, founder of *Bazme Khawateen*, feels that the Deoband *fatwa* had the effect of taking the community backward. "In any case working Muslim women seldom pay heed to opinions or *fatwas*,"—she said. A basic fact that has often been missed is that with changing times and India progressing towards becoming a global economic powerhouse, Muslim women have emerged as major players in the development process.[7]

Muslim women, thus, have to reckon with *fatwas* or opinions expressed by Islamic scholars in matters relating to education, employment and political participation. At least women belonging to not-so-affluent families or backgrounds cannot completely ignore this reality.

## Opposition to the Bill

Reverting to reservations, OBCs and Muslim women are not currently separately represented within the Women's Reservation Bill because there is no *general reservation* for OBCs and Muslims, and as such a sub-quota within the Women's Reservation Bill is considered unconstitutional. A Joint Select Committee formed in 1996 had informed a delegation of backward caste MPs that sub-reservations for OBC women were not legally permissible without Constitutional Amendment. While it might be possible to add a sub-clause, the Committee advised that the push should first be for a Constitutional Amendment that enables a general OBC quota and/or a non-secular quota for Muslims. In addition to a number of minor technical adjustments, the Committee recommended that the Bill be passed into law as soon as possible.[8]

The Women's Reservation Bill was strongly opposed by Sharad Yadav, President of Janata Dal (United) and other 'like-mined' parties like the Samajwadi Party led by Mulayam Singh Yadav and Rashtriya Janata Dal led by Lalu Prasad Yadav.[9] Sharad Yadav, who even threatened to commit suicide before allowing any such Bill without quota for Dalit women, claimed: "if there is no party whip, 90 per cent of the MPs will oppose the Bill, whether they are from the UPA (United Progressive Alliance led by Mrs. Sonia Gandhi) or the NDA (National Democratic Alliance); whether they are from backward classes or upper castes, whether they are male or women MPs."

While most of the seven JD-U Rajya Sabha MPs supported the Bill, the 20 party MPs in the Lok Sabha led by Sharad Yadav opposed it. JD-U leader and Bihar Chief Minister Nitish Kumar supported the Bill, saying that the legislation was one whose time had come. Sharad Yadav and Lalu Prasad's protest against introducing the Bill in the Lok Sabha received the indirect support of Mamata Banerjee's Trinamool Congress, whose two MPs abstained from the voting, in the Rajya Sabha.

The Janata Dal (United) and other parties opposing the Bill in its present form wanted a sub-quota for women belonging to other backward classes (OBCs) and minorities within the 33 per cent reservation, arguing that the Bill, without such sub-quotas, will only benefit a few elite women from the metros. Their argument was considered as a ploy to sabotage the Bill. Such protests have come handy for the UPA government, which took the stand that it would introduce the Bill only "after wider consultations" with all parties. If the Janata Dal (United) is for reservations for women from OBCs and minorities, will it nominate women from those sections in the elections to the assembly? Of course, Sharad Yadav had no straightforward reply: "We have been trying to empower women. But the selection of candidates depends on their winnability too."

When the Bill was passed in the Rajya Sabha in March 2010, a section of the Muslim women reacted positively. But, the All India Milli Council, the Muslim Welfare Organisation, Dr. B.R. Ambedkar Sewa Dal and *Samajik Nyay Morcha* and others contended that in its present form (without sub-quota for OBC and Muslim women) the Bill would benefit only those from the affluent sections. They demanded a sub-quota for women from weaker sections to ensure fair representation. At a convention in New Delhi, the organizations asserted that a quota without a sub-quota will perpetuate inequalities in the country and the Bill will fail to serve its purpose.[10]

On the other hand, a section of the Muslims believed that the Bill is a conspiracy to reduce the representation of the Muslim community in the legislature, stating that there is already a tendency to reserve the constituencies that have consequential Muslim population for SCs and STs. They apprehended that the women's reservation would further squeeze the community out. The following are the views of some of the Muslim MPs:[11]

- *Ejaz Ali, JD-U MP (Rajya Sabha, Bihar)*: "At present, 60 per cent of Members of Parliament are capitalists, 20-22 per cent belong to Scheduled Castes and Scheduled Tribes. Rest 17-18 per cent belong to the downtrodden sections of the society including OBCs and Muslims. Muslims constitute about 15-20 per cent of the population and OBCs 52 per cent of the population. Muslims are just 5 per cent in Parliament and none from the community is in several State Assemblies. OBCs and Muslims deserve political reservation".
- *Sabir Ali, Lok Janashakti Party MP (Rajya Sabha, Bihar)*: "Through this Bill, only women of creamy layer people and politicians will get elected because today without money and muscle power one cannot get elected to the Lok Sabha. When today it is difficult for Muslim men (as the community lacks money and muscle power as a whole) to get elected, how will their women reach Lok Sabha? The Bill will bring Muslim representation in the House to zero. We are not against women reservation per se, but we want quota for Muslim women in it".

- *Asaduddin Owaisi, MIM MP (Lok Sabha, Hyderabad)*: "We are not against political empowerment of women as such. If reservation is to be given it should be given to the most deprived sections of the society who have never been represented in the Lok Sabha or State Assemblies. ... ... The representation of Muslim women is very abysmal and apathetic. That is why we say if you are creating a quota for women, there must be a portion for Muslim women".

The main concern of Ejaz Ali and Sabir Ali was, thus, the impact the Women's Reservation Bill will have on the Muslim community and the reduced opportunities for Muslim men.

Assuming a separate sub-quota is created for Muslim women within the 33 per cent quota, will the Muslim community support Muslim women? All the three MPs assured that there is nothing wrong in Muslim women contesting elections. Ejaz Ali added that "some *Ulema* have said Muslim women should not go to politics. I do not think this is a good suggestion. In Hijab they can come to Parliament, Assembly and Panchayat."[12]

Dr. Mustafa Kamal Sherwani, Chairman of the Lucknow-based All India Muslim Forum, observed: "While the concept of women empowerment is laudable, in the absence of a separate proportionate quota for Muslim women, the measure in the Indian context can be seen as nothing other than further weakening the Muslim community's representative character, and to stifle even those faint voices of Muslim members, who sometimes, make a feeble attempt to cut across the party lines against the injustice to the community"[13]

Muslim leaders like Maulana Abdul Hameed Nomani of Jamiat ul Ulama-e Hind, Maulana Jalaluddin Ansar Umri of Jamat-e Islami, Maulana Mufti Mukarram Ahmad of Shahi Fatehpuri Masjid, Kamal Farouqui, Chairman of Delhi Minorities Commission, Dr. Qasim Rasool Ilyas of All India Muslim Personal Law Board, Dr. Zafar ul-Islam Khan, editor of *Milli Gazette*, Muhammad Ilyas Malik, Vice President of All India Minorities Coordination Board have all taken the stand that they are not opposed to 33 per cent reservation for women in Central and State legislatures, but there should separate quotas for Muslim and other backward class women within the 33 per cent quota.

It is obvious from the above that the concern of the Muslim leaders is centered mainly about a reduction in the representation of the

Muslim community *per se* if 33 per cent of the seats are set aside for women. By 'Muslim community' they mean Muslim men. Why cannot Muslim women compensate for any possible reduction in the Muslim male representation? No Muslim male leader has strongly demanded and wholeheartedly supported a separate quota for Muslim women. Congress MPs from the Muslim community, like Maulana Mohammad Asrarul Haque from Kishanganj in Bihar and Ismail Hussain from Assam, said: "We will have to abide by *whatever the high command says*". They did not demand separate quota for Muslim women, for fear of going against the Party. In opposing the Women's Reservation Bill in its existing form, their main concern seems to be that though the Bill may empower Indian women in general, it will also reduce the chances of Muslim men.

Muslim women's associations have supported the passing of the Bill in its present form as a first step. In a March 2010 rally in Delhi, Naish Hassan of the *All India Muslim Mahila Andolan* said that she was not against Muslim women reservation, "but this can be done later by amendment. There is no purpose to hold this at present stage. ... ... First let this Bill pass as it is, and then we will fight for quota for Muslim women. ... ... politicians who have no base are opposing this Bill. They are feeling insecure with this Bill." Similar views were expressed by Albina Shakeel, Member of the Delhi Committee of All India Democratic Women Association. She said that the AIDWA was "supporting this Bill because as women in the society, whether we are Muslim women or other women, we all face a lot of problems. And at a juncture when something is being done for women as a class, we should support it. First we are women; and then comes any affiliation with a community, caste or class."[14]

The concern that Women's Reservation Bill will reduce the opportunities for Muslim men is also voiced by Shaikh Ahmed Ali, a journalist, who points out that of the 543 Lok Sabha seats, 84 are already reserved for the Scheduled Castes and 47 for Scheduled Tribes. Once 33 per cent of the total seats are reserved for women, the Muslim leaders will be left with very few seats to contest and win. Although the intelligentsia argues that Muslim women can contest and win from the reserved seats, the chances of their being successful look remote. Ahmed Ali deplored that "India failed to produce a single Muslim women leader at the national level since independence" and that the few Muslim women who entered the Parliament "none have won the election on their own." He refers to three Muslim woman members in the 15th Lok Sabha to illustrate his point. "Malda MP Mausam Benazir Noor is the niece of Former Union Minister ABA Ghani Khan Chowdhury. Kairana MP Tabassum Begum is the widow of powerful Muslim BSP MP Munawwar Rana and Sitapur MP Qaiser Jahan is the wife of Sitapur's sitting BSP MLA J. Ansari."[15] If there is no single Muslim woman leader at the national level, it is the community that has failed its women by placing restrictions or not promoting them. Secondly, as we have already seen, those who have won have the elections have not done so on their own steam, but on the strength of their male relatives.

## Muslim Women's Arguments

With regard to the objections raised by the male members of the community over the Bill, Najma Heptulla (Rajya Sabha MP from the BJP) questioned: "As for the men expressing concern on our behalf, how many of them have actually worked towards ensuring our participation?" Similarly, K.S. Saleekha, CPI (M) MLA from Sree Krishnapuram in Palakkad district in Kerala blames the "religious orthodoxy and the bigotry of the Clerics for the poor representation of Muslim women in State politics. If the Bill is passed, all parties, including the Indian Union Muslim League, would have to field women in the reserved constituencies…and those who still renege on the legislative commitment would stand exposed."

On the other hand, a plea for passing of the Women's Reservation Bill in its present form was also voiced by Waquarunissa Ansari, Corporator/Councillor elected from Umarkhadi in Maharashtra. Demanding that the Bill should be passed, she said: "I do not think we need reservation within reservation. It is the quality of the women that matters, not just the caste or religion." Asma Shaikh, Corporator elected from Bainganwadi (Govandi, Mumbai) prefers a quota within quota. "I am here only thanks to the reservation in urban self-government bodies. We Muslims get elected only from Muslim areas because we are less educated than others. We may not stand a chance in general areas…. … Also, the community and families believe that if we work alongside other women, we too will become modern."[16]

There are very few Muslim women like Fauzia Khan, who is now a Minister of State in the Maharashtra Government, who have made it on their own credentials. Although she has no political family background, she was fortunate to be handpicked by R.R. Patil

(Nationalist Congress Party) Home Minister of Government of Maharashtra and groomed by Sharad Pawar, who was impressed by her grasp of issues relating to women and education. However, Fauzia Khan was not elected, but nominated as a member of the Legislative Council.

The profile of the elected Muslim women given above shows that, by and large, they need to belong to successful political families or have money and muscle power behind them to win elections. It is possible that if a sub-quota is made available for Muslim women, many more are likely to get elected as the electorate will have no option, but elect one of the contesting Muslim women. But, will the powerful Muslim politicians allow such quota be availed by Muslim women from ordinary families instead of one of their own? Speaking about the seats that may become available exclusively for women under the Reservation Bill, Bahjat Najmi, President of the Mufti Hafizur Rahman Academy, Jeddah, voiced apprehensions that the Bill (in its present form) was "neither going to help the general women of the country—mainly of the low castes—nor the Muslim women. It is meant for the upper caste Hindu families and the politicians who will take its optimum use by fielding their own daughters and daughters-in-law."[17]

Incidentally, how many seats will come in the way of Muslim women if a sub-quota is created within the 33 per cent quota? Out of the 180 seats that will accrue to women under the Bill in its present form, Muslim women may get only a few seats, which will be available to them throughout the country. According to the 2001 Census, Muslim women accounted for 13.46 per cent of Indian female population.[18] If seats are reserved for Muslim women on this basis, Muslim women will be entitled to only 24 seats out of the 543 seats in the Lok Sabha. Will the male Muslim politicians allow these seats to go outside their families?

The Muslim community itself has often placed impediments in the way of Muslim women desirous of political participation. For instance, it was contended that Muslim women's photographs cannot appear on voter ID cards.[19] There are also instances where the Muslim community has asked the mainstream parties not to encourage Muslim women. For example, when Aneesa Mirza, former Ahmedabad Mayor (Congress Corporator elected as Mayor of Ahmedabad Municipal Corporation in 2003) was being considered by the Congress as its candidate from Shahapur constituency in Ahmedabad, a group of

Muslim leaders met the State Congress party President and demanded that no Muslim women should be given ticket. They said that people from the minority community did not like its women contesting elections and it would have adverse effect on the results.[20]

Yet another example comes from Kerala. The Muslim League was the biggest beneficiary in the Muslim-dominated Malappuram district, where it is the dominant party. Following the reservation of one-third seats for women in the Panchayats and municipalities, the Muslim League's women headed 20 of the Panchayats and two municipalities, apart from hundreds of positions in Gram Panchayats, Municipal Councils, Block Panchayats and the District Panchayat. However, the Muslim League let down the Muslim women. KPM Basheer writes:[21]

> "The League holds immense possibility for emancipating Muslim women, which is closely linked to their political participation. But the same party, which made so much political capital out of the reservation in the Panchayati Raj Institutions ... ..., is opposed to the idea of one-third quota for women in the Lok Sabha and the State Assemblies. When the much-delayed Women's Bill came up in Parliament last time, the League, along with some other parties, opposed its introduction. The League masked its hostility to the Bill by demanding "reservation for minorities first." The League attracted flak when it failed to field women in the Assembly election in May 2001. The League, now the No. 2 in the UDF Government, had been allotted 23 seats as its share, but it refused to give ticket to a single woman. The CPI (M) set an example by fielding three Muslim women in the election—that the three seats were ones they expected to lose is another matter".

The Muslim League had fielded Ms. Qamarunnisa Anwar for the first time at the 1996 Kerala Assembly polls. Though she lost the election, the mere fact that the League had chosen to field a Muslim woman was considered a positive sign. But, in the 2001 Assembly election the party denied her ticket, even though she was the President of *Vanitha League*, the women's wing of the party. It is said that prior to the elections the party bosses took a decision that women should be fielded only if the Women's Bill was passed and reservation in

Assemblies became statutory. Bashir writes: "This decision was allegedly taken after a prominent Kozhikode-based Sunni leader, known for his anti-women viewpoints, had made a statement objecting to Muslim women's involvement in politics.[22] Ironically, the *Vanitha League* was launched by the party to take advantage of the reservations in Panchayati Raj Institutions. Despite its reluctance to promote women, the Muslim League had no option, but to field women in the PRI elections. "However, the *Vanitha League* is a paper organisation that comes to life only during elections. Its affairs are decided by the male leaders of the parent party. It hardly has a political role; its activists do not take part in *dharnas* and processions organised by the party. Had there been no reservation for women in the Panchayats, there would have been no *Vanitha League*".[23]

The Muslim League placed further restrictions on Muslim women, insisting on their wearing Islamic dress, restricting them from attending meetings and public functions after sundown and advising them to pay extra attention to their households, husbands and children. The women were even told to take care of their husbands' egos, lest the wives' positions trigger an inferiority complex or jealousy in them!

Reverting to the Women's Reservation Bill, in its present form the Bill provides for reservations for scheduled caste and scheduled tribe women within the women's quota. Looking at the poor performance of Muslim women in the Assembly and Parliamentary elections, a sub-quota within the quota for women belonging to the OBC and Muslim community appears to be a common sense demand.[24]

However, the government feels that even if this demand is agreed to, it would be difficult to implement the demand not only because it involves Constitutional Amendment, but also on account of the non-availability of data on the OBCs. Veerappa Moily, then Union Law Minister said at a Press Conference in Bangalore on March 25, 2010: "We do not have the data on which to base the reservations because no data has been collected on the OBCs since the 1930s. As the census is ready to start we will have to wait till the 2020 census for the data; analysis will take more time, so all this will likely cause 20 years delay to pass this amendment."

The noise made by Political parties and Muslim leaders over the Reservation Bill has little to do Muslim women's interests. The politicians, who opposed the women's reservation Bill on the ground that there is no separate quota for Muslim women, were aiming to attract Muslim votes in their respective constituencies. On the other hand, the Muslim leaders who were demanding separate reservation for Muslims were aiming at males only. When it is practically impossible for reservations for the Muslim community in the legislatures on the basis of religion, it becomes all the more important for the community to demand reservation for Muslim women. But with patriarchy ruling their thinking, neither the Muslim Clerics nor the intellectuals have spelt out their clear stand on Muslim women's entry into the legislatures. They have not yet given or even willing to give serious consideration to a quota for Muslim women in the Parliament. There is a feeling, as our study through a questionnaire indicates that illiteracy among the Muslim women makes them unsuitable to enter the Assembly or the Lok Sabha; they are good enough in the PRIs. Although, it is complained that the male Muslim members of the Assembly or Parliament have not been doing anything for the community, our respondents have felt that poorly educated and inexperienced Muslim women in the legislature may not effectively represent the issues of the community; a view with which we do not agree.

While Muslims as a whole are not proportionately represented in the Parliament, Muslim women are even more poorly represented. In the present Lok Sabha, Muslim women constitute just 1 per cent of the total elected Muslim representatives. The Reservation Bill for Women without a sub-quota will not bestow any political advantage for Muslim women. Separate quotas for Muslim women will at least compel Muslim males to not only allow Muslim women's participation in elections and elect them, but also helps in changing their stereotyped, conservative attitude and withstand *fatwas* against women's political participation, if they wish to ensure that sufficient number of Muslims is represented in the legislatures. It is contended that if there is no separate reservation for Muslim women, the likely political domination from the lower castes will prompt political parties to push non-SC/ST women against the 33 per cent reservation and that the beneficiaries will be women mostly from the existing ruling class, as there will be no compulsion to promote OBC and Muslim women.

In an opinion poll conducted by Outlook-MDRA among Muslim women on Women's Reservation Bill, the respondents were asked to identify the factors behind Muslim women's negligible presence in Indian politics. The following (Table 5.13) was the response:

**Table 5.13:** Percentage of Respondents of Muslim in Indian Politics.

| *Factor* | *Percentage of respondents* |
|---|---|
| Islamic norms | 28.0 |
| Muslim men | 25.5 |
| Lack of education and poverty | 20.8 |
| Muslim clergy | 13.1 |
| Not interested in politics | 7.7 |
| Other | 4.9 |

*Source:* Outlookindia.com, March 29, 2010. Available at http://www.outlookindia.com/article.aspx?264747)

The opinion poll has also revealed that (a) 64.5 per cent of the respondents felt that there should be separate reservation for OBC and Muslim women; and (b) 67.2 per cent of the respondents felt that rich Muslim women will corner the seats in the Lok Sabha after the passing of the Bill. Only a small percentage of Muslim women (7.7%) have expressed disinterestedness as the reason.

In connection with this project, we had sought the opinion of different strata of the Muslim community both in Karnataka and Uttar Pradesh, to know their opinion as to whether the Muslim community would encourage Muslim women if a separate quota is introduced. The respondents included women (students, research scholars, professionals and housewives) and men (professionals, *Ulema* and others). The responses are discussed in a separate chapter.

Our survey in Uttar Pradesh and Karnataka shows that over 70 per cent of the respondents (both male and female) are of the firm belief that if a separate quota is allocated to Muslim women, the Muslim community would definitely encourage the women to participate in the elections. The male respondents included some *Ulema* also.

It is true that the ground realities and challenges faced by Muslim women in politics are plenty. Hurdles that Muslim women have to overcome include patriarchy, conservatism, lack of education, absence of money and muscle power associated with politics, restriction on movement, need to observe Islamic norms, and lack of control over resources etc. There is also a general perception that Muslim women, being uneducated and lacking in exposure, are considered to be less competent to take-up politics. Some of our respondents point out that there are instances where men continue to usurp the functions and powers of elected women in Panchayati Raj Institutions. The women members of PRIs are yet to come into their own as far as performance of their expected roles in development. The strings of power continue to be with their spouses or other family males, making them virtually puppets. This is not possible in the case of women elected to the State Assembly or Parliament. Men, therefore, think that they would lose their hold on their women if they contest and win Parliament/Assembly elections. The Panchayati Raj Department organises training programmes for the elected women of the PRIs. But, the impact of this training and its curriculum content has yet to be analysed from point of view of gender equality. In any case, educated women appear to handle their political leadership roles relatively much better and it is the lower crust of the PRIs where female literacy and educational levels are extremely low and this makes them vulnerable. In such cases, family males exploit the situation to their own advantage.

The first opportunity for Muslim women to enter the election scene was provided by the 73rd and 74th Constitutional Amendments, which reserved 33 per cent of the seats in PRIs. Zoya Hasan writes: These elections were also presented an opportunity to non-Muslim women belonging to the poorer sections. Till now, there were several obstacles in the way of women's participation in elections. These included:

- Complex social environment like class, caste and gender hierarchies;
- Indifference of women rooted in the historic background of non-participation in governance;
- Non-inclusion of women in political patronage, as no political party proposed women's participation;
- Low levels of education and socio-cultural norms; and
- Poverty and lack of financial control of women.

If the above obstacles are common to all women, Muslim women had the added disadvantage of living in a highly conservative and patriarchal society. Muslim women, especially those belonging to the lower socio-economic strata, had to pay heed the society's restrictions and religious rulings issued by the Clergy. When elections to the PRIs were being held for the first time in 2005 after the introduction of reservations for women, the Darul Uloom Deoband was agitated to find that a number of Muslim women were offering themselves as candidates. The Seminary issued a *fatwa* which said that "Muslim women are not allowed to appear before men without a veil and under the Islamic law *"pardanashin"* women are only allowed to contest elections." Although, it was clarified that the Darul Uloom had only said that it did not oppose Muslim women from contesting elections, but only said that they must observe *purdah* and not mingle with the crowds openly when they seek votes. The Clerics regarded this as necessary to ensure the sanctity of Muslim social norms. The *fatwa* was issued a week before elections for over 14,000 village heads and thousands of council members in Uttar Pradesh. Why was it not a matter of concern when Muslim women were contesting Lok Sabha and Assembly elections? Joya Hasan answers: "The answer is obvious. Very few Muslim women contested legislative elections. It does not really matter; whereas large numbers of them have begun contesting local elections. The conservative lobby wants to stymie this process, since in the long run political empowerment can facilitate social and economic empowerment."[25] It is unfortunate that the Muslim 'leaders' did not attempt to persuade the Darul Uloom to withdraw the *fatwa* in the interests of Muslim women. Media reports show that Congress MP Rashid Alvi only said that if Muslim women do not contest elections, the entire community will lag behind and that they have to progress if the country has to progress. He did not say anything in condemnation of the *fatwa* unlike the non-Muslim leaders of Communist Party (M) and the BJP.

However, in spite of the *fatwa*, Muslim women could no longer remain mute spectators when women of other communities were availing opportunities presented by the Constitutional Amendments. As a result, over the years, thousands of Muslim women of Uttar Pradesh have begun contesting local elections; and not all of them have been paying heed to or following Darul Uloom's *Fatwa* both in letter and spirit.

Whatever may be the arguments that have stalled the passage of the Bill in the Lok Sabha, women continue to show interest in contesting elections to the local government bodies. Irrespective of the effectiveness of their participation in the PRIs, women now hold about 40 per cent of elected posts in the local bodies, contesting and winning even from general seats on the basis of their work for their communities.

Women represent about 48 per cent of the Muslim community. Besides problems common to women in general, Muslim women have their own religion-specific or community-specific problems, about which non-Muslim men and women representatives do not want to exhibit (undue) concern. But, being in politics Muslim women can ensure that their rights are upheld, and many women-specific and gender-sensitive issues are taken up more effectively and passionately. They could take-up issues that concern their children and ensure that their children do not remain uneducated and unemployed. The deep-rooted patriarchal practices and the feudal mindset of Muslim society do create hurdles in the emancipation of Muslim women, but with the growing political representation by the women, the sanctions on speech and behaviour could be considerably changed.

Finally, one of the problems associated with the demand of a separate quota for Muslim women's political representation is that the issue is linked to that of the OBC women. But, there is no dialogue between the two and they seem to be suffering, as Professor Muzaffar Assadi puts it, ghettoization.[26] In response to the argument that the political participation of Muslim women is hindered by *fatwas* issued by the Clergy, Professor Hasnat Mansur said: "the Muslim clergy is not the mind or body of the Muslim community and it is mainly interested to keep its hold on the community for its own benefits. Muslim women do not know from which forum they should speak about their problems. Even progressive friends do not take interest in the problems of Muslim women; they think that these should be solved by the Muslim community itself".[27]

The performance of some Muslim women in the local body elections shows that if one is sincere, voters do not care for the gender and religion of the contestant. This was proved when Razia Saleem Khan, a Muslim candidate, won the chairman's seat of Khurja Municipal Board (Uttar Pradesh) in 2000. She was the first Muslim to be elected to the post in the last election. She retained this seat by defeating a BJP candidate. Khan attracted a large number of non-Muslim votes too. Similarly, Reshma Afroz, the sitting chairman of Rampur Municipal Board (Uttar Pradesh), won the seat a second time. Naseebun Nisa won from Nanpara Nagar Palika Parishad. In Nagina (Uttar Pradesh) Tahira Begum was elected chairman. Shakeela Begum has won Muhammadi Nagar Palika Parishad (Uttar Pradesh). Atia Bano was elected chairman from Faridpur (Uttar Pradesh). A number of other Muslim women candidates have won from several other municipal boards. Their representation has also increased in corporations and municipal boards.[28]

By not encouraging or even discouraging Muslim women's

political participation, the community is wasting its immense potential. As Prof. Naznin Begum said, "50 per cent of the power, potential and resource embedded in women should never be allowed to go wasted. We have to pay more attention to the empowerment of Muslim women as they are lagging behind compared to others in spite of having very high potential. Their potential has become dormant due to negligence, isolation, non-recognition and various other reasons. It is a major setback to the community which has not been realized. It is necessary for all round development of the society and the community. Women should be involved in community development and make them share the responsibilities for the progress to compete with everything which concern our rights towards dignified life. A woman should have the caliber to face and tackle any challenge, any problem, any issue, or any situation of the surroundings".[29]

In the case of Muslim women, especially, the two interacting casual factors 'supply' and 'demand' seem to be responsible for their under-representation. The most common explanation for the supply-side factor is women do not come forward and/or they are not interested in politics. The demand side factor is related mainly to the selectors, or political parties, where such parties discriminate against women's nomination.[30] Added to this, Muslim women belong to that traditional culture in which women are reluctant to run for political office on account of the hostility from the community's political elites and the tough conditions imposed by the Clergy if they were to participate in elections.

This discussion will not be complete without a reference to efforts to form all-women's parties in the past. A women's political party was launched in Uttar Pradesh on January 4, 1998 as it was felt that it was the only option left for women to fight the elections.[31] Later in October, 2007, Suman Krishan Kant, the widow of former Vice President Krishan Kumar Kant, along with other influential women launched the United Women's Front to address issues such as women's illiteracy, early marriage and tokenism in Parliament. The aim of the party was to work for increasing the share of women in the Parliament. The Party's national general secretary claimed that it was for the first time in the history of India that a national political party has been formed by women. She even claimed that it is the only party of women in the world.[32] Nothing more is heard of both the parties, leave alone the question whether the parties would have improved the prospects of Muslim women's political participation.

In concluding this chapter, we would like to quote Husna Subhani, President of RJD's Mahila wing. "Even a mother does not feed her child till it cries. We, the neglected gender of a minority community, must scream to be heard. It is a majority-led, male-dominated politics in a man's world." She has cited her own frustrations: "a decade's active politics and never a ticket to contest elections. Four general elections and a Delhi State election—each time I have suffered last-minute denials. It is tough being a woman politician, let alone a Muslim one!"[33]

## NOTES AND REFERENCES

1. The Bharatiya Janata Party seems to be trying its best to woo the Muslims. Bibi ben Sama, for instance, was the only Muslim candidate of BJP to have wonin the polls for six municipal corporations across the State in Rajkot, once considered a Congress bastion. She attributed her success to the support by her husband, Habib Sama, leader of BJP's minority cell in Rajkot andvoters from both Hindu and Muslim communities. A class VI dropout, Bibi ben Sama said, "Despite being a Muslim woman, I was supported by people from all the communities. We will try our best to prove what a Muslim woman can do if given the chance." Her husband said that the Muslims had been voting for Congress for more than four decades, but the community felt it was time to look at things from a different perspective. "There is a perception that BJP is against Muslims, but this is not true. BJP is now focusing on Muslim-dominated areas. All it needs to do is to select proper candidates to bridge the gap between the party and the Muslim population." (Vijaysinh Parmar in *Times of India* (Rajkot) October 14, 2010. (Available at http://articles.timesofindia.indiatimes.com/2010-10-14/rajkot/28212911_1_muslim-candidate-bjp-party-office)
2. Bharuch in Gujarat, for example, has 23 per cent Muslim population. But, Dr. Roshanben Shabbirbhai Dudhwala, the only female contestant who fought the elections to the 13th Lok Sabha as an independent candidate secured just 0.23 per cent of the valid votes polled. The election was won by a BJP candidate (Male).
3. Islamic Clerics oppose women's reservation, in *Two Circles.net,* 11 March, 2010. Available at http://twocircles.net/2010mar11/islamic_clerics_oppose_womens_reservation.html)
4. *Ibid.*
5. *Ibid.*
6. *Ibid.*
7. *The Hindu,* 13 May, 2010. Available at http://www.thehindu.com/news/muslim-women-are-partners-in-development-process/article429106.ece)

8. *Women's Reservation: A Long Delayed and Much Needed Step*. Policy brief series: No. 3; July 2008, New Delhi: Centre for Legislative Research and Advocacy.
9. Mulayam Singh Yadav, chief of the Samajwadi Party, one of the staunchest opponents of the bill in its present form, had remarked in November 2012 that rural women will not benefit from the women reservation bill because "they are not as attractive as those from the affluent classes." This remark was a shade better than what he said in 2010; that if the women's reservation bill is passed it will fill Parliament with the kind of women who invite catcalls and whistles. Later he changed tracks and declared that he would support the Bill "if Dalits, Muslims and backward class are taken care of in it, we can consider supporting it." (Available at http://www.hindustantimes.com/India-news/Lucknow/Mulayam-Yadav-says-unattractive-rural-women-won-t-gain-from-reservation-bill/Article1-957345.aspx)
10. Dalit, Muslim bodies for sub-quota for women in Bill, *The Indian Express* (New Delhi), June 27, 2009.
11. Muslim MPs tell TCN why they oppose women quota Bill, in *TwoCircles.net,* 16 March, 2010. (Available at http://twocircles.net/2010mar16/muslim_mps_tell_tcn_why_they_oppose_women_quota_Bill.html)
12. *Ibid.*
13. Dr. Sherwani. Women Reservation Bill *vis-à-vis* Muslim Women, March 6, 2010, in *Ummid.com*. (Available at http://www.ummid.com/news/2010/march/06.03.2010/women_reservation_muslim_women.htm)
14. Reported in *TwoCircles.net*. (Available at http://twocircles.net/2010mar20/muslim_women_hold_rally_support_women_reservation_Bill.html)
15. Ahmed Ali, Shaikh. Why Women's Reservation Bill is anti-Muslim? March 12, 2010. (Available at http://ibnlive.in.com/blogs/shaikahmedali/2200/61628/why-womens-reservation-Bill-is-antimuslim.html)
16. A Veil lifted, by Anuradha Raman *et al.*, in *Outlook India.com*, 29 March, 2010.
17. M. Nasir Jawed, Women Reservation Bill: Time for Muslim women to act, in *Saudi Gazette*, 12 March, 2010. (Available at http://www.saudigazette.com.sa/index.cfm?method=home.regcon&contentid =2010031266049)
18. As per the 2001 Census, the total female population of India was 496,453,556. Of this, Muslim female population was 66,814,106. *Census of India* 2001, Population by religious communities. (Available at http://censusindia.gov.in/Census_Data_2001/Census_data_finder/C_Series/Population_by_religious_communities.htm) If 180 seats (as per 33% reservation).
19. A petition filed by one Ajmal Khan of Tamilnadu in the Supreme Court against the election commission's mandate to carry photo identity cards for voting. He contended that if a Muslim woman is contesting elections, posters carrying her photographs would be put up all over a constituency and it

was against the tenets of Islam for a Muslim woman to get photographed without a veil (*burqa*). He argued that a Muslim woman's face can only be seen by her husband or close relatives. The Supreme Court Bench of Justice K.G. Balakrishnan and Justice Deepak Varma was, however, not amused. Dismissing the petition, the Court said: If having photographs on election identity cards and electoral rolls defines religious tenets and betrays sentiments of a section of Muslim women, it is for them to decide whether to vote or not. The Bench asked: "What these women would do if they were to contest elections?" *DNA*, January 22, 2010.

20. *Gujarat Global.com* November 25, 2007.
21. Basheer, KPM, Where Muslim League lets Muslim women down, in the *Hindu,* 6 July 2001. http://www.thehindujobs.com/thehindu/2001/07/06/stories/0406211o.htm)
22. *Ibid.*
23. *Ibid.*
24. State of Democracy in South Asia: National Dialogue on Democracy and Human Security, 18-19 September, 2004, Prof. G. Ram Reddy, Centre for Distance Education, Hyderabad. http://www.democracy-asia.org/Hyderabad.pdf).
25. Hasan, Zoya. *Fatwa* as a Political Weapon. In *DNA* (Daily News and Analysis), Mumbai, 29 August, 2005.
26. Cynthia Stephen, Give us our Due, in *Infochange News and Features*, April 2010.(Available at http://infochangeindia.org/governance/analysis/give-us-our-due.html)
27. Ms. Hasnat Mansur was speaking at the Dialogue in Hyderabad on 18-19 September, 2004. She is associated with FEMWOB, a Muslim women's organisation in Karnataka.
28. UP Municipal Elections and Muslims, Syed Ubaidur Rahman in *Milli Gazette* http://www.milligazette.com/Archives/15-12-2000/Art1.htm)
29. Professor Naznin Begum is the National Vice President of the Social Democratic Party of India. (Available at New Delhihttp://www.popularfrontindia.org/pp/story/empowering-muslim-women-presented-prof-naznin-begum)
30. *Gender and Party Politics*, (Eds.) Joni Lovenduski and Pippa Norris, Thousand Oaks, Calif, 1993.
31. Haider, Saraswati. All Women s Political Party Launched in UP, in *Economic and Political Weekly,* Vol. XXXIII, No. 8, February 21, 1998).
32. Women's enews.org, 7 January, 2008. http://womensenews.org/story/080107/women-in-india-form-their-own-political-party#.Ujb5ZuvrbZ4)
33. Wadhwa, Soma. One-eighth will do. *In Outlook-India.com*, June 15, 1998. (Available at http://www.outlookindia.com/article.aspx?205701)

# 6

# Muslim Women's Political Participation

## Religious Aspects

The conspicuous absence of Indian Muslim women in the State Legislatures and Parliament leads one to believe that they are unable to muster adequate support from the community in seeking an elected office. As we will see later, unless a Muslim woman belongs to a political family or is highly influential through her family connections, ordinary Muslim women have hardly ever succeeded in elections to either the Parliament or State Legislatures.

Muslim women are also discouraged, if not totally prohibited, through *Fatwas* that place restrictions on their attire, mobility, getting photographed and interaction with voters. In the course of brief survey in Uttar Pradesh and Karnataka, the respondents were asked though a questionnaire whether Islam categorically prohibits Muslim women's political participation. In response, while a majority of the respondents said that Islam does not prohibit Muslim women's political participation, some respondents, both men and women, affirmed that Muslim women cannot participate in elections. On the other hand, a number of respondents said that they could do so by wearing *purdah* and staying within the limits prescribed by the *Shariah*. But, it appears that influenced by the *fatwas*, a bulk of the laity of the Muslim community seems to believe that Muslim women's political participation is un-Islamic and hence they should not encourage them by voting in their favour. This has resulted in most of the Muslim women contesting elections losing even from Muslim-dominated constituencies in the Assembly and parliamentary elections.

Maulana Saidur Rehman Azmi Nadvi, Head of Nadwatul Ulema, the biggest Islamic seminary in north India, for example, contends:[1]

> "Islam does not permit women to discard the *purdah*, deliver lectures in public (*taqreer*) and demand their due. They have clear guidelines to follow—stay at home in *hijab*, and take care of household chores. They are also free to get educated and serve the nation."

The Maulana rules out any compromise over their entry into politics, saying, "Contesting elections is by no means a cake walk. There is only one option for female aspirants—turn into *'mard'* (man)."

Can a Muslim woman assume leadership role? Is there really a prohibition in *Quran*? These are much debated issues and those who are not fully conversant with *Quran*, come up with a ready answer: No. On the other hand, *Qur'anic* scholars assure that the answer is clear in the *Quran*. "But, if one refers to and depends upon "man-made books (*Hadith* written 200+ years after the revelation of the *Quran*) a view of subjugation of women and denial of rights in the political system emerges."[2] In this chapter we propose to briefly consider this aspect.

Responding to the question as to why a Muslim woman running for office is controversial, Anne-Sofie Roald states that the reason is a *hadith* on female leadership. The *hadith* in question says: *"A people which has a woman as a leader will never prosper."*[3] While this *hadith* is interpreted in various ways, the most traditional and conservative scholars insist that it means that women can never be leaders and the leadership of women is "un-Islamic."

There has never been unanimity on the meaning and interpretation of this *hadith* among scholars, past and present. From the earliest days of Muslim scholarship, even the jurists who implicitly accepted the *hadith* as containing some injunction have differed on the meaning of *"placing affairs in the hands of a woman"*. Some scholars prohibit women from all public duties. Imaam Abu Hanifah permits a woman to hold public office, even to be a judge in matters in which her testimony is admissible i.e., all cases other than those involving fixed penalties (*Hudood*) and retaliation (*qiyas*). Ibn Hazm in his *Muhalla*, allows a woman to hold every office besides that of the Head of State based on this *hadith*.[4]

On the other hand, the most liberal scholars interpret this *hadith* from the historical context in which it originated and opine that the *hadith* means that it is the best person, regardless of gender, who should be the leader. Thus, at the "liberal" extreme, Imaam Hafiz Ibn Hajar indicates in *Fathul Bari* that Imam Muhammad Ibn Jarir Al-Tabari not only supported the unrestricted appointment of woman to judgeship, but also permitted her appointment as Head of State. A similar view is reported from Imam Malik Ibn Anas and adopted by some Maliki jurists. There was no unanimity even among the earliest scholars on this matter, although a vast majority barred women from holding the office of the Head of State.

The liberals consider that the *hadith* in question has been misunderstood and misinterpreted. Moroccan Sociologist Fatima Mernissi, for example, focuses on the political situation at the time the *hadith* was related by its narrator, Abu Bakr, in order to interpret its meaning. According to her, Abu Bakr related this *hadith* because he was forced to choose alliance between Caliph Ali and A'isha (the Prophet's wife) just before the battle of the Camel in 656; 24 years after the death of the Prophet.

Islamic scholars refute the general impression that the leadership of Muslims by women is a modern phenomenon; a result of Westernisation. In her book entitled *The Forgotten Queens of Islam*, Fatima Mernissi cites from historical texts the lives of several Queens in Muslim history. Mernissi documents the lives and reigns of 16 women who ruled between 1000 A.D. and 1800 A.D. as Governors, Sultans and Queens, throughout the Islamic world.[5] Some of them received the reins of power by inheritance; others won power in successful struggles with other heirs. Many women led armies into battle, won victories, and concluded armistices. Some had confidence in their competent Viziers, while others counted only on themselves. Mernissi writes: "Each had her own way of treating the people, of rendering justice and of administrating taxes." Coins were minted in their names and in mosques the *Khutbah,* the Friday sermon, was proclaimed in their names, as the Ruler of the land.

It is apparent from Mernissi's book that various Muslim communities at various times were *de-facto* or *de-jure* ruled by women. A group of *Kharijites*, the *Hudaybiyyah*, held that women were eligible for the office of Head of State as recorded by Ibn Hazm in *Kitabul Fisal.* Not only did they appoint their Imam's daughter as his successor, but the lady delivered sermons from the pulpit and led them in prayer and in the battle-field.

The famous thirteenth century Mamluk Queens Razia Sultana of Delhi and Shajarat Al-Durr of Egypt were not the only women sovereigns over Muslim communities. Ibn Battuta records that for forty years (from 1347 to 1388), Muslims in the Maldives were ruled by Queens. The first was Sultana Khadija the daughter of Sultan Salah al-Din Albendjaly who ruled for 33 years, followed by her two sisters, Sultana Myriam and Sultana Fatima. After the reign of Sultan Iskandar Thani, the Muslim kingdom of Aceh in Indonesia was ruled by four Princesses who succeeded each other as Queens between 1641 and 1699 viz., Sultana Tadj al-'Alam Saffiyat al-Din Shah, Sultana Nur al-'Alam Nakiyyat al-Din Shah, 'Inayat Shah Zakiyyat al-Din Shah and Kamalat Shah.

The Shiite dynasty of Yemen also produced two Queens, Asma Bint Shihab al-Sulayhiyya and 'Arwa Bint Ahmad al-Sulayhiyya. Each of them took the title *al-Sayyida al-hurra* and had the *khutbah* said in her name. There were also the Mongol Khatuns like Kutlugh Khatun and Safwat al-Din Khatun.

These examples refute the claims of those who believe that there were no Muslim women Heads of State before Benazir Bhutto of Pakistan. Women have ruled Muslim communities and their leadership was accepted and respected by the scholars of the communities of the period.

The role of woman in the history of the world is demonstrated in the story of Belquis, the Queen of Sheba. She has earned a place in the *Quran*, setting a precedent that a woman in a political leadership is not offensive to God. She was a democratic ruler who consulted her people before taking important decisions. She visited Solomon, talked to him and made decisions for herself and her people. After witnessing what God gave Solomon, she became a Muslim, while still being the Queen of Sheba. Sheba's history provides a lesson that God has placed no restrictions on a woman in a leadership role. Contrary to what the traditional Muslim scholars and man-made *Hadith* books advocate, a woman as a political leader or Head of State is not against God's system or against the *Quran*. It might be against the chauvinistic views of the men who wrote the corrupted books of *Hadiths*.[6]

Prophet's biography also reveals that women took part in political negotiations and discussions. One example of women's decision-making presence at the time of the Prophet could be found in the story about the second pledge of al-Aqaba. Here, while living in

Mecca, the Prophet goes with some 70 men and *two women* to negotiate with the people of Medina. This was a preparation for the coming *Hijra* to Medina.

Elaborating on Abu Bakr's *hadith*, Sanusi Lamido Sanusi, respected Islamic Scholar of Nigeria, writes that contemporary scholarship articulates the rejection of the *hadith* from different perspectives[7]:

> "The first, which for want of a better term I will call 'feminist', rejects the authenticity of the *hadith* in its entirety. This view is represented by Fatima Mernissi in her ground breaking book, *The Veil and the Male Elite: A Feminist Interpretation of Women Rights in Islam.* Mernissi in this book does the unspeakable by questioning directly the reliability of a companion of the Prophet as a narrator of *hadith*. She suggests that Abu Bakr, a former slave, joined Islam because of the promise of manumission. She argues that he prevaricated between joining Ali and joining Aisha in the civil war, and then after Aisha lost the battle he opportunistically 'remembered' a *hadith* spoken 25 years earlier to curry favour with the winning side. Finally, she stresses that the second Caliph Umar had ordered Abu Bakr flogged for false testimony. She therefore rejects the authority of Abu Bakr and with it the evidence of the *hadith* since to her it is a fabrication".
>
> "The second group adopts a different line of argument. Exemplified here by Justice Aftab Hussain in his book *Status of Women in Islam,* the central argument of this group is that it is clear that Abu Bakr did not understand from the words he narrated an injunction against the leadership of women. He was a companion of Aisha and followed her and fought among her troops and returned with her to Madina after her defeat. He remembered this *hadith* as he stated during the Battle of the Camel and yet neither left her side nor advised anyone else to. This group says that to insist that the *hadith* is an injunction against female leadership places this companion of the Prophet in very unbecoming light. Is it possible that a true companion would remember an injunction of the Holy Prophet and proceed in disobeying it as if he had never remembered? Would he be so impudent as to

> subsequently announce this recollection without any explanation for his non-compliance?"
>
> "The third group takes a different course. This group accepts the *hadith* as authentic, but insists that it was a prophecy relating to the Kingdom of Persia and had no legal implications beyond that. This group argues that the *hadith* must be read along with related ones, since, according to Hafiz Ibn Hajra, it merely completes the story of the Chosroe who tore the Prophet's letter".

It is evident that different scholars have interpreted the *hadith* in question in different ways. A Muslim who accepts the essentially inferior status of woman by Divine decree, or at least sees nothing wrong with according her a public status below that of man, readily accepts the interpretation which precludes her from political leadership. Such a choice is to him "Islamic" only because it conforms to his preconception and presupposition of the Islamic position on gender relations. But, a Muslim who sees Islam as an *essentially emancipating and egalitarian faith* accepts an interpretation which validates and concurs with his own subjective predisposition. He rejects the traditional interpretation only because he considers the subjection of women a historical aberration, an evanescent feature of a society striving to attain, but still short of realizing, its true potential.

Joining the discourse on the Islamic perspective on women in the Political system, Muslim Women's League asserts that the social responsibility in Islam is derived from the *Qur'anic* verse which states: *"And [as for] the believers, both men and women—they are friends and protectors of one another: they [all] enjoin the doing of what is right and forbid the doing of what is wrong."* (*Quran* 9:71).

This verse compels both women and men to act for the betterment of society. One is encouraged to take an active role in society rather than merely a passive one. Political involvement is a means to fulfil one's obligations to society. Involvement in the political system can take many forms, from voting in elections to holding a position as a legislator or a judge, to being a Head of State. Islamic history provides precedents for each of these roles for women.[8]

Since the beginning of Islamic history, women have had a voice in electing their leader. The leader of an Islamic state is confirmed by the people through a process known as *bai'ah (Bay'ah)*; a symbolic contract between the leader and the people wherein the leader promises to obey Islamic law and the people, in exchange, promise their allegiance. In essence, *bai'ah* is the election of a leader, for, without the *bai'ah,* the purported leader has no legitimacy and thus cannot act as the head of state. Prophet Muhammad received the *bai'ah* from the people. Conservatives argue that *bai'ah* is a *process of being chosen and not getting elected.*

The *Quran* addresses the issue of women giving the *bai'ah* to Prophet Muhammad and God tells Muhammad to accept the pledge of the women:

> *"O Prophet! Whenever believing women come unto thee to pledge their allegiance to thee...then accept their pledge of allegiance."* (*Quran* 60:12)

Traditionally, an aspect of leadership in Islam is the ability of the leader to lead the Muslims in prayer, i.e., act as the Imam. Those who are against women holding leadership positions base their argument on the belief that women cannot lead men in prayer. However, this argument is based on two assumptions. First, that one must assume that the leader himself or herself is obligated to lead prayer and second, one must assume that women cannot lead men in prayer. The word Imam as used in the *Quran* means *a source of güidance* (*Quran* 2:124). The meaning is not limited only to prayer. Thus, the leader *should be able to guide* the people along the path of Islam. In other words, the leader should follow the teachings of Islam in leadership and should act as a role model. Leading prayer is not a necessary criterion for leadership, although it is symbolically desirable.

Thus, it is held that the assumption that the leader must actually lead the prayer is not actually necessary. The criteria for leading prayer lie in one's ability to read the *Quran*, possess the knowledge of the *Quran*, and knowledge of the teachings of Prophet Muhammad. Thus, maleness is not the criterion. For instance, Umm Waraqa bint Abdullah, a companion of the Prophet Muhammad, was well versed in the *Quran* and the Prophet trained her and allowed her to lead mixed-gender prayers.[9] Similarly, a woman named Ghazala al-Haruriyya, in the 7th century A.D., led Muslim men and women in prayer.[10] She is reported to have recited the two longest chapters in the *Quran* during that prayer. Although many traditional Imams do not accept *Ghazala* as a legitimate precedent because she belonged to the Khawarij School, it does not necessarily invalidate her actions.

Muslim Women's League asserts that in view of the ample evidence in the *Quran*, *Sunnah*, and *Islamic history*, ignoring the contribution of Muslim women deprives the Islamic heritage of the valuable role models while continuing the stagnation of Islamic thought. It is argued that to exclude women from political involvement simply because they are women is an act of tribalism based on gender. The Prophet stated: "*He is not of us who proclaims the cause of tribal partisanship*..."[11]

### Women Leaders in Islamic History

We may once again recall that Islamic history gives several examples of women who undertook various forms of political activism, including fighting to defend Islam. Unfortunately, however, much of this history has been ignored.

- The first martyr in Islam was a woman, Sumaiya Zawgat Yasir, who was tortured and killed in the early period of Islam because of her belief in Prophet Muhammad.[12]
- Umm Umara defended the Prophet during the Battle of Uhud. (The Prophet is reported to have said: "On the day of Uhud, I never looked right or left without seeing Umm Umara fighting to defend me."[13]
- Nasiba bint Ka'ab also fought along with the Prophet in the Battle of Uhud. She was known as a courageous and dedicated warrior.[14]
- Umm Salama, one of the Prophet's wives, was instrumental in advising the Prophet during the crisis at Hudaybiya in 628 A.D. which prevented disunity among the Muslims after the Treaty of Hudaybiya and her opinion prevailed over that of many men, including Umar ibn al-Khattab.[15]
- An inquisitive student of Islam, Umm Salama asked the Prophet why only men were mentioned in the *Quran* and in response God revealed the following verse: "*Verily, for all men and women who have surrendered themselves unto God, and all believing men and believing women, and all truly devout men and truly devout women, and all men and women who are true to their word, and all men and women who are patient in adversity, and all men and women who humble themselves before God, and all men and women who give in*

*charity, and all self-denying men and self-denying women, and all men and women who are mindful of their chastity, and all men and women who remember God unceasingly: for all of them has God readied forgiveness of sins and a mighty reward."* (*Quran* 33:35).[16]

- Prophet's respect for the wise decisions of women is evident from the fact that when Umm Hani bint Abi Talib, who had offered refuge to two non-Muslim men who sought protection after the opening of Mecca and reported the incident to the Prophet, the latter told her: "We offer refuge to whomever you offered and we guarantee the safety to whom you guaranteed safety."[17] In this instance, Umm Hani bint Abi Talib was performing a significant political function, one often reserved only for the ruler, when she granted political asylum to these men.
- Aisha, wife of Prophet Muhammad, who was politically active, played a major role in the armed resistance against Ali, the fourth successor after the death of Prophet Muhammad.[18]

Thus, throughout time, Muslim women have served actively in their communities and impacted their societies. From the earliest centuries of Islam, women have been scholars, leaders, advisers, and businesswomen. Besides being wives and mothers who were supportive of the leaders, Muslim women have been leaders themselves. Some women stand out as exemplary role models of Muslim women.

Even in the recent times, women have served in the Muslim world as writers, doctors, scientists, politicians, and even Prime Ministers. For instance, Egypt's Zainab al-Ghazali was a twentieth century Islamic activist and promoter of women's Islamic rights. She founded the Muslim Women's Association, which reportedly had three million members by the time it was dissolved by a government order in 1964. With her belief that Islam allows women to be active in all aspects of public life, as long as it does not interfere with their first and most sacred duty, she petitioned for women's right to work, enter politics, and take an active part of public life.

Shirin Ebadi, a lawyer and judge who fought for human rights and democracy in Iran, was honoured with the Nobel Prize for Peace in 2003. Dr. Ingrid Mattson, a Canadian convert to Islam, is a Professor of Islamic Ethics and Legal Theory and Director of the MacDonald Center for Islamic Studies and Christian-Muslim Relations at Hartford Seminary in Hartford, Connecticut (USA). In 2006, she became the first female President of the Islamic Society of North America and held that position till 2010.

We firmly believe that the Muslim society should look to these role models as examples of the balance one can achieve between piety, personal growth, and service to humanity and encourage Muslim women's political participation; a right that accrues to them as the citizens of India. It is nobody's argument that Muslim women should, even when they enter politics, should forget that they are Muslims first; bound by Islamic traditions and culture. It is also nobody's argument that they should discard *hijab* once they take-up a political office. They could perform their duties to the society and humanity even if they wear the *hijab*. The 60 million Muslim women of India represent an untapped source of talent, which should not be allowed to go unutilised.

## NOTES AND REFERENCES

1. Muslim women cannot discard *purdah* for politics' in the *Times of India*, March 12, 2010). The Maulana is also a senior member of All India Muslim Personal Law Board.
2. *Women and Politics in Islam*, 18 November, 2012. (Available at http://www.submission.ws/women/women-and-politics-in-islam.html)
3. Roald, Anne Sofie. *Quran on Women's Leadership*. International Museum of Women. Anne-Sofie Roald is an Associate Professor at the University of Malmo, Sweden, a Program Director at Chr. Michelsen Institute in Bergen, Norway, and author of *Women in Islam: The Western Experience*. A historian of religion and convert to Islam, her main work has been in the field of Islamism, gender and migration studies. (Available at http://www.imow.org/wpp/stories/viewStory?storyid=1692)
4. *Women and Political leadership in Muslim Thought*, October 2001. (Available at http://www.islamawareness.net/Women/leaders.html)
5. *Ibid.*
6. *Ibid.*
7. *Ibid.*
8. *Ibid.*
9. Dehlawi, Zakaria. *Women Leaders have a History in Islam*, in The Daily of the University of Washington, March 2, 2009. (Available at http://dailyuw.com/author/zakariya-dehlawi)

10. Quoted in Sanusi, Lamido Sanusi. *Women and Political Leadership in Islamic Thought*. Available at http://www.islamawareness.net/Women/leaders.html
11. *Women and Politics in Islam*, in Submission. WS, 18 November, 2012. (Available athttp://www.submission.ws/women/women-and-politics-in-islam.html)
12. Sanusi, *op. cit.*
13. *An Islamic Perspective on Women in the Political System*, Muslim Women's League, September 1995. (Available at http://www.mwlusa.org/topics/rights/politics.html.)
14. Muslim Women: Past and Present in *Women's Islamic Initiative in Spirituality and Equality*. (Available at http://www.wisemuslimwomen.org/muslimwomen/bio/umm_waraqa_bint_abdallah/)
15. Available at http://www.islamicaweb.com/forums/blog/6/entry-136-ghazala-al-haruriyya/
16. Muhammad Asad, 1980, *The Principles of State and Government in Islam*, Dar Al-Andalus, p. 32 quoted in *Women in Society: Political Participation*, Muslim Women's League, September 1995 http://www.mwlusa.org/topics/rights/polirights.html)
17. Ashrof, V.A. Mohamad. (2005), *Islam and Gender Justice: Questions at the Interface*, Delhi: Kalpaz Publications, p. 12.
18. Ashrof, V.A. Mohamad (2008). *Islam and Gender Justice: Questions at the Interface*, Delhi: Kalpaz Publications, p. 13.

# 7
# Responses from the Field

As a part of this study, we conducted a survey to seek the views and opinions of a cross section of the Muslim community both in Uttar Pradesh and Karnataka, through a questionnaire. The questions related not only to the political participation of Muslim women, but also a number of other related issues. The respondents were chosen at random and included both Muslim men and women. Among the Muslim women were housewives, students, professionals, women who had contested the PRI/ULB elections and religious teachers and students of religious schools. Muslim men included Moulavis, Muftis, academicians and senior journalists.

The responses were collected by the Field Investigators though personal contacts and with the help of Muslim intellectuals who are disturbed by the poor performance of Muslim women in elections. In some cases, like Hardoi for instance, the questionnaire was got filled up by women who had participated in a seminar organised by the CSSS at Varanasi.

We admit that the survey is not scientific nor is by no means comprehensive. But, the responses, which we will discuss below, give an indication of how the community perceives the various issues involved.

## Uttar Pradesh

### *Jaunpur and Muzaffarnagar*

A majority of the respondents (22 out of 25) of Jaunpur were aware that Islam does not bar women from political participation. Only two

**Table 7.1**: Responses about Muslim Women's Participation in Politics

| *Respondents* | *Jaunpur* | | *Muzaffarnagar* | | *Total* | |
|---|---|---|---|---|---|---|
| | *Male* | *Female* | *Male* | *Female* | *Male* | *Female* |
| Teachers | 2 | 5 | 1 | 7 | 3 | 12 |
| Moulavis | 2 | – | 2@ | – | 4 | – |
| Housewives, students and Professionals* | – | 16 | 1 | 5 | 1 | 21 |
| **Total** | **4** | **21** | **4** | **12** | **8** | **33** |

*Note:* (*) Lady Doctors and lawyers (@) the two Moulavis were members of JUH also

*Source:* Author's Field Study.

males (one of them a Maulavi) and a woman believed that Islam prohibited women's political participation. The lady respondent asserted that Islam prohibits woman from participating not only in political, but also from administrative and judicial etc., occupations.

Similarly, only one Maulavi of Muzaffarnagar said: "Islam bars them from politics under present circumstances. I would advise them to keep away from politics over the issue of their reputation." All the remaining 15 respondents said that Islam does not prevent women from participating in politics, although six of them qualified their response by stating that Muslim women can participate in politics "by wearing *purdah*."

Some of the Jaunpur respondents who agreed that Islam did not prohibit women's political participation, elaborated:

(a) A Muslim woman can participate in male-dominated activities, only when she needs to go out for the survival of her family. For that she has to cover her whole body apart from her face and hands.

(b) One lady respondent (a Doctor) said that *Quran* and *Hadith* encouraged Muslim women to participate in political activity and quoted examples of Razia Sultan, Benazir Bhutto, Begum Khalida Zia and Shaikh Hasina.

24 of the 25 respondents of Jaunpur believed that a Muslim woman can take-up and discharge the responsibilities of a public office by staying within the limits of Islam. One lady respondent said that a Muslim woman *does not get a chance* to assume responsibilities

of public office. Similarly, there was almost unanimity among the Muzaffarnagar respondents to the above question. However, one Maulavi stressed that a Muslim woman should remain within *purdah*, meaning that she should not undertake such responsibilities.

Simultaneously, all the respondents of both Jaunpur and Muzaffarnagar agreed that Muslim women should not be denied of the opportunities available to women of other communities, although there was a grudging response from a Maulavi of Muzaffarnagar that a Muslim woman can take-up politics or social service by remaining within *purdah*. On the other hand, only one lady teacher from Jaunpur answered the question with a "yes", i.e., she positioned Muslim women separately from the women of other communities, even if it meant denying them of the opportunities available.

What is clear from the above responses is that the Muslim community is aware that Islam places no bar on women's political participation and that it does not want Muslim women to remain mere spectators of the modern times and watch helplessly as the others are availing the opportunities on offer. The community wants Muslim women to access political power and share the fruits of the modern world—but by maintaining their Islamic identity and remaining within *purdah*.

Accessing political power by contesting elections to the Assembly or the Parliament is one of the rights granted under the Constitution and opportunity available to both men and women in a democracy. There is no reason why Muslim women should be denied of such an opportunity. If Muslim women find it difficult to access such political power by competing with men and women of other communities, will the Muslim community support its women if a separate quota is made available to Muslim women, as demanded by some of the political parties. 18 of the 25 Jaunpur respondents and 9 of the 16 respondents from Muzaffarnagar thought that in such a case, the Muslim community would promote women's participation. While one respondent felt that even if there is a separate reservation, the Muslim society will not encourage Muslim women, two others said that "whatever women could do as per religion they could, and not that which is prohibited under the religion." Two respondents said that even if a separate quota is provided, Muslim women have to participate in the elections wearing *purdah*. One respondent felt that more than Muslim women, it is the community *per se* that is in need of reservation.

The above responses indicate that Muslim women's participation in public affairs is circumscribed by the condition that she limits her activities to "Islamic" mores and boundaries. Why should the community believe that increased social participation might result in decreased religious commitment?

The Election Commission data that we have presented in the earlier chapters show that Muslim women do have aspirations to enter the assembly and parliament. But, compared to women of other communities, why is it that the number of Muslim women contesting elections to the Assembly and Parliament is less? A majority of the respondents felt that lack of education and economic factors prevented Muslim women from contesting in elections to the Assembly and Lok Sabha.[1] Six respondents felt that the attitude of the Muslim society, oppression, domestic responsibilities and male domination were responsible if more Muslim women were not participating in the elections.

Only four respondents from Jaunpur and Muzaffarnagar believed that religion was solely responsible. Two of them elaborated that because of the *purdah* system and 'Islamic conditions', more Muslim women were unable to participate in elections to the Assembly and Parliament. Overall, the main reasons as to why there are fewer Muslim women in the elections to the Assembly and Lok Sabha are the following:

- Lack of education and financial means.
- Attitude of men.
- Inability to get nominated by political parties.
- PRI elections are local area specific as against Assembly and Parliamentary elections.

Among other reasons, one respondent from Muzaffarnagar said that when a Muslim woman gets elected to the Panchayati Raj institutions, her work is done by the male members of her family and this was not feasible if she is elected to the Parliament or Assembly. A Muslim woman is also looked at as one with no capacity to function as an MP or MLA. The male members of the family do not want to allow her such a broader independence.

It is in this context that almost all the respondents felt that it is not correct for the Clergy to issue *fatwas* on issues relating to politics or preventing Muslim women from participating in elections. One respondent however defended such *fatwas* and said that the media was unnecessarily defaming the clergy.

Compared to women in general, Muslim women have a number of religion-specific hurdles to overcome. In fact, the Muslim community itself has been facing a number of problems arising out of its socio-economic backwardness, which are expected to be taken up by the male politicians of the community in the Assembly/ Parliament. But, the respondents from both Jaunpur and Muzaffarnagar said that the Muslim male political leaders were not doing enough for the community and/or for the advancement of and solving the problems of Muslim women. Similarly, almost all the Jaunpur and Muzaffarnagar respondents felt that the Muslim political parties were neither interested in Muslim women's problems nor were promoting their political participation, as the parties are dominated by males and male chauvinism has been keeping the women away.

If that be the case, does not the community think that if there is adequate number of Muslim women in the Assembly/Parliament, they would take-up the community's issues in a better way? All the 25 respondents from Jaunpur and 16 respondents from Muzaffarnagar, both male and female, answered in the affirmative.

While there are no prominent Muslim political parties in India, except the Muslim League (Kerala State Committee), the ones that have been functioning in Uttar Pradesh have not encouraged Muslim women. At the same time, Muslim women have limited chances of getting nominated by the mainstream political parties. If it is not a Muslim political party, they have to turn to a political party which they consider secular. In fact, in response to our question, almost all the respondents said that they do not consider any of the existing political parties secular. Only two respondents named the Congress and Samajwadi parties as being secular. However, even those who considered that the Samajwadi Party was secular felt that the Party had started revealing its true colours.

In so far as BJP is concerned, less than 50 per cent (10 of the 25) of Jaunpur respondents and all the 16 respondents of Muzaffarnagar said that the party is not acceptable to the Muslims, even though there were Muslim leaders like Shah Nawaz Hussain and Mukhtar Abbas Naqvi in the party. Only two respondents of Jaunpur conceded that BJP is acceptable. Others did not have any opinion over the issue.

Finally, all the respondents of Muzaffarnagar and 23 out of 25 Jaunpur respondents felt that there is not only a paucity of Muslim women in the legislatures, but there are fewer women of all communities. They wish that more-and-more Muslim women enter politics and occupy elected positions. A respondent from Jaunpur said that the community has to stimulate the younger generation and provide them all opportunities so as to become equal to those of the non-Muslim communities.

The question on the need for Muslim girls acquiring technical and professional qualifications so as to find well-paying jobs, elicited mixed response. Fifty per cent of the respondents felt that Muslim girls should definitely acquire technical and professional qualifications so as to improve the socio-economic condition of their families. Three respondents insisted that girls should remain in *purdah* even when acquiring such qualifications. Others felt that Muslim girls can take-up jobs under 'extenuating circumstances' or when there is no alternative for the survival of the family.

In spite of the above response, all the respondents believed that secular education does not corrupt Muslim girls and as long as they maintain their religious identity they could acquire technical and professional qualifications. For, all the respondents felt that the community cannot keep itself away from the opportunities available in the modern world.

In their general comments, only two (one a lady teacher and another, a Maulavi) out of the 25 respondents from Jaunpur felt that Muslim women should not contest elections. On the other hand, all the 16 respondents of Muzaffarnagar agreed that Muslim women should participate in elections, with some adding that Muslim women should come up not only in politics but in all fields. They also felt that there should be separate quota for Muslim women.

**Table 7.2:** Hardoi, Saharanpur, Sitapur and Rae Bareilly

| *District* | *Female* | *Male* | *No. of respondents* |
|---|---|---|---|
| Hardoi | 2 | 4 | 6 |
| Saharanpur | 22 | 8 | 30 |
| Sitapur | 1 | – | 1 |
| Rae Bareilly | 1 | – | 1 |
| **Total** | **26** | **12** | **38** |

*Source:* Author's Field Study.

Of the 38 respondents of the above four districts, 33 said that Islam does not prohibit Muslim women's political participation. The remaining 5 respondents gave the following replies:

- Islam prohibits women from taking part in politics. (A Maulana from Saharanpur);
- Muslim women can enter politics under exceptional circumstances, like when Muslims are in danger. (Another Maulana, also from Saharanpur);
- "In the present political situation" it is better if women stay away from politics. (A Mufti from Saharanpur);
- She can take part in politics by wearing *purdah*. (Yet another Mufti from Saharanpur); and
- *In a country like India* Muslim women should stay away from politics. (A Muslim woman respondent from Saharanpur).

In response to the question whether Muslim women cannot take-up and discharge functions of a public office by staying within the bounds of Islam, 33 of the 38 respondents answered in the affirmative. However, the lady who had replied that *in a country like India* a Muslim woman should stay away from politics said that it is not possible in India for a Muslim woman to take-up and discharge social responsibilities. Similar view was expressed by a Muslim male respondent. One Mufti from Saharanpur felt that it would be better if Muslim women undertake social responsibilities by staying within *purdah*. On the other hand, yet another Mufti from Saharanpur opined that by staying within *purdah* a Muslim woman can take-up any job. One respondent gave an ambiguous reply, stating: "depends".

The responses show that the notion that the responsibility for upholding Islamic identity rests with Muslim woman weighs foremost in the minds of the community. While this author has no complaint about Muslim women wearing a *hijab* and/or dressing up modestly and observing Islamic norms, asking her to wear *purdah* means restricting her activity outside her home and denying her the right to utilize her talents and productivity for the betterment of her own family and community. Similarly, does the response that Muslim women should not take part in politics *in a country like India* mean that a Muslim woman should keep away from political participation in a secular society?

However, 35 of the 38 respondents said that it is not fair to deny Muslim women of the opportunities available to women of other communities. While one respondent said that it is not correct to say that Muslim women are kept away from opportunities available to women of other communities because of Islam, one respondent felt that Muslim women cannot discharge their responsibilities outside their homes as well as they do in their homes.

In so far as Muslim women's political participation is concerned, 29 of the 38 respondents felt that the Muslim community might promote women's political participation if a separate quota is made available to them. One respondent thought that only 80 per cent of the community may promote women's participation even if there is a separate quota. On the other hand, one respondent felt that if women do not violate Islamic laws, the society may promote them. Like some respondents in other districts, one respondent said that the government should set aside a separate quota for the Muslim community first than setting aside a separate quota for Muslim women. Two women respondents felt that the community will never promote Muslim women's political participation—quota or no quota. The rest were not sure as to how the community would respond to such separate quota for Muslim women.

It is apparent from the above responses that the community is not too keen on Muslim women's political participation. Although we specifically asked the reasons, apart from religion, two respondents were candid that the religious leaders want Muslim women to stay out of politics. Others cited illiteracy, patriarchy and lack of resources, *purdah*, lack of awareness, society's outlook, family restrictions, socio-economic backwardness, inability to take decisions, lack of support from the community, and lack of acceptance by the community as the major reasons as to why fewer Muslim women were participating in elections as candidates. One respondent said that even Muslim men were not winning elections.

However, all, but two respondents agreed that Muslim women can represent the community's problems better in the Parliament or the Assembly, as compared to representatives of other communities. While one respondent asked as to why Muslim men cannot speak up on behalf of the community, another felt that once they get elected, even Muslim women forget about the community and concentrate only on their own interests. 34 of the 38 respondents felt that Muslim men in the Parliament and Assembly were not doing anything about the community's problems. Three respondents felt that although the men were doing their best, they were unable to achieve much success.

Yet another factor responsible for the community not promoting Muslim women's political participations seems to be that there are no secular parties which could be trusted. Only 8 of the 38 respondents perceived Indian National Congress as secular, as against five, who named the Samajwadi Party. Only two respondents regarded the Communist Parties as secular. All the other 23 respondents felt that none of the existing political parties were secular.

If lack of education and exposure are some of the reasons for Muslim women's poor participation in politics, the community has to promote education; especially secular education besides religious education. But, secular education, especially for Muslim girls, seems to be an anathema. For, when asked whether they considered that secular education would corrupt Muslim girls, at least six respondents answered in the affirmative as against 32, who did not think that it would. Yet, a majority of the respondents felt that Muslim girls also should acquire technical and professional qualifications for the betterment of the socio-economic status of the community. There were a few who thought that Muslim girls cannot remain unaffected by the evils of secular education and hence should learn household work and stay at home. One respondent observed that while staying within the limits of Islam, Muslim girls may acquire technical and professional qualifications under 'difficult circumstances'. Obviously disgusted with the outlook of the Muslim community towards secular education, one respondent felt that the Muslim society was 'willingly or unwillingly' enjoying all the benefits and developments of the modern world, without contributing anything.

### Allahabad (10), Lucknow (26), Varanasi (14)

Out of the total 50 respondents, 13 from Varanasi (including three *Ulema*), 23 from Lucknow and 9 from Allahabad said that Islam does not prohibit women's political participation. Three respondents (1 from Varanasi and 2 from Lucknow) were not aware of the actual position in *Quran*.

- Five female respondents from Varanasi and one from Lucknow believed that Islam prohibits women's political participation.
- One *Ulema* said that Muslim women could only function as 'advisors' (but they cannot participate in elections);
- One respondent who agreed that Islam did not prohibit women's political participation, added that it is only the

'mean-mindedness' of some people in the community that was responsible for such statements (that Islam prohibited women from political participation);
- One respondent added that Muslim women were also entitled to their Constitutional rights;
- One female respondent from Allahabad said that a Muslim woman can participate in elections subject to observing certain prescribed norms.

Although a majority of the respondents were aware that Islam did not prohibit women's political participation, it is evident that almost 20 per cent of the respondents were not fully aware of the provisions of *Quran* on the issue.

The question whether a Muslim woman cannot discharge the functions of public office remaining within the bounds of Islam and maintaining their religious identity, received the following response:

- Seven respondents felt that Muslim women cannot discharge the responsibilities of public office if she were to remain within the bounds of Islam and retaining her Islamic identity;
- Two respondents said that because of the *purdah* system prescribed under Islam for its women, Muslim women cannot join politics. One of them said that Islam even prohibits men and women listening to each other's voices, which is not possible if women join politics;
- One respondent said that Muslim women can discharge the functions of public office if they get departments like health and education, where women can interact with women only; and
- One respondent from Varanasi was specific: even remaining within the bounds of Islam, Muslim women can work in hospitals, banks, or open or take-up jobs in children's schools—sort of thus far and no further.

Thus, there seems to be a belief among some of the respondents that it is not possible for Muslim women to discharge the functions and duties of a public office remaining within the bounds of *Shariah*. Some believed to the extent that it is not possible for a Muslim woman to hold a public office even if she strictly followed the *Shariah*.

In so far as Muslim women's contesting elections if there is a separate quota for them, the following were the responses:

- If there is a separate quota for Muslim women, the community will encourage its women to avail the quota and contest elections (37 out of 50 respondents);
- Not sure if the community will allow its women to contest elections even if there is a separate quota for Muslim women (5 respondents);
- As a Muslim, a woman should live under *purdah* and hence, the community should not encourage them to contest elections even if there is a separate quota (One respondent);
- Even if there is a separate quota for Muslim women, the community will get a *fatwa* issued against women venturing into politics. This makes Muslim women back out (one respondent);
- Setting aside a separate quota for the Muslim women would be difficult or can never happen (two respondents);
- Even if there is a separate quota, the community will not encourage women to contest (four respondents);
- The community should encourage women even if there is no separate quota (one respondent);
- Cannot guess how the community would react in the event of a separate quota being made available to Muslim women (three respondents); and
- One respondent, a Professor at that, said that unless a Muslim woman remains within the limits of *Shariah* and *Purdah*, she would become a Hina Rabbani Khar (Pakistan's External Affairs Minister) or Nazma Heptulla (former Indian Speaker of Rajya Sabha).

A majority of the respondents from the three cities were aware that religion is not the sole reason for the poor performance of Muslim women contesting elections. They cited the following as the reasons influencing women's political participation:

1. Lack of awareness/ignorance/social skills and confidence.
2. Lack of support from the family and society.
3. Restrictions from the family and community and need to stay in *purdah*;

4. Poverty, Lack of education /Illiteracy.
5. Fear of insecurity, political and societal discrimination.
6. Corruption.
7. Patriarchy and/or male domination.
8. Double burden.
9. Lack of good leadership.

Only five of the 50 respondents still felt that religion and the restrictions imposed in the name of religion (like *purdah*) are mainly responsible for the poor performance of Muslim women in the elections. This response implies that the Muslim voters do not take kindly to Muslim women who dare to contest elections despite *fatwas*. This is evident from the experience of Syeda Khushtara Banu, who lost the election to the Hassan Municipal Corporation (Karnataka in 1978 *by a single vote*) (See Karnataka Chapter).

Thus, in reply to the question whether it was correct for religious leaders to issue *fatwas* on political issues or preventing Muslim women from contesting elections, 40 of the 50 respondents felt that it was not right. Only six respondents believed that the religious leaders were right in issuing such *fatwas*. Two respondents observed that *fatwas* were only for guidance and it was left to the individuals to agree/comply with the rulings or not. Two respondents did not respond to the question.

But, the fact remains that in a community which is economically poor and educationally backward, and in which the women are far more uneducated, *fatwas* have far-reaching effects. It is true that *fatwas* are not binding, even on the person seeking a ruling on a specific issue. But, the poor and illiterate who have no knowledge of such issues believe that they have to abide by *fatwas*.

In spite of reservations about the chances of Muslim women's political participation, 40 respondents replied that they were confident that once Muslim women enter the Assemblies or Parliament, they can raise issues affecting the community more effectively than men and women legislators of other communities. One respondent did not have a reply. The following are other responses:

- Muslim women will not be effective, because of their religion and being a minority;
- One should not distinguish between male and female legislators; and
- Muslim women are backward and cannot be any more effective than others.

The response to this question indicates that a majority of the respondents feel that there should be adequate number of Muslim women in the legislatures so as to effectively raise issues concerning the community. That the Muslim community has a number of problems is very well known. But, while legislators of non-Muslim communities do not want be seen as interfering in the affairs of the Muslim community, even Muslim male members of the legislatures or Lok Sabha toe the Party line and/or do not wish to appear rubbing the religious leaders on the wrong side. For instance, Arif Mohammed Khan had to quit the Indian National Congress in 1986 due to differences over the passage of Muslim Personal Law Bill which was piloted by Rajiv Gandhi in the Lok Sabha.

Do the male Muslim politicians safeguard the interests of the Muslim women? Seema Alavi, Associate Professor of History in Jamia Millia, New Delhi, wrote in 1999:[2]

> "There is a complete invisibility of women's issues in even the lip service political parties pay to Muslim concerns. Political rhetoric is generally based on the assumption that the Muslim community is neither gendered nor culturally variegated. This premise informs the political construction of a community leadership which is inevitably male and located in the narrowly defined class of *Ulema* (religious head). Thus *muftis* of towns and *mullahs* of mosques are seen as the repositories of the community's best interests and its sole spokesmen. Alongside, even though we do not have religious electorates, Muslim MPs are invariably viewed by political parties as representatives of their religious community. This was most clearly evident in the Congress government's handling of the Shah Bano case in 1986, and more recently in the demand from Muslim MPs for a quota for Muslim women within the proposed Women's Reservation Bill. In both these cases the opinion of the Muslim patriarchs received political attention even as women demonstrated against the unrepresentative character of the self-styled champions of their interests."

The fact that the present Muslim male leadership is not doing enough to solve the problems of the community is also evident from the replies to our question. 48 of the 50 respondents replied with a resounding 'No.' Two respondents however said that the Muslim male leaders were 'trying their best'. But, obviously, their efforts are not enough. This is evident from the fact that when the Chairman of the Minority Education Commission scoffed at co-education for Muslim girls, including *Madrasahs*, no male Muslim leader voiced his opposition.

Muslim women's political participation is also circumscribed by the perception that the political parties who might offer tickets to Muslim women or whom the Muslim women may approach for tickets are not secular. Most of our respondents believed that no political party is secular and does not have the interests of all sections of the people in its heart. Some felt that the Indian National Congress, the Bahujan Samaj Party, the Samajwadi Party and the Communist parties were secular.

But, if the secular character of the existing parties is suspect, Muslim women could contest under the banner of the Muslim political parties that have come up, especially during the 2012 Assembly elections, in Uttar Pradesh. Some of these Muslim-based parties claimed to be secular and not meant to work for the welfare of the Muslim community alone. Election statistics reveal that such parties have not promoted Muslim women's political participation. The reasons for this phenomenon are stated to be:

- Many of the respondents have not heard of Muslim political parties;
- No Muslim political party has tried to promote women's participation in elections;
- Muslim political parties think that it is not right to promote women;
- Muslim political parties accorded a lower status to women and because of the backwardness in their thinking, they did not want women to either get educated or join politics;
- Muslim political parties being dominated by males are patriarchal and have no intention of promoting women's participation;
- The efforts of Muslim-based political parties, if any, are only limited. Even when the Muslim political parties tried to promote women, the community did not cooperate;
- The society is still male-dominated and conservative in approach and thought;

- Muslim men think that women are their property and hence will have to do everything on their behalf. Though the basic principle of Islam is equality between men and women, men still do not think so. Hence, they do not allow Muslim political parties to nominate Muslim women.

In this context, it has been observed that some Muslim women have contested, both in Karnataka and Uttar Pradesh, under BJP banner at the elections to the Panchayati Raj Institutions. Such instances have also been reported from Maharashtra and Gujarat as well. Even if such instances are small, does it mean that the Muslim community has come to accept the Bharatiya Janata Party?

- 31 of the 50 respondents said that BJP is not acceptable to the Muslim community, although a few Muslim women might have contested PRI elections under BJP banner;
- Nine respondents answered in the affirmative;
- Two respondents said that the Muslim community has 'started' to accept BJP or has not 'completely' accepted the party;
- One respondent said that though the Party is not acceptable, some of its leaders are;
- Other 7 were non-communial or did not know; and
- One respondent said that Shia Muslims have accepted the BJP, but not the Sunni Muslims.

As regards Muslim girls acquiring technical and professional qualifications that would enable them find better paying jobs so as to improve the socio-economic conditions of their families, apart from making them better candidates in elections, 47 of the 50 respondents did not have any objection or reservations. Some of them attached a rider: "girls may acquire technical and professional qualifications, but staying with the religious prescriptions." While two respondents felt that girls would be depriving boys from jobs, one respondent felt that if there are no separate institutions for girls, they would fall prey to evil.

If the Muslim community does not want its girls to acquire secular education, what is the reason? As most institutions, especially those offering higher education or technical and professional courses are co-educational, is that what that prevents them? Do they think that secular education in co-educational institutions is not preferable for girls as it may corrupt them?

- 39 of the 50 respondents said that secular education does not corrupt Muslim girls and that they can remain religious in their attitude and behaviour while acquiring technical and professional qualifications. However, two *Ulema* among them who replied in the affirmative added a rider that in doing so the Muslim girls should keep in mind the requirements under *Shariah*, i.e., wearing *Hijab*;
- Three respondents did not favour co-education, with a *Ulema* holding that secular education gives the Muslim girls the capacity for independent thinking, which in turn, makes them corrupt and makes them go astray; and
- Six respondents felt that co-education corrupts girls; and
- One respondent had no answer to the question and another was not sure.

Without acquiring education, the Muslim community will remain mute spectators of the developments taking place around them, as they will not be equipped to avail the opportunities. Can the community afford to remain untouched with the developments in the modern world and without availing the opportunities? A majority of the respondents realise that the Muslim community cannot afford to remain untouched by developments in the modern world and that the community should avail the opportunities offered and that the Muslim women should not be denied of the opportunities available to women of other communities. Some of the respondents equated 'modern' with 'western' and said that if the development is based on Western ideology, which is evil, it is better that the Muslim community remains aloof from such developments. However, two respondents added that Muslim women could avail such opportunities by staying within the bounds of *Shariah*. One of the respondents said that the opportunities should be 'reasonable' and in keeping with *Quran*. Two respondents were so much concerned about Muslim women transgressing the *Shariah* in availing the opportunities that they said that they did not mind if the Muslim women forgo the opportunities available to other women.

It has been observed that while a large number of Muslim women have contested in the elections to the Panchayati Raj Institutions both in Karnataka and Uttar Pradesh, it is not so in the case of elections to the Legislative assembly and Parliament. Election statistics reveal that thousands of Muslim women have contested in the elections to the PRIs, although the success rate is not unsatisfactory. But, when it comes to elections to the Legislative assembly and Parliament, not only the number of contestants is small, but the success rate is appalling. The winning candidates are invariably the close relations of male political leaders or from the *elite* class. Cannot the Muslim women translate their enthusiasm in participating in the elections to the PRIs to Assembly and Lok Sabha elections? The response to this question is varied.

- There is no need to enter Assembly/Parliament.
- There are very few educated women who could try and contest for Parliament/Assembly seats, but they are bound by the society's restrictions;
- Lack of Muslim leadership to promote women's entry into Parliament/assembly.
- Lack of society's support.
- Males support women's participation in Panchayat elections because they can dictate terms and even work on behalf of the elected representatives. When a woman is elected to a PRI, her work is done by her husband or guardian and she just becomes a puppet in the hands of men. Woman's role gets limited to signing of papers. This is not possible if a woman wins a parliament/assembly election.
- If elected to a PRI, the area of work is closer home and Muslim women can operate within their cultural boundaries.
- It is easier to participate in local elections and resources needed are not much. On the other hand, contesting Legislative/Parliamentary elections involves more money and women from ordinary families can never reach that level.
- One would also need a lot of political clout to get even nominated for Assembly/Lok Sabha elections.
- Male leaders would never like to give a strong position to women and are against women's upliftment.
- Religious restrictions and *Purdah* system does not allow women to reach Assembly/Parliament.
- Poverty, illiteracy and lack of awareness on the part of women.

- Muslim women have lesser chances of contesting Parliamentary/Assembly elections as they are not issued tickets by political parties.
- Reservations in the PRIs have helped Muslim women. Absence of such reservation in the parliamentary and assembly elections makes it difficult.
- Because of corruption, muscle power and economic power, women are unable to contest parliament and assembly elections.
- Male chauvinism prevents men to promote women to participate in Assembly/Parliamentary elections.

The respondents were asked for their view, in general, on Muslim women's electoral participation. Six respondents did not feel it necessary for Muslim women to participate in elections. However, a majority felt that Muslim women should participate in elections for the betterment of the Muslim community. One respondent even felt that while Muslim women were contesting elections, the percentage could be increased by constant encouragement. One respondent agreed that Muslim women should also contest elections, but staying within the boundaries of the *Shariah*. One respondent said that before contesting elections, a Muslim woman should get educated and learn to respect the *purdah*. If she does not respect the *purdah*, she cannot respect the community.

## Responses from the Field: Karnataka

With a view to ascertaining the views on Muslim women's political participation, we approached several Muslim women and men in Bangalore, Mysore, Mandya, Gulbarga, Bijapur cities of Karnataka through our Field Investigators. However, unlike in Uttar Pradesh, several of the Karnataka respondents did not want to be identified and some did not want to commit in writing. We also approached several Muslim intelligentsias including people well-versed in Islamic norms, *Shariah* and *Quran*, academicians and those connected with politics and social activists. The following is a gist of the views expressed by the following respondents:

1. Professor Abdul Aziz, formerly Head, Department of Economics, Institute for Social and Economic Change (ISEC), Bangalore.

2. Mr. Shabbir Ahmed Khan, Islamic Scholar and Council Advisory member, Jamaat-e-Islami Hind, Bangalore.
3. Maulana Wahiduddin Khan, Convener, Majlis-e-Ulema Karnataka and Rector, *Jamiyat-ul-Tayyibat* (*Madrasah* for girls).
4. Abdul Riyaz Khan, Chairman, Wakf Board Karnataka.
5. Dr. Abdul Hameed Maqdoomi, Veterinary Doctor and Social Activist, Gulbarga.
6. Iqbal Ahmed Saradgi, State Vice President, Congress.
7. Mirza Mehdi, State President, Indian Union Muslim League.
8. Akbar Ali., State President, Welfare Party of India.
9. Abdul Mannan Sait, BSP leader.
10. Hafiz Syed Shamsul Huda, Social Activist and BSP leader.
11. Moulana Imtiyaz Hyder, Renowned Shia Islamic Scholar and Editor of *Misbah* Magazine.
12. B.S. Junaidi, President, Bijapur District Congress Committee (Minority Department).
13. Ms. Fathima Peer Mohammed Girgavi, BJP Vice President, Basavana Bagevadi, Bijapur.
14. Ms. Sheema Mohsin, National Convener, Welfare Party of India and Social Activist.

Replying to our question, all the respondents said that Islam does not bar women from political participation. Some, though, said that such participation should take into account and be within the limits prescribed by the *Shariah*. Mr. Shabbir Ahmed Khan said: "Though the word 'political' is a recent phenomenon, women have the right to participate along with men on equal footing and it is so mentioned in the *Quran*. Even the word public office is recently derived administration jugglery. Every work entrusted of any nature is a 'responsibility' which has to be discharged by both men and women".

With regard to the poor performance of Muslim women in elections, Shabbir Ahmed Khan said that: "While in the contemporary era, a person contesting an election claims himself to be the competent person, in Islam the right person is not only to be elected, but with the specific characteristics features, he has to be chosen."

All the others attributed lack of education and patriarchy as the main reasons for the poor performance of Muslim women in politics. Maulana Imtiyaz Hyder pinned the blame for the poor performance of Muslim women in elections on the society. "Community or the society did not give them a chance to perform. Some people from the community think that women should not go out of the house and there is no need to enter into politics. That is wrong." On the other hand, Hafiz Syed Shamsul Huda believes that "the Hindu upper cast lobby has kept Muslims away from taking active part in politics. Besides this, wrong perception about Islam is equally responsible." In his view, "some Muslim *Ulema* divided Islam into two categories: *Deen* and *Duniya* and they kept politics in *Duniya* and considered it as mundane activity".

All the respondents were confident that once elected to the Assembly/Parliament Muslim women can more effectively raise issues related to the Muslim community as compared to members of other communities. Shabbir Ahmed Khan felt that raising issues related to the Muslim community in the Parliament or Assembly has no relation to the sex; whether it is men or women. Those who are deeply involved in the society alone can feel the pinch which makes them to rise to the occasion and place the feelings in an orderly manner.

Responding to the effectiveness of the male Muslim political leaders, Shabbir Ahmed Khan said: "Among Muslims there are two specific sections; one is Leader and second is *Qayid*. As narrated in Prophet Moses' history, Hazrat Taloot was chosen because of *Ilm* (Knowledge). Therefore, the *Qayids* are successful among Muslim community because they are backed by pre-requisition, i.e., *ilm,* whereas leaders who know little will have no depth as far as knowledge is concerned, with some exceptions." Others felt that the existing Muslim male political leaders were either not serving the community's interests as is expected of them or they were not successful in solving the problems of the community. One respondent scoffed: "We should not label them as community leaders; rather they are representative of their parties." Yet another respondent said that, "Rather Hindu leaders have more concern towards Muslim community than Muslim leaders."

With regard to Muslim-based political parties, the consensus was that the parties have not tried to promote Muslim women's political participation as they are male dominated.

As regards the secular character of the political parties, there was a wide consensus that none of the existing political parties were secular. Some, however, named the Congress and Welfare Party of India.

However, all the respondents opined that Muslim women should not be denied the opportunities available to women of other communities. Availing the opportunities of the present times necessitates acquiring education and suitable qualifications. While the Muslim boys usually enter the family business/trade after certain level of education, the Muslim society could allow the girls to acquire better educational qualifications. Almost all the respondents agreed that secular education does not corrupt Muslim girls and that they could acquire technical and professional qualifications and there is no prohibition in this regard; some adding that a Muslim girl should maintain her Islamic identity and keep in view the limits prescribed by the *Shariah*. However, one respondent felt that improving the socio-economic condition of the family is not a girl's basic responsibility; it is a wrong concept.

Shabbir Khan replied that "in the present day context the education is considered as 'pre-requisite for livelihood', but it is totally wrong … Islam does not restrict anyone from acquiring knowledge and even the word *'Iqra'* which was the first verse revealed by the Prophet, does not specify what type of knowledge. Therefore, the time and situation will decide the type of knowledge to be acquired."

All the respondents agreed that the Muslim community cannot afford to remain untouched with the developments in the modern world and remain a mute spectator, without availing the opportunities. They said that the community should take active part in the ongoing developments.

With regard to our inquiry whether it was correct for *Ulema* to issue *fatwas* on political issues or preventing Muslim women from contesting elections, Shabbir Ahmed Khan said that while there is no group called as religious leaders, persons who have acquired knowledge and are acquainted with the realities (Persons with *Taffaqqo Fiddeen'*) are not only competent, but are the right persons to come out with diktats to keep the society in the right track". He, thus, believes that it is right for the *Ulema* to issue *fatwas* even on political issues.

Other respondents were cautious in their responses. While one respondent said that a *fatwa* could be issued "if the need occurs", others either did not want to comment or opined that a *fatwa* should be in the light of *Quran* and *Hadith* or a *fatwa* could be issued on Muslim women's political participation if one is transgressing the *Shariah* limits. There was also a feeling that *fatwa* being an opinion, it may vary from one Mufti to the other and that it is not an order. Only two respondents said that the *Ulema* have no right to issue *fatwas* that hinder the political participation of Muslim women.

If there are no political parties that could be considered truly secular, have the Muslim political parties tried to promote women's participation in elections? If not, why? The responses varied. Several of the respondents said that there are no Muslim political parties in Karnataka like IUML in Kerala and *Ittehadul Muslimeen* in Hyderabad. One respondent felt that in the absence of Muslim parties in Karnataka, the community should form its own political party with honest leaders and unite under one banner. But, one respondent felt that "not just Muslim political party, but all political parties have poorly fielded women candidates as they do not want competition."

If some Muslim women have contested elections under BJP ticket, they were exercising their Constitutional right and for their own personal benefit. But, by and large, most of the respondents said that the BJP is not acceptable to the Muslim community. The main objections of the antagonists were:

- Muslim community wants that a secular party should come to power;
- If the BJP interferes with the personal liberties of the Muslim community, the latter will not accept the Party; and
- No Muslim can accept BJP ideology which is anti-secular and anti-Muslim.

Sounding disillusioned, some of the respondents said that the BJP was as good or as bad as the Congress and there was no difference between the two parties. On the other hand, some respondents felt that it is wrong to blame BJP and said that though people perceive it as a communal party, it is concerned with Muslim community too. It is obvious that the Bharatiya Janata Party has to work hard to erase its communal tag if it has to win over the Muslim community.

As regards their views, in general, on Muslim women's electoral participation, one respondent felt that the present situation in India is not safe for women. Sheema Mohsin, Member, Karnataka Waqf Board replied: "Muslim woman's electoral participation is poor as she has very little support and encouragement and is generally looked down by the society. Islam has given many rights to woman. Lack of awareness and mind-set has discouraged and deprived Muslim woman from performing and exercising them and over a period of time she thinks it is a man's arena and gives up altogether". Dr. Abdul Aziz feels that financial constraint and the vastness of the constituencies are some of the reasons for the poor performance of Muslim women in Assembly/Parliament elections. In spite of such constraints, Professor Abdul Aziz and some other respondents desired that Muslim women should not only vote in big numbers and contest elections, but they should also join political parties mobilize public opinion, lobby and canvas in favour of women candidates. They wanted the Muslim community to encourage women not only in politics, but in every other field. A few chose not to answer the question.

## Views of Muslim Women in Politics

The Project's Field Investigator visited Bijapur and Gulbarga districts to meet a number of Muslim women who had contested in elections to the Urban Local Bodies and seek their opinion on a variety of issues.

Our Field Investigator observed that as most of the women were either illiterate or poorly educated, almost every elected woman in both districts was manipulated by her husband or other male relatives. Even as an elected member of the ULB or other PRIs, she did not step out of the house or participate in any policy or decision-making meetings. Instead, the attendance diary was taken to her home for her signature. The Field Investigator reports: "they have been used as puppets and I felt they are proud of being used as such."

Although the questionnaire was more detailed, the respondents chose to answer only those which did not put them in an awkward position. The following is a gist of the responses elicited by the Field Investigator in Bijapur and Gulbarga.

- Shahnaz Begum Abdul Mubeen Inamdar, Bijapur had contested the ULB elections in 2007 on Congress party ticket, with the support of her husband, family and the community, apart from the religious leaders. Asked as to how the men treated women in the Party, she said: "Men think that women are not fit for decision-making. A woman faces problems from the party itself. Once a woman enters into politics, there would be no respect left for her." The main hurdles in contesting elections for a woman are poor educational status and lack of finance. She felt that there should be reservation for Muslim women.

- Bibijan Shanawaz Mangoli, Bijapur was an independent candidate at the ULB elections in 2007 from a ward reserved for women, as she was not given a ticket by the political parties. Her husband, who was in politics, encouraged her while the community offered manpower. However, in her opinion, men think that women are not fit for decision-making. She also cited lack of education and poor finances as the main hurdles for women in contesting elections. While a separate reservation for Muslim women might help, she feels that education is the first requirement followed by a pro-active role by the political parties towards women. She is aware that Islam does not bar women from political participation.
- Khaderbi Basheer Ahmed Hundgund of Bijapur was a contestant at the 2007 ULB elections on Congress ticket. Her husband said that although the constituency was dominated by women, he regrets his decision to make his wife contest as he found that the "local politics is full of dirt." In answer to the question as how she is treated by the men the ULB, she said: "The party members call the husband if needed and the attendance register is signed at home itself." Based on her experience, she says that Muslim women should not enter into politics especially in urban localities. They are treated as nothing, but a mere formality. Muslim women cannot survive in politics unless they have a god-father and is irreligious. Her view on empowering Muslim women: "She should be educated and serve the community, but without entering into politics."
- Yasmin Nisar Ahmed Patel, Bijapur had contested the 2007 ULB elections on party ticket and with the support of the family and community. However, she feels that men think that women are not fit for decision-making. In spite of the problems, she had plans to fight the next elections with a view to help development of the community and to solve women-related issues. She is aware that Islam does not bar women's entry into politics and she is given due respect if she really works for the upliftment of the society. But, first and foremost, women should be educated and there should be equal rights to both genders.

- Shaheda Kasimsaab Patwegar, Bijapur contested the 2007 ULB elections as an independent candidate, as she could not get party nomination. She feels that women should actively take part in developing the community. She is aware that Islam does not bar women from political participation. But education and necessary financial means are essential for contesting elections.
- Hasimbi Rajaksaab Ambarkhan, Bijapur. Contested 2007 ULB elections on Congress party ticket. She had the support of the family and community. She feels that exposure to the outside world and education play a very important role if Muslim women were to succeed in politics and said that a separate reservation for Muslim women will be an added advantage.
- Shahista Nayeem Serikar, Gulbarga won the 2007 ULB elections from a ward reserved for women on Congress party ticket. She had the support of the family and community. She feels that it is necessary that Muslim women should enter politics for the development of the community and to solve women related issues. She is aware that Islam does not bar women from political participation and she is treated with respect by the male members of the Party.
- Meharunnisa Abdul Samad Begum, Gulbarga is yet another woman who contested and won the 2007 ULB elections as an independent candidate, as she was not offered a ticket by any political party, including the Janata Dal (Secular). She had the support of her family and community. She is also aware that Islam does not bar Muslim women's political participation. She feels that a woman with good exposure and education can command respect from the males and there is no need to have a godfather to survive in politics.
- Malanbi Kasim Ali, Gulbarga. She contested the 2007 ULB elections under Congress party ticket and won. But she shifted her alliance to JD (S) after two years. She had the support of the family and community, but not the religious leaders. She is aware that Islam does not bar women's political participation. But, a woman should have sound education to command respect from the male members of the Party. But she confides that the Police from the area did not support her in any way (when needed).

- Nasreen Begum, Gulbarga contested and won the 2007 ULB elections as a Congress party nominee, with support from husband and community. Even the religious leaders lent their support. She is aware that Islam does not bar women from political participation. She feels that a separate reservation for Muslim women in Lok Sabha and Assembly elections may not benefit women as the men dominate women in every aspect.
- Jameela Begum, Gulbarga. She contested and won the 2007 ULB elections from a ward reserved for women on Congress party ticket. She was supported by her husband and the community, including religious leaders. As to the question of males' attitude towards women in the party, she says that "they do not even consider our opinions".

All the above women, who had participated in the ULB elections, were aware that Islam did not prohibit women's political participation. They emphasised that Muslim women were definitely interested in political participation and contest elections even as independents, as they feel that as an elected representative of the PRI or legislature, they would be able help the development of the community and attend to issues concerning Muslim women. It is obvious that the elected representatives continue to be dominated by men, who think nothing of even usurping the functions of Muslim women elected representatives. What comes out clearly is that unless a Muslim woman (any woman, for that matter) is educated and has wide exposure, she cannot command respect from the male members of the party nor have a say in decision-making. By and large, the society, especially the political class, Muslim or otherwise, is yet to realise that women have to be treated with dignity and respect and it a woman's right to be in politics.

## Respondents from Bangalore

Before considering the responses to our questionnaire from Muslim women of Bangalore City, we feel it is relevant to give a brief background.

Bangalore is the political and IT capital of Karnataka, with a cosmopolitan population. The city has a number of good educational institutions, including medical and engineering colleges, some established as a part of State-sponsored projects, which offer immense educational opportunities. With a number of IT companies, the city also offers a ready opportunity if one has right educational qualifications. It is for this reason that Bangalore has attracted qualified youth from all over the country, making the city polyglot.

Muslims of Bangalore have a high literacy rate, although lower than the city average and lower than other religious groups. However, a sheer high *literacy rate* does not necessarily imply enough education and qualifications to get a job of the formal sector of the economy.[3] For, a 1994 survey had revealed that 43.2 per cent of the educated Muslims of Bangalore were educated up to 7th standard and 12.8 per cent were educated above 7th standard.[4]

**Table 7.3:** Literacy Rates of Muslims in 2001 (%) in Bangalore, Karnataka, India

| | *Bangalore* | *Karnataka* | *India* |
|---|---|---|---|
| Males | 81.3 | 76.9 | 67.6 |
| Females | 77.2 | 63.0 | 50.1 |
| **Total Muslim population** | **79.3** | **70.1** | **59.1** |

*Source: Census of India*, 2011, quoted by Aminah Md. Arif, p. 292.

It is held that the educational policies of the State Government and economic growth have benefitted the Muslim community also, though not as much as the other communities.[5] Muslims have also established a number of educational institutions in Karnataka, most of which are run under the Al-Ameen movement, which also provides schools for the underprivileged. The establishment of these schools and colleges has, in turn, resulted in an educated middle class, which, in turn, has set up several other institutions like hospitals, interest-free banks and publishing houses etc.[6] Muslims of Bangalore/Karnataka have also established a good name in the real estate business. However, in the matter of higher education, Muslim girls are reported to be lagging behind. Bangalore-based Professor Hasnath Mansur who worked as Principal of a girls' college for 23 years was concerned with the dramatic absence Muslim women in higher education. Among the thousands of girls enrolled in the colleges where she served, she found that Muslim girls were just a handful. She discovered that "acute poverty was the main culprit". She found that except for a few households, most Muslims were poor and the parents could not afford the fees. "One of the biggest and enduring myths is that it is our religion that stands in the way of Muslim women's progress. But I can say with conviction that it is not Islam, but poverty that is the root cause. It was not only the many Hindus and Christians believed the myth that Islam imposed restrictions on women, but far more disturbing was that many Muslims too believe this myth. Professor Mansur deplores that poverty unfortunately kept the Muslim community not only poor, but backward, ignorant, superstitious and illiterate. This enabled a misguided section of the orthodox clergy to get away with their misinterpretations of Islam."[7] This situation is to be kept in view while considering the responses to some of our questions.

Besides higher education of Muslim girls, "as far as their political representation is concerned, Muslims are largely under-represented at all levels. However, Bangalore is home to a few major political figures, whose reputation crosses the boundaries of Karnataka, like K. Rahman Khan (former Deputy Chairman of Rajya Sabha and then the Union Minister for Minority Affairs) and Jaffer Shariff, former Union Railway Minister. The Muslim political leadership of Bangalore also includes local figures such as Roshan Baig, who has held different portfolios as State Minister and Mumtaz Begum, the first Muslim Mayor of Bangalore."[8] In 2009, Mumtaz Ali Khan became a Minister of Haj, Waqfs and Minority Welfare in the first ever BJP government in a South Indian State. He was responsible for the induction of Ms. Sheema Mohsin as a Member of the Karnataka Waqf Board, much to the consternation of the Muslim community that a Muslim woman has been made a member of the Board.

In spite of the opportunities available at their door-step, Muslims of Karnataka do not seem to have taken the initiative for various reasons. Some of the reasons will be evident from the responses to our questionnaire.

In the above background, we also elicited the views of 31 Muslim women from the city of Bangalore. The respondents included a 16 years-old secondary school student to housewives, teachers, professionals, entrepreneurs, business women and college teachers. The responses are summarised below:

1. 27 of the 31 respondents are aware that Islam does not prohibit Muslim women from political participation. One of them even said that "besides their religious rights and duties, Muslim women are also entitled to their Constitutional

rights." Some of the respondents however added that such participation should be subject to observing Islamic mores and *Shariah*.

Yet, there are still misconceptions in the minds of the community about Muslim women's electoral participation, as is evident from the replies of other respondents. For, while two respondents said that Islam prohibits women's political participation, one lady (a lecturer in the Engineering faculty) said that "in some places women are prohibited as long as certain conditions are met."

A 16-year old Muslim girl (student) said that though Islam does not categorically prohibit women's political participation, "in Islam certain positions are declared for men and women and as such women cannot go against such restrictions. If they do, it will only result in failure. Islam says that men should be at the front in every walk of life and women should be behind them. Islam says that a woman should be fully covered and should not expose herself. Islam does not give permission to women to participate in elections. (For), participating in elections (has) many risks ... ... (for), it is not just entering one's name, but one has to follow all the rules. (She elaborated saying that while a man can undertake canvassing, meeting people, including men, address gatherings etc., "a woman cannot walk through the roads and ask people to vote for her.").

One respondent said that Muslim women are restricted from public appearance and contesting elections in Islam mainly with her safety in mind. "Our country is not open to accepting a woman with *hijab* as a contestant in elections."

2. However, 28 of the 31 respondents said that a Muslim woman can take-up and discharge the functions of a public office while maintaining her Islamic identity. Of these, one respondent added that a Muslim woman can take-up and discharge the functions of a public office if the family and the society permit and two respondents who had answered in the affirmative, felt that it would be difficult. One respondent declared that given a chance and if restrictions are not imposed on each and every movement of a Muslim woman, she will definitely make changes for the better. But, to be able to do so, she should be educated in the first instance.

One respondent felt that a Muslim woman cannot discharge the functions of a public office and yet remain within the bounds of Islam and maintain her Islamic identity. Another lady commented that "most of our community are illiterate, chauvinistic and will not allow women to undertake the responsibility of a public office."

3. Responding to the question on secular education, the respondents agreed that secular education does not corrupt Muslim girls as long as they retain their faith in Islam and that they can acquire technical and professional qualifications which would enable them improve the economic status of their families.

   A respondent commented that if more Muslim girls get educated and join the mainstream, it would change the view of other communities towards the Muslims. But, some respondents entertained apprehensions that if Muslim girls attain higher education "they may get carried away with the temptations around them." But there were others who said that higher education instils confidence in girls. In any case, all the 31 respondents agreed that the Muslim community cannot remain untouched with the developments in the modern world and allow the world go by. If this were not to happen, the community has to concentrate on education.
4. 30 of the 31 respondents agreed that it is not fair to deny Muslim women the opportunities available to women of other communities. One of the respondents said: "If each one comes forward with different rules to be followed, it restricts the freedom of Muslim women and makes it difficult for them in the path of progress. That is the biggest problem." The respondent questioned: "Right from the commoner to the biggest religious leader, everyone has a comment or judgement on Muslim women's actions. Why?" Only one respondent (a housewife) held a different view. She answered the question with a "yes." Meaning that it does not matter if a Muslim woman is denied the opportunities available to women of other communities. She did not elaborate.
5. To the question whether the Muslim community will encourage its women contest elections if a separate quota is made available, five respondentsdid not think so. One respondent explained: "Till date we have men in our

community who do not want their wives, sisters or daughters to go out of the house. As the women are dependent on men even for the smallest things, they are scared to face the world. Unless a woman is permitted to face the world and take part in conversation with other people right from the beginning, no matter what quota is introduced, it is going to be of no use." Two respondents were sure that even if there is a separate quota for Muslim women, the society will not encourage them. The rest 24 respondents believed that the Muslim community would encourage its women if there is a separate quota.

6. While almost all the respondents attributed lack of education, poor finances, lack of awareness of affairs outside the home, low self-esteem, domestic responsibilities and want of support of the family and society as the main reasons for the poor performance of Muslim women in elections, some respondents attributed it to male chauvinism in the Muslim society, which, as one of them insisted, "is more than 100 per cent true." The latter felt that men of the community need to be sensitised to the fact that "women are not objects to be grounded at home." But, there was a wider consensus that Muslim women can take-up issues relating to the community more effectively in Assembly and Parliament than others. There were a few who did not think that Muslim women would be able to effectively represent the community's issues in the Assembly/Parliament.
7. However, all the 31 respondents agreed that the Muslim male politicians were either doing nothing or were not doing enough to solve the problems of the community. One respondent said that even if there are a few good leaders, "they have been told that working for the Muslim men and women was no use and it was not going to work." Only one respondent named Mr. Roshan Baig (Congress), Minister for Haj, Waqfs and Minority Affairs in the present Karnataka Cabinet), who has taken interest in providing basic amenities to the poor.
8. Similarly, the respondents were not happy with the performance of Muslim-based political parties and said that such parties have not tried to promote Muslim women either

due to male domination or due to sheer neglect of Muslim women, on account of egoism and religious limitations. [9]

9. All the respondents agreed that secular education does not corrupt Muslim girls and they can pursue professional and technical courses of study and help in improving the socio-economic status of their families. A few, however, cautioned that the girls should not give in to temptations and remain firmly bound to their Islamic values. The respondents also agreed that the community cannot remain untouched with the developments in the modern world, without availing the opportunities available.
10. Most of the respondents played safe by not responding to the question whether it was correct for religious leaders to issue *fatwas* on political issues and/or preventing Muslim women's political participation. The few that responded said that it was not correct, although, they added, *fatwas* may be necessary in the interests of Islamic values. One respondent however said that "the religious leaders cannot be raising their voice for every second thing that a Muslim woman does… because she is not doing anything that is against her religion." Yet another respondent said that a "right and authentic *fatwa* is always welcome."
11. Most respondents felt that the Congress Party was secular. Others cited Janata Dal (Secular), Janata Dal (United) and the new entrant, the Aam Admi Party. Others either did not respond or said that they had no idea. As regards the Bharatiya Janata Party, the respondents were almost unanimous that it was not acceptable to the Muslim community, even if some Muslim women have contested elections under BJP banner.
12. A large number of Muslim women have been participating in the elections to the PRIs as compared to the elections to the State Assembly/Parliament. The respondents adduced different reasons for this phenomenon. Male ego, women's safety, need to wear *hijab*, largeness of the Assembly/ Parliament constituencies as opposed to the PRIs constituencies etc., were cited as the reasons. Only one out of the 31 respondents said that she does not favour Muslim women entering politics or contest elections.
13. While four of the 31 respondents said that Muslim women should stay away from politics, others felt that Muslim

**Table 7.4:** General Opinion on Muslim's Politics Participation in Respondents

| | *Respondents* | | | *Among male respondents* | | | |
|---|---|---|---|---|---|---|---|
| | *Male* | *Female* | *Total* | *Maulvi* | *Mufti* | *Local politician* | *Others* |
| Chamrajnagar | 21 | 4 | 25 | 7 | 1 | 2 | 11 |
| Mandya | 13 | 12 | 25 | 4 | 2 | 1 | 6 |
| Mysore | 14 | 11 | 25 | 3 | 3 | 5 | 3 |
| **Total** | **48** | **27** | **75** | **14** | **6** | **8** | **20** |

*Source:* Author's Field Study.

women should be encouraged to actively participate in politics "because they are patient, capable of understanding problems better and are good at multi-tasking. Remaining well within Islamic boundaries women can do wonders in any field, provided they are given support, respect and freedom by their family and community, especially their male counterparts."

## Responses from Chamrajnagar, Mandya and Mysore

Responses to the questionnaire were collected from 25 respondents each from Chamrajnagar, Mandya and Mysore of the State. The respondents were as given Table 7.4.

Only two Moulavis (one each from Chamrajnagar and Mysore) and one Mufti (Mandya) said that it was correct if Islam categorically prohibited women's political participation. Among the others, only 5 respondents, including one woman, said that Islam was right in prohibiting women's political participation. All the other 67 respondents said that Islam did not prohibit women's political participation. When we sought their general opinion on Muslim women's political participation, of the two Moulavis, only one Maulavi said that they should not participate in elections while the other said that a Muslim woman will only lose if she contests an election. All the other respondents were in favour of women's political participation.

20 of the 75 respondents, including 10 Moulavis and Muftis, felt that Muslim women cannot discharge the functions of a public office and yet stay within the limitations prescribed by Islam.

What is interesting is that 68 of the 75 respondents said that it is unfair to deny Muslim women of the opportunities available to women of other communities. Such opportunity includes political participation and aspiring for an elected office. Only two Moulavis did not mind if Muslim women are denied such opportunities.

23 of the 75 respondents did not believe that the community will promote Muslim women's political participation even if a separate quota is made available to them. Four respondents had no opinion to express on the question. The responses to the question shows that a sizeable number of the respondents were still not sure whether the community would encourage Muslim women's political participation.

However, it is observed that a major part of the community's reluctance or unpreparedness to allow its women to participate in Assembly and Parliamentary elections has nothing to do with religion. Only two of the respondents attributed religion to the disinclination of the community. All others felt that illiteracy of the women, poverty, lack of awareness of politics, absence of support from the families and community, influence of religious leaders, minority status of the community etc., as the main reasons. Some respondents felt that a majority of the electorate being Hindus, Muslim women were unable to win. But, as we have seen in the earlier chapter, Muslim women were unable to win or poll a respectable number of votes even in Muslim-dominated constituencies.

Keeping in view the educational backwardness and lack of exposure, 20 of the respondents felt that Muslim women members will not be able to represent the community's issues effectively in the assembly or parliament. On the other hand 53 respondents reposed faith in elected Muslim women representatives. Only two respondents did not have any answer. The reason may be due to the fact that 34 of the 75 respondents felt that male Muslim leaders were doing their best to highlight the community's problems. While 4 respondents did not answer the question, the remaining 37 felt that the Muslim male politicians have failed the community.

As to the secular character of the political parties, 16 respondents felt that there were none. However, 18 respondents named Janata Dal (Secular) and as many as 38 named the Congress Party. Only one respondent named Janata Dal (United) as the secular party, although it has no presence in Karnataka. Others did not have an opinion. At the same time, 50 of the 75 respondents opined that the Muslim-based political parties had no interest in promoting Muslim women's political participation. 14 respondents did not reply to the question while the rest attributed the disinclination of the Muslim parties to male domination and the bias against women. Only 10 respondents believed that Muslim parties were helping to promote women's political participation. One respondent said that there were no Muslim political parties in Karnataka, although the Welfare Party is supposed to be a Muslim-based political party. On the other hand, 14 respondents, including 2 Moulavis and one Mufti, felt that the Bharatiya Janata Party was acceptable to the community. It is obvious that a majority did not favour BJP although Muslim women have contested the ULB/PRI elections on BJP ticket in the past.

The question of religious leaders issuing *fatwas* prohibiting Muslim women's political participation or placing restrictions elicited a clear response. 53 of the 75 respondents said that it was not correct. The respondents included 8 Moulavis and Muftis. On the other hand, 2 Muftis and 7 Moulavis thought it was correct for the religious leaders to issue such *fatwas*. Others had no opinion to express.

As regards the question whether secular education corrupts Muslim girls and whether Muslim girls cannot acquire secular education by retaining their religious identity, a majority of the respondents answered that Muslim girls could acquire technical and professional qualifications without losing their Islamic identity. Only 4 Muftis and Moulavis felt otherwise. By and large, the opinion was that Muslim girls could acquire technical professional qualifications so as to access better jobs and improve the socio-economic status of their families.

A number of reasons were cited for fewer Muslim women contesting Assembly/Parliamentary elections. The reasons included poverty, lack of finances, oppression by males, lack of support (of the family and society), fear of losing, minority status and poor sponsorship by political parties. Some of the respondents felt that when even Muslim males were losing elections, Muslim women stood no chance of a victory.

Finally, the general opinion of the respondents was that Muslim women should enter electoral politics. One lady replied that it is the male opinion that counts more than what the women hold, demonstrating the major role played by the Muslim males in deciding whether Muslim women should enter electoral politics or not. Only one Moulavis felt that Muslim women should not participate in elections.

The responses from the field reflect the ambitions and aspirations on the one hand and the dejection and helplessness of the Muslim women on several aspects; not only political participation. The responses also reflect the confusion; between the religious obligations and life's realities.

## NOTES AND REFERENCES

1. According to the Rules, a candidate has to offer Rs. 25,000 as security deposit when contesting for a Lok Sabha seat and Rs.10,000 for an Assembly seat. A candidate cannot also spend more than Rs. 25 lakhs for fighting election from a Parliamentary constituency in States like UP and Bihar and Rs.10 lakhs from an Assembly constituency. However, one MLA said: "between Rs. 50-70 lakh is the average amount of money that goes into the total electoral process for any serious candidate. Just vehicle rentals can cost about Rs. 5 lakh. There are other things in campaigning like posters, banners and workers and voters, all of whom have to be kept satisfied. There is other expenditure which we cannot discuss openly." Mail Online India, 1st November, 2013 (Available at http://www.dailymail.co.uk/indiahome/indianews/article-2483842/How-elections-really-cost-Delhi-MLAs-admit-campaigning-costs-20-TIMES-declared-past-candidates.html)
2. *Indian Express*, On the Internet. (Available at http://expressindia.indianexpress.com/ie/daily/19990921/iex21050p.html)
3. Aminah, Mohammad Arif (2012), Muslims of Bangalore: A Minority at Ease? In *Muslims in Indian Cities: Trajectories of Marginalisation* (Ed.) Laurent Gayer and Christophe Jaffrelot, London: C. Hurst & Co., pp. 291-92.
4. *Ibid.*
5. *Ibid.*, p. 293.
6. *Ibid.*
7. In *The Weekend Leader*, Vol. 3, No. 3, 23rd March, 2014. (Available at http://www.theweekendleader.com/Causes/931/Late-bloomer.html)
8. Aminah, Mohmmad Arif, *op. cit.*, p. 294.
9. Charles Kurzman and Ijlal Naqvi, who have analysed the performance of 48 Islamic political parties in Muslim-majority countries in the past 4 decades have come to the conclusion that "It is far more common for Islamic parties to lose (and except for handful of high-profile cases) and finds that most Islamic parties are unable to attract more than a small fraction of Muslim voters. Just over a third of the parties explicitly call for equal rights for women. The 2002 platform of the Justice and Development Party in Turkey devoted a sub-section to women's rights and said: "All necessary measures shall be taken to encourage women to participate in public life. Women shall be encouraged to enrol as members to our Party and to play

an active role in politics. Support shall be provided to associations, foundations and non-governmental organizations related to women. Organizations dealing with women's problems will be consulted when legal arrangements will be made on the subject of women. The prevention of violence, sexual and economic exploitation against women shall be included among priority policies of our Party...." The 2002 platform of the Felicity Party in Turkey, by contrast, mentioned women's rights in passing within a section on family issues, and concludes that "women's most important problem is the dilemma of [combining] work and family life. ... ... On the issue of women's rights, four parties added support for full equality for women (the Salafi Islamic Association in Kuwait, Hizbullah in Lebanon, the Jamaat-e-Islami in Bangladesh, and the Party of Justice and Development in Morocco), and only one downgraded from full equality to a distinct role for women (the Muslim Brotherhood of Egypt, which also sparked controversy with its draft platform of 2007, which made a point of saying that a woman could not serve as head of state, among other shifts). (Kurzman, Charles Kurzman and Ijlal Naqvi, *Islamic Political Parties and Parliamentary Elections*, Working Paper, United States Institute of Peace, January 15, 2009. University of North Carolina, Chapel Hill).

# 8
# Conclusion

In one of its reports, the United Nations warns that it will take more than 50 years for countries like India to achieve gender balance in politics if women's participation in Parliament does not improve. Although women are turning up to vote in increasingly large numbers at each election, they are still not seen as politically important to find a place on the ballot paper. Their votes are taken for granted as the political parties assume that their voting patterns are mostly influenced by the male members of the family or community. As women constitute nearly half the electorate, they would remain excluded from the decision-making process if they are not adequately represented in the legislature. No political party has shown enthusiasm in addressing this important issue.

Although there are complaints of discrimination against Indian women in general in various fields, such discrimination is more conspicuous in politics. For, even after 70 years of independence, the presence of women in the Parliament has not exceeded 10 per cent and they account for even less in the State Assemblies.[1]

It is no consolation that in Indian women enjoyed an exalted position in the society in ancient times and they were treated at par with men even in political and philosophical spheres. Even Muslim women enjoyed such status right from the Prophet's time. However, over the centuries, the position of women has deteriorated and politically they are pushed to the background. It is not that they have retreated on their own volition; they had no choice in a man's world.

Women represent roughly 50 per cent of the population. Being in politics they can ensure that their rights are upheld and many women-specific and gender-sensitive issues are taken up more effectively and passionately. Crimes against women can be curbed and laws meant to protect women can be strengthened if there are women in authority to address them. Women's entry into public space and exercising authority will improve their self-esteem. Also, compared to men, women are generally less corrupt and more committed. Given the right opportunity, they are capable of cleansing the system. But it is highly essential that adequate number of women from all important segments of the society should come together for this cause and assert themselves. It is also equally important that women are provided a secure and honorable space to enhance their performance so as to facilitate many women to engage themselves in politics without hesitation. Thus, unless specific conditions are met, women face multiple hurdles and find it difficult to participate in the political process that has so far remained a male bastion. The reasons for this not happening are gender-specific. Besides historical prejudices, women are less mobile than men as their domestic responsibilities places limits on the time they can spend outside their homes. Consistent efforts will have to be made over a period of time to engender the political processes, institutions and issues that are critical to such exercise.

As the political parties are unlikely to accommodate more women on the ballot paper without compulsion, there is no alternative than extending reservations, of one form or the other, for women as has been done in many countries. But the Women's Reservation Bill in India is yet to become a law even after more than 15 years of its introduction in the Parliament. Having received the assent of the Rajya Sabha, it is yet to be passed by the Lok Sabha. The oft repeated reason, that efforts to get the Bill passed in the Lok Sabha is stalled for want of political consensus, is a euphemism for lack of political will. Getting the bill passed now rests with the new government that will be in position after the 2014 elections.

*** *** ***

Within Indian women, Muslim women are almost unseen in the country's Parliament and State Legislatures despite forming 12 per cent of India's female population. It is an accepted fact that without being proportionately present in the political system, not only the nature of the representative system, but also a given group's ability to influence policy-making becomes limited. This is more so with the large Muslim women population, who have their own religion-specific problems and issues that affect their socio-economic conditions. Non-Muslim members of the Parliament, including women members (who, in any case, are few in number), do not wish to raise the problems of the Muslim women in the legislature for fear of being blamed by the Muslim community of interference in its internal affairs. The Muslim male members of the Parliament/ Assemblies assume that Muslim women have no problems and even if there are any, the legislature is not the forum to address them. Hence neither the non-Muslim nor the Muslim MPs or MLAs raise issues that are specific to Muslim women. But, without a bold initiative of the community, it will be difficult to get a fair representation for Muslim women. A look at the figures of Muslim women in the 15 Parliamentary elections held so far makes it clear that it is almost impossible for a Muslim woman to get elected; even from constituencies dominated by Muslims.

It is held that the Muslim society in India continues to be male dominated as there have been no social and economic reforms and Muslim women still do not fully enjoy the rights granted to them under *Quran*. Pointing out that they have fewer rights than those available to Muslim men under the Muslim Personal Law, Late Dr. Asghar Ali Engineer, an Islamic scholar, had observed that most large Muslim organizations are against granting Muslim women more independence and do not want to reform anti-woman personal laws. He wrote:[2]

> "Muslim women are suffering both from internal and external oppression. Muslim men practice what they themselves believe is Islamic and oppress their women and refuse to entertain any thought of change. Many educated Muslim women thus start believing there can be no liberation within Islam and seek their freedom through secular laws. I conduct workshops for rights of Muslim women and when they listen to what is written in *Quran*, they say they never thought *Quran* liberates them. They thought Islam enslaves them. Thus those who attend our workshops become activists for their Islamic rights".

The Sachar Committee, which studied the socio-economic status of the Muslim community and highlighted the fact that in spite of being India's largest minority group, Muslims have been left out of the development trajectory, had stated that Muslim women were doubly disadvantaged. The Committee had said:

> "The *hijab* and other regressive practices make it difficult for (Muslim) women to break the old shackles and come out into the open. Muslim society does not motivate its women to venture out of the home. With this kind of constricted social base, it will be difficult for Muslim women to make use of any legislation based on affirmative action."

## Education and Muslim Women

Sociologists point out that formal education is strongly associated with political participation for both men and women and that education is an especially powerful predictor of political participation. The importance of women holding leadership positions in the context of even Peace and Conflict Resolution was stressed by Anne Marie Goetz, Chief Advisor to the UN on Peace and Security (UN Women), in her speech in New York, 22 September, 2013.[3]

> "Peace requires that women are seen as leaders, not victims. Peace will come when women have equal access to jobs and to land. When there are as many women as men who are politicians and heads of corporations. When there are as many men as women caring for homes and children. Peace will come when we listen to everyone who has been affected by conflict—not just to the belligerents."

The Sachar Committee noted that Muslim women were woefully lagging behind their counterparts in the other groups in education. Some young Muslim girls who testified before the Sachar Committee blamed the conservative Muslim organizations which were more concerned about the dress code for Muslim women than issues relating to education and employment. However, the conservatives of the community opine that for a Muslim girl, *Madrasah* education is good enough. While the *madrasah* curriculum could still be modernised so as to enable the Muslim children leaving the *madrasahs* shift easily to mainstream education, again, a section of the Muslims does not want the government to interfere with the *madrasahs*. While there is a slow change in the community on this issue, the government could still set up schools offering good quality education, especially for girls, in Muslim-dominated localities and appoint female teachers to improve the educational status of Muslim girls. Merely offering financial assistance in the form of scholarships is not enough if there are no schools for the girls to attend.

It is not that the Muslim community was not aware of its poor educational status as the main reason for its backwardness until the Sachar Committee reported. The community also knew that Muslim girls were far behind other communities in this aspect. At a meeting organised by the *Tehreek Islah-e-Moashra* Committee of the All India Muslim Personal Law Board, on 15 April, 2013 at Lucknow, Dr. Asma Zehra, Member of the Executive Committee of the Board observed that educational backwardness was largely responsible for most of the problems faced by the Muslim community, and added that if women of the community are educated, things would change as women are the axis of Indian families.[4] The meeting however did not discuss the necessity of political participation of Muslim women as a means of their empowerment.

If the main reason behind the poor socio-economic conditions of the Muslim community *per se* is its educational backwardness, it is all the more reason with Muslim women (Table 8.1).

**Table 8.1**: Literacy Rate by Religious Communities, Census of India, 2011

| *Religion* | *Literacy rate (Total)* | *Literacy rate (Males)* | *Literacy rate (Females)* |
|---|---|---|---|
| Hindus | 65.1 | 76.2 | 53.2 |
| Muslims | 59.1 | 67.6 | 50.1 |
| Christians | 80.3 | 84.4 | 76.2 |
| Sikhs | 69.4 | 75.2 | 63.1 |
| Buddhists | 72.7 | 83.1 | 61.7 |
| Jains | 94.1 | 97.4 | 90.6 |
| Other religions | 47.0 | 60.8 | 33.2 |
| **India** | **64.8** | **75.3** | **53.7** |

*Source:* *Census of India*, Drop-in-Article on Census—No. 4, (Available at http://censusindia.gov.in/Ad_Campaign/drop_in_articles/04-Distribution_by_Religion.pdf)

There are various reasons for the educational backwardness of Muslim women; economic, social and cultural. Muslim women remain backward due to the need for adhering to “Islamic traditions.” Leave alone higher education, often even primary education is not easily accessible to girls from poor Muslim families. Girls are often discouraged to go in for higher education as most such institutions are co-educational. There is also an apprehension that if a girl is highly qualified the chances of finding a suitable husband for her become slim, as boys tend to drop out to take-up the family business/trade—small or big. Muslim women and girls from less affluent families are also conditioned to accept the decrees passed by religious leaders. Earlier in this study we have referred to the orders passed by the Department of Minority Education prohibiting co-education for Muslim girls resulting in a large number of Muslim girls being taken off from the rolls of even co-educational *Madrasahs* in Uttar Pradesh.

Our respondents, both in Karnataka and Uttar Pradesh, agree that Muslim girls need to acquire technical and professional qualifications so as to help improve the economic status of their families. Our survey has shown that there are still some (even among women) who think that secular education corrupts Muslim girls and they may *"give in for the temptations"* and maybe led astray. But, a majority of our respondents felt that secular education does not corrupt Muslim girls as long as they dress modestly and remain true to their religious beliefs. Almost all the respondents agreed that Muslim women should not be denied opportunities available to women of other communities; but, to avail the opportunities, one needs suitable education.

We have no argument with the edict that Muslim women (for that matter any woman) should be modestly attired at all times. But, if the socio-economic status of the Muslim community has to improve, it is necessary that even Muslim girls also acquire an education that would help them not only access gainful employment, but also, as mothers, chart the course of their children in the right path. One of our respondents argued that a family's economic status need not depend on a girl's earnings. But, acquiring good education is not necessarily to support the family, but it also can fetch a decent job giving a girl the much needed confidence and helps her to take-up a job if circumstances warrant.

As such, barring Muslim girls from acquiring educational qualifications or working in public and private sectors on the presumption that they would stray away from Islam does not appear to be a sound argument. A cross-section of the Muslim women feel that trivial issues such as dress code or earning to make a living makes no impact on the determination of the contemporary and educated women, who feel no qualms in contributing to the family's income. Muslim women feel that since Islam does not discriminate between men and women, there is nothing wrong if a woman contributes towards the household's income. The emerging educated middle class among Indian Muslims is well aware of the changing times and the need for changing the lives of Muslim women.

While education is necessary for social advancement and improvement in the economic status of the Muslim community, it is not *essential* to contest elections and seek political office. Analysing this aspect, Anne Marie Goetz said:[5]

> "The absence of a strong linear relationship between women's educational attainments and their numbers in formal politics suggests that there must be something specific political institutions that discourage female participation, Jayaweera suggests that it is no great mystery: women's many time constraints from their domestic and other work commitments, and "gendered perceptions of political and community leadership" mean that women both elect to stay out of politics, and are not considered admissible as representatives, even if they do wish to participate."

Even if the educational aspect is ignored or does not count, there still remains the gendered perception of women by the political leadership, which is common to all women, irrespective of their religion. But Muslim women have an additional factor to contend with; that of restrictions arising out of their religion. Though the Sachar Committee has gone into the question of Muslim girls' education, it has not gone into the issue relating to Muslim women's political participation; or the reasons as to why there are hardly any Muslim women in the Parliament or on the need for Muslim women's representation in the legislatures.

Apart from the Sachar Committee, even when prominent Muslim women talk about the status of Muslim women in India, the accent is mainly on their poverty, lack of education and subjugation by the conservative society to which they belong. For instance, Dr. Syeda Saiyidain Hameed, Islamic scholar and member of the Planning Commission of India, had an occasion to observe: "Muslim women in India suffer "double jeopardy" on account of their gender and as members of a minority community."[6] She drew as much from *Quranic* verses and Urdu poetry as she did from the Sachar Committee Report and the approach paper of the 11th Planning Commission to make a case for equitable growth that cuts across barriers of gender and religion. Drawing from her interaction with Muslim women, she said:[7]

> "The condition of Muslim women really pains me because as a Muslim I know that Islam never ordained the injustices which are being committed against women in the name of religion and as an Indian and as a part of the government, I know that the discrimination suffered by Muslims are against the letter and spirit of our Constitution."

If the condition of Muslim women in India has not only stagnated, but has steadily declined, she blamed it on misinterpretations of *Quran* by interest groups that have propagated male dominance and ushered in caste practices which had no religious sanction.[8] Does it mean that the Muslim society will continue to be guided by the religious leaders with regard to Muslim women? Dr. Hameed has no solutions to tear the Muslim women away from such 'interest groups' and 'male dominance.' Her helplessness is evident from her statement: "Commissions come and go, but these things remain the same."[9]

A concerned Professor Nusrat Andrabi, Member of the J&K Muslim Wakf Board, desired that young women should be a part of political and economic forum. She said:[10]

> "Women are under-represented not only in politics, but in all other spheres as well. The political arena is not considered safe and secure because of the stigma on the political role of women. Women should have a say in politics and should not be subjugated by their male counterparts."

Rehana Yusuf a student of Political Science at the University of Kashmir makes a point: "The women that join politics here are usually through family routes. They grow up in political set up and imbibe a political mind-set. I do not have any political background; hence, the only way to understand politics is to study politics. I really want to join politics; for, a woman's presence in politics may serve as a boost to women's rights and much more."[11]

The need for more-and-more women, including Muslim women, entering politics is being understood along with identification of the constraints. But, there is helplessness all-round to remedy the situation. During an interaction with young women of Uttar Pradesh in December 2009, Rahul Gandhi, Congress Vice President said that women should take part in active politics. He stressed that "the country needs a society which is not male-dominated." He wanted young women, those below 35 years of age, to become national leaders, while simultaneously confessing that "the country's political system is difficult for women and if a woman wants to enter the politics, this system is closed for them." He advised the audience: "If you want to bring some change, participate in the process, it will not only benefit you, but would also provide a chance to learn as well." As Rahul Gandhi rightly said, "People talk about upper caste and lower caste, but there is no discussion about women. They are most discriminated and the only way to end this is by getting into politics..."[12]

In the absence of representation in the legislature, Muslim women have remained totally excluded from governance. The problem has become compounded in the absence of support from Muslim-based political parties and Muslim male politicians with genuine concern. It is necessary that Muslim women are represented in the legislatures in adequate numbers if the long-term interests of the Muslim community are taken care of. However, although since the 1980s Muslim women have been trying to enter the Parliament and State Assemblies by contesting elections in large numbers, they have not been successful. Most of our respondents said that the reason for this is the poor educational status and ignorance of the Muslim women. With education comes confidence. Arguing that Muslim women must first have access to education, Dr. Shabistan Gaffar, Chairperson, Committee on Girls' Education, Government of India said:[13]

> "The social tradition and misunderstanding that prevailed within the community regarding education has prevented many girls from being educated. Poverty is a huge additional deterrent. ... Girls need to participate fully in the economic activities; otherwise the process of economic development cannot be accelerated in the country like India. There is need to recognize the fact that the engagement with engineering and technology, management and law disciplines are vital for the advancement of girls."

Similarly, Maulana Kalbe Sadiq, reputed Shia scholar, admits that "no society where women are subjugated and not allowed access to education can be called civilised. The educational empowerment of Muslim women can potentially work as a catalyst to modernize the entire community in India. But this can happen only if they are empowered by education and new thinking to confront the traditional barriers set for them." Besides poverty and absence of girls' schools nearer to their residences, some of the respondents in our study said that the institution of *purdah* was a big stumbling block in Muslim girls' education.

By all accounts, improvement of the socio-economic conditions of the Muslim community and political participation of Muslim women hinges on especially girls' education. This calls for not focussing narrowly on cultural practices such as *purdah*, but instead availing the opportunities made available by the government under the new 15-Point Programme and other such schemes so as to educate their children. It is only with education and accessing well-paying jobs that Muslim women can gain self-confidence and gender equity. As women gain economic power, they will also gain social rights. It is heartening that we have observed during the course of our study in Uttar Pradesh and Karnataka that parents' resistance for girls' education is lesser today, if only they can afford to send the girls to schools.

## Factors Affecting Political Participation

This study was undertaken to examine whether Muslim women have ambitions of seeking an elected office and if so, what are the factors that hinder their electoral participation and who or what is preventing or discouraging them from seeking an elected office.

A number of respondents, both male and female, from Karnataka and Uttar Pradesh who replied to our questionnaire said that illiteracy and/or educational backwardness are the prime reasons as to why Muslim women hesitate to venture into politics. As a number of respondents said, such women lack confidence to venture into politics. But, while poor educational background is not confined to Muslim women alone, there are quite a few educated Muslim women who have also been contesting and losing elections; often repeatedly.

A second reason for poor participation of Muslim women in Parliament and Assembly elections is their poverty. Again, although contesting an election to either the State Legislature or Parliament costs substantial sums, absence of financial means alone is not the sole reason which deters Muslim women.

A third factor responsible is the neglect of Muslim women by the mainstream political parties. The mainstream political parties, even those who have promised 33 per cent reservation for women and whose leaders express concern in public meetings, have not been nominating and supporting a respectable number of Muslim women.

Fourthly, being nominated in large numbers alone is not going to guarantee victory unless the voters, especially of the Muslim community, support the contesting Muslim women.

Finally, Muslim women from ordinary families i.e., who are neither affluent nor belong to high profile political families or to the elite, have to keep in mind the *fatwas* issued by the religious class. No ordinary Muslim family normally dares to challenge *fatwas* against Muslim women's electoral participation.

Thus, this study has tried to ascertain the views of the Muslim society and Muslim political parties on Muslim women's political participation in the States of Uttar Pradesh and Karnataka keeping in view the above factors.

*** *** ***

Muslim women all over the Islamic world are fighting for their rights; so are Indian Muslim women. It is not that the Indian Muslim women are impervious to modernization (as opposed to westernization) and social change. They are also against denying Muslim women the opportunities available to women of other communities, particularly when the Islam's objective was and continues to be, to modernize the thinking, and striving for women's upliftment and emancipation in the society. Muslim women could remain religious in their outlook, but need not necessarily be confined to the homes. The post-Independence generation, which is not affected by the trauma of partition as did their parents, is determined to join the mainstream in securing its Constitutional rights. Contesting elections to the Parliament and State Assemblies is one of their Fundamental rights, which the Muslim women of post-1947 generation are eager to achieve. Such thinking substantiates the increasing number of Muslim women contesting elections since the 1980s.

There is a growing political awakening among Muslim women, who have for too long been told that they are not capable of or meant for a political career. Some of the social problems that the Muslim women face are common to women of all religions in India, including the concept that they are secondary to men. But while the situation among the other communities is changing, the situation is not so bright with Muslim women. Some of our respondents said that *"in a country like India"* Muslim women should not participate in elections. We were also told that in Islamic countries women may become members of the legislature as they will have a separate place and could participate by wearing *purdah*, which is not possible in India. As long as a Muslim woman, or any woman for that matter, dresses up modestly, we fail to understand the argument. Even a most conservative society like Saudi Arabia has nominated women to the Shura Council, the most influential political body in the Kingdom.[14] Why should Muslim women lag behind "in a country like India", which offers them more space?

Our field studies in Uttar Pradesh and Karnataka show that Muslim women are as much interested in contesting elections and occupy, and even fight for, decision-making positions like women of other communities and in achieving their objective, are prepared to challenge the patriarchal forces as well as the powers that be. However, in doing so, Muslim women are not becoming irreligious or losing their faith and continue to remain devout Muslims. Thus, besides lack of education, poverty, awareness and lack of exposure, what affects their political ambitions is the conservative attitude of the religious leaders, neglect by the community leaders, male chauvinism and the Muslim society itself.

## Political Parties and Muslim Women

Muslim women's political participation has never been considered an issue; by the government, political parties, Muslim leaders and the Muslim society. A male-dominated polity which has not been able to enact the Women's Reservation Bill for the last almost two decades, could not be expected to worry about Muslim women, even though they comprise almost 60 million of the country's population.

The electoral participation behaviour of Muslim women in Uttar Pradesh and Karnataka follows the classic Supply and Demand formula identified by Pippa Norris and Joni Lovenduski.[15] The supply side factor is highlighted by the fact that Muslim women do not come forward or are not encouraged and/or they are not interested in politics. The demand side factor is related mainly to the selectors, or political parties, who fail to nominate Muslim women, advancing any number of reasons. Prospective candidates are also discouraged to put forward their names from the anticipation of failure. As is the case with traditional cultures, Muslim women are also reluctant to run for political office when the political elites appear hostile to women by imposing tough selection criteria.

However, Election Commission's statistics show that Muslim women, especially those far removed from the partition days have come a long way in entertaining ambitions of electoral participation like non-Muslim women. This is evident from the fact that over 7,000 Muslim women sought to enter PRIs in a State like Uttar Pradesh during the 2012 elections and 26 per cent of the women elected were in the 21-30 age group and about 61 per cent in the age group of 30-50 years. Similar enthusiasm is also observed in Karnataka elections to the Panchayati Raj Institutions. For these women, it was not a cake-walk as they belonged to middle to lower-middle class families, mainly house-wives, and with some basic educational qualifications. A substantial number of them were even illiterate or educated at home.

Similar participation is also observed in the elections to the Legislative assembly and Parliament, though there were fewer women, due to various factors besides the expenses involved. While their performance in the elections to the PRIs and ULBs is satisfactory, Muslim women have not been successful to the same extent in Assembly and Parliament elections, even when the contestants were well educated. Karnataka Muslims sent just one Muslim woman in about 60 or 70 years to the Assembly! The voters, even Muslim voters in predominantly Muslim constituencies, have refused to repose faith in the contesting Muslim women either out of sheer contempt to their gender or under the impression that Muslim women are incapable of entering Assembly/ Parliament. Thus, the main reason for the failure of the Muslim women to poll a decent percentage of the valid votes polled, and thereby lose their deposits, lies with the Muslim society itself.

One of the reasons adduced by our respondents was that the mainstream secular political parties were not sponsoring adequate number of Muslim women. It is true that the mainstream political parties, despite their swearing by women's empowerment, have failed to nominate adequate number of Muslim women in the elections to the State Assemblies and Parliament. It is another matter that they have failed to nominate non-Muslim women also. The usual lame excuse offered is that in spite of their best intentions to nominate more qualified women, very few come forward. The incident that we have quoted from Karnataka, where the State Congress selection committee initially included only one women in its list of candidates submitted to the Congress High Command for approval for the 2013 general elections to the Assembly, but later revised the list and included the names of 10 women explains the reluctance of the political parties to nominate women. Where did the State Congress Committee find the additional women, whom they could not find initially? In the revised list the State Congress unit could have included at least one Muslim woman;, but, it did not.

However, even Muslim women put up by perceived secular parties and Muslim-based parties have not been able to win. Is it because the Muslim society does not want its women in the State Assemblies and the Parliament on the grounds that they are not competent or is it that they do not want to go against religious rulings? A majority of the respondents said that illiteracy, poor economic status, lack of exposure, patriarchy etc., as the main reasons as to why lesser number of Muslim women have contest in the Assembly and Parliament elections. The respondents also pointed out that when a Muslim woman wins a PRI election, her work is done by the husband or other male members of the family and she just marks attendance. This, they said, is not possible if a Muslim woman gets elected to the Assembly or Parliament. As an elected member of the Assembly or the Parliament, she will be far away from home, for longer periods of time and the husband cannot accompany her. Such phenomenon is reported among Hindu women members of the PRI also.

The data presented in the previous chapters show that a number of Muslim women have contested elections as independent candidates, as the secular parties did not sponsor Muslim women even when they were approached. On the other hand, most of our respondents said that there was no secular party, although some of them named the Congress and Samajwadi partiers, with a few naming the Leftist parties. However, the Samajwadi party seems to be losing its secular credentials. Most of the respondents said that the BJP is not acceptable to the Muslim community, although a few women might have contested under the BJP banner. However, there are instances from Karnataka, where a number of Muslim women have contested PRI elections under BJP ticket and won with enviable margins. Some Muslim women have also contested under the banner of Karnataka Janata Party (floated by B.S. Yeddyurappa). Those who have so contested said that they do not consider BJP as communal.

If the mainstream political parties are not nominating Muslim women or if the community does not have confidence in the secular credentials of the existing mainstream political parties, can they have their own Muslim-based political party?

There have been attempts in the past to form separate Muslim-based political parties. But, "since 1947, moves by sections of Muslims to form their own political party at the national level have met with suspicion, condemnation, opposition and resentment from different quarters, including the Muslim intelligentsia. After Partition, the Muslim League in India was rechristened as Indian Union Muslim League with the objective of becoming an All India party. It never received country-wide acceptance, but it did survive and got respectable standing in Kerala."[16] The Muslim League claims: "Since independence, many organizations have come with tall claims to represent the Indian Muslim politics, but most of them vanished failing to withstand the test of time.[17]

Other Muslim-based political parties include the *Insaf Party* floated by Syed Shahabuddin in 1989 (which failed to attract Muslims and was wound up in 1990), the Peace Party, the Welfare Party of India launched by the Jamaat-e-Islami Hind, the AIMIM in Andhra Pradesh, the Assam United Democratic Front, and the *Ulema* Council etc. But, a section of the Muslims apprehend that such parties may be branded communal. Others feel that "the community needs to become more active in politics and join mainstream parties and assimilate. You cannot lock the community into a religious straightjacket like this."[18]

The main cause of the failure of these parties is reported to be the diverse nature of the Indian Muslim community which is sub-divided into many other religious, linguistic, and regional groups. In any case, Muslim-based political parties do not mean that they would promote Muslim women. Shahida Lateef wrote:[19]

> "Most Muslim political parties do not have any specific plans for women, although they do have women's sections. These are actually used to maintain the *status quo* and play on the fears of religious and political nature. They prefer to

> perpetuate ignorance rather than to attempt the more challenging task of promoting change."

Although the IUML has a women's wing (Vanitha League), which is very active in organising training programmes for women, the foray of Kerala Muslim women seems to end with contesting elections to the PRI. Our inquiries in Uttar Pradesh and Karnataka show that none of the Muslim-based parties have (some questioned: where are Muslim political parties?) tried to promote Muslim women in as much as the parties are headed by men and male chauvinism comes into play.[20]

The problem, thus, lies in part, to the absence of a Muslim-based political party with wide support base and which could serve as an alternative to the mainstream parties and the absence of a credible Muslim leadership acceptable to the entire Muslim community; a leadership with Muslim women's interests in mind. Our respondents said that the few Muslim leaders who are associated with the mainstream political parties have not done anything for the community in as much as they have to necessarily toe the party line. Consequently, the Muslim community does not seem to have thrown up any leader demanding induction of more Muslim women into politics. Speaking about the present Muslim leadership in India, Rahman Khan (Former Deputy Chairman of Rajya Sabha and Former Minister for Minority Affairs) said:[21]

> "It is a fact that the sort of political leadership that Muslims need, one that emerges from the grassroots and is organically related to the Muslim masses, does not exist and shows no sign of emerging. This is to say, the Muslim political leadership in India is one that is imposed by various political parties. Existing Muslim political leaders are generally handpicked by various political parties and are dependent on these parties for their survival. Hence, it is these parties, and not these 'leaders', that ultimately determine the Muslim agenda."

Rahman Khan bemoaned that the "Muslim political and religious leaders and intellectuals are a hopelessly divided lot. Together, they have worked to keep the Muslims embroiled in controversies that shut them from the rest of the Indian society. Sometimes, they create these controversies, at other times these are imposed on them from without".[22] He also blamed the Muslim leadership for continuing to harp on "the same set of issues that they have been harping on for the last sixty-odd years—emotional or emotive issues like discrimination, reservations, the status of the Aligarh Muslim University, Muslim Personal Law, Urdu and so on. These are issues that cannot be resolved overnight. They would take ages to be solved".[23]

In so far as empowerment of Muslim women is concerned, Rahman Khan opined:[24]

> "My personal position is that Muslim women too must be educationally and economically empowered. They must be enabled to play their role in the public sphere as well. In this regard, I agree that sometimes Muslim organizations do actively work against Muslim women's empowerment. Thus, for instance, today they are demanding that there should be a separate quota for Muslim women in seats for elected bodies that are to be reserved for women, but at the same time you have this recent *fatwa* from a leading *madrasah* which, in practical terms, makes it virtually impossible for Muslim women to function in such roles".

Shujaat Bukhari, Editor of *Rising Kashmir*, who analyzed the situation, has not been able to come up with an answer either. He concludes:[25]

> "Today, Muslims in India are orphans at the political level, and they deserve a strong leadership, which could move towards undoing the injustices brought out by the Sachar Report and also facilitate their living as proud Indian citizens. This is the biggest challenge the leadership faces."

Unfortunately, there are no Muslim women leaders also and the few that were there or are still there in politics, have either not done anything for promoting Muslim women's political participation or are not looked at by the community with favour. Like the Muslim male leaders, the Muslim female leaders also cannot go against the party-line. As soon as the Rajya Sabha passed Women's Reservation Bill to provide for 33 per cent reservation for women in Parliament and State legislative assemblies, political parties and politicians who did not want the Bill to be passed suddenly thought of OBC and Muslim women to support and bolster their demand. Najma Heptulla, Former Deputy Chairperson of the Rajya Sabha for 17 long years and left the Congress to join the BJP, criticised the leaders demanding a sub-quota for OBC and Muslim women. She asked:[26]

> "Just because women have now come up as a force, these people want to divide this force into bits and pieces. If they want to put up Muslim and backward class women, let them do it and help them, but they should make an effort to find such women, train them and make them capable of contesting elections. How many men from the minority community have they put up in Parliament that they are now suddenly worried about Muslim women?

The political parties demanding a sub-quota for Muslim women needed the support of Muslim women leaders and started searching for one, or of making one, if possible. Unlike the earlier approach of looking for enlightened people who would liberate them, Muslim women were now being asked to be leaders.

The fact is that there have been few women leaders from the community. Most of those in this minuscule group were either from political families or belonged to the upper crust. Their presence in politics was just symbolic. As the community did not try to encourage Muslim women, it has no Muslim woman leader of the calibre of Sushma Swaraj, Brinda Karat, Late Jayalalithaa or Mayawati in 70 years of Independent India. "More importantly, Muslim women are missing from the debate about themselves. They are so disempowered that they need someone else to represent them even to voice their views in public and through the media".[27] In fact, some of our female respondents looked down upon some of the Muslim women leaders, as they go about unveiled and hair shorn. They even were sarcastic about Benazir Bhutto, Begum Khalida Zia and Shaikh Hasina, as if they have committed a sin by occupying the positions that they held. Obviously, these respondents were not fully aware of the rights granted to Muslim women in *Quran*.

We have already seen that in all the 15th General elections held so far, there were only 19th Muslim women out of the total 549 women elected to the Lok Sabha; and six Lok Sabhas did not have a single Muslim woman member. Following the 2009 elections, the three Muslim women elected to the Parliament from Uttar Pradesh were related to powerful male politicians. Would they have been nominated by the parties if they were not so related? Mainstream political parties justify their inhibitions about giving women tickets by arguing on the basis of the winnability factor. When there is no alternative, women are put up in such seats where there is less chance for the party to win or use women as dummy candidates in a 'friendly fight' with the opposition party. If the women fail to win, the party can make it the basis for denying a ticket to a woman in the next election. Even if a sub-quota is created for Muslim women within the Women's quota, such seats are more likely to be usurped by powerful Muslim leaders to nominate their own wives/sisters or such other female relatives.

## Religious Conservatism

Though the Muslim orthodoxy is aware that there are Muslim women competent to serve in the legislatures and the Parliament, what appears to frighten the orthodoxy is that given the liberty, Muslim women might cross the limits of *Shariah*. If Darul Uloom had reluctantly permitted Muslim women to contest elections wearing *purdah*, the Indian Union Muslim League had asked Muslim women to "dress according to Islamic norms" in order to maintain "religious discipline". Though the women's wing of the IUML, opposed the dress code, it had no option than obeying the "elders." The IUML claims that it is not orthodox, as, if it were so, it would not have allowed women to enter politics. However, IUML's Kerala State Secretary, KNA Qader said that "there are many in our society who feel that women entering politics is *haraam*."[28]

Participation in election and accessing elected office improves women's self-esteem besides giving them an opportunity to serve the community at large and Muslim community in particular. A number of even uneducated Muslim women have excelled themselves as Sarpanches of Gram Panchayats in several parts of the country.[29]

One of the problems faced by Muslim women, especially the illiterate or poorly literate, in electoral participation relates to restrictions imposed in the name of religion. Most of the Muslims in India are artisans and/or self-employed. Rural Muslims are engaged in the agricultural sector as labourers or in related operations. These categories of Muslims tend to have a restricted world-view and conservative in their outlook. Unaware of the *Quran* or *hadith,* they believe in the local Imam for guidance in religious matters. Most often, the Imam of the mosque, who also comes from a poor family, may have a very limited knowledge of theology and *Shariah*. Consequently, his *fatwas*, based on ignorance and conservative view, often go against women's interests if he declares that Muslim women should not contest elections.[30]

India being a secular democracy there is much more social and political space available to Muslim women compared to their sisters in many other Muslim countries. To avail of this social and political space, Muslim women should have a greater awareness of their *Quranic* rights. Simultaneously, they should also know their civic rights as citizens of India. This is possible only through education; both religious and secular. Thus, with no political leader to support them, Muslim women's political empowerment can come about only when they know their *Quranic* rights and respond to patriarchy and conservatism. While the religious leaders recommend religious education for girls, they frown upon secular education.

The poor representation of Muslim women in Indian politics in the initial years of independence shows that the concern for religious identity and the rise of fundamentalism (Hindu and Muslim) made Muslims shun secular education and confine their women to the home. The divisive environment continued to affect Muslim women, who were considered solely responsible for preserving the community's identity. Political participation of Muslim women is also circumscribed by the absence of competent Muslim leaders who are well-versed in *Quran* and *Hadith* and capable of guiding the community in the proper direction. There is a need for leaders with a liberal outlook and who have a good education; both modern as well as Islamic. They must have strong, organic relations with the Muslim masses, know their problems and concerns, and capable of representing them.

Besides political leaders, there is a need for more Muslim NGOs to work with the community as well as with people and organizations of other communities. While the number of Muslim women activists and NGOs is on the increase, they should become socially relevant for the Muslim community and work in diverse fields such as health, modern education, employment, and protection of the environment etc., instead of harping on religion-related issues alone. Late Dr. Asghar Ali Engineer opined: "There is also a great need for internal critique and at least educated Muslim men should attempt an honest criticism of condition of women in their community and consolidate efforts for change and reform. They also tend to be defensive and reactive. Time has certainly come to be proactive for improving Muslim women's status in India."[31]

Whether it is a question of girls' education and employment or women's political participation, it is often a *fatwa* issued by an Islamic scholar that acts as a deterrent. Most of our respondents both in Uttar Pradesh and Karnataka felt that it was not correct for the religious leaders to issue *fatwas* on political matters or women's political participation. But, there are some who feel that the religious leaders are right in issuing *fatwas*. It is true that accepting the advice tendered (*fatwa*) with reference to a specific question rests with the person who raised the question. It is not necessary that he should heed the *fatwa* and a *fatwa* is not applicable to the entire community. With more-and-more *fatwas* being issued on a variety of subjects in the recent past, more than 300 Islamic scholars (including leading *Ulema* from South Africa, Afghanistan and the Gulf countries) converged in Gujarat's Bharuch city for three days in March 2014 at the Islamic *Fiqh* (jurisprudence) Academy of India. The gathering "asked the clerics to resist from issuing '*fatwas*' at the drop of a hat and cease issuing edicts in favour of any political party, particularly in the election season."[32] The gathering also recommended a thorough revision of the curriculum of *madrasahs* and increasing the duration of the Muftis' course from one to three years to allow them to gain expertise in jurisprudence and social issues before they set out to issue any edicts.

What has been observed in the recent years is that *fatwas* against Muslim women studying, working or participating in politics have not driven them out from the public sphere, from jobs, from institutions of higher learning. In fact, Muslim girls' enrolment in institutions of higher education is higher than that of Muslim boys in large parts of India, because Muslim boys often drop out as soon as they enter their teens and take-up jobs in order to supplement their families' incomes. Interestingly, the *burqa* has played a facilitating, rather than restraining, role for some Muslim girls who don it because their parents feel that they are thereby protected and safe and so allow them to attend college.

Besides championing gender-just understandings of Islam and reforming Muslim Personal Law, a Muslim woman should be accorded the status due to her under the *Quran,* i.e., as one with equal rights as man. In the course of our study both in Karnataka and Uttar Pradesh, barring a few, all the respondents, men and women, including Moulavis, said that *Quran* does not prohibit political participation of women, although some of them added a rider that they should do so by following the Islamic norms. Almost all the respondents have also said that staying within the Islamic norms Muslim women can undertake and discharge the responsibilities of any public office. Muslim women are claiming this *Quranic* right and have shown that they will not shy away from the public sphere.

Elections to the local bodies in the past 10 years have shown that Muslim women have both the willingness and competency. Since the Constitution does not permit religion-based reservation, Muslim women cannot have reserved seats. But, if there is a quota for them within the quota for women, it will bring more Muslim women into the political sphere. In spite of the *fatwas* and frowning clergy, Muslim women of Uttar Pradesh have taken a pro-active stand at the 2012 general elections to the Assembly, making Muslim women and girls realise the value of their vote and educating the community about the importance of participation in the democratic process and urging them to vote in the elections.[33] Those that spearheaded the campaign persuaded the male members of the families and mustered their support for sending the women of the family to cast their vote on the polling day.

One of the reasons as to why Muslim women are not encouraged by the community is the apprehension that once in politics the women will have to necessarily interact with men. Madhu Kishwar elaborates:[34]

> "In a culture where even formal interaction with men unconnected to one's own family is frowned upon, women are severely handicapped in politics because they cannot cultivate close association with men without jeopardising their position in the family. A woman operating on her own strength in a party filled with corrupt politicians who think nothing of slandering their own women colleagues would find the going very tough, even if she can somehow mobilise other compensatory resources by her own special efforts. The fact that politics is dominated by the most unsavoury kind of men makes most women themselves reluctant to break

taboos regarding free intermixing with men. A woman risks her reputation by even being seen with many of them, whereas a man does not have to prove his credentials by such fierce avoidance.

Yet another reason as to why women, including Muslim women, hesitate to participate in elections is the breakdown of institutional politics from a high level of decorum and decency into a situation where politicians are no more decorous or decent. This makes it difficult especially for Muslim women, given the strict regime of restrictions that they are made to live under. Even though Indian men might favour women's political participation, this does not easily translate into relaxing restrictions on the women in their own families; more so in Muslim families.

But years of democratic practice have encouraged women to break free on Election Day and turn out in large numbers to vote. Panchayati Raj and gender sensitive programmes have given women a better understanding of their rights. Women do not vote for their self-interest, but in the interests of the society. As women have families on their minds, they are given to thinking of the future, of the long term, as, unlike men, women would want a school, a hospital, even a college, so that their children could prosper in the future. Hence, elections where more women line up to vote reflect the "felt aspirations" rather than "felt needs". It is also the reason why more women should be in politics; for the betterment of the community.

## Political Parties

Political parties, which have a larger role to play in women's political participation, are still reluctant to field women at the National level. A political party being an authentic institutional voice in a democracy, in a multi-party democracy like India, the role of political parties in elections, in mobilizing public opinion and also in governance process cannot be overemphasized. Therefore, the backing of a political party for the success of a candidate in election is imperative. This is evident from the fact that the chances of women contestants winning when they are fielded by political parties are better than when they contest as independent candidates. It follows, therefore, that getting more women into the legislature depends upon the willingness of the political parties to nominate more women.

In spite of mainstream political parties not sponsoring them, Muslim women have started to fight elections either as independents or under the banner of regional parties. Besides the difficulty in securing nomination by established political parties, the low-key participation of Muslim women in elections to the Parliament and assemblies, is due to the importance attached to their maintaining Islamic identity, as the religious leaders insist upon Muslim women wearing the veil if they have to participate in elections, either as candidates or voters.[35] But, young and educated Muslim women have started to express the urge to be a part of the development. Nargis (22), who was elected *Pradhan* of Gunasi village Panchayat in 2010, said that she wants to change the perception of women being domestic slaves. "I not only want to prove people wrong that women cannot join the politics of development, but in a conservative rural society they can also be leaders like men. If you can change the face of a village, you can change the face of the country." During her election campaign, she promised the rural voters that development funds would be utilized in a transparent manner.[36] Her ambitions are reflected in her statement: "The Panchayat is the gateway to state and national politics."

Muslim women cannot forever remain mute spectators when women of other communities are availing opportunities presented by the constitutional amendments. As a result, over the years, thousands of Muslim women of both Karnataka and Uttar Pradesh have begun contesting local elections; and not all of them are unduly worried about *fatwas*. The bold step taken, especially, by the Muslim women of Uttar Pradesh is exhilarating in view of the fact that in spite of being illiterate or poorly educated, they have exhibited courage in daring conservatism.

Though the Muslim middle-class is expanding even in North India, it is still not very articulate, caught in dilemmas and insecurities. It is stuck between respect for the *Ulema* on the one hand and the necessity of disregarding them when their *fatwas* come in the way of improvement of their lives. While the middle-class does not want to lock horns with the *Ulema*, it does not also consider them as leaders, having come to understand the politics that some of them play. Several educated Muslims have voiced their concern at some of the *fatwas*, which they consider are redundant and based on narrow sectarianism. Not all the Muslims are in the grip of the Moulavis, although poor and illiterate Muslims cannot dare to ignore them. Yet, they feel, as our respondents said, that the Moulavis should not issue *fatwas* relating to politics and confine themselves to truly religious issues.

**** **** ****

A country cannot be considered to have 'developed' in any meaningful sense if either systemically or culturally or through neglect a sizeable section of its population is deprived of access to knowledge and effective political representation. It is also an established principle of democratic policy that all of those (and all of the interest groups) who are likely to be affected by the politico-economic and socio-cultural decisions taken by the state ought to participate in such decision-making processes. This means that all the socio-cultural and economic groups should be represented in the governance process, at the local, state and national levels. That being the case, it will not be wrong to argue that all the social groups including the religious minorities should find a place in the governance process which means that they should be adequately represented in the national Parliament, State legislature and in the rural and urban government bodies. This means that the Muslim women should have a separate quota in the Women's Reservation Bill.

If women, in general, have a right to be involved in all aspects of development processes, even Muslim women have such right ("even in a country like India"), especially on account of their numbers. Over the past decade, gender equality and women's empowerment have been explicitly recognised as vital not only to the social, economic and political well-being of civilised societies, but also as key elements in social and economic advancement. While political parties make tall promises in their election manifestos, no effective steps are taken to fulfil such promises once elections are over. Addressing gender issues in politics also depends on how many women candidates are endorsed by parties and how they choose candidates. A political party being an authentic institutional voice in a democracy, the backing of a political party for the success of a candidate in election is imperative. It follows, therefore, that getting more women into the legislature depends upon the willingness of the political parties to nominate women; including Muslim women.

But, things are not totally stagnant on Muslim women's front. An educated middle class is emerging among Indian Muslims which is well aware of the need for change in the lives of Muslim women. The educated Muslim women are becoming aware of their rights and are no longer prepared to accept what is being imposed on them in the name of religion. But, the empowerment of Muslim women and ushering in social reforms should also be accompanied by an improvement in the general economic condition of the community. This can however be achieved only through improved educational status of not only Muslim women, but men too. There is also a great need for internal critique and at least educated Muslim men should attempt an honest criticism of the conditions of Muslim women and consolidate efforts for change and reform. When changes are occurring all over the Muslim world, there is no reason why Indian Muslim women should remain untouched, especially in a secular democracy.

Finally, we would like to reiterate that the responsibility of improving the socio-economic and political status of the Muslims in India rests with the Muslim community itself. The community has to take steps instead of depending on the government or the political leaders. As Aijaz Ilmi, Chairman of the Executive Board of *Siyasat Jadid*, Urdu Newspaper published from Kanpur said:[37]

> "I do not deny that successive governments have been neglectful of Muslims, but my point is that blaming the government alone is a convenient way to absolve the Muslim haves of their complicity in reinforcing Muslim backwardness... self-styled Muslim leaders and well-to-do Muslims have done precious little for the community's economic and educational advancement, continuously harping on emotional, identity-related and what are narrowly conceived as religious issues...what the Muslims need today is effective community leaders and social activists, and not just politicians, to make sure that the government schemes reach the grassroots and their intended beneficiaries."

The extensive data on elections to the PRIs, State Legislatures of Uttar Pradesh and Karnataka as well as the Parliament (Look Sabha) that we have gone through and the responses to our questionnaire show that:

- Muslim women of both Uttar Pradesh and Karnataka have exhibited a lot of interest and enthusiasm in taking part in elections as contestants.

- From the first elections in 1952 to 2012, there has been a steady increase in the number of Muslim women contesting elections to the State legislatures and Lok Sabha from both the States.
- Muslim women's ambition to enter the State Legislatures and Parliament has been making them contest the elections even as independents, knowing fully well that they are bound to lose.
- Muslim women have been more successful at the PRI-level that at the general elections to the State Legislatures and Lok Sabha.
- Non-Muslim voters have no problem in electing a Muslim woman if she had proved her commitment to social service. Some of them have been elected unopposed and have been chosen to handle responsible positions in the PRIs.
- Muslim families seem to permit their women to seek an elected office in the PRIs and ULBs more readily than in the State Legislatures and Parliament.
- Muslim society does not appear to repose faith in sending its women to the State Assemblies and Parliament.

Dr. A. Mohamuda Begum, Member, Syndicate, Cochin University of Science and Technology, Kerala summarised the status of Muslim women thus: "Their presence is shrouded and they stay as simple vote banks. Empowerment of women as whole needs multiple level task involvement."[38] The term 'shroud' says it all. The sad part is that nobody has bothered or bothers about Muslim women. In a detailed analysis of the performance of Muslim winners and losers to the Karnataka Assembly elections of 2013, Md. Ismail Khan has reached the first and second runners-up among Muslim males. But no attempt has been made to ascertain the reasons as to why the Muslim women lost.[39] Does not Muslim women's loss or gain mean anything? The fact that the Muslim women do not invite any concern from their own community is evident from the following statement of Satya Pal Ruhela:[40]

> "During my last 27 years' service in the Faculty of Education, Jamia Millia Islamia, New Delhi, I never saw a politician, leader or rich Muslim industrialist, actor, actress, social worker or the like coming to inquire about the social

backgrounds, hardships, aspirations, educational problems of the Muslim girl students."

In concluding, we feel that it is high time that the Muslim society takes a more practical view of the *Shariah*. Rigid rules are all very well in an Islamic state, but if Muslims living in India try and bring everything into an Islamic framework, they will lose out.

## NOTES AND REFERENCES

1. In 2010, Rajasthan had the highest percentage of women legislators at 14.5 per cent followed by Andhra Pradesh, with a little over 12 per cent and West Bengal with 11.5 per cent. Nagaland had none. Only eight State assemblies crossed the 10 percent mark. Apart from West Bengal, Rajasthan and Andhra Pradesh, the others were: Madhya Pradesh (26 out of 231), Chhattisgarh (10 out of 90), Bihar (26 out of 243), Assam (13 out of 126) and Haryana (nine out of 90). Despite its highest rate of literacy, Kerala Assembly had just 5 per cent women. Karnataka had only five women in the Assembly of 225 seats and there were only 27 women legislators in a 403 member house of Uttar Pradesh. Ten States had less than 5 per cent women in their Assemblies. These figures show the bleak picture of women's representation.
2. Engineer, Dr. Asghar Ali. Muslim Women in Indian Society, in *Indian Muslims*, 23 March, 2007, (Available at http://www.indianmuslims.info/articles/asghar_ali_engineer/articles/muslim_women_in_indian_society.html)
3. Goetz, Anne Marie, at a function in New York. She is the Chief Advisor, Peace and Security, UN Women. (Available at http://www.unwomen.org/ca/news/stories/2013/9/speech-by-annemarie-goetz-lantern-dedication
4. *Muslim Mirror*, 16 April, 2013. (Available at http://muslimmirror.com/eng/empower-women-with-education-to-uplift-muslims-dr-asma-zehra/)
5. Goetz, Anne Marie (2003). Women's Education and Political Participation, Background Paper prepared for the *Education for All*, Global Monitoring Report, 2003/4, Gender and Education for All: The Leap to Equality, New York: UNESCO.
6. *The Hindu*, Bangalore, January 24, 2007.
7. *Ibid.*
8. *Ibid.*
9. *Ibid.*
10. Dr. Andrabi was the leader of 10 member delegation to attend the historic peace dialogue in Muzaffarabad in 2012. Reported in *World Pulse*, June 7, 2013. (Available at http://worldpulse.com/node/72339). She was reflecting

the aspirations of young Muslim women of Jammu & Kashmir, where, according to reports, the number of Muslim girls opting for Political Science and Law courses has been on the increase.

11. *Ibid.* Several such voices are heard from Aligarh, New Delhi, and Bangalore etc.
12. *The Hindu*, December 8, 2009. (Available at http://www.thehindu.com/news/national/women-should-join-politics-rahul/article61810.ece)
13. Gaffar, Dr. Shabistan. Empowerment of Women through Education, in *New Age Islam*, January 13, 2012. (Available at http://www.newageislam.com/islam,-women-and-feminism/empowerment-of-women-through-education/d/6370)
14. Saudi Arabia has steadfastly refused to permit women function in the public space; including driving cars. Although King Abdullah, a reformist, has been cautiously pressing for political reforms, but in a country where conservative clerics and some members of the royal family resist change, liberalisation has been very gradual. In September 2011 the King announced: "Because we refuse to marginalise women in society in all roles that comply with *sharia*, we have decided, after deliberation with our senior clerics and others... to involve women in the Shura Council as members, starting from next term. Women will be able to run as candidates in the municipal election and will even have a right to vote." (Women in Saudi Arabia to vote and run in elections, reported in BBC Middle East, 25 September, 2011. (Available at http://www.bbc.co.uk/news/world-us-canada-15052030)
15. *Political Recruitment: Gender, Race and Class in the British Parliament*, Cambridge University Press, 1995.
16. Mir Ayoob Ali Khan, Will a Muslim Political Party work at National Level? in the *Times of India* (Hyderabad), 26 May, 2012.
17. Indian Union Muslim League, *IUML Vision* 2020. (Available at http://www.indianunionmuslimleague.in/#sthash.cdrAynvm.dpuf)
18. Kolhatkar, Neeta, quoting Irshad Ilmi, Editor of Kanpur-based *Siyasat Jadid*. Should Muslims have their own Political Party? In *DNA* (Mumbai) 26 April, 2009.
19. Lateef, Shahida, (1953). Modernization in India and the Status of Muslim Women in *Modernization and Social Change among Muslims in India* (Ed.) Imtiaz Ahmad, Delhi: Manohar, p. 165.
20. A prominent member of the AIUDF opined: "'the society still does not accept women as leaders in the political sphere. We can consider women if she is influential, rich and belongs to a family that has political legacy like Anowara Taimur. We will consider women only if there is a mandatory provision like 33 per cent reservation". Yet another example comes from Andhra Pradesh. In the bye elections for the Greater Hyderabad Municipal Corporation (Ward No. 104, Borabanda, reserved for women) held in March 2013, the AIMIM, which is a Muslim political party, put up a non-Muslim female candidate against a Muslim woman of the Congress party. It could

have sponsored a Muslim woman. The AIMIM candidate defeated her opponent.)

21. Rahman Khan in an interview with Yoginder Sikand, Muslim Leadership in India, 26 May, 2010, in *Countercurrents.org* (Available at http://www.countercurrents.org/sikand260510.htm)
22. *Ibid.*
23. *Ibid.*
24. *Ibid.*
25. The Question of Muslim leadership in India: Is Asaduddin Owaisi the only hope for Indian Muslims? Asks Shujaat Bukhari, in the *Milli Gazette,* Published Online: Sep. 22, 2012. (Available at http://www.milligazette.com/news/4107-the-question-of-indian-muslim-leadership)
26. Najma Heptulla in an interview by Nilima Pathak of *Gulf News*. Najma Heptulla is the great grandniece of Maulana Abul Kalam Azad, a prominent Indian Freedom Fighter and Islamic Scholar. (Available at http://www.thefreelibrary.com/INTERVIEW+Women+need+a+aelevel+playing+ground.-a0222289725)
27. Sherwani, Arfa Khanum. Beyond Burkha politics, in *DNA*. Mumbai, 24 June, 2010. (Available at http://www.dnaindia.com/analysis/main-article_beyond-burkha-politics_1400905)
28. There have been instances in Gujarat, Andhra Pradesh and elsewhere, when the local Muslim leadership and Clergy strongly opposed the nomination of Muslim women in Assembly elections and even canvassed against them. It may be recalled that in the 1965 Presidential elections in Pakistan, opposition parties put up Mohtarma Fathima Ali Jinnah against General Ayub Khan. Her supporters also included a number of religious-political leaders, who had earlier been adamant that a woman could never become the Head of an Islamic State. In justifying their stand, they said that a woman could become Head of State under extraordinary circumstances. Not to be outdone, Ayub Khan got a series of *fatwas* issued by another set of religious leaders against electing or appointing a woman as Head of an Islamic State. The election was won by General Ayub Khan.
29. Alka Madhok cites examples of Muslim women in Rajasthan who did yeomen service to the community as heads of Gram Panchayats. Natho Begum, for instance, as Sarpanch took the initiative to improve the infrastructural facilities in the village and establishment of a school in the village. Fatima Bi, yet another Sarpanch bagged 25 awards, the most prestigious one being the title of Uttam Sarpanch, an award given on Independence Day and UNDP's Race against Poverty Award for Asia-Pacific region from United Nations Secretary General. Madhok, Alka. Panchayati Raj: Participation of Muslim Women, in *Status of Muslim Women in India* (Ed.) Hijra Kumar, Sarojini Naidu Centre for Women's Studies, Jamia Millia Islamia, New Delhi (2003): Aakar Books.
30. In 2009, Jaleel Khan, former MLA, who could not get re-nomination by

the Congress for Vijayawada West assembly seat, deployed some Muslim scholars to speak against Congress party's official nominee, Mallika Begum. A few religious leaders deputed by Jaleel, said they would be issuing a '*fatwa*' to Muslims in the city to vote against Mallika Begum. However, they retracted when the media people grilled them on their "authority" to issue a *fatwa*. They clarified that they were not issuing any *fatwa* and were only appealing to Muslim electorate not to vote in favour of Mallika since she is a woman. "As per Islamic law, women are not eligible to contest the election. So, we are requesting all the Muslims to vote against this woman for defying the Islam," said Abdul Khadar Rizwi, Moulana of Jumma Masjid at Canal Road. [Reported in *Times of India* (Hyderabad), April 2, 2009]. (Available at http://timesofindia.indiatimes.com/city/hyderabad/Jaleel-appeals-Muslims-to-vote-against-Mallika/articleshow/4347012.cms?referral=PM)

31. Engineer, Dr. Asghar Ali, *op. cit.*
32. Go Easy on *Fatwas*, Muslim Scholars tell Clerics, in *DNA*, Mumbai, 3 March, 2014.
33. Muslim Women Campaign for India Elections, 4 February, 2012, (Available at http://www.onislam.net/english/news/asia-pacific/455659-muslim-women-campaign-for-india-elections.html)
34. Kishwar, Madhu. Women's Marginal Role in Politics, (Available at http://www.manushi-india.org/pdfs_issues/PDF%20files%2097/women's_marginal_role_in_politics.pdf)
35. According to reports, the villagers of Katiya Kammu in Saharanpur district of Uttar Pradesh have not exercised their franchise for an estimated three decades. According to the village Pradhan "several years ago, during panchayat elections, in a move to check impersonation, women were asked to remove their veils and identify themselves. It was then decided that no woman would vote in future. Village where women do not vote reported in Indian Express, February 29, 2012. The village consisted of 1,256 voters, with 400 women, a majority of whom were Muslim women. (Available athttp://www.indianexpress.com/assembly-election2012-news/a-village-where-women-dont-vote/917903)
36. Farzan Ahmed, Uttar Pradesh: Young India stands up, in *India Today.* in, December 25, 2010. (Available at http://indiatoday.intoday.in/story/young-india-stands-up-in-uttar-pradesh/1/124455.html).
37. Ilmi, Aijaz. Chairman of the Executive Board of Siyasat Jadid, Urdu Newspaper published from Kanpur in an interview with Yoginder Sikand.
38. *Empowerment of Women*. (Available at http://www.vanithaleague.com/index.php/en/articles/28-artempwomen)
39. Khan, Md. Ismail. Analysis of the Performance of Muslim Winners and Losers in Karnataka Assembly Elections, in *TwoCirles.net*, 8 May, 2013.
40. Ruhela, Satya Pal (Ed.) in Preface to, New Delhi (1998): MD Publications Pvt. Ltd.

# Executive Summary

1. This study examines the status of electoral participation of Muslim women in Uttar Pradesh and Karnataka, seeking representation in the Panchayati Raj Institutions and the respective State Legislatures and Parliament. While there are several studies in India and abroad on the socio-economic conditions of the Muslim women, there are hardly any studies devoted exclusively to their political participation.
2. Muslims constitute about 13.4 per cent of the country's population (2001 Census). But, their representation in the Parliament and state legislatures is disproportionately low and that of the Muslim women is abysmally low.
3. In the absence of a religion-based quota, the chances of Muslims, both men and women, getting elected to the legislatures depend upon the mainstream political parties. The political backwardness of the Muslim community is also due the lack of effective Muslim leadership.
4. Muslim women's problems in electoral participation are community-specific. They are told that Islam prohibits women from politics and their primary duty is to look after her husband and children. By and large Muslim families do not encourage their women to take-up politics, unless they are "political families."
5. Muslim women have realised that while they may stand some chance if the Women's Reservation Bill becomes an Act, they have been desisting demanding a quota based on religion as it is not permissible under the Constitution and such demand will only delay the passing of the Bill.

6. By the 1990s, many Muslim women had become educated, financially independent, and becoming increasingly conscious of the gap between their human rights and social needs on the one hand, and their objective conditions, on the other.
7. Muslim constitute 12.72 per cent of the population of Karnataka with a literacy rate of (2001 Census) 70.1 per cent; higher than that in Uttar Pradesh. Muslim female literacy rate varied from 52 per cent (Rural) to 70.61 per cent (urban). Reports show that there is an educational awakening among Muslims in Karnataka and the rate of enrolment in high schools has increased since 2010 by 15 per cent.
8. The participation of Muslims as candidates in the elections increased from the 1962, with most candidates flocking to the Congress party, which was considered secular. For the first time a Muslim womancontested the 1978 Assembly election from Bangalore as a Congress candidate, but lost.
9. Although there was no explicit prohibition against electoral participation, Muslim women of Karnataka do not seem to have evinced interest in participating in the elections nor the community promoted their participation. Consequently, Muslim women did not contest in the elections held to the Assembly during 1952, 1957, 1962, 1967 and 1972.
10. Between 1951 and 1985, only eight Muslim women contested Assembly polls and only one was elected in 1985. But, the increasing number of independent candidates showed the rising interest, although the Muslim community did not favour them even in Muslim-majority constituencies. Not a single Muslim woman from Karnataka has ever made it to the Lok Sabha.
11. A large number of Muslim women have contested PRIs/ULB elections reflecting their political ambitions. Unlike in Uttar Pradesh, they had no *fatwas* to contend with. A number of Muslim women have also been elected unanimously. None of the Muslim women elected, through contest or unanimously, are related to any senior political leader unlike in Uttar Pradesh.
12. BJP or Karnataka Janata Paksha (floated by B.S. Yeddyurappa) does not seem have prevented Muslim women seeking nomination. They considered BJP as secular as any

other party. *Hijab* also does not seem to have stood in the way of Muslim women contesting an election, or running administration.

13. Uttar Pradesh has a high Muslim population (about 18.5% of the total population). The literacy rate of Muslim females both in the rural and urban areas of Uttar Pradesh is far behind the national average. Only 48 per cent of the State's Muslims are reported literate; the literacy rate ranging from 57 per cent among males to 37 per cent among females. The main reason for educational backwardness of Muslim girls is the abject poverty of the parents, absence of schools providing quality education in Muslim areas and absence of lady teachers and sanitary facilities. The role of religion in the educational backwardness especially of Muslim girls, cannot be totally ignored.
14. The role of Muslims in the economic activity in Uttar Pradesh is marginal, with most of them engaged in informal skills and trades with poor productivity, primarily because of low levels of education.
15. A number of Muslim women, from Uttar Pradesh, have made supreme sacrifices right from the first war of independence in 1857. From the point of view of electoral participation of Muslim women, Uttar Pradesh has fared poorly since the first elections after independence.
16. Muslim women, of Uttar Pradesh have made a delayed entry into the electoral politics. Besides the trauma of Partition, they lived in a different socio-cultural setting, compared to Karnataka.
17. Chapter 4 gives the details of Muslim women contesting in the 15 general elections to the UP Assembly since 1952. Their average representation in the Assembly has been a mere 4.4 per cent. However, despite social restrictions, increasing number of women havecontested elections, even as independent candidates, for want of nomination by mainstream political parties. In spite of the *fatwas* and frowning clergy, Muslim women of Uttar Pradesh have realised importance of participation in the democratic process not only by contesting elections, but also by urging Muslim families to vote.
18. Election results show that a high percentage of Muslim

women have either lost the election or forfeited their deposits. Muslim women had no guarantee of success even while contesting from districts which had substantial Muslim population as in the case of Karnataka. The community has disregarded even educated Muslim women.

19. Muslim women who entered Parliament from Uttar Pradesh were either from the political families or elite. No woman from an ordinary family has ever been elected.
20. It is not easy for Muslim women to contest even in the PRIs elections as they have to secure the consent of their spouses/ parents, and gauge the reaction of the society. Besides the expenses involved, they were also to keep in mind the religious leaders.
21. At the 2012 elections to the PRIs in Uttar Pradesh, over 7,000 Muslim women contested the elections seeking to become members of the various Nagar Panchayats, Nagar Palika Parishads and Nagar Nigams of the State and over 1,300 of them were successful. Muslim women have shown courage in contesting elections, ignoring the *fatwas*.
22. The age profile of Muslim women contesting PRIs elections shows that the elected women Sarpanches were around 50 years of age or even less. Most of them were in the age group of 30 to 40 years and married. The younger generation, (21 to 30 years), opting for political participation denotes a sign of change.
23. It is difficult for Muslim women to get elected without a separate quota within the Women's Reservation Bill. Even if they are allotted a separate quota, the number of seats that would accrue to Muslim women would be small and is likely to be usurped by Male politicians to sponsor their own family members.
24. Chapter 7 gives the responses to a questionnaire from a cross section of the Muslim community in Karnataka and Uttar Pradesh. The respondents included religious figures, housewives, students and professionals. Most respondents are aware that Islam does not prohibit women's political participation and that it is not correct for the religious leaders to issue *fatwas* preventing or placing restrictions on women's political participation.

25. The main reasons for the poor performance of Muslim women are reported to be poverty, lack of support from families and society, lack of education etc. As a prelude to political participation, it is absolutely necessary that Muslim women should concentrate on education and the Muslim community has to give a serious thinking to this aspect.
26. The study shows that no Muslim male political leader has been genuinely concerned about the community and no Muslim political party has been encouraging M:islim women for various reasons. Under the circumstances, Muslim women have to join hands with other women's groups and fight for their rights.

# Bibliography


## Books and Edited Volumes

Afkhami, Mahnaz and Erika Friedl (1997). *Muslim Women and the Politics of Participation: Implementing the Beijing Platform*, New York: Syracuse University Press. (Available at http://www.questia.com/PM.qst?a=o&d=59644978)

Ali, Quazi Arshed (2012). *Karnataka Muslims and Electoral Politics*, Bangalore: Bookware.

Ashrof, V.A. Mohamad (2005). *Islam and Gender Justice: Questions at the Interface*, Delhi: Kalpaz Publications, p.12.

*Baseline Report: Women and Political Participation in India*, Report of the Core Group, 1998, National Institute of Advanced Studies, Gender Studies Unit, Prepared by NIAS *et al.*, and Coordinated by IWRAW Asia Pacific.

Bernard Lewis (1997). *The Middle East: A Brief History of the Last 2000 Years*, New York: Simon and Schuster Inc.

Bhatty, Z. (1985), Socio-Economic Status of Muslim Women in Z. Siddiqui and A. Zuberi (Eds.) *Muslim Women: Problems and Prospects*, New Delhi: Manohar Publishers.

Chopra, J.K. (1993). *Women in the Indian Parliament: Critical Study of their Role,* New Delhi: Mittal Publications.

*Gender and Party Politics* (Eds.) Joni Lovenduski and Pippa Norris, Thousand Oaks, Calif (1993).

*Government of India*, Socio-Economic and Educational Status of Muslim Community in India: A Report, New Delhi (2006) (Sachar Committee Report), pp. 50-51.

Hasan, Zoya and Ritu Menon (Eds.) (2004). *Unequal Citizens: A Study of Muslim Women in India,* New Delhi: Oxford University Press.

Iftekhar, Pumma. *Muslim Women and their participation in Public Life: A Case*

*Study of UP*, Doctoral Thesis submitted to Jamia Millia Islamia. February 1998.

Iqbal A. Ansari (2006). *Political Representation of Muslims in India, 1952-2004*, New Delhi: Manak Publications Ltd.

Karlekar, Karin Deutsch (2005). Muslim Women in Indian Politics during the period 1947 to 2002, *In a Minority: Essays on Muslim Women in India*, (Eds.) Zoya Hasan and Ritu Menon, New Delhi: Oxford University Press.

Lateef, Shahida (1983). Modernisation in India and the Status of Muslim Women, in *Modernisation and Social Change among Muslims in India*, (Ed.) Imtiaz Ahmad, New Delhi: Manohar, pp.152-183.

Lateef, Shahida (1990). *Muslim Women in India: Political and Private Realities*, New Jersey: Zed Books.

Lateef, Shahida (1998). Muslim Women in India: A Minority within a Minority in *Women in Muslim Societies: Diversity Within Unity*, (Eds.) Herbert L. Bodman, Nayereh Esfahlani Tohidi, Boulder, Colorado, USA: Lynne Reinner Publishers Inc., pp. 251-272.

Madhok, Alka, Panchayati Raj: Participation of Muslim Women, in (Ed.) Hajira Kumar (2002), *Status of Muslim women in India* (Ed.) Sarojini Naidu Centre for women's studies, Jamia Millia Islamia, Delhi: Aakar Books, p.78.

Mary E. John, The Politics of Quotas and Women's Reservation Bill in India, in Miyoko Tsujimura and Jackie F. Steele (Eds.) (2011), *Gender Equality in Asia*, Japan: Tohoku University Press, pp. 169-195. (Available at http://www.cwds.ac.in/Politics%20of%20quotas%20and%20WRB-MJ-Ch.8.pdf)

Menon, Visalakshi (2003). *Indian Women and Nationalism: The UP Story*, New Delhi: Har-Anand Publications Pvt. Ltd., p.29.

Mohan, Vasundhara (2010). Political Participation of Muslim women in India in Women and Politics in Asia: A Springboard for Democracy? (Eds.) Andrea Fleschenberg and Claudia Derichs, Berlin LIT-Verlag)

*Muslims in Indian Cities: Trajectories of Marginalisation* (2012) (Eds.): Laurent Gayer and Christophe Jaffrelot, London: C. Hurst & Co. (Publishers) Limited, p. 5.

Rahman, Farhat Naz. *An Islamic Perspective on Women in the Political System*, Islamic Research Foundation International Inc., Louisville, KY (USA). (Available at www.irfi.org/articles/articles_251_300/an_islamic_perspective_on_women.htm)

Raman, Vasanthi (2006), Identity Formation, Nationhood and Women: An Overview of Issues, in *Identity Formation, Nationhood and Women*, (Ed.) Anshu Bharatiya, New Delhi: CWDS, (Available at http://www.academia.edu/1308011/Identity_Formation_Nationhood_and_Women An Overview of Issues)

Samiuddin, Abida and Rashida Khanam. (Eds.) (2002). *Muslim Feminism andFeminist Movement: India*, Delhi: Global Vision Publishing House, pp. 47-73.

Shirin Rai (2002). *Class, Caste and Gender: Women in Parliament in India*, International IDEA, Women in Parliament, Stockholm (http://www.idea.int)

(Available at http://www.cccindia.co/corecentre/Database/Docs/DocFiles/cs_india.pdf)

Singh, Pritam (2003). *Women Legislators in Indian Politics*, New Delhi: Concept Publishing Co.

Zahid, Naghma (2002). *Political Participation of Muslim Women: A Case Study of Delhi*, PhD Thesis, Delhi: Jamia Millia Islamia.

## Working Papers, PhD Theses and Special Reports

Bird, Karen. The political representation of women and ethnic minorities in established democracies, Working Paper presented for the Academy of Migration Studies in Denmark, Aalborg University, 11 November, 2003. (Available at http://www.hks.harvard.edu/fs/pnorris/Acrobat/stm103%20articles/Karen%20Bird%20amidpaper.pdf)

Dittmar, Kelly. *What is the Hold up? Women's delayed entry into Political office,* Centre for American Women and Politics, Rutgers, January 8, 2013. (Available at http://cawp.rutgers.edu/foornotes/whats-the-hold-up-womens-delayed-entry-into-political-office

Dr. Sherwani. Women Reservation Bill *vis-à-vis* Muslim Women, March 6, 2010, in *Ummid.com*. (Available at http://www.ummid.com/news/2010/march/06.03.2010/women_reservation_muslim_women.htm)

Goetz, Anne Marie. Women's Education and Political Participation, Background Paper prepared for the Education for All Global Monitoring Report 2003/4, *Gender and Education for All: The Leap to Equality, 2003*. (Available at http://unesdoc.unesco.org/images/0014/001467/146770e.pdf)

Karat, Brinda (2005). Survival and Emancipation: Notes from Indian Women's Struggles, Gurgaon, India, Three Essays Collective, p.142). (Available at http://www.pucl.org/Topics/Gender/2003/reservation-bill.htm)

Nayar, Usha. An Analytical Study of Education of Muslim Women and Girls in India, October 1, 2007. (Available at http://www.jeywin.com/wp-content/uploads/2009/12/An-Analytical-Study-of-Education-of-Muslim-Women-and-Girls-in-India.pdf)

Parveen, Shaista. *Political and Social status of Muslim Women in Western Uttar Pradesh: A Case study of Saharanpur and Muzaffnagar Districts,* Aligarh Muslim University. (Available at http://jmi.ac.in/upload/Research/ab2012_polsc_shaista.pdf)

Raman, Vasanthi. The Implementation of Quotas for Women: The Indian Experience, Paper prepared for workshop hosted by International Institute for Democracy and Electoral Assistance (IDEA) on 25 September, 2002 in Jakarta, Indonesia. (Available at http://www.quotaproject.org/cs/cs_india.pdf)

Roald, Anne Sofie. *Quran on Women's Leadership*. International Museum of Women. (Available at http://www.imow.org/wpp/stories/viewStory?storyid=1692)

Shaheed, F., *et al.*, *Women in Politics: Participation and Representation in Pakistan*, Special Bulletin, Lahore, May 1988.

Sheikh, Mehraj-Ud-Din and Qamar Jahan. Literacy Rate of Muslim Women in Uttar Pradesh (India), in *Educationia Confab*, Vol. 2, No. 4, April 2013 (Available at http://www.confabjournals.com/confabjournals/images/652013817437.pdf)

*Situation of Muslim women and girls* ( Available at http://ncw.nic.in/pdfReports/Gender%20Profile-Uttar%20Pradesh.pdf)

*Women and Political leadership in Muslim thought*, October 2001. (Available at http://www.islamawareness.net/Women/leaders.html)

*Women and Politics in Islam*, 18 November, 2012. (Available at http://www.submission.ws/women/women-and-politics-in-islam.html)

Women's Representation, Effectiveness and Leadership in South Asia, February 2005, Fifth South Asia Regional Ministerial Conference, Celebrating the Beijing Plus Ten, Islamabad, Pakistan, 3-5 May, 2005, Women's Representation, Effectiveness and Leadership in South Asia, Khawar Mumtaz (Available at http://www.unifem.org.in/PDF/Women_representation.pdf)

*Women's Reservation: A Long Delayed and Much Needed Step*. Policy brief series: No. 3; July 2008, New Delhi: Centre for Legislative Research and Advocacy.

## Journal Articles

Dehlawi, Zakaria. *Women leaders have a history in Islam*, in The Daily of the University of Washington, March 2, 2009. (Available at http://dailyuw.com/author/zakariya-dehlawi)

Fatima, Nikhat. Muslim women activists in Hyderabad discuss history, politics, and society in *The Milli Gazette Online*, Jun 17, 2011.

Goudreau, Jenna. A Few Reasons Why Women Should Not Go Into Politics, in Forbes Woman, 7 July 2011. (Available at http://www.forbes.com/sites/jennagoudreau/2011/07/07/why-women-shouldnt-go-into-politics-michele-bachmann-sarah-palin/)

Haider, Saraswati. All Women s Political Party Launched in UP, in *Economic and Political Weekly*, Vol. XXXIII, No. 8, February 21, 1998.

Halder, Nomita. "Female Representation in Parliament: A Case Study from Bangladesh" in New Zealand Journal of Asian Studies, 6, 1 (June 2004):27-63, (Available at http://www.nzasia.org.nz/downloads/NZJAS-June04/6_1_3.pdf.)

Islamic Clerics oppose women's reservation, in *TwoCircles.net*, 11 March 2010. Available at http://twocircles.net/2010mar11/ Islamic_clerics_oppose_womens_reservation.html)

Jalali, Nazia. The Role of Women in Politics *Khilafah* magazine, (August 2003 edition), (http://www.oocities.org/zq83_uk/archives/women_in_polity. htm)

Jalil, Rakhshanda. Educating Muslim Women in Modern India: Problems and Perspectives, in *Dialogue,* January-March, 2010, Volume 11 No. 3.

Kamat, A.R., Literacy and Education of Muslims: A Note, in *Economic and Political Weekly*, Vol.6, No.23, June 6, 1981.

Kishwar, Madhu. Women's marginal role in politics, in *Manushi*. (Available at http://www.manushi-india.org/pdfs_issues/PDF%20files%2097/women's_marginal_role_in_politics.pdf)

M. Nasir Jawed, Women Reservation Bill: Time for Muslim women to act, in *Saudi Gazette*, 12 March 2010. (Available at http://www.saudigazette.com.sa/index.cfm?method=home.regcon&contentid=2010031266049)

*Muslim Women and their representation in South Asian Politics in Islam and Muslim Societies,* Vol.6, No.2, 2013) (Available at http://www.muslimsocieties.org/Vol_6_No_2_Muslim_Women_and_their_Representation.html

*Parawansa, Kofifah Indar. Obstacles to Women's Political Participation in Indonesia* (International IDEA, 2002, Women in Parliament, Stockholm) (http://www.idea.int/publications/wip/upload/CS_Indonesia_Parawansa.pdf)

Siddiqui, Farasat Ali, Nazmul Hussain and Akram Hannan, Literacy and work participation among Muslims in Uttar Pradesh, *Journal of Geography and Regional Planning,* Vol. 4(6), pp. 305-325, June 2011 (Available online at http://www.academicjournals.org/JGRP)

UP Municipal Elections and Muslims, Syed Ubaidur Rahman in *Milli Gazette* http://www.milligazette.com/Archives/15-12-2000/Art1.htm)

## Web Articles

Sikand, Yoginder. Muslims in Kerala and Elsewhere: Accounting For the Difference, in *Countercurrents.org*, 30 June, 2007. (Available at http://www.countercurrents.org/sikand300607.htm)

*An Islamic Perspective on Women in the Political System*, Muslim Women's League, September 1995. (Available at http://www.mwlusa.org/topics/rights/politics.html.)

Muhammad Asad, The Principles of State and Government in Islam, Dar Al-Andalus, 1980, p. 32 quoted in *Women in Society: Political Participation*, Muslim Women's League, September 1995 http://www.mwlusa.org/topics/rights/polirights.html)

Quoted in Sanusi, Lamido Sanusi. *Women and Political Leadership in Islamic Thought*. Available at http://www.islamawareness.net/Women/leaders.html

*Women and Politics in Islam*, in Submission. WS, 18 November, 2012. (Available athttp://www.submission.ws/women/women-and-politics-in-islam.html

# Index

Abu Bakr, 201, 203
Affluent families, 252
Age profile, 140, 149–50, 281
Aligarh Muslim University, 23, 263
All India Anna Dravida Munnetra Kazhagam, 175
All India Indira Congress, 172
All India Ladies Conference in Ahmedabad, 100
All India Majlis-e-Ittehadul Muslimeen, 130, 175
All India Milli Council, 7, 183
All India Minorities Coordination Board, 184
All India Minorities Front, 172, 178
All India Muslim Forum, 184
All India Muslim Mahila Andolan, 185
All India Muslim Personal Law Board, 13, 184, 251
All India Women's Conference, 4
Anglo-Indian community, 90
Anti-Muslim
  pogroms, 14
  violence, 110
Anti-woman
  reform, 249
  viewpoints, 189
Arab Muslims, 33
Arab traders, 33
Area Intensive Educational Development, 91
Artificial political barriers, 45
Asmita Resource Centre for Women in Hyderabad, 85
Aspirations, 24, 116, 169, 213, 245, 274
Assembly Elections, 42–44, 46, 49–50, 52, 61, 105–7, 109–14, 137, 151, 188, 193, 223, 227, 256, 279
Assembly polls, 43, 48

Babri Masjid demolition, 46
Backward communities, 40–41, 58, 92
Backwardness, 37, 102, 223, 251
  economic, 36, 39
  political, 278
Bahujan Kranti Dal (BKD), 171
Bahujan Samaj Party, 47, 49–50, 130, 151, 223
Ballot paper, 247–48
Bangalore City Corporation, 85
Bangalore Municipal Corporation elections, 53
Bangarappa's Karnataka Congress, 47
Battle of Uhud, 206
BBMP elections, 72
BDC members, 134
Better Education Through Innovation (BETI), 117
Bharatiya Janata Party (BJP ), 46–47, 50–53, 60, 72, 151, 175, 186, 193, 214, 224, 231, 241, 244, 260–61, 279

Bicameral legislatures, 90
Brihat Bangalore Mahanagar Palike, 84
Buddhist, 33
*Burkha*, 68, 137–38
Bye-elections, 125, 177

Candidates
- better, 224
- dummy, 265
- elected, 117
- independent, 22, 44, 60, 72, 103, 106, 111, 125, 169, 171, 177, 233–34, 260, 269, 279–80
- male, 42
- minority, 49
- non-Muslim, 43
- winnable, 118
- winning, 226

Career politicians, 154
Caste
- quotas, 2
- reservation, 59

Central Government Scheme, 91
Centre for Law and Governance, 123
Charitable organizations, 36
Charter of demands, 86
Child Development Ministry, 105
Christians, 30, 33, 37, 35–36, 40–41, 57, 91, 237
City Corporations, 61, 63, 72–73
Civilised societies, 271
Civil society, 6
Clean society, 138
Coastal Kerala, 33
Co-education, 97–98, 223
Co-educational madrasahs, 252
Communal-based reservations, 4
Communication skills, 36
Communist parties, 223
Communist Party, 51, 101, 171, 193, 218
Community
- activities, 3, 102
- backward, 181
- development, 195
- dominant, 38
- leadership, 38, 222, 253
- marginalized, 67
- non-Muslim, 55, 215, 222
- religious, 93–94, 222, 251

Congress and Welfare Party of India, 229
Conservatism
- political, 60
- religious, 95, 265

Conservative
- Islamic injunction, 37
- Muslim, 96
- society, 253

Constituent Assembly, 2, 5, 30
Constitutional Amendments, 59, 133, 182, 189, 192–93, 270
Constitution of India, 31, 90, 181
Core Group, 28
Councillor Election Results, 70
Country-wide acceptance, 261
Cultural development, 39
Curriculum content, 192

Dakshina Kannada, 31, 33
Darul Uloom, 15, 111, 134, 136–38, 193, 265
- *fatwa*, 193

Democratic
- process, 116, 118, 268, 280
- society, 181

Demographic developments, 99
Deoband, 97, 136–38
- fatwas, 138, 181
- Dar-ul-Uloom Islamic University, 137

Department of Minority Education, 252
Department of Political Science, 23
Devaraj Urs, 41–44
Development funds, 270
Disparities, 93, 95

Distractions, 97
District-wise participation, 151
Doha Debates, 7–8
Domestic responsibilities, 2, 134, 213, 240
Dominant parties, 188
Door Darshi Party (DDP), 171
Dress code, 60, 181, 250, 252, 265
Drinking water problems, 84

Economic
  activities, 96, 98, 255, 280
  development, 39, 86, 255
  factors, 27, 102, 213
  group, 271
  status, 239, 252–53
Educated women, 3, 69, 133, 181, 192, 253
Education/Educational
  accessing, 95
  acquiring, 38, 225, 230
  advancement, 272
  awakening, 38, 279
  backwardness, 38, 93, 96–97, 243, 251, 256, 280
  basic, 27
  early childhood, 37
  facilities, 102
  formal, 36, 97, 250
  hinder, 95
  ideal, 96
  institutions, 92, 236
  loans, 39
  low levels of, 92, 98, 280
  opportunities, 38, 236
  policies, 236
  pre-Partition, 93
  primary, 98, 252
  problems, 274
  professional, 99
  regular, 96
  religious, 13, 67, 96, 218, 266
  secondary, 98
  vocational-*cum*-school, 100
Election Commission, 16, 103, 125, 168–69, 213, 259
Elections
  contested, 61, 231, 241, 260
  democratic, 1
  fresh, 44
  local body, 62, 194
  mid-term, 126, 171
  municipal, 66
Electoral politics, 16, 21–22, 244, 280
Elite families, 21
Empowerment, 10, 23, 85, 117–18, 136, 251
  educational, 256
  political, 26, 184, 193, 266

Faculty of Education, 273
Family restrictions, 217
*Fatwas*, 68–69, 117–18, 136–38, 181, 192–94, 199, 213, 220–21, 230–31, 241, 244, 257, 266–68, 270–71, 279–81
  authentic, 241
  controversial, 181
  withstand, 190
Female participation, 253
Feminist Interpretation of Women Rights in Islam, 203
First war of independence, 100, 280
Freedom movement, 100

Gandhi, Indira, 42–44
Gender, 21, 24–25, 27, 29, 115, 194, 201, 206, 233, 253–54, 259, 269
Gendered perceptions, 38, 253
Gender roles, 27
Government-aided schools, 96
Government of India Act, 4, 90
Government policy, 1
Government schemes, 272
Gram Panchayats, 59, 132–33, 139, 152, 188
Gulf countries, 267

Human development, 45
Human resource development, 39, 91

Identity Formation, 24–25
Illiteracy, 8, 26, 35, 95, 102, 190, 221, 226, 243, 256, 260
Independent political outlook, 104
Indian Congress-Socialist (ICS), 171
India's freedom struggle, 66
Indonesia, 25, 27
Indonesian Muslim, 27
Industrial centres, 14
Institute for Social and Economic Change (ISEC), 45, 227
Institutional voices, 269, 271
Inter-community harmony, 68
Islam
  bars, 211
  bounds of, 216, 219, 239
  divided, 229
  forgotten Queens of, 201
  Indianisation of, 13
  and Muslim Societies, 23
  spirit of, 97
Islamic
  activist, 207
  conditions, 213
  dresses, 189
  Fiqh, 267
  framework, 139, 274
  heritage, 206
  history, 204, 206
  identity, 212, 216, 219, 230, 238–39, 244
  law, 136, 138, 193, 205, 217
  norms, 191, 227, 268
  position, 204
  rights, 207, 249
  seminary, 136, 200
  tradition, 208, 251
  justifications, 12
  permit, 180
Islamic Research Foundation International Inc, 24

Jains, 33, 91
Jamaat-e-Islami Hind, 98, 228, 261
Jamia Millia Islamia, 28–29, 273
Janata Dal, 46–51, 84, 103, 171–72, 182, 234, 241, 243
Janata Party, 43–44, 137, 171–72
Jurisprudence, 267

Karnataka Janata Party's (KJP), 51, 54, 84
Karnataka Kranti Ranga, 43
Karnataka Legislative Assembly, 15, 49
Karnataka Panchayati Raj Act, 45, 151
Karnataka State Minorities Commissions, 38, 40
Karnataka Waqf Board, 231, 237
Khawarij School, 205
Kshetra Panchayat, 133

Labour Force Participation Rate (LFPR), 98–99
La Martiniere Girls College, 117
Leaders
  cooperative mafia, 123
  enlightened, 66
  honest, 231
  independent, 54
  male, 26, 185, 189, 223, 226, 263
  non-Muslim, 193
  purported, 205
Leadership
  female, 137, 200
  male, 222
  political, 3, 14, 104, 202, 204, 237, 253, 262
  role, 200, 202
  strong, 263
  vacuum, 66
Leftist parties, 260
Legislative
  Assembly, 1, 7, 90, 104, 125, 264
  Council, 55–56, 90, 187

Like-mined parties, 182
Literacy, 93–95
  levels, 93–95
  rate, 32, 34–35, 92–95, 251, 279
Local bodies, 69, 134–35, 193, 268
Lok Sabha, 2, 6, 56–57, 123, 125–32, 168–69, 171–72, 175, 177, 182–88, 190–91, 222, 248, 265, 273
Madrasahs, 14, 96–97, 223, 228, 250, 263, 267
Mainstream politics, 85
Majlis-e-Ulema Karnataka and Rector, 228
Male-dominated Parliament, 11
Mandatory reservations, 134
Man-made Hadith books, 202
Minorities, 5, 12, 20, 24, 39, 91, 117, 125, 182, 188, 221
  ethnic, 1
  religious, 5, 271
Minority
  status, 243–44
  votes, 49
Minority Development Corporation, 53
Minority Education Commission, 223
Minority Groups International, 28
Minuscule group, 264
Modern education, 14, 37, 39, 68, 266
Modern society, 104
Monthly per capita expenditure (MPCE), 99
Moradabad and Barabanki districts, 96
Moral responsibilities, 44
Municipal Corporations in Karnataka, 62
Muscle power, 183, 187, 191, 227
Muslim
  Arab, 33
  artisans, 97
  based parties, 223, 260, 262
  based political parties, 223, 229, 240, 243–44, 261–62
  bodies, 86
  Brotherhood, 7
  candidates, 21, 42–44, 52, 55, 118, 194
  clergy, 194
  clerics, 190
  constituencies, 259
  contestants, 31, 47, 49–50
  dominated constituencies, 49, 111, 135, 179, 199, 243
  electorate, 22, 112
  elite, 13, 117
  female literacy, 35
  industrialist, 273
  intellectuals, 210
  intelligentsias, 66, 227, 261
  leadership, 66, 93–94, 169, 201, 226, 263
  literacy, 95
  male-dominated, 179
  migration of, 34, 99
  nominating, 167
  orthodoxy, 265
  participation of, 42, 279
  patriarchs, 102, 222
  political participation of, 16, 21
  politics participation, 242
  quota, 41
  resurgence of, 27
  rural, 265
  scholarship, 200
  urban slum-based, 38
  voters, 21, 48, 135, 221
  well-to-do, 272
Muslim woman
  abandoned, 69
  absence, 236
  activists, 85
  arguments, 186
  aspirations, 12
  association, 207
  of Bangalore City, 235
  bar, 234
  candidate, 22, 52
  courageous, 137

deprived, 231
electoral participation, 41, 179, 227, 231, 238, 257
employment, 181
empowerment, 10, 69, 195, 263, 272
encouraged, 211, 214
entertain, 127, 131
failure, 29
*fatwa* barring, 136
interests, 189, 262
involvement, 189
of Karnataka, 15, 44, 56, 58–59, 72, 86, 179, 279
leader, 264
lone, 44, 46, 106, 125
organizations, 134
participation, 15, 59, 61, 100, 105, 138, 151, 190, 211–12
patriotic, 100
positioned, 212
prohibited, 181
promoted, 223
in *Quran*, 264
representation, 7, 253
reservation, 185
sponsor, 260
of Uttar Pradesh, 15, 101, 106, 118, 124, 134, 136, 193, 268, 270, 280
Nadwat-ul-Ulema, 58, 180
National Commission for Minority Educational Institutions, 35
National Council for Minority Educational Institutions, 97
National Democratic Alliance (NDA), 128, 182
National Front Government, 48
Nationalist Congress Party, 51, 112, 187
National-level parties, 118
National Policy on Education (NPE), 91
Nationhood, 24–25
Non-affluent families, 179
Non-Congress government, 43
Non-Muslims electorate, 9
Non-political associations, 36
Not-so-affluent families, 181

OBC quota, general, 182
Opinion polls, 22, 190–91
ORG-Marg Muslim Women's Survey, 35

Panchayat
elections, 226
leaders, 59, 61
Pan-Indian level, 66
Parent parties, 189
Parliamentary polls, 48
Partition, trauma of, 106, 257, 280
Patriarchal Indonesian society, 25
Patriarchal readings of religion, 102
Patriarchal society, 192
Planning Commission of India, 253
Political activism, 206
Political activity, 36, 104, 211
Political advancement, 105, 151
Political aide, 123
Political ambitions, 6, 258, 279
Political analysis, 36
Political arena, 2, 5, 25, 134, 138, 254
Political behaviour, 13, 22
Political career, 110, 258
Political class, 116, 235
Political clout, 226
Political consensus, 248
Political development programmes, 39
Political discourse, 14
Political dominance, 13
Political engagement, 36
Political equations, 42
Political families, 3, 11, 45, 123, 168, 199, 257, 264, 278, 281
Political institutions, 253
Political longevity, 110

Political mobilisation, 14, 26
Political movements, 85
Political negotiations, 4, 202
Political participation, factors affecting, 256
Political parties
  main, 104
  national, 195
  north Indian, 49
  role of, 21, 269
  separate Muslim-based, 261
Political patronage, 192
Political posturing, 99
Political power, 212
Political process, 2, 5, 22, 55, 132, 153, 248
Political pulse, 116
Political representation, 1–2, 5, 23, 25, 86, 194, 237
Political reservation, 183
Political rights, 13, 43
Political Science, 23, 254
Political situation, present, 216
Political struggle, 12
Political visibility, 85
Politicians, 6, 25, 45, 49, 117, 175, 178, 183, 185, 187, 189, 207, 250, 264, 272–73
  corrupt, 153, 268
  male, 2, 12, 15, 153, 214, 240, 243, 255, 265, 281
Politics
  active, 104, 181, 196, 255
  dynastic, 123
  formal, 253
  inclusive, 21
  institutional, 269
  joining, 137
  male-dominated, 196
  quota-based, 117
Popularity, 43, 137, 150
Post-Independence generations, 257
Post-partition
  generations, 43
  period, 14
Prophet Muhammad, 205–7
Proverbial statement, 94
*Purdah* system, 21, 101, 180, 213, 219, 226

Qamarul Islam, 47
Qayids, 229
Quality education, 280
Queens in Muslim history, 201
Quota
  minority, 116
  non-secular, 182
  religion-based, 9, 278
  separate, 2, 58, 168, 184–85, 189, 191, 194, 212, 215, 217, 220, 239–40, 243, 263, 281
  special, 5, 12
  for women in politics, 23
*Quran*, 69, 93, 117, 200, 202, 204–7, 211, 218–19, 225, 227–28, 230, 249, 254, 266, 268
*Quranic* rights, 266

Rajya Sabha, 124–25, 180, 182–83, 237, 248, 263–64
Rani Chennamma Party (RCP), 53
Rashtriya Janata Dal, 172, 182
Regional group, 261
Regional parties, 9, 126, 128, 130, 151, 270
Religion-based
  impediments, 180
  reservation, 11, 268
Religion-related issues, 266
Religious
  affiliation, 3
  beliefs, 252
  calculations, 115
  class, 257
  discipline, 265
  electorates, 222
  fanaticism, 38
  figures, 21
  group, 91, 236

identity, 9, 48, 215, 219, 244, 266
limitations, 241
orthodoxy, 186
restrictions, 226
rights, 237
sanctions, 254
symbolism , 26
teachers, 210
texts, 12
traditionalism, 37
Renowned Shia Islamic Scholar, 53
Representation, 1, 8, 10–11, 26–27, 29, 43, 103, 139, 168, 183–84, 194, 255, 278
average, 103, 280
fair, 86, 168, 183, 249
functional, 90
male, 185
Representative Assembly, 30
Republican Party of India, 43
Reservation Bill, 2, 12, 58, 187, 189–90
Role models, 134, 205–6, 208
Role of religion, 97, 280
Round Table Conference, 4
Royal family of Rampur, 128, 178
Rural areas, 34–35, 37, 93, 136

Sachar Committee, 22–23, 35, 92, 117, 249–51, 253–54
Samajwadi Party, 51, 111, 124, 151, 171–72, 182, 214, 218, 223, 260
Samata Party, 172, 175
Sample size, 16
Secular democracy, 266, 272
Secular State, 5
Separate proportionate quota, 184
Separate quotas for Muslim women, 190
Shia Muslims, 224
Sikh communities, 37
Social development, 39
Social problems, 258
Social responsibilities, 204, 216
Societal discrimination, 221
Societal problems, 11
Socio-economic development, 12
South Asian Countries, Election in, 9
States' Reorganization Act, 30, 56
Sunni Muslims, 224
Supply-side factors, 195

Take-up jobs, 68, 215, 219, 267
Tribal partisanship, 206
Trinamool Congress, 182

UDF Government, 188
Ulema Council, 261
Universal adult franchise, 4
Urban areas, 4, 15, 34–35, 95
Urban centres, 13, 98–99
Urban Local Bodies (ULBs), 16, 59, 61, 63, 65, 72, 134, 149, 232–33, 259, 273

Valid votes, 44, 46, 49, 106, 111–12, 118, 259
Value-based Politics, 44
Vanitha League, 189, 262
Voter
cooperation, 72
first-time, 117
ID cards, 187
non-Muslim, 273
rural, 270
turnout, 115

Welfare Party of India, 228, 261
Winnability factors, 265
Women
led group, 13
leaders in Islamic history, 206
related issues, 233
representatives, 135, 194
brigade, 100
franchise, 26
Indian Association, 4
sovereigns, 202
tickets, 265
voters, 113, 115

Women and Child Development Ministry, 105
Women's Research Action Group, 29
Women's Reservation Bill, 2, 6, 11, 16, 51, 58, 105, 124, 167, 179–82, 184–86, 189–90, 222, 248, 258
Work-force participation, 15

Zamindari, 101
Zamindari Abolition Act, 93
Zilla Panchayats, 59, 133
Zilla Parishads, 133